DEGREES OF FREEDOM

DEGREES *of* FREEDOM

*The Origins of Civil Rights
in Minnesota, 1865–1912*

William D. Green

UNIVERSITY OF MINNESOTA PRESS

MINNEAPOLIS
LONDON

The University of Minnesota Press gratefully acknowledges assistance provided for the publication of this book by the John K. and Elsie Lampert Fesler Fund.

The University of Minnesota Press gratefully acknowledges financial assistance provided for the publication of this book from the Office of the Provost, Augsburg College.

Published by the University of Minnesota Press
111 Third Avenue South, Suite 290
Minneapolis, MN 55401–2520
http://www.upress.umn.edu

Green, William D.
Degrees of freedom: the origins of civil rights in Minnesota, 1865–1912 / William D. Green.
Includes bibliographical references and index.
ISBN 978-0-8166-9346-7 (hc)
ISBN 978-0-8166-0933-8 (pb)
1. African Americans—Civil rights—Minnesota—History.
2. Civil rights movements—Minnesota—History.
3. African Americans—Minnesota—History.
4. Race relations—History. I. Title.
F615.N4G74 2015
323.1196'0730776—dc23   2014043932

Printed in the United States of America on acid-free paper

The University of Minnesota is an equal-opportunity educator and employer.

25 24 23 22 21 20 19   10 9 8 7 6 5 4 3 2 1

To Judi, with every waking and adoring breath,
I dedicate this book.

CONTENTS

PREFACE

On a cold evening in February 1873, Frederick Douglass, by now the most famous African American in the country, was finishing his speech to a crammed auditorium of enthusiastic St. Paulites. The thunderous applause and throaty huzzahs that had punctuated various points of the message now filled the room like a tidal wave, drowning out the jeers and catcalls from a hostile crowd that had assembled outside. As he took in the adulation, his friend and one of the hosts of the occasion approached to congratulate him for his successful address before offering to put him up in a room in his hotel, the Metropolitan, the most prestigious of its kind in the city of St. Paul. Later that evening, four years and one month after the celebration of the approval of the black suffrage amendment to the state constitution, Douglass, a confidant to the Great Emancipator himself and conscience of the Republican Party, was denied a room by a clerk simply because he was black.

This was an example of a white patron who supported—indeed, sincerely embraced—African American freedom, equality, and dignity who nevertheless chose not to translate those principles into the policies he used in governing his business. For many of his ilk, "freedom" only seemed to mean being unshackled from chains of servitude, not having the means to pursue the full enjoyment of opportunity. "Equality" meant having access to the ballot, but not being served at a restaurant downtown. "Dignity" meant that white men used the appellation of "mister" to African American men with middle-class bearing, while tolerating a society that demeaned the entire black race. It was the nature of this kind of "sincerity"—multifaceted and often paradoxical, myopic and sometimes self-congratulatory—that characterized the tepid relations between blacks and whites in postwar Minnesota.

Although this brand of sincerity rested on well-deserved laurels of the Republicans who forged a new society that eventually benefited themselves, it was not one that was socially and economically integrated. Rather, this form of sincerity was the kind that allowed Republicans to tout the hyperbolic promise of social Darwinism as a legitimate test of character over adversity only to condescend when African Americans did not widely succeed because, they felt, it was their race and not the racialized system that was flawed. Also, during the period examined in this book, this brand of white Republican sincerity mired race leaders within the weblike duty to be grateful. A clear example is illustrated by the Frederick Douglass incident in that Douglass chose not to criticize the discrimination he had faced across the North at places like the Metropolitan that were often owned by Republican patrons. After all, one could never forget—nor would one be permitted to forget—that the patrons had been the willing instruments of *the fateful lightning of His terrible swift sword.* Minnesota, to be sure, was not Mississippi. It was this nature of race relations that black leaders in the state who sought to advance true opportunity would seek to redress over the next forty years, and that this book seeks to examine.

I began this work hoping to understand how Minnesota's reputation for black–white tolerance evolved. This was a state with a small black population, yet it provided the national civil-rights movement with leadership by figures such as Hubert H. Humphrey, Walter Mondale, Donald Fraser, Roy Wilkins, and Whitney Young, who launched his career in civil rights with the National Urban League while a graduate student at the University of Minnesota. Minneapolis was the first city in the nation to have an antidiscrimination ordinance. And going back to the turn of the century, during the most violent period against African Americans the nation had ever witnessed, when white supremacists acted with legal impunity, Minnesota legislators twice amended the civil-rights law and opened the state capitol to Booker T. Washington, W. E. B. DuBois, Ida B. Wells-Barnett, and others to debate the national agenda for civil rights. In the St. Paul home of attorney Fredrick McGhee, DuBois got the idea for the Niagara Movement, precursor to the National Association for the Advancement of Colored People (NAACP) that would later be led by Roy Wilkins, who cut his teeth on racial-justice activism as a student at the University of Minnesota. In 1921, the state legislature made lynching a crime decades before Congress enacted a similar law. And although other states extended voting rights to black men by legislative enactment or judicial decree,

Minnesota was the first state in the Union to do so at the ballot box, where only white men could vote, two years before ratification of the Fifteenth Amendment. What was it about the Land of 10,000 Lakes that seemed to breed a consciousness for social justice for the African American?

I started this examination in my first book, *A Peculiar Imbalance: The Fall and Rise of Racial Equality in Early Minnesota,* and found that the seed was planted with the influx of settlers who migrated from New England and the upstate New York region where reform sentiment was strong. But the geographic location of Minnesota also was a factor. Noted historians—Eugene Berwanger, John Hope Franklin, Leon Litwack, Eric Foner, and Jacque Voegeli to mention a few—observed that Northerners during the antebellum years living within border regions of slaveholding states often displayed antiblack attitudes, partly in reaction to their vigilance against fugitive slaves who could see and were tempted to cross over into the Promised Land just across the river. Fearing that slaves and even free blacks would degrade the local white labor capacity to earn a living, Northerners in the border regions of their states looked at the African American with hostility.

Richard Dykstra in *Bright Radical Star: Black Freedom and White Supremacy on the Hawkeye Frontier* found the same tendencies when he studied the attitudes of Iowans living just across the Missouri border. With Iowa as a buffer, Minnesota shared no border with a slaveholding state. For most Minnesotans, the African American—slave or free—was an abstraction. Immigrants increasingly satisfied the need for cheap labor. With the infusion of the attitudes of New Englanders and upstate New Yorkers, Minnesota developed a liberal bent that willingly joined other Northerners in the struggle for emancipation, but took the lead in the struggle for enfranchisement. Although many interests competed for control over the party apparatus, by the mid-1860s political and business leaders, as well as the editorial voices of three of the most prominent newspapers of the state, threw their weight behind both initiatives. It seemed then that Minnesota's policy makers had well prepared the ground for racial advancement.

A Peculiar Imbalance ended on a high note when black Minnesotans gained the right to vote, a chance for a better education for their children, and the opportunity to participate in public service. *Degrees of Freedom* picks up the story and moves it forward by examining how, despite having the political franchise and contacts with important men, genuine opportunity and social and interracial acceptance remained largely elusive. Indeed, the challenges blacks encountered were both unprecedented and unexpectedly disappointing. Although the vestiges of freedom and citizenship had become law of the land, the new order did very little to erase prejudice that had taken centuries to form in the hearts and minds of white men and women. Even the most benign patrons failed to understand the corrosive effect of the daily assaults on dignity that black people routinely faced. Not even membership in the middle class shielded black people from such insults. Some patrons equated the racism that African Americans faced and the obstacles it posed with being a white man surviving the hardships of owning a business or working a farm. That this dynamic existed in a society controlled by the Republican Party, whose leaders shared some of these same beliefs of racial superiority, only compounded the challenge the race men—black men who worked to advance the dignity and rights of African Americans—had to confront. Looking skyward at what should have been a sunny new day, they could already see dark clouds on the horizon.

Republican ethos, during the post–Civil War period, held that a man could become whatever he wanted if he was willing to work hard enough for it. Full citizenship inevitably led to full opportunity. Within this framework, if the black man remained inferior to other men after he had been granted full citizenship, it was entirely his fault and an issue of character, and nothing more could or should be done for him. If his skin color provoked white men to discriminate and exclude him simply because of his race, then the bite of stigma was his only to endure. If his own agenda for racial advancement and choice of leadership was overridden by the paternalism of white Republican patrons, then he was at least to feel grateful that Minnesota was not the South, where lynch law was commonplace. Throughout the 1880s, to the casual observer, black Minnesotans generally seemed to be doing well when portrayed in stories written by white editors. Candor between blacks and whites was precluded from civil discourse.

And yet a small community of black Minnesotans, despite the complex relationship they had with white patrons, did enjoy a degree of social and economic progress. A vibrant middle class that evolved in the 1880s formed religious, social, literary, educational, and political groups, as well as a black-owned newspaper. Soon St. Paul attracted a small but growing professional class that included black lawyers and enterprising business-men, many of whom would become the race men of Minnesota, who were interested in staking their claims within one of the smallest but most promising African American communities in the country. These were the people and activities many white Minnesota patrons saw as indication that life was indeed good for the few black people fortunate enough to live in the state; that the state had removed all obstacles, which in turn provided opportunity for those willing to work hard enough at it; that, through the eyes of self-satisfied boosters, Minnesota had done what no other state had been able to do—resolve, at least within its own borders, the Negro Problem.

But it was a misleading portrait. Upward mobility in Minnesota was not widely available to its African American citizens. Even the black middle and professional class—indeed, the political elite—had brought their sense of station, and in many instances their education and capi-tal, when they relocated to the state from elsewhere. At the same time, the vast majority of the state's African Americans were lower class, fro-zen in poverty because job training was largely out of their reach. White employers—even those who characterized themselves as patrons of the black community—were disinclined to hire them for anything other than manual labor.

By the end of the nineteenth century, as race relations worsened across the nation and white-on-black violence increased with impunity, the worried black elite in Minnesota considered the most effective means to protest, though they paid far less attention to the condition of the local poor. For many of them—especially those who relied on the kindness of white patronage to support their businesses, for the state's African Amer-ican population was too small to support black-owned enterprises—to criticize the white patrons was too much like walking on thin ice at the beginning of a Minnesota winter. Indeed, as reflected in their acceptance of the cakewalk—a racially demeaning spectacle that was popular at the time in white quarters—it was unwise to be too closely associated with the black lower class. Relatively speaking, by the end of the century, Min-nesota was safer than most states.

Having come from places where racial abuses had occurred, many African Americans knew just how unpredictably and suddenly tragic situations could erupt. Even though they appreciated the relative sanctuary of tolerance within the North Star State, they knew that while living among a growing white native-born and ethnic working class who faced increasingly desperate and uncertain economic times, within a national climate that made it easy to make black men the scapegoat, it was unwise to lower their guard. In two separate instances during the early summer months of 1896, a mob nearly lynched a black man accused of attacking a white woman. Both attempts took place in St. Paul, one of which occurred only blocks away from the state capitol. In contrast to official complaisance and to some degree in compensation for it, the Minnesota legislature eight years later availed the chamber for the House of Representatives as a place to meet for a national convention of civil-rights leaders. This was the beginning of a new era with the advent to national leadership of W. E. B. DuBois, an era that rejected accommodation as the solution to the so-called Negro Problem and replaced it with new principles for racial advancement that included better education, jobs training and employment, and an end to racial violence, an era that began in the home of a St. Paul attorney. *Degrees of Freedom* documents this complex and often nuanced story.

In Part I, "The Barbers," the book sets the context of this history by following the early life of Jim Thompson, a black man brought to Minnesota as a slave and freed in 1839. Through his life we see how the perception of his race dimmed as the region transitioned from frontier to territory to state, as American settlement increased and as race-exclusionary laws governing citizenship followed. Indeed, his fortunes, in terms of property ownership and social standing, diminished as the world he knew gave way to white settlement. It was a different kind of black man who in 1865 would play a critical role in the long campaign to extend the state constitution to grant suffrage rights to black men. This new black man was a man of the city, a refined man whose stock-in-trade was not hunting game and hewing a log, but cutting hair and trimming a beard. In Part I we are introduced to the first generation of race men.

Part II, "The Entrepreneurs," documents the extent to which white patrons were willing to support the black community. Once civil and political rights were established, the hard work to prepare a recently freed and impoverished people to enter into the promising postwar economy lay ahead. White patrons were not willing to do this, and viewed this instead as the obligation of the very people who had no resources. Minnesota was about to enter into its own reconstruction era with the emergence of new economies, the reintegration of a white Minnesota labor force, and the heavy influx of foreign-born and native-born settlers. As the black population was dwarfed in contrast to a vast and expanding white population who felt that enough had been granted to freedmen and -women, it was easy for patrons to limit support to far less inflammatory social and cultural activities. Black Minnesotans would have to persevere through the slights and rejections on the streets and in restaurants, res- olutely presenting a good face and finding comfort in dignified celebra- tions of racial pride and community building, making certain to invite white friends—many of whom sponsored the events—to share in the fes- tivities. Yet it is during this period that a second generation of race men recognized that political equality and racial discrimination were expected to coexist within a segregated society, and that certain opportunities, however limited, were still worth pursuing. With the formation of a black press, the African American community at last gained its own record of note—the *Western Appeal,* later renamed the *Appeal.*

In Part III, "The Radicals," we are introduced to a new generation of race men who established black social circles, negotiated the treacher- ous rapids of acquiring and maintaining political leverage, and connected a largely isolated black community with the national debate on black advancement. This effort was led by two men who at times were rivals— Frank Wheaton (from Maryland) and Fredrick McGhee (from Mississippi, by way of Chicago). Part III also recounts the battle of principles between Booker T. Washington and W. E. B. DuBois. At the national convention of the National Afro-American Conference, controlled by Washington, we see the final rupture between McGhee, chief counsel to Washington's organization, from his mentor, often referred to as the Wizard of Tuske- gee. From there, McGhee and DuBois launch plans to form the Niagara Movement, a precursor of the NAACP. Theirs would ultimately be a new direction—indeed, a *radical* direction, as it was seen then, that insisted that black Americans deserved their place within an integrated society.

To better understand this era I thought it necessary to consider the manner in which the race men and their white patrons talked to each other about racial advancement. Throughout much of the period covered in this book, and especially at the turn of the century, it would appear that they rarely in fact did. Rather, the manner of conversation that occurred tended to be without debate, calcified in civility, free from candor, rife with pretense, conveying only a highly starched, self-satisfied sense of racial harmony, Victorian in style, paternalistic in tone, rigidly confined within a belief that the opportunity to move beyond the status quo was the most radical and therefore subversive of notions. It was within this context that white patrons tended only to signal their judgment on the tactics that the race men chose to pursue, through whether they donated funds or turned a cold shoulder. This nuance-laden manner in which supposed allies interacted on the issue of race and strategy is what I have sought to explore in this book. But it would be wrong to conclude that this book seeks to document the history of Minnesota "Nice," the stereotypical behavior of white residents of the state who were characterized as amiably reserved yet passive-aggressive when interacting with black people. The dynamic of the late nineteenth and early twentieth centuries was not about that at all: it was one based on control. This book explores how the race men maneuvered within the political arena governed by those constricting rules of engagement.

I am using the term "race men" for the admittedly indelicate purpose of labeling black men who dedicated themselves to advancing the welfare of their people because it was widely coined by African American men and women during the nineteenth century. Ida B. Wells, for example, referred to her father as a race man because he had inculcated within her a reverence for education, a sense of political independence, and a passion to confront racial injustice, and freely adopted the term that reflected the sensibilities of a time when leadership was typically delegated to men. The term, however, does not obviate the fact that she led campaigns (that included male supporters) for universal equality and the end of lynching (Paula Giddings, *Ida: A Sword among Lions*). She was not alone as women nationwide worked in their respective communities to advance the race. Such historians as Kate Masur (*An Example for All the Land*), Barbara Welke (*Recasting American Liberty*), Janette Thomas Greenwood (*First Fruits of Freedom*), Leslie Schwalm (*Emancipation Diaspora*), and Martha S. Jones (*All Bound Up Together*) provide thorough studies of the work of black women in resettlement efforts, fraternal organizations, Freedmen's Bureau, education, and the African Methodist Episcopal Church.

In Minnesota, black women worked in many of these same areas, though exhaustive research has yet to be done. Such a study would have to include Adeline Taylor, who, with her husband, spirited fugitive slaves to St. Paul and beyond in the early 1850s, and Emily Grey, who led a posse to free Eliza Winston in 1860. In 1887, Mrs. J. J. Wiley was arrested for allegedly causing a disturbance after white men accosted her during a procession for President Grover Cleveland. She successfully sued the county to have her arrest record expunged. Nellie Francis, who became active in the state Republican Party and a leader in the woman's suffrage movement in Minnesota, successfully lobbied the state legislature to enact an anti-lynching bill that would predate the federal effort by decades. In 1921, Lena O. Smith, a former hairdresser who became the first black female licensed attorney in Minnesota, a founder of the Minneapolis Urban League, and first woman president of the Minneapolis chapter of the NAACP, championed issues such as equal protections, equal access to housing, and the right to join labor unions. Nellie Stone Johnson, activist and labor leader, would later cofound the Minnesota Democratic-Farmer-Labor Party.

"Race" work, in other words, was not the exclusive province of men. Yet, history records that the relationship between black men and women activists was not usually smooth during the late nineteenth and early twentieth centuries. Even DuBois, a supporter of women's rights, had to reluctantly concede in 1906 to the prevalence of male chauvinism by fashioning a women's auxiliary to operate as a branch of the Niagara Movement. This was a step forward because women were not included at the inaugural meeting a year earlier. In Minnesota it would not be until the late 1880s that women branched out from traditional work in social, educational, community, and church activities into political activism. Even so, most black women were relegated to laboring inconspicuously in menial tasks that limited their ability to participate in a group that had an advocate for them. Indeed, most were like Martha Clark, who worked for Senator Alexander Ramsey for more than twenty years. The day after getting married, she was required to leave her new husband behind in St. Paul to accompany her employer when he returned to Washington. Essentially, the kind of work to which most black women were relegated infringed on their right to pursue happiness. The history of the black women of Minnesota is layered and complex, and reflects experiences uniquely saddled by sexism, racism, and classism. Thus, it deserves its own treatment at another time.

To write this history I relied on primary and secondary resources that included letters, memoirs, government documents, court records, statutes, speeches, census data, articles, books, and newspaper articles. Of these sources, I found newspapers especially helpful in providing context to the drama. I always sought to verify the accuracy of the article and understand the bias of the writer, but I found that they shed light on historical moments often glossed over in other sources. For example, we only know the existence and, more important, the work of the race men discussed in the first two chapters from newspaper accounts. The same applies to the events surrounding Frederick Douglass's 1873 speech in St. Paul mentioned earlier. Legislative journals of the state house and senate only summarized parliamentary maneuverings of key bills as they worked their way to enactment or defeat, but newspapers transcribed the speeches and debates, complete with the color of the response from the gallery and other legislators. One could often discern the thinking of major politicians, who otherwise refrained from speaking or writing on certain issues, by reviewing editorial comments of the major newspapers, for it was common practice for the newspapers to serve as the politicians' "organ." And with the publication of the *Appeal,* black Minnesotans, who otherwise received spotty coverage from the white press, spoke for themselves for the first time. More than conveying news and opinion, newspapers often reprinted letters from black Minnesotans, which preserved correspondence that otherwise did not survive the passage of time. All of this is to say newspapers were integral pieces to a puzzle without which the whole picture would be incomplete.

I am grateful to the Minnesota Historical Society for its wonderful collection of newspapers, letters, memoirs, census data, county records, and recorded interviews, and especially to Debbie Miller, Hampton Smith, and all the other MHS staff too numerous to name who helped me scale the numerous roadblocks I encountered. I extend my appreciation to Earl Spangler, David Taylor, and Paul Nelson, whose pioneering research first peered through the veil of nuance so characteristic of race relations in Minnesota at the end of the nineteenth century, to Brendan Henehan, whose research on black newspapers and lawyers was invaluable, and to Douglas Bristol, who explored the complex manner in which black barbers leveraged their role of service to fashion to one of civic leadership. It is indeed on their shoulders that I was able to frame the right questions and see the bigger picture. Finally, I thank Erik Anderson for believing in this book and my vision, for it was his ever-welcome advice, calming manner, and (just as valued) easy conversation that made bringing this project to fruition relatively pain free.

PART I
the
BARBERS

1

WHEN AMERICA CAME TO ST. PAUL

"Be it enacted by the Legislative Assembly of the Territory of Minnesota,
That all free white male inhabitants over the age of twenty-one years, who
shall have resided within this Territory for six months next preceding an
election shall be entitled to vote at any election for delegate to Congress
and for territorial and county officers..."

—An Act to prescribe the qualification of voters
and of holding office, Chapter IV, Laws of Minnesota, 1849

Jim Thompson, a former slave who had lived in Minnesota for more
than a decade and one of the first residents and a respected member of
the small French-speaking community that would soon be called St.
Paul, lived in a cabin near the Mississippi River. It was here, on the evening of January 25, 1841, that a man named Jean-Baptiste Deniger, in the
company of a ten-year-old mixed blood girl named Ursula Labissoniere,
stopped to warm up against the winter's chill. Deniger was drunk and
the girl looked afraid of him. Sensing Thompson's suspicion, Deniger left,
speeding away in the sleigh he had parked outside. Time passed before
Thompson was able to borrow a horse and sleigh from a neighbor and
give chase. When he finally caught up with Deniger he found the man
already in the act of raping the girl. Thompson pulled Deniger away from
the girl and carried her back to his cabin.[1]

On February 13, Henry Hastings Sibley, newly appointed Justice of the Peace to Clayton County, Iowa Territory, issued a warrant for Deniger's arrest, basing probable cause on the affidavits of Jim Thompson and friend and neighbor Jacques Lefevre.[2] At the hearing François Chevalier, another neighbor of Thompson's, testified that he heard Deniger say that he intended to "do something." Chevalier's testimony, along with that of Thompson, Lefevre, and Monjeau, all but assured a finding of guilt.[3]

Within his community of Pig's Eye, then named for the French Canadian loner with the squinty eye who had lived there before anyone else, Thompson was likely recognized as l'homme noir or l'Américain, but these descriptions did not diminish his status as un homme de caractère, a man of character. He had been with his neighbors when they first set foot on this expanse of land that sloped to the bend in the river. By the end of the year, their little community would become "Saint Paul," named for the apostle of nations. In this rugged place, racism was a foolish indulgence for survival relied on kinship. The sharp edge of the law was blurred in the mist of great distance between civilization and the frontier outpost.

Thompson was born a slave on the Virginia plantation of America's fifth president, James Monroe, and was brought in 1828 to Fort Snelling by his subsequent master Lieutenant William Day. At the fort he was a "mulatto slave," and later when, as a freedman, he worked at the Methodist mission at Kaposia, he was designated a "negro." In fact, official documents, census data, records, and chronicles kept by Americans referred to him by this racial designation. However, the court record of the Deninger hearing and Sibley's arrest warrant referred to Thompson conveniently as "deponent" far out of view of settled Iowa Territory where the legislature had just passed a law that mandated "a negro, mulatto, or Indian, shall not be a witness in any court or any case against a white person."[4] Racism, within this context, was impractical, if not pointless.

To Iowans south of Prairie du Chien the reason for these prohibitions was simple: they wanted to do nothing that gave blacks legal benefits that might, in turn, stimulate black immigration into the region. Iowa also banned interracial marriages in 1840. Historian Eugene Berwanger wrote, "Iowa's proximity to [slaveholding] Missouri and the fact that many Iowans considered free blacks the most wretched and miserable element of the population, guided the actions of the Hawkeye legislators."[5] At the first state constitutional convention in 1844 many Iowa delegates, not content with denying the ballot and membership in the state legislature and militia, also demanded, unsuccessfully, the incorporation of a black exclusion provision in the territorial constitution. One delegate, a former New Yorker, said he would "never consent to open the doors of our beautiful state [to Negroes] . . . If free Negroes were not prevented from settling in Iowa, the neighboring states would drive 'the whole black population of the Union' into it."[6]

But Mendota and Pig's Eye were situated far from Des Moines, the territorial capital. Thompson, the mulatto, the man of African descent, the Negro, did indeed testify against Deniger, the white man. Indeed, Minnesota country was still wilderness, despite the civilized trappings of county designations and juridical appointments of the courtroom. The American flag fluttered over the confluence of the Mississippi and Minnesota rivers before the national identity and social custom of prejudice was firmly established, not only within the enforcement of the law, but, more significantly, the hearts and minds of residents.

"Civilization," as legal historian Lawrence Friedman wrote, "advanced in undulating waves, generally along river valleys . . . The land was not empty before the Americans came." Nor was it so after they first arrived. For a time, in practical terms, Americans reluctantly had to coexist with other social systems. The Dakota still controlled much of their territory, and "[i]n the Mississippi Valley, a cluster of Frenchmen lived by a half-remembered form of the law of France."[7] The inhabitants of Pig's Eye clearly were not concerned about being overrun by free blacks and fugitive slaves, let alone Americans. Jim Thompson, who apparently learned to speak French, was the only man of African descent living among them, and yet he in effect had become one of them.

A man of considerable abilities, he learned to speak Dakota and, while still a slave, married Mary—Marpiyawecasta—daughter to the Dakota chief Cloud Man whose village sat on the shore of what was later named Lake Calhoun.[8] He himself was a man who was half-black, half-white, had a Dakota wife and, by 1842, a three-year-old daughter and newborn son named George, who coincidentally bore the name of Jim's first master. In 1856, Thompson succeeded in getting his children, Sarah and George, who were both one-half Mdwankanton Dakota, listed as official members of the Lake Pepin Mixed Blood Reservation.[9] To Thompson, race consciousness seemed to be fluid. He represented preterritorial, "precivilized" Minnesota.

However, to the Yankees who transformed St. Paul from an outpost into an American city, Thompson, a man for whom many claimed great admiration, was simply a "colored" man and "the African."[10] As an American once again living among Americans he once more became a man whose "blackness" relegated him to live within limits and a state of inferiority. History reveals the relative speed at which Minnesota moved in order to stand at last at the threshold of territorial status. The first step was to satisfy the requirements of the Northwest Ordinance of 1787, which required that five thousand free adult male inhabitants live in the region. Even the black man Jim Thompson was included in the count. As soon as a district qualified, a legislative assembly had to be convened of which one house should be popularly elected. The ordinance encouraged settlers to build schools, admonished inhabitants to be just to the Indians, required common highways to forever remain free to all citizens of the United States, and mandated that new states would be forever a part of the Union and that its inhabitants should bear their portion of the federal burdens.[11] The Ordinance prohibited the expansion of slavery into the region. As the district became a territory and later formed into a state, the new society would be dedicated to "the fundamental principles of civil and religious liberty."[12] Under the Northwest Ordinance there was no concern about race (provided, of course, that the man was non-Indian) or even whether a man was a citizen of the United States; he only needed to inhabit the region. As an inhabitant under that rule, Jim Thompson was equal to any man and therefore was included in the count.

The next step required compliance with the Organic Act, which authorized qualified residents to elect a territorial legislature that then drafted a constitution for the territory.[13] Under this act, those eligible to vote for the delegates were *white* males over twenty-five years of age. It was ironic that all of the male inhabitants of color who were needed to make Minnesota "eligible" for territorial status would be denied their civil rights by the very law that they helped to make possible. Such was the nature of civilization that was being introduced onto the Minnesota frontier. Although the Organic Act excluded black men from voting for a representative to the first legislative session, a provision in section 5 empowered the territorial government to reassign to inhabitants of color suffrage rights that were extinguished when the Organic Act replaced the Northwest Ordinance as the basic charter of government for the Minnesota Territory. What rights the Organic Act had taken away from Thompson could theoretically be returned by enactment of the territorial legislature.

This action, of course, was not likely to be taken. Each week brought steamboats laden with new settlers from northern and Midwestern states that had enacted "black laws," reflecting the antiblack sentiment that characterized the Jacksonian Era, and many of these people were the same ones who had endorsed such legislation.[14] Nonetheless, the debate really involved more than whether inhabitants of color should be able to vote: it was a clear indication of Minnesota's evolving notion of race, the black community's value to society, and an expression of the territorial self-interest and self-image.

In those early days, the "white"-only language of the Organic Act had to seem peculiar, for it scarcely reflected the reality of race and color in early Minnesota. Observing the residents of St. Paul in 1845, Fletcher Williams wrote: "At this time, by far the largest proportion of the inhabitants were Canadian French, and Red River refugees, and their descendants. By 1847, there were only three or four purely American (white) families in the settlement . . . English is probably not spoken in more than three or four families."[15] The people here were "a curious commingling of races, the old Scotch, English, and French settlers having married with the Crees and Chippewa, and crossed and recrossed until every shade of complexion, and a Babel of tongues, was the result."[16]

There was a sense that the community had a duty to educate a child regardless of race. In a letter written in 1846 by the Reverend Thomas S. Williamson, a physician and missionary seeking a teacher for a school he had established, he wrote: "[The teacher] should entirely be free from prejudice on account of color, for among her scholars she might find not only English, French and Swiss, but Sioux and Chippewa, with some claiming kindred with the African stock."[17] Williamson had to be referring to Thompson's children, who were eight and five.

Still, one was as likely to hear French spoken on the street as English. The town in 1849 was very much an outpost, with French voyageurs and half-breed "attachés" (Franco-Indian trappers affiliated with the American Fur Company). The newly formed Court of the Third District that included St. Paul convened in the latter part of August. Judge David Cooper presided and Henry Sibley was foreman of the grand jury. Judge Cooper read the jury an elaborate charge, which Sibley said only three of the twenty-odd members understood, because the rest were French. Major William Forbes, also a member of the first Territorial Council, had to translate.[18]

This was a place that would soon receive the "American stamp." The *Pioneer* excitedly reported on a recent arrival of the *Highland Mary* that carried five hundred passengers, a common load for those days. "On Friday morning . . . the smoke of a steamboat was visible at Saint Paul, and the very heart of the town leaped with joy . . . As she came up in front of Randall's warehouse, the multitude on shore raised a deafening shout of welcome . . . Such has been the anxiety here before the arrival of steamboats, that nothing else was talked of. Saint Paul seemed likely to go to seed."[19] With each boatful of settlers came the racial bias of the nation. An editorial on the same day said, "Let us do everything in our power to welcome, encourage, and build up those who have come to unite their fortunes with ours," and further recommended that, as hotels were overcrowded, citizens entertain the strangers at their homes until they could build "tenements." In June 1849, 840 people lived in St. Paul. One year later the population had grown to 1,289 residents.[20]

Nine years earlier, Thompson was attracted by the space he saw in the clearing called Pig's Eye. Now, within the limits of St. Paul, the space was rapidly disappearing. The ninety-acre tract called St. Paul Proper included all the principal business parts of town and the most thickly populated neighborhoods. The names of the proprietors of those lots were some of the most prominent names of early Minnesota—Robert, Lambert, Jackson, Brunson, Cavalier, Sibley, Bass, Larpenteur, Forbes, Simpson, Rhodes, LaRoche, Coty, Guerin—and Thompson was their neighbor.[21] But even though he knew men who would soon become Minnesota's power elite and now did well for himself as a carpenter and roofer, his standing as an Old Settler would not transfer to New Citizen.

On September 27, 1849, twenty-six-year-old Benjamin Brunson passed his next-door neighbor Thompson's home on his way to the Central House, a hotel where the territorial legislature was convening. Brunson had had a long relationship with Thompson because his father, Methodist missionary Alfred Brunson, had purchased and then freed Thompson in 1837 to work as an interpreter at the Kaposia mission on the opposite bank from latter-day St. Paul. Thompson later provided lumber to construct the first Methodist church in St. Paul, and the site of a school. Thompson had been, in other words, a fixture in the Brunson family history. However, on September 27, 1849, under his arm was a bill that granted suffrage rights only to white men over twenty-one years of age. On November 1, Representative Brunson's restrictive bill became law.[22]

The effect of the law was both immediate and expansive. By denying Jim Thompson and all other nonwhite men the franchise to participate in territorial, county, or precinct elections, the law barred them from serving on county juries because such service required that jurors be selected from voting lists. In time, this law also denied all nonwhite men from serving as a referee in civil cases and from holding office in villages because such candidates had to be "qualified as a juror."[23] In 1851, the law would expand to bar blacks from running in village elections by providing that any person elected to office had to be "entitled to vote at the election at which he shall be elected." A similar law in 1853 prohibited black participation in town meetings. Although these subsequent laws were not necessarily intentional expressions of antiblack sentiment, but rather logical increments of citizenship, the cumulative effect was to increase restrictions on the rights of Minnesota's free black inhabitants.[24]

In 1854, the entire St. Paul delegation in the territorial house supported Bill No. 34, "a bill to provide for the good conduct of Negro and mulatto persons." Modeled on an 1807 Ohio law, it required all blacks intending to permanently reside in the territory to post a personal bond of three hundred to five hundred dollars as a guarantee of good behavior, practically barring people with meager resources from further settlement. The bill failed by a vote of six to ten. Following the defeat, St. Paul representative John H. Day, angered at St. Anthony–area legislators who opposed his bill, gave notice that during the next legislative session "he would introduce a bill to compel all the negro population of the Territory of Minnesota to reside in St. Anthony and Minneapolis."[25] Dr. Day's segregation bill, however, never materialized.

In 1856, the target of discrimination extended from black adults to their children when the city's school board began efforts to segregate black children from their white classmates, relegating the black children to the worst facilities available.[26] In fact, antiblack sentiment was so rigid that when school superintendent Benjamin Drew discovered that a "quadroon" boy was attending a white school, he told the teacher that "she had done wrong to receive him as [the boy] would not be allowed to remain."

The teacher responded, to no avail, that the mixed-race boy—one-quarter black—"is no darker than many [mixed-blood Indians] who were here."[27]

Six years earlier, three schools were established to provide "ample means for the education of *all* the children in town," and one of the schools was in the basement of the Methodist church that Thompson helped to construct and finance.[28] Now Thompson's son was being denied an education because he was one-quarter black. It was about this time that Old Settlers Jim and Mary Thompson moved their family away from the St. Paul they no longer knew.[29] But this was a new age.

In 1861, Minnesota was not only a state, but it was at war with the South, which included the state of Thompson's birth. Minnesotans had also become predominantly white, Protestant, and unambiguous in their sense of superiority over the black, red, and brown man. And yet, by 1865 these same ignoble white men had nobly fought to end slavery and lay the groundwork for equality.

But did Thompson feel that being able to vote would make him equal? Although he left no record of his thoughts on the matter, he was a practical man. That was how he had survived this far. Thus, it would seem that to him, "equality" was not just a word on a document, or even a right to cast a ballot, but the extent to which the white man respected his stake and his right to possess it. One knew the men with whom an agreement was made, and it was sealed not by a document, but by a handshake. As long as he knew the men and they knew him, the law did not matter. Indeed, as more people came to town, jostling for their stake in a place with diminishing opportunities, politics became necessary and it only worked if one had friends. By the mid-1860s, his French friends were gone. Many of the Anglo-Minnesotans who had been his friends either acquiesced or actively supported racialized laws and practices. The Dakota had been removed from the state. And he had nothing in common with the black people now making their homes in the town he had helped to found. When America, itself a foreign culture to the region, had come to the St. Paul he knew, he had watched his opportunities wane and his fortunes diminish, and with them evaporated the prospects for his children; and it wasn't so much because of the law, for racial exclusionary law had come with the flag in the 1820s, but because of the men who eventually flooded into the region.

Thompson, the product of the old St. Paul, was black, but different, for his speech pattern, after so many years of speaking French and Dakota, probably made him sound vaguely foreign to the recent arrivals—both black and white. In all likelihood, they would not have known him to be from St. Paul, certainly not the city they knew. Their city had been built on top of the ground that sloped to the bend in the river where he had first stepped out of his canoe in 1840 with the first band of Red River refugees, where he watched it grow from Pig's Eye to a village named for the Apostle of Nations, to a time when he was a neighbor of Sibley and Ramsey and son-in-law of a powerful Dakota chief. By the 1860s, his St. Paul had become fully civilized, but it was a civilization that relegated him to a status of inferiority. Within a growing community, he must have lived increasingly in isolation, possessing knowledge of how to survive in a precivilized world, and knowing things that no one else could know—the full range of relationships between the black man and the white. This made him a stranger in a strange land, a foreigner within his own country, within the town he helped build, in what had once been home, a place the new Negro had called the Promised Land, a curious place where a wealthy black man who became a leader for black advancement secured his stature by serving white men only. A strange land indeed.

2

Maurice Jernigan Takes a Stand

"We the undersigned colored residents of the State of Minnesota, respectfully petition your honorable bodies to amend the constitution of this State, by striking out the word 'white' believing it not only superfluous, but prescriptive in its terminology—a mark of degradation, and the great auxiliary in supporting the unilateral prejudice against us who have committed no crime save the wearing complacently the dark skin our Creator had seen fit in his all-wise providence to clothe us with."

—Maurice Jernigan, A. Jackson, H. Hawkins, Ed. James, and W. Griffin (The Black Barbers of St. Paul), *St. Paul Press*, 1865

During the nineteenth century, if a black man had enriched himself as a barber from a thriving business located in the city's best neighborhood and serving a clientele comprised of the city's social, political, and financial elite, and he wanted to improve the welfare of African Americans, he had to carefully straddle the thorny polarity of competing interests. Against the odds of racial prejudice he had acquired the American dream—something few white native-born or immigrant men could say—by securing the patronage of white men of influence whose community standing built firmly a platform of status quo. In order to continue drawing his high-paying customers, the black barber had to accommodate men who benefited from or were complaisant to a society that held African Americans in a perpetual state of inferiority. Beneath his congenial demeanor and skill with razor and scissors, he knew that his prosperity, his survival, his capacity to help his race rested on his quiet access to the white power elite and on his ability to charm. This essentially was the paradox in which he operated. Through the prism of nineteenth-century republican ideals, especially on the free soil of the North, barbering, despite offering black men the only avenue to personal advancement, was considered an "unmanly" occupation, one steeped in the application of fine scents and tonics that catered to the vanities of fashion and bourgeois conceits of a privileged few, applied deftly as the barber often indulged, if not in abject racial stereotype, at least with jolly sycophancy.

No black barber, argued black leaders Frederick Douglass and Martin Delany, could ever expect to be equal to the white man or earn his respect. As long as the black man relied on servant status, argued Morton Wilkinson, a supporter of black suffrage and the U.S. senator from Minnesota, the black man and his race would be relegated to perpetual subservience. Yet, upon closer examination, looking past the nonthreatening veneer that barbers necessarily perpetuated, despite the stigma from republican values, individual black barbers, under the cloak of adaptation, would prove to do more to help their black kinsmen in getting jobs and the ballot than any single intellectual, leader, or politician, black or white. They were, essentially, a living and breathing paradox in that they were better situated to change the status quo not just by working within it but by supporting it. Their middle-class pretensions, their desire for respectability and moderation, their sometimes conservative views on race relations made them easy to be misunderstood, denigrated, and even mocked by insensitive white customers and impassioned reformers of both races alike. Yet, as illustrated in Minnesota, they kept on trimming hair until, in time, they became the recognized leaders whose voices, even more than those of Douglass and Delany, validated the next bold step to equality.

Relative to the social and racial constraints of St. Paul in the 1850s, the small number of black men living in town could be seen engaged in useful work either as laborers or as barbers, with the presumption by most white people seeing them that they were free. But another class of black men also inhabited St. Paul, men who had violated the law of servitude by running away from their masters. Such men had reason to cover their tracks, seek the protection of friendly souls, and sometimes lead a paradoxical existence of being hidden in plain view. This too was a manifestation of the time when American civilization came to St. Paul, for the long reach of Southern slaveholders increasingly followed the great Mississippi northward. Although slavery was prohibited, there was no guarantee of safe harbor for the fugitive. Still, fugitives trickled into town.

Stealthily, a slave could make his way northward by staying in a series of safe houses where he would receive the name of another person further up the line who in turn would help him to freedom. Usually such routes, depending on who "conductors" knew, ran northeasterly toward Chicago or Detroit, anywhere where the fugitive could easily blend into the large and generally safe population, or into Canada. However, during the early 1850s a few fugitives followed the North Star up the Mississippi. Joseph Farr, an African American who resided in St. Paul at the time and participated in this effort, described how it worked. A fugitive would arrive at the Illinois home of Eugene Berry, a black man who lived by the river. When the time was safe—for slave catchers could be anywhere—Berry would lead the fugitive to "our agent in Galena," a black laborer named James Garret Johnson working on the wharf, who would then stow the fugitive among the freight onboard the *Dr. Franklin* bound for St. Paul. "When the boat came into St. Paul my uncle . . . would be at the wharf and the fugitive would be brought to my uncle's house, where I lived."[1]

The St. Paul in which Joseph Farr lived with his uncle and aunt was wide open, a place that during the months when steamboat traffic was possible was dusty and noisy with all the virtues and vices of a raucous frontier boomtown; streets and boardwalks filled with all manner of folk: settlers, town burghers, dreamers, and drifters. A growing number of them came from eastern and Midwestern states. Many were immigrants, but almost all of them were native-born and reflected every attitude in America, good and bad, about the African American, except belief in slavery. And although the town was vibrant, it was still quite small, so when a black man—any black man—walked the streets, he was noticed, and Farr's uncle was a black man of considerable note. In one account, while his aunt harbored a recently arrived fugitive, the slave master entered his uncle's barbershop. Farr, at the time an eighteen-year-old working in the shop, recalled that the man dressed "as Southerners were always dressed in those days, with a wide-brimmed light hat and expensive black clothes," and said to his uncle, "See here, I understand that you know all about the fugitives that come here," and offered him thirty dollars to help him reclaim one. While they stalled him, Aunt Adeline sneaked the slave woman away to safety.[2]

What is notable, beyond the heroic act of Farr's uncle and aunt, as well as his partner and fellow "conductor" James Heighwarden, another black barber formerly of Virginia, is that the slaveholder who had traveled so far from home to retrieve his slave, and was presumably unfamiliar with St. Paul, knew that William Taylor, the black barber whose shop was next to the post office on Third near Minnesota, was the man he should see.[3] Someone had to have told him about Taylor. Anyone could have seen him escort fugitives up from the levee, their telltale demeanor of walking as if their lives depended on vigilance, always looking over their shoulders or downward to avoid the gaze of white folks, as if doing so might make them invisible, but not realizing that trying to be invisible on the streets of St. Paul in the early 1850s only assured their detection. And even if people never saw Taylor with a fugitive, he nevertheless remained quite notice-able, for he dressed well and owned his own business, all of which made him seem superior to common laboring white men within a white man's territory of Minnesota. And even if he had had nothing at all to do with fugitives, his race made him guilty by association for bringing the cheapest of unskilled black workers to compete against white laborers. St. Paul legislators, reflecting this fear, introduced a bill similar to Ohio's black code that would discourage blacks from entering the state by requiring a bond of five hundred dollars for good behavior. The bill failed.[4] Nonetheless, St. Paul's mood toward the African American—or rather, that of the majority of white men on the street who didn't have, and were not likely to ever have, what Taylor possessed—was evident.

A power shift was now occurring within territorial politics. From here on, territorial and later state law would not reflect the values and fears of the majority of white men on the streets of St. Paul. With every new wave of arrivals that transformed Minnesota into a Republican territory, St. Paul conversely became a Democratic stronghold. It would be reasonable for a Southern master—himself, of course, a Democrat—to expect support from fellow Democrats who no more than he wanted fugitives in their midst, especially if the fugitive could take a job. The man on the street, resenting the legislative failure of the black code bill, had reason to feel that if the territorial leaders would not protect him against the black man, then he must protect himself, and in doing so join his interests with that of the Southerner, as Congress apparently had intended in a recent enactment.

The Fugitive Slave Act of 1850 was intended by Northern political leaders to create a sectional truce, but it simultaneously created "an atmosphere of fear" in African American communities throughout the North, for it empowered slaveholders, with the assistance of any willing civilian, to speedily reclaim fugitives, and punished anyone who aided the fugitive with a fine and imprisonment. The captive had no legal safeguards such as a jury trial or other legal proceeding. In fact, the new law awarded ten dollars to the commissioner if he ordered the captive's return, but only five dollars if he ordered the captive's release. Although the paperwork involved in the two transactions supposedly justified the difference, critics called it an open bribe. It also posed an obvious threat to free Northern-born African Americans, especially those viewed to be a threat to white interests. Any of them might be "mistakenly" identified as fugitives or simply "kidnapped" and carried to the South because the law made it nearly impossible for black people to prove that they were in fact free. Encouraged by the law, Southerners like the master who approached William Taylor appeared in Northern communities or employed agents to reclaim runaways. Across the North paid informers of both races "identified" fugitives. "Even among the ex-slaves [within Minnesota] there were traitors," Farr reported. Some "traitors" gave false testimony. All of this exacerbated tension under which Northern African Americans lived. An estimated twenty thousand fled to Canada between 1850 and 1860. However, "most Negroes," as Leon Litwack wrote, "chose to remain in the North and resist the precarious nature to their freedom." Barber Taylor was one such person in that he flaunted the proscriptions of the law rather than cower to it. From the year he first arrived in St. Paul—the same year federal law mandated that he desist in trafficking fugitives, or at least be discreet in his actions—Taylor set up shop and waited to receive the first arrival of a slave running away from bondage, seemingly impervious to the fact that he acted in clear violation of federal law.[5]

It would seem, therefore, that Taylor could be easily prosecuted or worse, "mistakenly identified" as the runaway; that the Southern master could get any number of men on the streets of St. Paul to collaborate in reclaiming his property. Instead, the master chose to be discreet. He first tried bribing Taylor, and when that failed he simply moved on, apparently understanding that the barber was no ordinary Negro. This black man owned and operated an establishment on one of the main streets of the business section of St. Paul. "[A] very well-known character and the leader of the colored people here in those days," his establishment was "up to the increasing luxury, style, and elegance of the growing metropolis of Minnesota."[6] Such a place could only operate if his customers were numerous and, given the demographic of St. Paul during the first half of the 1850s, white—and not just white men, but, as his own experience with successful black barbers dictated, white men of status. Even in the Deep South, where slavery was the foundation of the economy and an integral part of the culture, and racial stigma was law, black men skilled at barbering had thriving businesses in such cities as Charleston, Mobile, Savannah, and Natchez, Mississippi. In Alabama during the 1850s, a free black man and barber named John Rapier was so successful that he could afford to travel throughout the United States and Canada as well as send his sons to college. All of them could not have thrived without the support and protection of very influential white men.[7] And Taylor was indeed known by St. Paul's social elite. This was a place where balls and dancing parties were about the only proper amusement available, without which "the long winter months would have probably been intolerably tedious." For such events, William Taylor was in great demand as a popular ball musician. With "a very musical voice," he notably "called figures" for hundreds of balls and dances.[8]

Presumably, the St. Paul society that enjoyed his talents was comprised of Democrats and Whigs alike and both wanted cheap labor to do the work as the territory's economy grew. Among the Democrats was one notable leader, Henry Hastings Sibley, who had sent agents south "to engage Negroes as deck hands on the steamboat" after their white deckhands struck for higher wages. At the time, Minnesotans were fighting two wars—one against the Confederates and the other against the Dakota—and these hostilities compounded the need for Sibley's steamboats carrying supplies for troops to operate unimpeded by aggrieved white laborers. The financial vitality of St. Paul and the gentlemen of the city who benefited from it likewise relied on uninterrupted steamboat service.[9] It was a situation in which white laborers acting under color of federal law could theoretically protect their perceived interests when Democratic leaders could not—or would not.

In 1855, one year after the black code bill failed in the Minnesota legislature, the *Dr. Franklin,* the steamboat on which the Virginia-born Joseph Farr worked as a cabin boy before moving to live and work with his uncle in St. Paul, and lifeline to so many runaways looking for freedom in the North Star State, sank; and with that ended the Minnesota leg of the Underground Railroad. Years later, Joseph Farr would write: "Oh I can't tell how many slaves we got away." Nationally, it was estimated that fifty thousand slaves escaped the South through the Underground Railroad. Few of the men and women who made it to William Taylor's home in Minnesota registered their names and there was no way to identify them, making it virtually impossible to trace whether they moved on or whether they stayed. They had no reason to cooperate with census takers working for the same government that enacted and enforced the Fugitive Slave Act. They had every reason to be discreet in a town where slave catchers roamed and duplicitous whites and blacks were everywhere waiting for the chance to turn them in for a reward. Within this fog of history lies the story of Maurice Jernigan, who illustrates key elements of the history of black barbering.

Black barbering in America began during the earliest years of the colonial era, in the master's household, where work as a private servant exposed the slave to the changing Anglo-American culture. By the 1600s, American colonists had begun adapting the cultural practices of the European aristocracy to the circumstances in the New World, importing genteel culture in pursuit of higher status. Historian Douglas Bristol explains: "Whether they built brick houses or, as in the case of Benjamin Franklin, merely ate their porridge out of a china bowl with a silver spoon, America's great merchants and planters brought with them or began to acquire the trappings of genteel living." When people could not attain higher social standing in European courts, by learning new manners and adopting different styles of presentation, they could in America transform themselves from rude provincials into cosmopolitan members of "polite society." Copying the grace of aristocrats established genteel practices in the colonies. George Washington reflected this sensibility when he copied out 110 "Rules of Civility," thereby acquainting himself with proper behavior that dated back to the Renaissance.[10]

Fundamental to genteel values was the conviction that outward behavior and appearance reflected the inner self. A spiritual divide was thought to exist between genteel people and common folk, with the former thought to possess keen sensibilities and a more refined sense of beauty, while the latter supposedly lacked well-developed intellectual and emotional faculties and stood lower on the scale of human development. These distinctions justified a sense of inequality by presenting class differences as the natural order of things. "To be acknowledged by others, as genteel," Bristol observed, "validated one's claim to membership of the ruling class. Hair assumed a prominent role in displays of gentility." Deriving from styles adopted by European monarchs, a link was created between hair and social hierarchy. In this context, the barber and hairdresser assumed an important role in helping the socially ambitious maintain a genteel appearance. As a seventeenth-century English critic observed, "May I not truly say of too many . . . that the barber is their chaplain; his shop, their chapel; the looking glass, their Bible; and their hair . . . their God."[11]

Society expected its barbers to be witty, adept at clever flattery, and able to entertain clients. Writers as far back as Plutarch described the pleasant nature of beard trimmers, highlighting the success of the barber as based in part on his ability to create an atmosphere in which courtiers and the upper classes felt at home. "Drawn by the opportunity to relax and exchange ideas, poets, merchants, and intellectuals joined the crowd, leading one barber to boast that the barbershop was 'a place almost within the precincts of the Temple of Learning.'" But even here, the nature of trade imposed great limitations on the social mobility of the barber, even one who had acquired popularity and patronage from the privileged, even when he had leveraged these contacts into prosperity. Because of their status as personal servants, notwithstanding their skill and sensibilities, it was not uncommon for barbers' customers to treat them with contempt. Throughout the seventeenth and eighteenth centuries, the trade carried that stigma regardless of the continent (European or North American), race (black or white), or status (free or slave). Nonetheless, although a barber could not expect to be viewed as an equal, he could, considering his relationship with his master, enjoy a greater degree of camaraderie than any other member of the servant class. Yet he was still a servant. As a result, wrote Bristol, "the barbering trade became associated with the dependence of indentured servants and slaves and the degraded status of free blacks." Especially as it related to free blacks, in the minds of many black leaders, including Frederick Douglass and Martin Delany, barbering—indeed, all "menial" labor—reinforced the conviction among white people "that colored men are only fit for such employment." Because many black barbers, deferring to the prejudices of white customers, barred African Americans from their shops, they were, in the opinion of delegates to the 1852 Ohio Colored Convention, much worse than a white man who refuses to eat, drink, ride, walk, or be educated with the colored man because they themselves were African Americans.[12] Farming, in contrast, symbolized not only emancipation, but manhood.[13]

Black barbers angrily rejected charges that their work degraded the race even as they embraced the trappings of white class sensibilities. A good reputation allowed them to win the confidences of white customers and gave them the credentials to preside over commercial parlors in first-class barbershops. In turn, the income they earned from their thriving businesses allowed them to meet nineteenth-century standards of manhood by keeping their wives at home and their children in school. They also enjoyed the leisure time to participate in community organizations and the resources to support their activities. Thus, despite the criticism, they rose to positions of leadership. And through their customers they were often able to get unskilled blacks jobs. "Despite the occasional embarrassment or humiliation that came from serving white men, they expressed pride in their accomplishments as barbers, men, and leaders."[14] Nonetheless, in the view of critics, there was little fundamental difference between the free black man choosing to degrade himself and the slave.

At the core of the relationship between master and slave barber was the latter's ability to ensure that his master look his genteel best by polishing his boots, shaving his beard, and cutting his hair. Slave owners seemed to value this last skill above the rest. Once they had earned the trust of the master, "waiting men," as barbers were often called, were permitted to run errands, allowing them to become familiar with neighboring people, expand their awareness of the community, meet a wider range of personalities, learn more of the social graces, and adopt a greater degree of polish. All of this contributed to the slave barber's quest to become exceptional, for he knew that his master, especially if the master owned a plantation, considered himself to be an aristocrat in need of a retinue. "The knowledge of social etiquette and genteel fashion made the waiting men

[barbers] the most completely acculturated slaves in the colonial period
. . . The ability to interact comfortably with powerful whites established
distinctions between slaves."[15]

Indeed, acculturation proved to be such a valuable asset that waiting
men sometimes took great pains to display their refinement, and in many
instances contributed to fostering close bonds between master and servant, reflecting the assumption that closeness was loyalty, which was not all
together unreasonable. Thus, masters felt little compunction about having
the slave accompany him on travels west or even north. But possessing the
airs of privilege was a double-edged sword, for while the slave barber's position allowed him opportunities that few slaves received, he was aware that
he could and should have more, that he should be free. Although barbers
were a small portion of the slave population, they accounted for a disproportionate number of the skilled fugitives listed in runaway slave advertisements in South Carolina and Virginia between 1730 and 1801. Unlike
field hands, who typically stayed near their plantations when they ran away,
slave barbers and other skilled fugitives tended to seek out urban areas
where they could blend into the black population. In other instances, they
received indirect assistance from non-slaveholding whites who employed
them without asking too many questions.[16] Or, if they could make it—as
possibly in the case of Maurice Jernigan—skilled fugitives might find sanctuary within a relatively benign community of white people.

Jernigan's first appearance in any official record was in 1863, thirty-one
years after his birth in North Carolina, when, in St. Paul, he registered for
the federal draft, and in the same year was listed in the St. Paul *City Directory*
as a barber at the Merchant Hotel.[17] On the surface these notations might
seem unremarkable, but he was one of a host of men who reflected the
ethnic and occupational diversity of the Second Congressional District
that included St. Paul, and he was not the only black barber listed in the
business directory. Yet, on closer consideration, the notations hint at a
more complex chapter in Minnesota history. There was no record of what
Jernigan did for the first thirty-one years of his life. He did not appear in
census data or city directories anywhere in the nation, nor did he leave
letters, journals, or a memoir, as some free blacks who barbered did during
the antebellum period. Neither he nor the people who knew him talked

about his past. While the lives of most African Americans—free or slave—were lost to history, he especially had a reason to live a life largely unseen if he had run away from his master. Even in the North, after 1850, life was perilous. Masters and their agents roamed the streets of cities and towns secure in the knowledge that federal law and coins of silver protected their right to claim their fugitives, even on the free soil of Minnesota. There were even African Americans, as "the colored man" Joseph Farr recorded, who, in "taking care of the escaped slave, heard of a reward, came into town, and gave the poor wretch up."[18] In this context, one may reasonably surmise that Jernigan's past is obscured because he wanted it that way. A man with a documented past left tracks. A man without a past could redefine himself to suit his needs for the day. Jernigan could well have come to Minnesota in the early 1860s as a free man, but it is implausible that a black man, so recently arrived in St. Paul, could have had the capital and contacts needed to establish a barbershop at one of city's most prestigious hotels and have the steady patronage of the right customers who could provide him with a thriving business. Capital and affluent customers required time to accumulate and he was a man without a past and with too little time to create a relationship. Thus, Maurice Jernigan probably came to Minnesota as a fugitive, arrived sometime during the 1850s, and with Taylor's help gained access to men who saw his talent, protected him from capture, and introduced him to the right people.

It would have taken a circuitous route for the North Carolina–born Jernigan to arrive at Minnesota during the 1850s. Masters often brought favored slaves on trips to the North and West. Jim Thompson had been brought west by his Virginia master; then, after being sold to a second man in Kentucky, he was brought up the Mississippi River to Fort Snelling in the late 1820s. Similarly, Jernigan might have accompanied his master westward, and at some point along the Mississippi River made his escape north to St. Paul, possibly by way of Galena with the assistance of the free black network. Still, in this northernmost region a fugitive was not safe, especially if his skills enhanced his value to his master enough for him to be pursued. He would need to be exceedingly careful. Yet, as a runaway who was articulate and possessed refined skills and social graces, and presented himself in a charming and articulate fashion, he would likely receive protection that could yield opportunity for his advancement when the time was right.

In 1857, the time was not right. Those who enjoyed Jernigan's services—even Democratic leaders he likely served—would have known to be discreet, for in that year the U.S. Supreme Court handed down its decision in *Dred Scott,* based on a slave who claimed his freedom because he had lived in Minnesota, which underscored masters' right to ownership of their slaves on free soil.[19] Slaveholders seeking reprieve from the hot summers in the South found the climate and spring waters of the free state of Minnesota quite desirable, but it was the notable portion of the population who expressed tolerance for practices of visiting Southerners that made their ventures North welcoming. To show the desire for Southern patronage, state senator Charles Mackubin of St. Paul, acting on a petition signed by six hundred citizens from St. Paul, St. Anthony (at the time, St. Anthony was a separate town situated on the east bank of the Mississippi River, near the Falls of St. Anthony), and Minneapolis, introduced a bill securing a right to slave ownership by Southern tourists "for a period not to exceed the time of five months." Even though the senate declined to act by a wide margin, the message nonetheless remained that numbers of Minnesotans welcomed the tourist trade of masters bringing their slaves in tow.[20]

Abolitionists banded together in St. Anthony to form the Hennepin County Anti-Slave Society and carried out a series of confrontations against the Southern visitors, vowing to free slaves from their masters. The Minneapolis *Plain Dealer* castigated them as extremists, exhorting "the good and true men of the North [to] take care of the Abolition fanatic here."[21] Not even the Republicans liked abolitionists. It was one thing to help fugitives in their quest for freedom after they had escaped from their master in some far-off state, as William Taylor had done, and quite another to actively "kidnap" slaves accompanying their masters who visited the area. To the abolitionists, this was a difference without a distinction. By the summer of 1860, the war of words had intensified. Northerners had coined the phrase "bleeding Kansas" to describe the violence that had erupted there between proslavery and antislavery forces. Those who had watched Kansas bleed saw similar clouds form over Minnesota. Conflict seemed inevitable. The continued freedom of Jernigan as a runaway would increasingly rest on the paradox of his being known but not seen.

During the summer of 1860, most African Americans living in St. Paul, St. Anthony, and Minneapolis had reason for concern. On the evening of July 17, Henry Sparks, a body servant of Martha Prince, a vacationer from Mississippi, walked away from the International Hotel and disappeared into the night. With the assistance of unknown free blacks, he escaped to the Farmer's Hotel, located on the road to St. Anthony. After a couple days, white men entered the hotel and forcibly took the runaway and allegedly threatened to "blow his brains out." Within hours, he was seen aboard a steamboat sailing southward "to the silken patriarchal yoke of slavery."[22] Abolitionists brought charges against the "kidnappers" for having taken the man against his will and demanded that Martha Prince be brought to court. In her defense, she claimed that she did not have custody of Sparks, who was then on his way to Mississippi. She was released. The state then turned its attention to the "kidnappers," relying exclusively on the testimony of John Freeland, a free black man who had stayed with Sparks at the Farmer's Hotel, who claimed that St. Paul police officers and their captain forcibly took the fugitive away. They denied the allegation. The defense even called Mayor John Prince (unrelated to the slaveholder in the case) who knew nothing of the facts but nonetheless attested that he had ordered the police "not to meddle with the case." Charges were dropped and the police were released. Then the judge determined that Freeland's charges were groundless.[23] For this he was tried and found guilty of perjury. St. Paul's message to its black residents was clear: keep your head down, know your place. A month later, Minneapolis and St. Anthony would convey a harsher message.

When Republican Governor Alexander Ramsey posted a reward for the capture and return of the slave kidnappers, the Southern guests at the Winslow House in St. Anthony, a short distance upriver from St. Paul, discussed whether they should withhold their business and leave the state altogether. By the end of August that decision would dramatically be made for them when a black woman named Emily Grey rode at the head of a sheriff's posse that included abolitionists to take custody of a slave woman named Eliza Winston. Colonel Richard Christmas, a Mississippi planter, had brought his family to vacation alongside the St. Anthony Falls, for months now a hotbed for abolitionists. When he heard of a plot to take his slave, he relocated the family to a small resort on the shore of Lake Harriet. It was there the posse took Winston into custody and to court before District Judge Charles Vandenburgh. In a boisterous courtroom crowded with white laborers who relied on the tourist trade, the judge heard argument first from John Freeman, former attorney general of Mississippi, another guest at Winslow House and counsel for Colonel Christmas, who argued the federal law preempted state law and in that it dictated that Christmas had a right of ownership over Winston; Christmas therefore had the right to reclaim her. F. R. E. Cornell, representing Winston, disagreed, arguing that because Minnesota law prohibited slavery, Winston was a free woman. The judge, a law partner to Cornell, declared that she was free. The decision ignited a riot that lasted for days. Shops and homes of known abolitionists, including the seamstress shop that Emily Grey owned, were destroyed. For weeks, the residents of Minneapolis and St. Anthony walked the streets with weapons cocked, poised for civil war over the issue of slavery. These were dangerous times indeed.[24]

As the politics of slavery polarized Minnesota, a man like Jernigan could easily be caught in between if he was not careful. Barbering gave him shelter, a way to secure relations with men of influence who otherwise faced off against each other. As the skilled runaway, Jernigan probably surreptitiously continued trimming hair and charming customers, making himself known to the right people with possible assistance from William Taylor, who already had such contacts, as the word quietly spread of this remarkable man. His expertise and genial qualities mixed with a cultured Southern demeanor that he had acquired from working among the storied Southern aristocracy would have given him an exotic allure, especially in the plainspoken frontier community of St. Paul. And yet, nothing was certain, especially if one was in any way associated with the politics of the day.[25] During the riots that followed the Winston court decision, the barbershop of Ralph Grey on Main in St. Anthony was greatly damaged, even though he was not listed on the Abolition Society rolls, housed no antislavery petitions, and was not prominent in rescuing Eliza; but he was married to Emily Grey, the black woman who launched a plan to free the slave woman—made the contacts and led the posse—and his shop was next door to his wife's. He lost everything. The white laborers who rampaged through the streets felt they were attacking those who threatened Southern tourism. But it was more than that. It was Grey's barbershop that represented a special grievance: black men doing well in St. Anthony would surely attract more blacks—free and fugitive alike—to move in and snatch up business opportunities that rightfully belonged to the white man. Such a flinty circumstance had to inspire pessimism in black barbers.

Bristol observed a similar development in the Cincinnati riots of 1829 that "symbolized the beginning of erosion of northern race relations." The city had come to be an economically vibrant city with considerable opportunity, and its black population grew from 2 percent to 10 percent over the decade. With that growth, white anxiety intensified. One newspaper editor proclaimed that "we shall be overwhelmed." Reacting to rumors that hordes of African Americans would soon stream into the city, officials dusted off a series of "black codes" that had been dormant since they were enacted twenty years earlier. All black residents had thirty days to register, show proof of residency, the ability to support themselves, and furnish a bond of five hundred dollars "for good behavior." The true aim, however, was not black registration but black exclusion from the city. "In addition to job competition from African Americans, whites in Cincinnati may have resented the progress the African American community had made toward equality, receiving public funds to educate their children and establishing two churches of their own." White workingmen began attacking the black community called "Little Africa." At the climax of the raids on August 22 two to three hundred white men invaded the district. African Americans, seeing that they could not expect protection from city officials, armed themselves. Fighting between blacks and whites ensued for nearly two days and tensions simmered afterwards. By the end of the year, an estimated 1,100 African Americans had left the city for safe harbor in Canada. Until the Civil War, Northern white mobs in such cities as New York, Philadelphia, and Pittsburgh targeted African American institutions and property of well-to-do black residents, and barbershops were the most identifiable target. "The abolition movement also incited the white community, which explained why John Vashon a [Pittsburgh] black barber and mob victim, was targeted."[26]

Then, in April 1861, Confederate forces fired on the U.S. installation in Charleston harbor, Fort Sumter. The Civil War had begun. Suddenly, in the three largest cities in Minnesota, there were no slave catchers roaming the streets, no St. Paul officials catering to the whims of slave masters and mistresses, no obvious signs of slavery on Minnesota's free soil. Yet, as the young men of Minnesota raced to enlist to defeat Southern secession, the same teeming resentment of white urban laborers roiled against the threat of black men competing for their share of the American dream. In May 1863, the fugitive slave Robert Hickman along with seventy-six runaways—men, women, and children—from Missouri were repelled at the dock in Lowertown by a mob of white workingmen. A week later, when 218 fugitives attempted to dock, another white mob attacked them. Each time they had to be transported upriver to Fort Snelling where they could disembark safely.[27] That same year, in contrast to this reaction of St. Paul's workingmen to black arrivals, and not far from their sight, Maurice Jernigan, listed as "'Morris' Jernigan," opened his barber salon in the Merchant Hotel, one of St. Paul's most prominent establishments. In doing so, he not only became the first black barber to have a first-class establishment; he was the first barber of either race to do so.[28]

As a practice, black proprietors of first-class barbershops guaranteed their accessibility to affluent white customers by purchasing or leasing buildings in first-class neighborhoods, a trend that existed in both Northern and Southern cities. In the Charleston neighborhood where the city's successful merchants, upwardly mobile tradesmen, and white-collar workers resided, black barber Francis St. Marks "stood out not only for his skin color but also for occupying a brick house, in sharp contrast to the wooden houses of his white neighbors." Similarly, barber Thomas Green of Baltimore lived on Light Street in the merchant district. In 1859, two black barbers in Philadelphia—James Auter and Josiah Eddy, known to be the wealthiest barber in America—established businesses in the upscale neighborhoods of the city "with a continuous supply of desirable customers close at hand," and one barber secured a place on Broadway opposite City Hall. Bristol noted, "That they could occupy these prime locations shows that black barbers had become fixtures on the principal streets of America's cities."[29] Likewise, that Maurice Jernigan could operate his establishment in the Merchant Hotel illustrated the support he enjoyed from influential whites of the city, his skills being valued higher than those of the runaways from Missouri.

It is important to remember that the life of Jernigan as a runaway is speculative, aside from his date and place of birth. What is known is that 1863 was the first recorded year in which he operated a barbershop and that it was in the Merchant Hotel. One can parallel his experience with those of so many other black barbers in the North and South during the antebellum period to see how the business provided him with opportunities and contacts that otherwise did not exist for black men—the ability to acquire property, perhaps even wealth, and, as will become apparent, stature within his own community. Writing about black barbers in general, Bristol noted, "[They] met objective economic standards of middle class status . . . As long as affluent white men kept coming to their shops, they could afford to let their wives remain home, educate their children, and serve as deacons in their churches—in short, they could enjoy the trappings of middle class respectability."[30] "Respectability" meant, as Jernigan seemed to feel, coming out from the proverbial shadows. He appeared for the first time in the *City Directory*, a prudent business move. And in 1863, with a thriving business in a prime location, and a new wife for whom he could now provide a comfortable lifestyle, he took yet another step out of the shadows—he registered for the draft.[31]

By the end of 1862 Union forces had endured a number of military defeats at the hand of a smaller, more ill-equipped but better-led Southern army. Even the reputed victory at Antietam was really more pyrrhic than real for Union casualties had nearly equaled those of the Confederates. With the passing of each week, it seemed, Northern resolve to prosecute the war effort waned as hostilities, which many had initially felt would be short-lived, began the second year, with no end in sight. Soon voices in some of the North's largest cities were for an end to the war, and when Lincoln showed no interest in doing this, some voices, such as protesters in New York, called for secession from the Union. When Lincoln issued the Emancipation Proclamation in January 1863, thereby transforming the purpose for the war from a struggle for national unity to a struggle for human freedom, Northern critics questioned whether emancipation ran counter to their interests. Freed slaves, they felt, would be let loose on Northern cities where they would compete with white laborers for unskilled work, and this was unacceptable. With enlistments into the army declining, and fissures widening in Northern communities over the direction of the war, the Union faced an internal crisis that, if left unattended, would surely result in the dissolution of the nation. If men were no longer volunteering to serve, then they needed to be drafted. Those subject to the draft were "every male citizen and those immigrants who had filed for citizenship between the ages of twenty and forty-five."[32] Although the need for the draft was evident, the provisions of the Conscription Act, enacted in March 3, 1863, were ill-conceived by allowing men who could afford it to pay a substitute to enlist in their place, in effect transforming the army for national unity and freedom into one of poor workingmen most threatened by emancipation. This circumstance sparked the New York draft riots in which nearly a hundred African Americans were killed, and black churches and homes were destroyed. Lincoln had to dispatch troops, fresh from the battlefield at Gettysburg, to put down the rioting. Rumors of rioting could be heard in other cities: in St. Paul, a provost guard was posted in the city for several weeks.[33]

It was in this context that Maurice Jernigan registered for the draft, the only black man in Minnesota to do so, and this act revealed another aspect of his character. What he had to do to establish his barbershop suggests that he was talented, charming, shrewd, and had a strategic sense. He knew how to make the right connections, had a refined taste, and measured each step he took with prudence and discretion, so that by 1863 he may have been the wealthiest African American in Minnesota. Each customer enjoyed a manly though elegant barbering experience with good conversation, so characteristic of the most successful of black barbers in America. Jernigan had accomplished all this at a time when black men, free and slave, were swelling Union ranks in a desire to fight for their freedom, but, once wearing the Union blue, were consigned largely to custodial duties. Throughout the next year, black soldiers died by the thousands, not on the battlefield but from disease, as many were sequestered in filthy outposts along the lower Mississippi River.[34] A Protestant Irish immigrant from Le Sueur County commanding a regiment of colored infantry lost so many men that the regiment joined with another equally depleted colored regiment to create one full complement.[35]

When at last they were able to join the fight, black soldiers engaged the enemy with honor. But however ennobling giving the last full measure was, the theaters in which they fought were slaughter fields, and it was in a colored regiment that Jernigan would have served. By registering for the draft, he was offering himself to a heroic and likely martyred fate. Nothing in his known past would have foretold his decision to enlist; few of those who knew him would have predicted it. He had reached the pinnacle of professional success, possibly becoming the best-known and wealthiest black Minnesotan, and certainly the most sought-after barber, black or white, working in the capital city. According to federal law, he was not eligible to register for the draft because he was neither a state nor a federal citizen. But enlistments that spring were low and officials probably were not inclined to refuse a willing body during the national emergency. Besides, black men were already serving in the army and their numbers were increasing by the month. Still, legally, it was one thing to volunteer for enlistment, as the Militia Act of 1862 had authorized, and quite another to be subject to the draft, which was limited to "citizens" and "immigrants who had filed for citizenship," as the Conscription Act of 1863 prescribed. Unless Congress amended the draft law to include African Americans, black men would not be eligible for the draft for another three years when the Fourteenth Amendment conferred citizenship on them. And even if Jernigan's registration was lawful, it did not mean that he would be drafted. Still, his name was accepted and recorded, so he could be drafted regardless of his race.

The question was, why did he register?

Except for a few details that have been entered into official documents about Jernigan, one can only speculate. He left no writings. However, his life and the work of scholars on black barbers shed light on what could have been his motivation. He seemed ready to step out of the shadows, for he knew that a free man stood proudly with his face to the sun. Yet, over years of preparing for the opportune moment to advance himself, Jernigan had, as Bristol wrote of black barbers, "peered into the eyes of white customers and gained an awareness of white insecurities that prevented them from being snarled in the measuring tape that white men used to judge African Americans."[36] He understood that their patronage of him did not mean that they saw him as their equal. In fact, in nineteenth-century America, even though they may have felt genuine affection for him, he remained to them a black man and a barber, whose battles white men were expected to fight. His draft registration was a statement to his customers, who probably never expected him to step forward, and with this came its own kind of respectability. He may have felt a sense of duty. The war had become a struggle for his freedom. He was willing to respond to the call to arms, although he was by now a man of means who could buy his way out just as white men of wealth had been doing and as the law permitted. "We are now called upon in this coming draft," he would later write in a petition for black suffrage, "as we have been here before in preceding drafts to stand our chances in presenting our black bosoms as a rampart to shield our country's nationality from all harm."[37] A special grace was granted to those who did not have to serve but chose nevertheless to do so. Up to this point in his life, Jernigan's fate had been to live a life of duplicity, governed by an awareness of the difference between how blacks appeared to white men and their own racial identity, what W. E. B. DuBois would later describe as "double consciousness." At this point in his life, and in what would follow, he could determine his own character by cautiously integrating his true self with his public self. He could help white men see his success and work as a race man as validation of their own work as founders of a new republic. He could be a race man—one who advocated for black civil rights—with the security of respect from white men.

So, why not enlist? To achieve material success, Jernigan had to be a realist. To achieve his aspirations, as the next several months would make evident, he needed to be tending to his business. He would serve if called, but until that day, he would strengthen his contacts, not only to build up his personal wealth, but to be in the best position to uplift the jobless African Americans who were trickling into the city. With contacts, he could find them jobs. As a businessman, he could show them how money was made and property acquired. With the quality of his temperament, he could model the values and racial character that would secure not just cordiality but respect from white men of power. But by enlisting he would likely be deployed to a colored regiment in the distant South and his business would surely flounder. For as long as circumstances would permit, he needed to be at work, not just for the affluence it created, but for what it promised for the advancement of his race. And until that moment came, he would take every opportunity to lay the groundwork to cultivate his leadership within the small but cohesive group of black barbers whose white clientele set a new agenda for Minnesota that would include black political equality. It was through this network that Jernigan and Charles Griswold, a state representative from Winona, would meet.

When Charles Griswold, a thirty-three-year-old Connecticut-born clergyman from St. Charles Township in the southeastern river county of Winona and member of the house, came to St. Paul for the 1865 legislative session, he stayed, as many legislators did, at the International Hotel, the other prominent hotel in the city, where the cost of staying in one of its rooms easily stretched the modest income of a Minnesota country pastor, but he was worldly enough to know that if he was to accomplish his preordained work as a servant of God whose mission was to bring justice to his fellow man, he needed to be in the midst of where deals were secured. He had indeed come to the legislature for one reason. When in 1857 Republican delegates hammered out their draft for a new state constitution, they had refrained from pressing the case for black suffrage, deferring to voters to decide at a later time. Expediency had required them to do so. Although they held a bare majority over the Democrats during the constitutional convention, their constituents were an amorphous collection of interests who could not be relied on to support black suffrage, and getting a constitution approved was paramount. But since that time, Minnesota had become a state and its young men had fought valiantly to free all men from slavery.[38] Now, in January 1865, Charles Griswold had decided that there was no better time to bring the question to the voters. To do this he needed to get a bill passed in both houses to ask the voters to amend the constitution. Despite a Republican majority, there was no guarantee that the bill would pass; although they supported the war effort, it was uncertain whether enough of them would support black suffrage.

Reverend Griswold was cast from the same mold as Reverend David Secombe, the passionate Congregational pastor from St. Anthony (a village soon to be incorporated with Minneapolis) who, with his brother Charles, was one of the founders of the Minnesota Republican Party; like Secombe, and contrary to many of his fellow clergymen, Griswold had shown no compunction about preaching politics from the pulpit. In fact, Secombe's sermons had been the reason why a black woman named Emily Grey had joined his congregation.[39] Just as Secombe had preached for the abolition of slavery during the 1850s, Griswold preached for black equality, and his efforts bore fruit in an extensive campaign for a bill to remove *white* from the state constitution. He introduced three petitions from Winona, Hastings, and Rochester in favor of black suffrage and was joined by F. M. Stowell, who submitted a petition of 150 residents from Anoka, and Charles Taylor, who presented a petition from Rice County. Griswold was clearly the leader on this issue and he had the votes.[40]

However, he felt that the campaign lacked integrity without a formal endorsement from the very men for whom this right was being established. Like most white men in Minnesota—especially those coming from rural parts of the state—he probably did not know any African Americans, and those he may have seen on the occasional farm or in a town, and certainly at the hotel, were primarily laborers disinclined because of their station in life, or more immediately the work at hand, to venture into a honest conversation with a white man they did not know. The integrity of the endorsement would be based on whether the men giving it had demonstrable breeding, and were not just articulate but were used to communicating to a white audience. Although he may have heard about some black men who could help, within the few weeks of residing at the International Hotel, he knew of only one black man he could conveniently approach, someone who probably knew the kind of men who could give a proper and ideal face to the intelligent and industrious African American man. Thomas Jackson, the barber at the hotel and a quality man in his own right, knew of other such men.[41]

If breeding, refinement, industriousness, and material success were indicators of the kind of men who personified the mid-nineteenth-century Lincoln Republican ideal of what freed bondsmen could become if they were granted the opportunity to be politically equal, the black barbers of the St. Paul business district fit the bill. They shared several common features—their race and occupation, of course, but also their common sense of purpose. What made them leaders, however, even more than their sense of purpose, was a commitment to a singular means of action. It took the form of an organization they cofounded that was dedicated to unlocking the chains that barred black people from a promising future: the Golden Key Literary Society. To the outsider the group seemed innocuous, even laudable in its apparent commitment to books and ideas. But it was more than that. Like other literary societies during the antebellum period in Northern African American communities, when Golden Key members read the argument of slaveholders in order to refute the legitimacy of the peculiar institution, harnessing, as Frederick Douglass wrote, "the mighty power and heart-seeking directions of truth penetrating the heart of the slaveholder," they sought to achieve the same purpose by persuading those who opposed or were ambivalent about black equality. The literary societies in Philadelphia were examples of this focus and it may well have been R. T. Grey, a Pennsylvania native, who brought the concept to St. Paul. It was through the power of the word and the force of the argument that they would lead their people. At a time when the community lacked numbers and resources, the effectiveness of leadership rested on poetic articulation. This small group of black men prepared themselves for the moment they knew would come. They could see from the news and from what their white customers were saying about the war effort that the Confederacy was on its last legs. Jackson's message to Society members was that the time had arrived.[42]

Still, at this moment there were powerful reasons to decline to participate. St. Paul remained a Democratic stronghold. The same men who attacked Robert Hickman's band in 1863 walked the streets today. Besides, much of Jernigan's effort on behalf of black men had involved discreetly persuading white men, including the proprietor of the hotel, to provide them with employment. Even though Republicans dominated the legislature, they would all disperse at the end of the two-and-half-month session, leaving Jernigan to repair relations with Democratic clients who now saw him in a new light and would remember his collaboration with their political rivals. By openly supporting black suffrage, he in effect brought controversy into the barber's chair. His openly expressed opinion held that the Democratic client was wrong. Even if the Republicans could deliver the vote that fall so that Jernigan could become a full-fledged citizen, what good was citizenship if he could not continue to thrive, keep his business, or even earn a living? Furthermore, how could a black man's endorsement in a state where he could not vote sway an election? Why would his opinion have more weight with white male voters than that of their own Republican leaders? In any event, his shop was in Democratic territory, where he risked losing it all. But white men too were making fortunes and losing them as quickly. He could act with caution yet still lose everything. And the world was especially unforgiving to a black man who overreached.

Jernigan may have experienced fatigue from a lifetime of being careful of every word he uttered, always considering how the white man would take his meaning, at times modifying his meaning to the point that it was not how he felt but rather what he thought the white man wanted to hear. John Rapier, the wealthy black barber from Alabama who traveled throughout the country and Canada and sent his three sons to college, a man who "had everything that a free black man could reasonably hope for in Alabama in 1857," wrote to his son that year saying that he had had enough with barbering. "To tell the truth," he declared, "I hate the name barber. A farmer I look on as a superior occupation to a barber . . . The time has come for me to act."[43] But the white men with whom Rapier had to contend, similar in ways to those Jernigan served, were unlike Reverend Griswold, the white man who had come to sit in Jernigan's barber chair, his customer, a lawmaker, who had told him that he wanted a law that would make Jernigan equal to any man, and asked Jernigan to help make it so. How could Jernigan say no? What kind of man would he have been if he had said no? How could he be respected as a black man—no, as a man—if he had said no?

On January 20, the day Griswold introduced his bill, Thomas Jackson and Ralph Grey joined Jernigan in a barbering partnership at the Merchant Hotel, and with four other black men published a petition to the state House and Senate. "We the undersigned colored residents of the State of Minnesota," it began, "respectfully petition your honorable bodies to amend the Constitution of this State, by striking out the word 'white' believing it not only superfluous, but prescriptive in its terminology—a mark of degradation, and the great auxiliary in supporting the unilateral prejudice against us who have committed no crime save the wearing complacently the dark skin our Creator has seen fit in his all-wise providence to clothe us with." They sought to assure the legislators, and the general public, that Minnesota's African Americans were fully committed to being good citizens, embracing sober middle-class values and the virtues of education. They marveled at the inconsistency between Minnesota's practice and principle: "It seems to us incompatible with the spirit and genius of American civilization; when we reflect that we are taxed to support the State exchequer and its territorial subdivisions, without any recognition of identity—our citizenship." They wanted to tell policy makers that, far from the stereotype that all black people were penniless, the class owned property, itself a sign of civic validation. "Our property is taxed without representation—a division of the great moral principle that should more properly underlie the fabric of our glorious Government."[44]

During the recent war, black families had sacrificed every bit as much as white families. "[I]n their fiery ordeal through which our happy country is being forced, we will as we have, give it all the aid and sympathy of which we are capable. We have given to the suppression of this unholy rebellion our best blood, the 'dearest households,' in common with our white citizens." And despite this sacrifice, they wrote in the most candid, unrestrained manner, perhaps for the first time in their lives. They referred to the undeserved yet stultifying impact of prejudice: "We have given all of our talents, from the most illiterate to the best educated . . . We do feel that our white citizens have imposed a stigma on us, that dampens our ardor in pursuing everything that is eminently best for the exemplary citizen to follow; that blunts the better susceptibilities of our common nature, and turns aside all that is civilizing and patriotic which belongs to American destiny . . . And your petitioners will ever pray"[45]

On February 7, in a vote strictly along party lines, Republicans in both houses in the legislature passed the bill that proposed a referendum to strike *white* from the suffrage provision. Despite strong opposition from the Democrats, the bill passed by a large margin.[46] With such support Griswold believed that the electorate—white men all—was ready to pass a referendum for black suffrage during the November elections. "The fortunate moment has arrived. If we do not improve on it now, it may never come again."[47] The voters of Minnesota—all white men, the majority of whom were Republicans—would decide the fate of black citizenship in November.[48] But such optimism gave way to the spark of racism that immediately spread throughout the electorate like prairie fire on a hot summer day. Not even Republican voters within this most Republican of states could withstand the histrionics of the Democratic press when it resorted to personal attacks on the bill's sponsor and the bill itself. For example, the Mankato *Free Press* called Griswold a "Negro at heart," and contended that because he devoted "his exclusive time and talents to legislating for the Negro, we shall not be surprised to learn . . . that he had painted himself black and became a Negro . . . [A] change of skin color was all that was necessary to complete his transformation."[49] The implication was obvious: a man seeking to help the Negro could never be a true white man who was loyal to his own race. This proved to be an effective tactic in defeating the measure in the November election.

Democrats would couple the tactic with another, more incendiary swipe at black suffrage. The Chatfield *Democrat*, for example, promised a bleak prospect for the white race—interracial sex:

> It don't mean that the privileges of Sambo are to cease when he shall march to the polls and offset your vote with his, but you must take him to your home, have your wife wait on him, let him kiss your sister, set up with your daughter, marry her if he wants her, and raise any number of tan-color grandchildren . . . Negro suffrage is but a steping stone

to universal equality for everything, even to the detestable and God-forbidden principle of miscegenation.[50]

This theme may have been particularly biting since Jernigan's wife of two years, Alice, was white, but it is hardly likely that the barber was the intended target. The Chatfield editor, on the occasional trip to the state capitol, could well have received a trim from the stylish barber at the Merchant Hotel and liked both the handiwork and the artist who performed it with ease and grace and witty conversation, without knowing that Jernigan had even read his statement or was even capable of reading, let alone that he had joined other black barbers of St. Paul in a petition voicing passionate opposition, and without considering that while getting a trim and shave he exposed himself to any potential menace from the black man's razor. Of similar moments, one astonished English visitor observed "Nothing struck me more forcibly than an American under the razor . . . Shrinking usually under the touch of a nigger as from the venomed tooth of the serpent, he here is seen . . . placing his throat at his mercy."[51] In the curious logic of a racist, this was what a man would do: not miss the opportune moment to give consequence to his disrespect, not miss the chance for revenge. The accommodating black barber hardly posed a threat, and that was the point. Despite all the ease and wit and skill, Jernigan, by being accommodating, could never be the white man's equal. Rather, the editor's target audience was not just Democratic readers who were already predisposed to vote against the measure, but every Republican who fought to preserve the Union but remained ambivalent at best about the feared consequences of making the freedman truly equal to himself. The editor knew his audience well. He could touch that nerve and drive a wedge between the Republican electorate and their leaders. "Miscegenation" was a theme to which Democrats would revert in the coming years because it worked. That November, by a vote of 14,651 to 12,138, black suffrage failed.[52]

Griswold, on the other hand, a man of the cloth and more hopeful of the generosity of his fellow man at the start of the campaign, may have been stung by the level of vitriol and low-level characterizations directed at him. He no doubt felt exhausted, especially when he realized that black suffrage was unpopular even within his own county, as would become clear in the disappointing returns that November. His county would overwhelmingly support William Marshall, the Republican candidate for governor, but defeat the black suffrage measure.[53] But, perhaps already in February, seeing the clouds forming on the horizon, he may have concluded that politics and justice were incompatible, even among men he thought he knew and who knew him well enough to elect him to the legislature. On February 27, he formally requested, and was granted, a leave of absence from the session.[54] Hearing of this, the barbers, perhaps taking yet another step out of the shadows, wanted to publicly express their appreciation for his taking on, as the press termed it, "this good work." The next night, a delegation called on Griswold's room at the International Hotel to wish the legislator well and to give him a gift—an elegant gold-handled cane.[55]

R. T. Grey, Jernigan's partner from Minneapolis (he now shared Jernigan's space at the Merchant Hotel), and his wife, survivors of the first time in state history that a black man was the target of mob violence, had the honor to speak:

> We have been deputed by the colored people of St. Paul, to present you their respects and thanks for the very manly qualities which we have observed in our intercourse with you, as well as the invaluable service you have rendered our race and posterity by breaking the last link that bound our State to the old regime of the pro-slavery dynasty.[56]

Grey added:

> We now place you in the long list of illustrious men who have battled for the rights of the weak against the machinations of the powerful. You, too, shall become historic in our minds and memories. If it is characteristic of our race to forget injuries, it is an irresistible instinct to yield our hearts most where gratitude goes to those who befriend us. It is perhaps here, a most fitting moment to return our sincere thanks to the legislature of Minnesota, and particularly to the noble and brave Colonel Colvill and Mr. Stovall of the House, and Messrs. Nutting and Shilleck, of the Senate.

In closing, referring to the reason why Griswold received his leave, Grey said, "When you return to your home you can rest satisfied that—we will become exemplary citizens." With great emotion, Representative Griswold responded:

> I thank you gentlemen for this testimonial. It was somewhat unexpected, and if I had received nothing of the kind the fact that I have tried to do my duty would have been sufficient regard. I have been in the minority for a long time, have been called a fanatic and have had all kinds of opprobrium heaped upon me, but I feel no bitterness toward those who have treated me as it was the fault of their education. I should have introduced the measure, if mine had been the only vote in its favor, but I am proud to say that Minnesota is resolved to wipe out this relic of slavery which stains her Constitution.

At this he looked at the few members of the legislature who had gathered in the hall to witness the speeches. He continued:

> The bill passed the Legislature by strictly party vote and by an overwhelming majority. I do not think it is necessary to exhort you to disabuse the prejudices which have existed, for I can see by your countenances that you will do your parts like men. This prejudice is the result of slavery, the last vestige I thank God will soon be wiped out.

Then, addressing the barbers, he concluded, "I again thank you gentlemen, for this kind offering and I pray that God may bless you."[57]

To be sure, the white supporters of black suffrage were greatly disappointed by the defeat of the suffrage bill in the election. They had thought that high-minded sentiment tinged with reason might win over racism, that voters inspired by the heroism of their troops on the battlefield culminating in the surrender of Robert E. Lee and the tragic loss of their beloved president would be motivated to fully embrace the right side of history. Instead, the supporters learned that too many of their own constituents in otherwise solid Republican areas were not yet ready to destroy the last relic of slavery—abject racism; more needed to be done to correct "the fault of their education." It was therefore heartening that when the legislature convened in January, the Republican leaders vowed to try it again. The party leadership, if not most of their constituents, was ready for a new campaign. The black barbers of St. Paul were ready to do their part.

In Northern cities where the African American community was relatively large, their contribution could be significant, especially when their barbershops catered to black customers. Inside the shop there was no compunction about circulating petitions, and black men assembled for camaraderie as much as for a trim, for a chance to air their issues, swap stories, voice their complaints without reprisal, and debate issues of political concern; the barber as well was free to express his feelings. As an established fixture in black neighborhoods, the barbershop was the first and most enduring of black-owned businesses, which often resulted in the barber being able to assume a position of leadership. But in cities where the black community was exceedingly small, the black barber—especially one catering to the higher end of the economic spectrum—necessarily continued to derive his income from white customers. Even if his barbershop was well established, he needed to remain cautious. Even though black barbers might play leading roles and seek nothing short of total equality, they had to be mindful that their status could change at any moment. Well-paying customers could always take their business elsewhere. Thus, as Bristol observed, "they labored under the burden of their occupation, and, more generally, by their conservative approach to race relations." They had to balance their proud identity as black men and businessmen against their determination to maintain their status of respectability; and "respectability" meant segregated barbershops. Especially for those who had played a long-term role in abolition activities, they readily embraced the Republican Party and the Union victory. "For them," Bristol explained, "obtaining the right to vote was the culmination of a long effort to be deemed worthy of citizenship, that symbol of nineteenth-century American manhood."[58] This was what motivated Jernigan and the black barbers of St. Paul.

They had played a leadership role in black suffrage while maintaining a thriving business. Jernigan's establishment at the Merchant Hotel allowed him to maintain both access and customers who influenced policy. But because his name had appeared in the most widely read newspaper in the state, his name was public knowledge. Other black barbers whose names appeared on the petition moved in and out of the prestigious hotels. Grey, who partnered with Jernigan in 1865, returned to Minneapolis the next year. Thomas Jackson, who relayed Griswold's request for an endorsement from Golden Key Literary Society members in 1865, left his barber's chair at the International Hotel and was replaced in 1866 by two white barbers. Only Maurice Jernigan retained his place at the Merchant. For the remainder of the decade, his business continued to thrive. In 1867, true to the entrepreneurial spirit of postwar Minnesota, Jernigan formed a partnership with R. J. Stockton after cornering the barbering trade by acquiring the shop in the International Hotel, adding to his holding in the Merchant Hotel. When a fire destroyed the International in 1869, Jernigan began negotiating for a space in the soon-to-be-built Metropolitan Hotel, while he continued to invest in the shop that Stockton operated at the Merchant Hotel. By the beginning of the new decade, he had emerged as the premier black barber in town, the senior leader of Minnesota's black business elite, and he used his stature to make connections that would lead to the black male suffrage vote in 1868. And yet, his prominence as a black leader did not come from being selected by the whole of the African American community. While he encouraged white employers to hire black laborers, he deferred to attitudes of his customers and the hotel owner and did not serve black men in his barbershops. Nor did his prominence come from being the most articulate member of the Golden Key Literary Society. He seemed to prefer letting other Society members speak. Rather, his stature, until 1870, came from being the most enduring example of black potential in the minds of Minnesota's white Republican political and financial elite. He received neither tribute nor fanfare, yet his currency for leadership came from using discretion well. C. D. Gilfillan, one of the most powerful financial and political leaders in the city and state Republican Party, and owner of the Merchant Hotel, appreciated this quality in his character.[59]

3

ON BECOMING A GOOD REPUBLICAN

"Be men, hard-handed, laborious men."

—THE HONORABLE MORTON S. WILKINSON,
Convention of Colored Citizens of Minnesota, 1869

Three years after the first failed campaign for black suffrage, voters did what had never occurred in any state of the Union at any time of its history—they extended the right to vote to the black men of Minnesota. On January 1, 1869, virtually every major Republican officeholder celebrated with the newly formed Colored Citizens of the state. This was a time for great rejoicing, as the keynoters at its convention noted: the ballot had removed all obstacles, and with very hard work, the opportunities were limitless. But already there had been signs that racism was resilient in Republican postwar Minnesota, and the ballot and commitment to hard work were not enough to purchase a farm, secure an apprenticeship, or avoid the creation of an urban underclass.

January 1, 1869, was indeed a glorious day as members of the political elite of Minnesota's ruling party took turns at the podium in St. Paul's Ingersoll Hall. They were there to welcome the state's newest citizens to the political fold. Less than two months earlier a majority of the voters had supported the statewide referendum that extended the vote to black males, reflecting the Republican Party's commitment to black freedom and equality. The victory had been hard won. Two earlier referenda were defeated as much by lack of coordination on the part of Republican candidates waging their own campaigns as by a general reluctance of white voters to see black men as deserving the franchise.[1] By the fall of 1868, all of that had changed as each popular Republican candidate told his constituents that a vote for black suffrage was a vote for him, the Union, and the memory of Abraham Lincoln, their great martyred leader. Even so, it could hardly be considered an overwhelming victory, for of the 69,614 ballots cast 39,493 white Minnesota men voted in favor of the question. But a victory was a victory, and in the election of 1868, a majority voted for enlightenment and justice and against their baser selves. It was truly a day of great celebration.[2]

Ingersoll Hall, festooned by banners displaying likenesses of Lincoln, Grant, Sheridan, and Frederick Douglass, was animated by an enthusiastic and demonstrative assembly who rocked with cheers and laughter and tearful pride as the governor, the mayor of St. Paul, and state and congressional legislators—Republicans, all—gave colorful orations on their political legacy, the duty of black citizens to themselves and their community, the virtues of hard work, God and middle-class values, the loyalty that the party now deserved, and the Democrats, who deserved nothing but suspicion.[3]

Sharing the stage with these august political leaders were many of the black barbers who had helped to make the reason for the event a reality. Indeed, it could not have happened without their having created a commodious atmosphere where the state's business was done, transactions made, bills negotiated, relationships formed, favors promised and realized, power and riches secured—for which they might receive gratuities from grateful patrons in the form of money, land, or access. In turn, the black community came to see such barbers as those who could help new arrivals find work, lodging, and, on occasion, protection.[4] In this sense, barbering became a conduit between the black community and the white political and commercial establishment, which allowed men like Maurice Jernigan, R. T. Grey, and R. J. Stockton to uplift their race and become acknowledged leaders of their community and models of commercial and middle-class success. These men, because of what they had achieved through the skills they had perfected, personified what the black race could be within a new civilization—a new *Republican* civilization—that advanced itself when citizens advanced themselves. The success of the campaign for black suffrage and this convention that was a celebration of their handiwork was not dampened by the sentiment of the most prominent supporter of black suffrage, whose message had reason to give them pause.

Morton S. Wilkinson of Mankato was the first Republican to represent Minnesota in the U.S. Senate (from 1859 to 1865), a confidant of President Lincoln, and congressman-elect. He had been a long-time supporter of the abolition of slavery and universal male political equality, arguing during the first territorial constitution convention that *white* should be removed from the voting provision and vigorously campaigning for the amendment since the 1865 referendum. Just months earlier he had delivered a speech in southern Minnesota tying black suffrage to his campaign for Congress.[5] When the voters approved the suffrage amendment, it was as much his victory as it was for the black men of Minnesota. No white man deserved time to speak more than Wilkinson. When he visited St. Paul, he lived in the International Hotel, where Jernigan's second and newly opened emporium was located, and the senator was likely a frequent customer. As a successful politician who surely benefited in backroom dealings while sitting in barber chairs, amid the aroma of tonic and cigars, his anticipated comments characterized a romanticized vision of what it meant to be free and enfranchised and the inevitability of good fortune through hard work. He was introduced to the throng to enthusiastic applause. To the men and women seated before him that day—many of whom, as former slaves, knew something of hard labor—he said:

> You must carve your way through the solid rock, as the Caucasian has done, and rise to be dominant among the nations of the earth. It is work that will do it. Do not be content to be barbers and porters in hotels, but be men, hard-handed, laborious men. It was for such men that the homestead was passed.[6]

To Wilkinson, the Homestead Act, in its way, was as important as the abolition of slavery. On the same day that Lincoln issued the Emancipation Proclamation, the Homestead Act of 1862 went into effect.[7] Both were intended to free men, legally and economically, and though both received the enthusiastic support of Senator Wilkinson, it was the Homestead Act that offered his state the more immediate, widespread benefit. He embraced the Jacksonian ideal of a society that empowered the common man against the privileged few and the Jeffersonian ideal of the superiority of agriculture as a means to that end. Thus, as he had argued during the debate in April 1860, that it would be "scarcely necessary to remind the Senate that the monopoly of land by the few, as against the many, and the parceling out of public domain in immense tracts among venal courtiers, have been, all over the world, the most powerful auxiliaries of absolute and despotic power." The result had been that "the monarchies and the aristocracies of all ages have been enabled to hold the masses subject to their will." "Millions of the human family," he continued, "have been reduced to penury and degradation, because they were deprived of the right to earn the subsistence from the common earth, which was intended alike for the rich and for the poor."[8]

This was not an abstraction for Wilkinson but an urgent contemporary problem: in the United States, "even now, with all of our vast expanse of territory, labor is outweighed by capital, and the rights of the settler are but slightly regarded when brought into comparison with the money of the speculator." He argued that the homestead measure would be directed to "the laboring masses of the country, to those who are most often crushed down by the cruel and unequal conflict between capital and labor; to the poor man who earns his bread from day to day by the sweat of his brow; to him who feeds upon the uncertain crumbs which fall from the rich man's table."[9]

He then shifted his argument to the conditions of poverty in the urban North and challenged his fellow senators "to pass through our great cities" where they would "see the boys of all ages who swarm around the streets, many of them willing and anxious to labor, but finding nothing for their hands to do." They were "exposed to temptations of every kind, day after day looking upon the equipages of wealth with the hungry and cannibal eyes of poverty." Thus, he declared, the Homestead Act was "the measure of the working, suffering class of our people; those who were struggling on from day to day, from week to week, and from year to year, vindicating the dignity of labor against the oppressions and aggressions of capital."[10] The language that limited homesteading to white men was dropped. Now, the added weight of the Fourteenth Amendment made African Americans eligible.

A poor man intending to be a homesteader needed to be the head of a family, twenty-one or older, a citizen of the United States or one who formally intended to be, as required by the naturalization laws of the United

States; who had never born arms against the government or given aid and comfort to its enemies; who registered the appropriate paperwork and paid a nominal fee. The applicant, above all, needed to pledge that "the application was made for his or her exclusive use and benefit, and that such entry is made for the purpose of actual settlement and cultivation."[11] In other words, these public lands were reserved for farmers, not speculators and corporations, a provision that sought to guarantee that the common man stood a chance at acquiring the land.[12] The spirit of the Homestead Act was simple: it was about equal opportunity. Senator Wilkinson argued:

> The men who immigrate in youth to the western country, to build up for themselves a fortune and a reputation, are the men of all others to whom the most liberal provisions of the act should apply. We need their services. They are in plain fact, the vanguard of civilization upon this continent. They penetrate the wild solitudes far beyond the safety and comfort of society. They traverse and explore regions in which, for the time being, families could not reside securely. They pitch their tents and build their houses, break up and improve the soil, and open the broad acres to occupancy and culture. They furnish a far more and sure protection to our western frontier than can be given by all the armed soldiers along the borderline. Coming mostly from the different States of the Union, they bring with them a deep and permanent attachment to the institutions of our country... Such as some of the labors and dangers—such are some of their achievements. Why, then in the name of fairness, and of common sense, should this class of active and energetic young men be entirely ignored and cast aside . . . ? Laws, in order to be just, must be equal in application.[13]

The act authorized the distribution of public lands in plots up to 160 acres to citizens or intended citizens who paid a minimum filing and registration fee. After five years of residency and the completion of prescribed improvements to the land, the homesteader would receive title.

In practice, however, the law, when applied, and subsequent congressional enactments shifted the advantage of acquiring good land to corporations and speculators, just as Wilkinson feared. Vast acres of public land were effectively removed from access to Americans and new immigrants, but the congressional enactments that soon followed passage of the act took up the promise of homesteading in the western farmland of America.[14] Indeed, the desperate reality of the type of settler for whom the act was intended—the farmer whose only currency was his willingness to work hard—placed him in a position of being in debt, for he needed to borrow for seed, feed, and basic necessities until the time when his harvest could repay the creditor. Banks and merchants could prosper while homesteaders lived a Sisyphus-like existence.

Other congressional actions, such as those designed to promote railroad interests (like the Union Pacific bill that Wilkinson voted against) and facilitate the development of colleges and universities, exempted vast amounts of public land from homesteading. Homesteaders also lost to speculators and corporations that grabbed great swaths of the best parcels of the public domain through inventive, if unscrupulous and illegal, tactics in the West and elsewhere. Corporations quickly found out that they could, for example, use proxy filings by individuals as a way to accumulate vast acreage of western land; tried and true methods of graft and corruption often proved just as successful.[15]

Passed the same year as the Homestead Act, the Land Grant Act (also known as the Morrill Act for its sponsor Justin Morrill, a congressman from Vermont) offered states parcels of public land to use as funding sources for new institutions of higher education. A number of western congressmen opposed the measure, either through an apparent lack of interest in establishing schools or hostility to the act's potential loopholes. In the latter category, Kansas senator James H. Lane insisted that passage of the act would "ruin" his state. Minnesota's Morton Wilkinson railed against speculators as "a remorseless class of vampires," who he was certain would benefit most from the legislation.[16]

It was Wilkinson's desire to ensure against the encroachment of speculators that prompted him to oversee the sale of Winnebago lands. On the other hand, he too may have been touched with the fever of heady entrepreneurialism so prevalent at the time. It would seem that "[s]erendipitously, the senator was to benefit quite handsomely from the sale of Winnebago land. Given the oversight of reservation land sales, he embarked on a 'happy relationship' with firms that handled the subsequent appraisals and financing."[17]

A few facts are clear. John Usher, secretary of the interior, and a close friend of Wilkinson, appointed the senator to make the arrangements for distributing Winnebago land. Wilkinson nominated the appraisers and Usher continued "his happy relationship" with the senator by summarily approving those nominations. One of the firms authorized to finance the land sales, Thompson Brothers of St. Paul, was the old firm of another close friend, Indian Superintendent Clark Thompson. In short, Wilkinson supervised everything, including advertising. Lincoln, placating the man whose state had undergone the crisis of the Dakota War of 1862, placed his approval on the whole transaction. On August 23, 1864, Lincoln signed the order for the sale of fifty-four thousand acres of Winnebago land.[18] Wilkinson now had influence over who could purchase land on the former Winnebago and Dakota reservations. He was in a potentially lucrative situation, which was the very nature of the sale of Indian lands, and a possible reason for requesting a presidential appointment to commissioner of Indian Affairs when the current officeholder—William Dole—left office.[19]

The Dakota removal act of March 3, 1863, provided that the Dakota reservation be surveyed, appraised, and then offered for sale at its assessed value, with proceeds to go to the displaced Indians. As in the Homestead Act and the Winnebago removal act, the third section of the act directed "that before any person shall be entitled to enter any portion of the said land, . . . he shall become a bona fide settler." Speculators were persona non grata and entry was restricted to those persons who would settle and cultivate the land. In June 1865, with the completion of the survey and appraisal, the area was opened to entry at the St. Peter Land Office, which would also be assigned the task of selling Winnebago land.[20] About the same time, a small Mankato investment firm named J. J. Thornton & Company was formed to get in on the action. Wilkinson, one of five directors who served on its board, was in a position to authorize firm president John Willard to begin making bids by the end of the year.[21]

During the first thirty days after the St. Peter Land Office opened for business, only four persons filed claims on the Dakota reserve. Three of the four men were public officials and friends of the senator—John B. Downer and Henry Swift were officials of the St. Peter Land Agency. Downer was Receiver of Public Moneys and Swift, a former territorial governor, was registrar of land sales. Another public official was Judge Charles Vandenburgh, who had presided in 1860 over the Eliza Winston case, the only slave emancipation trial to occur in Minnesota. The remaining months of 1865 saw no significant increase in claims filed.[22] Thousands of acres of land remained unclaimed and open for auction. Land, apparently, was available to anyone who wanted it.

In late March 1865, three months before the St. Peter Land Office opened, twenty-three-year-old Lieutenant Thomas Montgomery of nearby Le Sueur County and an officer with the 67th Regiment, U.S. Colored Infantry, wrote to his father about an interesting letter he had received from Abner Tibbets, agent of the St. Peter Land Office of Nicollet County. Tibbets had known the Montgomery family for some time through previous land dealings. Now he seemed to be writing not so much as an opportunist, entrepreneur, or even trusted friend, but with a higher motive, for he was offering Montgomery's soldiers—black men who had nobly used their freedom to fight for the preservation of the nation—the opportunity to own free and clear rich Minnesota farmland. He was a civil servant but also a businessman at a time when land acquisition and self-advancement were the rule of the day, but the war for him was not a mere staging area for avarice. Having visited Montgomery's unit in St. Louis in early 1864, he saw firsthand the character of former slaves who rushed forward to take up arms against their former masters.

But although Montgomery's motivation to write the letter in 1865 was probably prompted by the new opportunity for acquisition of Dakota land, for Tibbits the seed may have been sown during the preceding August as a result of a brief time he spent with Elizabeth Estell. Montgomery had sent Estell, his servant, from Louisiana to help his mother on the family homestead in Le Sueur County. The final leg of the journey was the stage ride from St. Peter. As a favor to Montgomery, Tibbets, who lived there, met Estell and helped her transfer to the connecting stage.[23] During that time together, they probably talked—a curious Minnesotan having perhaps his first real conversation with a black woman, so-called contraband, who huddled against all the unfamiliarity around her and braced against the chill of Minnesota's autumnal air. She was a married woman and had fine character and was industrious.

Slavery and the war had separated her from her children and her husband, who, willing in the name of freedom to give the last full measure, was still in the South fighting under the lieutenant's command. It was hard to imagine that anyone who could be so blind as to enslave such a people would ever come to see her in any other light. It was hard to imagine a South where black people like Elizabeth and her husband William could ever live in freedom. Clearly, their best opportunity for a bright future resided up North in Minnesota. Although he was not bearing arms, Tibbets could offer Montgomery's men the opportunity to acquire the soon-to-be available land parcels on the Dakota reservations.

Montgomery wrote to his father, and curiously not to Tibbets, asking for more information about the land, the fees, the status of titles, taxes, "claims for who might die in service; whether the land will be timber or prairie, high or rolling, or wet and marshy, good soil or poor, convenient to market or to the Minnesota River . . . Was good water found easily? How far and in what direction [is the land] from St. Peter?" He wrote that his men were excited at the prospect:

> I spoke to the men about it and they seemed to be gratified that any person had taken such an interest in their future welfare. I have no doubt but I could form a good colony but the men as well as myself want to know on what conditions . . . we are to base our action . . . Of course they are wise about the climate.

But he knew that such a venture could be controversial and vouched for their integrity and solid republican spirit:

> I am anxious to do all I can for them *but I will not involve myself in any trouble.* All my men are without homes and are desirous of procuring them and they could bring their friends along. Some are tradesmen. All of them I have no doubt will make good industrious citizens. I don't want to have them misled. I think they will be quite willing to go to Minnesota. One of them said, "We will go anywhere to get away from them sesech." The plan is a good one and it will induce them to save their money.[24]

In the end, there evidently was "trouble," for Montgomery wrote nothing more about the venture. The Land Office received no bids from the black veterans. There is no record of Tibbets's superiors quashing the deal. Moreover, even though President Lincoln had assigned full authority to Wilkinson to oversee all of the land acquisition of the Dakota and Winnebago reservations, there is no indication that he intervened in any way. It is, however, implausible that he knew nothing of it. Bids—even prospective bids—from black veterans would have been noteworthy, especially in that for the remainder of 1865 few others stepped forward to bid on the land. Nonetheless, although initially there was little competition for land, the inquiry on behalf of black troopers somehow got lost in the shuffle. But there was a clue as to where Wilkinson stood on the matter. The year before, as a U.S. senator, he had voted against a concerted effort to relocate large numbers of freedmen and women to Northern states.

By spring of 1864 there were no signs that the South intended to lay down its arms. Confederate armies and guerrillas continued to frustrate the Union, for despite its victories blue armies could still not secure the territories won. But this was more than a military problem. The Emancipation Proclamation issued by President Lincoln in 1863 had freed the slaves in rebellious states. Now, hundreds of thousands of freedmen and -women without the protection of their masters or the invading Union army found themselves living without protection. On June 28, 1864, Republican Senator Waitman T. Willey of West Virginia observed:

> Take Virginia for illustration. About half the state is now within our lines, I mean on this side of our main army; and yet there is not a farm anywhere where it would be safe to place any of these freedmen, where they would be allowed to work, much less a year or so as to raise a crop, without strong military protection. Mosby's guerillas would hunt on any lands of the farm almost anywhere in our lines within Virginia. I imagine the same state of things exists elsewhere.[25]

In other words, considering the present state of the war, the federal government could not realistically secure for freedmen and -women the full enjoyment of new opportunity. Rather, genuine opportunity existed not in the South, but in the Northern and western states. Willey proposed an amendment authorizing the Commissioner of the Freedman's Bureau to initiate correspondence "with the Governors of States, the municipal authorities of the States, with the various manufacturing establishments, and farmers and mechanics," to begin the process of relocation:

> Homes might be provided for them, and they might not only find good homes but humane persons and employment at fair compensation, and it might supply to these districts that lack of labor which has

been occasioned by the withdrawal of laboring men in the ranks of our armies . . .

It seems to me that here is a proposition which will accomplish more good for the freedmen, find them more homes and better compensation and with a great deal less trouble and expense, than the whole machinery when it is in the fullest operation will ever find for them upon the abandoned plantations in the South.[26]

The amendment divided the Republicans and produced an unusual alignment across party lines. The Democratic archconservative Willard Saulsbury Sr. of Delaware joined with antislavery men such as B. Gratz Brown of Missouri in supporting the Negro relocation plan, although Saulsbury took a circuitous route to his position: "I could not vote for the amendment of the Senator of West Virginia as an independent proposition; but as an amendment to an obnoxious bill, with a view of perfecting that bill, I shall vote for the amendment." On the other hand, conservative Democrat Charles Buckalew of Pennsylvania denounced it as "monstrous," arguing that "our states to the North may well object to any such exertion of power . . . of this Government. Certain of the Northern states prohibit the introduction of this element of the population within their borders. I think they have the perfect right to establish and maintain their own policy on the subject." Charles Sumner, the "best friend of freedmen" in the Senate, who Willey no doubt was seeking to persuade, set the tone for Radical opposition when he said, "with great reluctance," that the amendment "went too far":

[W]hen I learned from his speech that he proposed to organize a system of migration, of transportation, of colonization in different States of the Union, under the auspices of the proposed bureau, I must confess I saw his proposition in an entirely different light. It seems to me the whole idea is entirely untenable, it is out of place on this bill. I hope, therefore, that it will be voted down and that we shall proceed with the bill.[27]

However untenable the amendment was, the dire facts were that by summer 1864, Union armies, even with superior numbers, had not shown that they could defeat Lee in the field, let alone protect the multitude of freedmen still living on Southern soil, whether occupied or not. At any rate, Willey said that the amendment was being misconstrued as compulsory relocation:

> I propose the honorable Senator does not understand my proposition yet. There is nothing compulsory in any of its provisions. It expressly says that [the commissioner] shall perform the duty prescribed to him in the section I propose, "so far as may be practicable;" and . . . that he should ascertain where labor is wanted, both in the insurrectionary States and out of those States, in Massachusetts, in Tennessee, in any other State; ascertain where labor is wanted, where the people desire to employ laborers of this character . . .
>
> It is not my design to organize a system of compulsory emigration; it is not my design, nor will the section bear the interpretation, that these commissioners are compelled necessarily to force upon any community that it does not desire this kind of labor from freedmen. The whole design and spirit of the section is that it shall be a matter of mutual consideration between the three parties—the commissioner, the freedman himself, and the person who desires to employ him.[28]

This was Willey's strongest argument and one that had to appeal to Republicans who worried about the growing number of voters back home who were tired of war, angered at mounting casualties, and lacked confidence in Lincoln and the Republican Party. And now, the prospect of black relocation with the influx of black laborers competing for work heightened the likelihood of continued racial violence, which they had witnessed in the last year in New York, Detroit, and even St. Paul when mob violence erupted upon the arrival of steamboats carrying fugitives from Missouri. Weeks later, a provost guard was ordered when it was learned that more riots would ensue, this time against the draft. Implementing the Willey amendment would require that reasonable white men at home with an investment in a stable community and vital local economy would be the ones to make the deal, not bureaucrats and out-of-touch politicians in Washington. Indeed, under the best of circumstances, the proposition offered an additional benefit—it could transform the brutish former slave into a productive member of society. Willey, perhaps being a touch disingenuous, expressed surprise at the controversy:

And I did think that such was an obvious advantage to the freedman himself in securing a home where he would obtain the protection of the law, the kindly sympathies of the people around him, and good labor at fair compensation, that there could hardly be an objection from any quarter to it.[29]

The cranky Senator Saulsbury was more blunt. In the wake of Congress's approving the resolution to send to the states the proposition for the Thirteenth Amendment, he argued that those who supported the abolition of slavery were hypocrites if they rejected the Willey amendment:

> Sir, tell me not, tell not the honest people of this country that the professions of the abolitionists are sincere; and they are honest in their efforts to set free this race unless they are willing to take them home, and give a practical illustration to the world of their sincerity by admitting them to an equality of rights to themselves.[30]

On this point, Saulsbury hit a nerve, for no Northern state as yet had approved black citizenship by popular vote. The friends of the freedman, it seemed, could support emancipation so long as the emancipated did not live among them. Racial equality was good as long as freedmen lived among white Southerners. The Delaware Democrat continued to scold the Radicals:

> I am surprised that any man or any party professing to have at heart so much the interests of the negro race should refuse to avail of the privileges offered by the amendment of the Senator of West Virginia. Sit not quietly in your homes and shed crocodile tears over the barbarism of slavery and the inhumanity of slaveholders when you have the opportunity to go and take this oppressed race not only to live in your midst, but to take them to your heart and to cherish them as philanthropic men should cherish the object of their pity.
>
> Sir, it would be one of the most sublime spectacles ever witnessed on the face of the earth; it would be one of the strongest proofs that could possibly be furnished in the people of this country and the people of other lands if the abolitionists of this country now, in evidence of their sincerity of the doctrine which they have preached, would say,

"Yes, we have a beautiful heritage up here in the North; our mountains are green; our valleys are fertile; our towns furnish innumerable workshops where this species of labor can be employed; our political institutions are free; we know no inequality among God's children; after preaching equality, we now evidence our sincerity by throwing open to you our own States and the employment of the same political and social advantages which we ourselves enjoy."

If this amendment be rejected by such votes as I have indicated, I apprehend that it will be impossible hereafter to make even the most stupid believe that modern abolitionism is anything else than absolute hypocrisy.[31]

What indeed made the provision untenable—even more than the logistics—was the widespread antiblack sentiment in the North. Since the start of serious emancipation efforts in 1862, black migration to the North had been a controversial issue, and though many freedmen had made their way north, there was strong opposition to government actions to assist their relocation. In the fall of 1862, the war department, facing great resistance, abandoned efforts to arrange for the employment and support of black refugees in Illinois. Nor was eastern opinion more favorable to blacks on this issue than western, as Governor John A. Andrew of Massachusetts showed in declining the offer of Union commanders to send two thousand blacks to the New England states.[32]

Indeed, Northern prejudice made congressmen acutely sensitive to the issue of black migration from the start of the freedmen's bureau planning. In the first meeting of the House Select Committee on Emancipation in December 1863, Representative Godlove Orth of Indiana proposed that no action should be taken to encourage emigration by freedmen. Democrat Anthony Knapp of Illinois shared this view and moved an amendment to the bureau bill, stating that nothing in it should authorize the introduction of any persons of color into any state whose laws prohibited them. Massachusetts congressman Thomas D. Eliot's committee rejected this motion by a vote of six Republicans (including Orth) to one Democrat, but the result signified a desire to steer clear of the issue rather than support for the migration of blacks.[33]

By June 1864, the issue of black relocation had become political theater. Republican opponents of the Willey amendment acknowledged political reasons for avoiding any reference to black migration in national legislation. To open public correspondence on the subject, Samuel C. Pomeroy declared, would enable "a political party to make A FUSS about it, and it will become an unpopular thing." Henry Wilson of Massachusetts held that the provision for official correspondence with state governors was open to misrepresentation and would excite opposition. Wilson said he supported black relocation, but, mindful that it could result in more contention in Northern communities, only if it were carried on by private voluntary means. Considering that antiblack sentiment was particularly strong in the West, many felt that some western Republicans actually supported black migration in order to embarrass easterners who voted against a bill for black advancement. After all, the amendment was primarily not so much about homesteading, but about labor, and urban labor at that, where white laborers had already demonstrated a penchant for mob violence. Nonetheless, other westerners knew that for many settlers the town could be a springboard to homesteading, a lifestyle ordained to the white man and that the freedman was to remain a creature of the South. In any event, many senators anticipated that the House would not approve the provision.[34] The Willey amendment vote would thus quietly fade away.

This did not need to be a party-line vote. Senators could vote any way they wanted on the matter. The Radicals had displayed their bona fides in the struggle for freedom when they approved the resolution to send the Thirteenth Amendment to the states for ratification in April with a vote of thirty-eight to six; and it was a defining vote, one that each senator knew would be on the right side of history. The Willey amendment was of a different stripe, compelling senators to vote against allies. On June 28, the Senate approved Willey's amendment, nineteen to fifteen. It was one of the few issues on the freedmen confronting the wartime Senate when men within the same caucus opposed each other. Such was the case with the senators from Minnesota. Ramsey voted to approve the amendment and Wilkinson voted to reject.[35]

Wilkinson did not seem to feel that the argument he made for the Homestead Act applied here. Still, it may not have been an easy vote for him to cast. But by January 1865, when the legislature agreed to submit the black suffrage amendment to Minnesota voters, he had to know how much more volatile the measure would be if a measure to facilitate black homesteading in the region was to be adopted. Even Lincoln Republicans would be ambivalent at best, as reflected in a letter from Lieutenant Montgomery: "I am anxious to hear the decision of the election this fall. I hope [William] Marshall is elected but I think it will be a close run on account of the point at issue—negro suffrage."[36]

Black suffrage did indeed fail, and given the prevailing racial sentiment in 1865, Wilkinson understood that black homesteading, viewed as the logical consequence of black suffrage, could foment racial tension on Minnesota's farmland. It is a reason he as a senator had voted against the Willey amendment. The signs were evident. "Because of Negro suffrage" an editor wrote in February, "we will have a wholesale immigration of that class of person. While there are doubtless some respectable and worthy exceptions, they are, as a people, ignorant, indolent, and addicted to petty thieving."[37]

Wilkinson knew his people. He understood the value of political timing, and the timing was wrong for him to be effective. He was no longer a man possessing the gravitas of a U.S. senator, for he had just lost a re-election bid that January. He was now a man without portfolio, an adornment to others whose political fortunes were just then in ascendance. Sectional peace had been declared, but the events of 1865 that followed in Minnesota ushered in tumult for which Wilkinson was not prepared. In this context, the problematic Tibbets–Montgomery plan was best left ignored. Montgomery, likewise understanding the stakes, was prepared to oblige when he wrote: "I am anxious to do all I can for [my men] *but I will not involve myself in any trouble*"; and nothing more was mentioned on the subject.[38] In Nicollet County, where the Montgomery–Tibbets plan was likely to be implemented, Marshall won the election and the Negro suffrage measure failed.[39]

It would not be until the middle of 1866 that immigration into Blue Earth County began to grow. In June and July alone more than 6,200 acres of land of the Winnebago reserve were sold at the St. Peter Land Office.[40] In August, J. J. Thornton & Company had established a railroad to carry freight between Mankato and Owatonna.[41] On July 12, 1867, several thousand acres of Winnebago land were sold, mostly to speculators, ranging from $7.00 to $7.20 per acre.[42] In the same year there were more bids on the Dakota land, none of which came from African American bidders. At public auctions between December 2 and 16, the sale held at the St. Peter office drew a crowd of small-tract entrymen who bid from $1.50 to $4.00 an acre. On the whole, speculators did not like competitive bidding, and most remained away from the auction. John Willard of J. J. Thornton was the sole speculator who bid on land and acquired 4,000 of the 25,000 acres sold. During winter, sales were suspended—speculators could not get to St. Peter, so bidding resumed in May 1868. By summer, 125,000 of the 275,000 acres remaining after December were sold.[43]

Between December 1867 and December 1869, fifty purchasers entered 159,202 acres, 2.3 percent of the total land area offered after the auction. Because 28 percent of those bought only 750–1,000 acres, Stewart observed, "It is possible that the group included a few actual settlers. But the purchase of three to four times the amount of land a man could farm would seem to indicate entry of speculators." The names of many of those purchasers appeared again and again as entrymen for lands in other parts of Minnesota, as well as in other states. One example was J. W. Sprague, who bought only two sections in the Dakota reserve. A few years later he was on the Pacific Coast buying up tens of thousands of acres of Washington timberland.[44]

Eight of eleven buyers were Minnesota residents: William F. Davidson (a colorful steamboat operator with a paralyzing grip on shipping trade on the upper Mississippi and Minnesota rivers (16,917 acres), J. W. Paxton (16,303 acres), George B. Wright (12,530 acres), Henry W. Lamberton (9,398 acres), and John Shilloch (5,338 acres). John Willard increased his holdings to 14,619 acres and bought an additional 10,008 acres in a partnership with Alpheus Hewitt and James Hubbell. Thus, 135 square miles of the Minnesota Valley passed into the hands of eight men.[45]

The news that thousands of acres of Minnesota that could become good farmland had been put on the block soon caught the attention of eager eastern promoters. Rock-bottom prices, no acreage limits, and the hope of turning a tidy profit attracted wealthy and ambitious men. By 1868 they appeared in St. Peter. The first arrival was Mark Howard from Hartford, Connecticut, who bought 2,000 acres and promptly left. Then came Merrill and Gilman Currier from Boston, William Porter from Philadelphia, Thaddeus Ault of St. Louis, and a dozen others from Baltimore, Cincinnati, and New York. Although none was a heavy buyer, they nevertheless gained 50,000 acres, approximately 20 percent of all land sold on the Dakota reserve.[46]

Acreage in the Dakota reserve had lost some value. Ten years earlier (1858) Sioux agent Joseph Brown had estimated the fair value of the reservation at $5.00 per acre. Yet only 2 percent of this land brought more than $2.00 per acre and the secretary of the interior permitted almost 75 percent of it to go at the bare minimum of $1.25.[47] On the nearby Winnebago reservation, the St. Peter land district sold farms to actual settlers for $2.25 to $3.00 an acre.[48] The Dakota and Winnebago lands were not strictly comparable because much of the Winnebago reserve had been under cultivation by the Indians.[49]

The land officers enjoyed manifest advantages denied other buyers. They could, if they wished, withhold the more desirable tracts from the public, and enter the lands themselves. Available for their private use were the confidential field notes and plats of the U.S. deputy surveyor who had measured the Dakota reserve. Armed with such useful information, they could be selective about what they bought. This is what happened with Downer and Swift.[50]

As Stewart concluded, the reserve was a speculator's paradise. The asking price for acreage was unaccountably low for land as prime agricultural property, and the federal government's hands-off policy served only to penalize citizens who hoped to improve and populate the broad areas of the West. By selling 160,000 acres in the Minnesota River Valley to speculators, the federal government in effect was forcing 1,100 to 1,200 future settlers to deal with a middleman.[51] Yet, the prospect of owning land attracted thousands to Minnesota's farmland.

Boosters for settlement in Minnesota were already looking for men who most closely resembled the man emblazoned on the official seal of the state, the epitome of the Minnesota spirit as native-born and European-born settlers streamed into the state to farm. In the 1864 Congress, Ignatius Donnelly rose to speak, in effect, to the world: "With more than a billion acres of unsettled lands on one side of the Atlantic and with many millions of poor and oppressed people on the other, let us organize the exodus which must come and build if necessary a bridge of gold cross the chasm that divides them, that the chosen races of mankind may occupy the chosen lands of the world."[52] Clearly, many of the white settlers, whether native- or foreign-born, were impoverished when they crossed the border into Minnesota, and the state had invested its energy and resources into creating an agency whose focus was on white and European immigration; it was their racial and ethnic characteristics that would color the farming regions of Minnesota, where culture and language created solid communities.

The "bridge of gold" was manifest with the creation of the Board of Immigration which sent out pamphlets in Norwegian, Swedish, German, and Welsh, as well as English, to be dispatched by agents who fanned out throughout states in the east and northeast as well as Europe. The board cooperated with railroads in efforts to get cheap fares for immigrants and their families and built immigrant-receiving settlement houses for their temporary accommodation. Swedish-born immigrant Hans Mattson, appointed as the board's secretary, went to Sweden in 1868 to recruit immigrants, and described his adopted home as a land of milk and honey. While in Sweden he organized two shiploads of immigrants to accompany him to Minnesota. In 1871, Mattson, now an immigrant agent for the Northern Pacific Railway, returned to his native country to search for prospective settlers, and returned in 1873 with another contingent. Agents representing the state were also sent to Milwaukee and Chicago to give aid to immigrants, and one was delegated to give them protection and advice when they reached St. Paul.[53]

In addition to the work of the board to attract immigrants, Minnesota encouraged other efforts to promote the state. Paul Hjelm-Hansen, a Norwegian journalist, wrote a series of articles that appeared in Norway and Norwegian-American communities touting the beauty of Minnesota. Other writers gave exaggerated accounts of Minnesota's fresh air and healthy climate. Eduard Pelz and Albert Wolf, German immigrants who worked as agents of the St. Paul and Pacific Railroad and later the Northern Pacific Railway, wrote pamphlets and articles about the "humanistic and public-minded effort to concentrate German emigration to Minnesota." These and other immigrant homesteaders all whetted the appetites of their countrymen, who established ethnic communities that dotted the state. As Blegen observed, "The Yankee, German, Norwegian, Swedish, Irish, Czech, Welsh, and other settlements and 'colonies' that took root in the 1850s expanded in numbers and deepened in their special character in the decades after the Civil War . . . More revealing of the complexion of the people [of Minnesota] is the fact that by 1880 seventy-one per cent of the total 'represented European blood of the first and second generations.'"[54]

In contrast, African Americans faced a tougher row to hoe in establishing themselves as Minnesota homesteaders. By 1870, 759 African
Americans lived in Minnesota. Anoka, Blue Earth, Dakota, Goodhue, Le
Sueur, Rice, Pine, and Winona counties each had at least fifteen blacks,
though most were laborers.[55] Forty years later, 8.7 percent of the African
American population in Minnesota lived in rural areas, but only twenty-nine farms out of 156,137 were operated by black families. "Of these,
sixteen were owned by the operator, 12 were farmed by tenants and one
was managed. The combined acreage owned by blacks was only 2,362, a
decrease of nearly 2,000 acres from 1900."[56]

In an agricultural state, black farmers had a harder time sustaining
themselves. If "freedom" meant farming successfully, as Republicans like
Wilkinson felt, then, as Richard Kluger wrote, "[T]he black man was
clearly going to need help to make his freedom a fact as well as a right."[57]
But the Freedman's Bureau, once launched, addressed land redistribu-
tion and black ownership as a Southern matter.[58] Formally known as the
Bureau of Refugees, Freedmen, and Abandoned Lands, the agency was
assigned the immense task of providing food, clothing, and medical care
for refugees, both black and white; their resettlement on confiscated and
abandoned lands where available; overseeing the transition of freedmen
to workingman status with full contractual rights with landlords; and
establishing schools to achieve minimal literacy as rapidly and widely as
possible. With meager funding and a one-year mandate, which needed to
be renewed annually, the ambition of the bureau gradually faded.[59]

One month after its initiation, Lee surrendered at Appomattox. Five
days later, Lincoln was dead. With the suddenness of presidential succession, the fate of the agency passed to Lincoln's vice president, Andrew
Johnson, a Democrat, former slaveholder from Tennessee, and opponent
of the bureau. By the time Wilkinson spoke before the Convention of
Colored Citizens of Minnesota, the fervor of the congressional radical
Republicans for black land ownership had long since waned. No effort
was made to launch a plan for freedmen and -women to relocate to the
North. And even the policy that centrally targeted the South and guaranteed former slaves forty acres and a mule was doomed.[60]

As "colonies" for foreign settlers took root on Minnesota's farmland,
no settlements of black homesteaders existed during the same period.
John Alfred Boone and John Green, who were veterans of Company K

of the 67th Regiment and served under Montgomery, and who may have been part of the group for whom Montgomery wrote, did move to Le Sueur County in 1865. Both were laborers.[61] In another instance, in 1870, a man named Dr. H. W. Ward proposed another colony in the Lake Osakis area, but after encountering "a number of difficulties," he abandoned the scheme.[62] Not until the late 1890s were efforts once again made to attract black settlers to rural Minnesota, only to fail.

As early as 1863, Minnesotans viewed blacks coming to the state not as potential farmers but as laborers who would satisfy the labor shortage. The Republican St. Paul *Daily Press* boasted, "The people of the State are prepared to welcome a large accession of Negroes to our laboring population." Farmers were to prosper with the "hired Negro labor" for they—the black man and woman—in comparison to the existing often derided laboring class of Irish workers, were "more efficient . . . more tractable and docile." Indeed, in the view of some Republican opinion makers, it was this class of black laborers who could actually civilize the raucous character of white laborers who had come to feel that the unskilled jobs they held were their birthright as white men.[63] Two privates in Minnesota's Eighth Regiment brought a boy named Samuel Chambers who later worked in Minneola Township on the Albert Basset family farm.[64]

Also in 1863, Benjamin and Daniel Densmore of Goodhue County each received officer's commissions from the recently established Bureau of Colored Troops. While training new black enlistees, it occurred to them that they could help their friends and neighbors back home by transporting freed slaves to Red Wing to work as servants. In response to one such request, Benjamin wrote about his search for a "pair of Africans" for a Hastings family.[65] To another family seeking "contraband," he wrote:

> I will endeavor to make the best selection possible. At present I have in view to offer the opportunity to one of our colored soldier's wives—it will be difficult to find a "man and wife" of the right sort, and willing to go at the same time.[66]

The Densmores also considered putting a former slave to work in their Red Wing family home, as well as assist in their mother's effort to provide "a sympathetic welcome and warm meal" for returning soldiers passing through Red Wing. Their sister Martha thought that an honest and active "darkey woman" might do nicely.[67]

Meanwhile, the family hired a Swedish woman to clean and cook, but she soon left after learning that a former slave would be working with her; she did not want the black woman to be viewed as her equal. In August 1864, one month after the Swedish woman left for another job, former slave Mary Prist arrived in Red Wing, where she expressed disappointment that "so few colored people" lived in the city. Orrin Densmore, on the other hand, wrote his son Daniel, saying, "Our contraband is doing well and seems contented to stay . . . She may prove coarse but fully meets our expectation and we hope will meet our wants."[68]

A few black men could and did escape the limitations of farm labor if they possessed the skills to barber and moved to town, where they could attract well-paying customers. Prince Honeycutt, for example, had served during the Civil War as camp boy for Captain James Compton. After the war, Compton brought Honeycutt home with him. In time, the former slave became a barber, married a white woman, and spoke out against the rise of antiblack activity that had appeared in the Fergus Falls area, where he lived out his life. Perhaps the best-known black man in the region lived in nearby New Ulm, in neighboring Brown County. Mark Cane had been sold as a slave for a thousand dollars to become an orderly in the Union army and later moved to New Ulm, where he learned to speak German and became a barber; his wife was a hairdresser.[69]

In 1868, Mankato became an incorporated city. The J. J. Thornton investment firm that began in 1865 now became the First National Bank of Mankato with Willard as its president, and Blue Earth County experienced unprecedented growth and economic vitality.[70] Although homesteaders could be found in virtually every corner of the old Winnebago reservation, according to census data of 1870, none were African American. Even so, it is worth noting that more Blue Earth voters—all males—supported the black suffrage amendment than there were black men, women, and children residing in the entire state; and the margin of victory in the county was greater than it was the year before. The same was true in Nicollet County. In contrast, the amendment failed in neighboring Le Sueur County, where Lieutenant Montgomery's Cleveland home was situated, by a near two-to-one margin in 1867 and 1868.[71] Wilkerson's own Blue Earth County voted decisively in favor of black suffrage, even though African American residents numbered only a fraction of 1 percent of the total population, most living as unskilled workers in the city or as laborers on farms.[72]

In three years the opportunity for black settlers to homestead the public land in Minnesota evaporated as speculators and white settlers poured into the region. Conversely, most blacks living in the region had no opportunity other than to work for a white man or woman. Within the Republican region of southwest Minnesota, it hardly seemed conceivable that a black man could be an independent farmer because virtually none were. Those who inquired into owning land were met not by mobs or harassment, but by no response. However, Lieutenant Montgomery, who in 1865 wrote on behalf of his black troops, would find his own fortune in the land by going into real estate immediately after returning from the army. By 1868, he would have a thriving business in St. Peter.[73]

An episode in 1870, in Todd County, illustrates the controversial nature of black relocation on Minnesota's farmland. Despite support for black suffrage, white Minnesotans did not like blacks homesteading in their midst.

T. Harris Ward, who, like Montgomery, had served as an officer in the Colored Infantry and was known for his sympathies for black people, ran against the incumbent county commissioner, Abraham Brower, whose supporters circulated a handbill alleging Ward's interest in creating a colony of up to seven hundred black settlers. Although there was no evidence that Brower authorized the handbill, the notice of the so-called plan was enough to incite Todd County voters to defeat Ward. Edward Pluth notes that from this episode "We see citizens, including outspoken Republicans, grappling with the potential impact of new civil rights for freed slaves."[74] In fact, Todd County, in contrast to neighboring Stearns and Morrison counties, had voted in favor of black suffrage in 1868.[75] Nonetheless, on a sweeping scale that included Montgomery's experience, V. Jacque Voegeli was blunt: "The blend of antislavery ideals and racism manifested by the [Midwest's] leading Republicans mirrored clearly the views of their followers. At the least, African Americans would be viewed as unwelcomed competitors for homestead land."[76]

Not until the end of the century did African Americans attempt to form a colony. In the summer of 1896, the Grand Army of the Republic held a national encampment on the state fairgrounds in St. Paul. Two real-estate agents distributed promotional materials among black veterans from Kentucky extolling the virtues of Fergus Falls. Representatives of a group from Greenwood, Kentucky, visited the city later that year and about fifty others arrived in April 1897, intending to settle there. Unable to find suitable homesteads or steady employment, some left at the end of the summer, moving to Aitkin County, Akeley and Nevis in Hubbard County, or to Sioux Falls, South Dakota. Although a few farmed, most of the original colonists felt it necessary to find work on larger, more established farms or move to the city.

Despite the disappointing venture, a Mille Lacs County real-estate broker in 1899 persuaded twenty-five additional Greenwood families to homestead in nearby Wealthwood, Minnesota, an undeveloped township with poor soil. This venture failed as well, forcing the majority of them to find work in the cities, their only real option being to leave behind the hard labor of farmwork for a white boss, which resembled what they had left in the South.[77] A black man with good character, means, and the ballot could not force a white man with good land for sale to do business with him. The city seemed to offer a better chance for advancement, or at least the security of a black community.

When Wilkinson admonished the black assembly to "make your children mechanics, make them blacksmiths, make them house builders, make them stonemasons," he was portraying a Minnesota in which apprenticeships to skilled labor and a customer base were within their grasp. Therefore, he reasoned, all barriers that remained were those of their own making.[78] But just as he saw farming and hard work as the antidote to a wretched future of poverty and disrespect, Wilkinson, carried away by the passion of the moment, forgot his own personal history with the practical application of policy and the African American. The world outside the walls of Ingersoll Hall on January 1, 1869, was far different from the one he portrayed. Antiblack sentiment in the trades, not just in Minnesota but throughout the North, from where the vast majority of urban Minnesotans came, had a long history.

In 1831, Alexis de Tocqueville observed about race relations in Jacksonian America that "The prejudice of race appeared to be stronger in the states that have abolished slavery than in those where it still exists; and nowhere is it so intolerant as in those states where servitude has never been known." A clear example of this was the opposition of the white Northern tradesmen against affiliating with black workmen. In Philadelphia, Cincinnati, New York City, and many smaller cities of Illinois, Indiana, Ohio, New Jersey, and Pennsylvania, white workers seriously objected to black competition. In a number of places, but Pennsylvania in particular, many violent antiblack demonstrations took place. The effect of that violence, especially in Philadelphia, and the loss of economic position during the 1830s and 1840s, drove so many African Americans from the city that the black population had actually decreased by 1850.[79]

In New York City in 1863, antiblack sentiment spiked higher with the importation of black strikebreakers, especially among Irish workers, the African Americans' closest competitors. Prior to the mass arrival of the Irish, most personal service and common labor was done by black men and women whose wages for such work were comparably high. The new immigrants undercut the "Negro scale" and pushed the black workers out of their jobs. A deadly hatred resulted, which manifested itself in quarreling and fighting between the two groups.[80]

The fear of competition with black workers among some white workers in the North led many to oppose emancipation. Racial prejudice ran so high in Pennsylvania that the legislature was urged in 1860 to reenact the laws permitting slavery. A union meeting that convened in Philadelphia in 1861 protested against antislavery legislation and urged the repeal of all state laws that had placed obstacles in the way of the enforcement of the Fugitive Slave Act. In New York City, the Democratic Party, dominated by the Irish and supported by unskilled Germans and other immigrant groups, purported to represent the city's workingmen. It opposed the freeing of slaves on the grounds that emancipation would result in the migration of thousands of freedmen and -women to Northern states, increasing competition for jobs and reducing wages even lower than the already-underpaid job market dictated.

In 1863, as mentioned earlier, bloody fights occurred in New York City, Buffalo, and other eastern cities (including Boston in 1867), between striking white longshoremen and blacks brought in to break the strike. One year earlier, in Minnesota, the St. Paul and Galena Packet Company, along with the La Crosse Company, dispatched agents to St. Louis "to engage Negroes as deck hands on the steamboats" after their white deckhands struck for higher wages.[81] That same year, a host of white laborers received a raft full of Missouri contraband with rocks and clubs at the docks in Lowertown, St. Paul. As the Republican newspaper, the St. Paul *Daily Press*, reported, "The Irish on the levee were considerably excited, and admitted by their actions that the negro was their rival, and that they fear he will out-strip them."[82]

This issue of black competition had festered since 1854 when the laboring class had urged their representative to sponsor a bill that would create a black code in Minnesota, and it nearly passed. The matter was revived in 1859 when legislators introduced a bill to prevent the migration of free blacks and mulattos into the state and require the registration of those already in residence. Like their predecessors, these legislators insisted that blacks would compete for jobs customarily held by poor whites, thus denying this class of citizens a livelihood. Moreover, they argued, whites forced to work with blacks might resort to violence. Worse still, they reasoned, black people would become paupers and wards of the state.[83]

The St. Paul experiences also showed how the rhetoric of the employers seemed to be intent in inflaming the situation if it meant they could acquire the cheaper labor of black workers. Faced by hostile whites, blacks seeking protection from their employers were not in a position to demand wages or reasonable working conditions. "We happen to know," wrote one employer, "that agricultural occupations, as indeed in many others, hired negro labor is more efficient, and more tractable and docile, than the class of white labor which is usually available for such purposes."[84] The *Daily Press* parsed the notion that the least efficient white labor was "low Irish":

> This fact, which is established by experience, is further corroborated by the testimony of true Celtic "hewers of wood and drawers of water," who, by the intense savage hostility which they were everywhere manifested to the introduction of negro labor, virtually confessed their inferiority to compete with it on the lowest functions of industry, and thus frankly acknowledge themselves the inferiors of their black counterparts.[85]

Despite the opportunity for work, it was the sort that kept them impoverished. Black–white labor tensions kept wages at the lowest level. In 1867, black ship caulkers were brought up from Portsmouth, Virginia, to Boston to defeat the white workers' struggle for an eight-hour day. Across the North, a few labor leaders attempted to mitigate racial tensions between two peoples who would benefit as allies by couching the issue of labor in terms of class consciousness rather than race; skilled workers, on the other hand, tended to forestall competition by altogether excluding blacks from workshops.[86]

Well into the 1870s, similar practices were evidently in play in St. Paul, for most of the jobs that African Americans could obtain involved menial work in restaurants and hotels. Indeed, the only contacts that a newly arrived African American—usually penniless and unskilled—made tended to steer him to this kind of work. In characterizing the dynamic of this period, Earl Spangler noted:

> Without money or friends, the objects of the open antagonism of workers already established, and depended almost entirely on the humanity and justice of white employers, these illiterate black people turned their hands to whatever job they could find to do and availed themselves of every opportunity for their business advancement and enlightenment.[87]

This was the reality African Americans had endured. This was the reality African Americans would continue to face for the remainder of the century. There would be no violence, no intimidation, but more frequently the cold shoulder. Unaccustomed to limitations that were not imposed with the whip or closed fist, the newly arrived African Americans missed the subtlety of rejection within postwar Minnesota. With homesteading and skilled labor foreclosed to them, the standard for respectability that Wilkinson held up was unattainable. But his purpose at the Convention of Colored Citizens was not to tell them what they already knew about the injustice they had long endured, but to inspire them to forget the history of racism and slavery that had brought them to this day. Only African Americans had the ability to win the respect of the white race:

> It has been said that the white race was the dominant race of the world, and with some degree of truth. The white race have been dominant, and the solution of that is to be found in the single word WORK. The right of the franchise cannot elevate you to respectability among men. If you would be respected in the sight of the nation, you must work; if you will be respected by good men, you must hew out your own fortunes.[88]

Listening to Wilkinson's words and the cheers that interrupted his speech, Robert Hickman was no doubt inspired by the total experience of the moment. Still, there may have been something more that filled him with joy, something that may have drowned out the words, the preachy expectation, the otherworldly simplicity of the challenges his race now faced, that made this moment good, precious, and eternal, that gave him a sense of deliverance. That "something" may have been the sheer power of being this close to a great man like Wilkinson who, as a confidant to President Lincoln, may have given Hickman a direct link to the Great Emancipator himself, whose spirit was actually there in Ingersoll Hall; and if this was true, Wilkinson's words and tone, and his overreaching belief that imbued the ballot and the promise of hard work with a power they did not have, meant, for the moment, very little. Hickman knew something about hard work as well as the indefatigable nature of racism, for he was a man, like so many seated around him, just five years out of slavery.

It was Hickman and his followers who had come upriver from Missouri on a raft in 1863 and were subjected to mob violence at the docks of Lowertown, but had nevertheless come to reside in St. Paul, not to take jobs from white laborers but to make a life in the new age of freedom. The most prominent newspaper in the state, the *St. Paul Press,* had heralded their arrival—"*Colored Workers for Hire*"—and they, accustomed to hard work, had not come this far to slough off the opportunity to make their way. If he shared the joyful reaction of the audience around him, Hickman now seemed willing to dismiss Wilkinson's naïveté or patronizing manner, and an evident need for closure. A new chapter was indeed about to begin. For Hickman, two facts were irrefutable: he was no longer in the South, and the white men of Minnesota had given him the right to vote. For that moment, and for only a moment, he would drift along on the optimistic currents of brotherhood.[89]

4

THE SONS OF FREEDOM

"You must carve your way through the solid rock."

—THE HONORABLE MORTON S. WILKINSON,
Convention of Colored Citizens of Minnesota, 1868

The success of the black suffrage campaign and the January 1 celebration that showed the value that Minnesota's most prominent leaders placed on black citizenship filled African Americans with optimism in confronting the immense challenges their race faced. Still, even with the ballot their small numbers undercut their ability to leverage the potential of a black voting bloc into real political power. Indeed, the ballot alone could not help them attain full opportunity. As Richard Kluger wrote about the national condition of African Americans, "[T]he black man was clearly going to need help to make his freedom a fact as well as a right."[1] It was no different in Minnesota. Black citizens still needed the support of powerful white Republicans. This was a period in which black Minnesotans, like African Americans throughout the North, began to celebrate racial pride through organized social and educational activities, and as a community without capital, they relied on white patrons for many such activities. The question was whether the Sons of Freedom, the only organization that addressed jobs skills and property ownership and record keeping of educational progress—three areas of specific interest to party leaders as referenced in their speeches at the convention—would receive support to do the work needed to advance black Minnesotans.

But in the climate of social Darwinism, the words that Senator Wilkinson spoke at the Convention of Colored Citizens of Minnesota—"We have done our part"—echoed loudly off the walls that effectively barred them from even the opportunity to own farms or acquire viable job skills. For a people recently emancipated from slavery, living in a society that stigmatized them because of their black skin, education—especially when black children learned alongside of whites—could, in the long run, bring down those walls.

In October 1865, nearly one month before voters rejected black suffrage, the St. Paul Board of Education adopted a resolution stating that "the mingling of children of African descent with those of white parentage is obnoxious to the views and feelings of a large portion of our citizens." Therefore, for the good of all children and families involved, the board resolved, "It is the patriotic duty of American citizens to extend to the African race all reasonable facilities to develop their intellectual and physical capabilities." Thus, the board directed the superintendent of schools to find by the beginning of the school year a suitable teacher and accommodations for the colored children of the city, "and that no children of African descent be thereafter admitted into any public school." More than 4,800 children between ages five and twenty-one resided in St. Paul that year, forty-five of whom were of African descent.[2]

Thus began the first policy for school segregation in postwar Minnesota. St. Paul had attempted to segregate black children during the 1850s with a provisional (and largely ineffective) policy that required that a separate school be available if thirty—then later, fifteen—black children wanted a formal education, but it was not one that could be enforced. Because of the high cost of fighting the Civil and Dakota wars, St. Paul could not afford to maintain an adequate and separate facility for its black children. In turn, teachers ignored the policy and allowed black children into their classrooms, to the consternation—in some instances, violent protests—of white parents. In one instance in October 1864, a "wild Irishman" had to be arrested after disrupting a classroom upon seeing a black child in his child's classroom. Fearing for the safety of their children, a few black parents kept their children in the woefully substandard colored-only school. In August 1865, a small group of black veterans issued a complaint against the conditions in which their children were forced to learn and the board of education decided to enact a more draconian policy. Whereas before, when a set number of "colored scholars" were required for the segregation policy to go into effect, now segregation would be absolute. Teachers could no longer feign ignorance of whether a certain percentage of African American children were enrolled in St. Paul schools, or, more likely, could disregard an egregious and unenforceable policy. The new policy made it clear: no children of African descent would be permitted in the same classroom with white children.[3]

Within two days of adopting the resolution, Superintendent John Mattocks announced that a site had been secured in Morrison's Building on Jackson Street, opposite the Methodist church, the rent being seven dollars a month. "The colored school would be in operation this week." A suitable teacher "and a warm friend to the colored people" was hired at fifty dollars a month. Almost immediately, the district neglected it. Soon after classes began, the board of education heard of "problems of maintaining and operating" the school, but allowed the school to limp forward, receiving an average of twenty students from month to month. In November 1867, the *Pioneer* exposed the dilapidated conditions at the school:

> The colored children of this city are excluded from the free schools which are located in convenient and comfortable buildings, well-supplied with maps, charts, blackboards, and the usual equipment of such institution, and are placed in a separate department, which is devoted to people of color ... Some of the windows have been broken out, the plastering is falling off and the keen air of winter will find entrance in many a crack and cranny. To keep out a part of the cold that would otherwise find entrance, the windows had been partly boarded up, so that while the benefit of increased warmth is attained, the disadvantage of a decreased light has to be submitted to.[4]

No equipment, no light and warmth (especially critical to newly arrived Southern-born children during Minnesota winters), and by 1867 no teacher effectively denied black children an education. District records continued to reflect that less than half of St. Paul's African American schoolchildren attended classes. Segregation placed these children out of sight and out of mind. Maurice Jernigan and other members of the emerging group of race men in Minnesota and legislators concluded that St. Paul schools, the only place in Minnesota that imposed a policy of segregation, could not be trusted to maintain the educational welfare of children of African descent. There needed to be oversight of what happened to these children in city schools. This was one of the issues on which the Sons of Freedom would seek to focus.

On the morning of January 1, 1869, hours before the Convention of Colored Citizens began, Jernigan, along with R. J. Stockton, R. T. Grey, and other members of the original Golden Key Literary Society, drafted a constitution for a new organization they named the Sons of Freedom. It was to be the first statewide organization that would address three fundamental issues that would serve as the foundation of opportunity and advancement for Minnesota's African American population: help to get blacks into jobs and into the trades, provide assistance in managing personal property and acquiring real estate, and keep records of African American children in and out of school. Membership was limited to black men of the whole state, and no membership fees would be charged.[5]

Founded on the principles of self-help—black people elevating themselves through their own devices—it was the kind of organization that fit within the values of nineteenth-century republicanism. But it represented more than a philosophical alignment with allies and patrons in politics and business; its agenda seemed to equate opportunity and advancement with racial independence. If a man could manage his own affairs and improve his standing in the community, he could wrest himself free of the stigma of perpetual inferiority. He could make his own decisions without fear of displeasing white men of influence. He could make alliances with whomever was better situated to meet his needs—whether Republican or Democrat. This was why the group called itself the Sons of Freedom. Having a job in the trades positioned black men to acquire capital that could be invested in property to enhance financial stability and personal independence. A good education allowed children to build on what their parents left them, to position themselves securely within the middle class. In the second half of the nineteenth century, being middle-class was synonymous with being American, and public education was the most American of institutions.

In the North and West throughout the antebellum years, public education was seen as the great uplifting force and harbinger of a bright future. Horace Mann, Henry Barnard, and other supporters of compulsory education argued that public schools were the seedbed of civic-minded-ness and a sense of national unity, the spread of humanitarian and egalitar-ian values, the "homogenization" of citizens from every ethnic, religious, and racial group, and the enhancement of human efficiency in building a wiser electorate in the land where universal male suffrage would be prac-ticed. Accordingly, a public education was the birthright of all citizens.[6]

That public education was a birthright was generally accepted throughout the North and West. What was not as well settled was whether the character of the ever-diversifying populations in the North and West should be reflected in the classrooms of the public schools. The road to racially mixed schools was circuitous. Despite the egalitarian mood of the age, the children of the middle and upper classes received education from elite schools, typically from private academies or public schools in mid-dle-class neighborhoods, so that the notion of "public school" came to mean where children of the working class attended. In cities in the North and West, those populations were usually predominately white. Diversity was defined in terms of religion and ethnicity, without the consideration of class and race.

Whether to integrate black children became a difficult proposition even for the friends of the African American. Prior to the move to pro-vide for tax-supported public education, middle- and upper-class parents paid for their children's education. Early in the nineteenth century, edu-cation for the poor was largely provided by benevolent societies. Because the free schools supported by philanthropists were regarded as a system for educating the poor, the friends of free blacks turned them away from these institutions, fearing they might be reproached for becoming a pub-lic charge, and deeming it wise to provide separate schools for them. However, the stigma of charity dissipated as a result of the widespread acceptance that free schools should be subsidized at public expense. Black parents thus concluded that it was not dishonorable to send their chil-dren to schools that they paid for through their taxes. But these schools were filled with the children of the hostile white working poor. As Carter G. Woodson wrote, "Unable then to cope with systems thus maintained for the education of the White youth, the directors of colored schools requested that something be appropriated for the education of Negroes." Complying with these petitions, boards of education provided for col-ored schools that were partly or wholly supported at public expense. But abolitionists soon saw that they had made a mistake in supporting a policy that was intended to protect black children against white harassment, for the amount appropriated to support the colored schools was generally inadequate to supply them with the necessary equipment and competent teachers, as boards of education bowed to the pressure in communities where white parents regarded the coeducation of the races as undesirable. "Confronted then with this caste prejudice, one of the hardest struggles of the Negroes and their sympathizers was that for democratic education."[7]

From the 1830s on, the legislatures of northern and western states established public education but generally left to local districts whether the races would be separated. New York, New Jersey, Ohio, many of the New England states, and the Pennsylvania that Ralph Grey as a native knew intimately had laws that expressly left to districts the authority to decide. Black children in Indiana received formal education only if they could attend a private or mission school. The Illinois constitution of 1847 expressly limited funds to the education of black children; though in communities where there were few black children, local districts casually looked the other way as black children were permitted to attend public schools with white children. A few states, however, demonstrated moral courage. In Michigan, after blacks were permitted to vote at school meetings in 1848, black children were allowed to attend public schools. In 1855, the Massachusetts legislature enacted a law that prohibited school segregation after the state high court five years earlier had validated Boston's policy. Two years later, in 1857, Iowa banned school segregation, as did Wisconsin in 1871. Except for Massachusetts, where the black population was relatively large, most northern and western states within the region formerly known as the Old Northwest territories, with few African Americans, could more easily resolve a problem that proved thorny for states with larger populations.[8]

In 1869, Minnesota, with a small black population, was well situated to have an antisegregation law. By then it had an active cadre of race leaders who had helped to pass the first black suffrage amendment ever to be approved by the voters of any state, and had created an organization that had as one of its objectives to improve the education of black children. The convention that they had held to positive reviews from all the major newspapers in St. Paul and Minneapolis, including the Democratic *Pioneer,* kept the ball in motion.[9] It could have been argued that school segregation contravened the tradition of a nonracial sense of duty to educate every child. In 1846, Harriet Bishop was invited to come to Minnesota to teach because she was "entirely free from prejudice on account of color, for among her scholars she might find not only English, French and Swiss, but Sioux and Chippewa, with some claiming kindred with the African stock."[10] The children "claiming kindred with the African stock" belonged to Jim Thompson, who may have donated his lumber and labor to build St. Paul's first schoolhouse.

With a Republican majority in both houses, whose members represented districts with few if any African American children and educated them without controversy with white students in the same classrooms, the new school law should pass without problems. But an additional factor may have contributed to the inevitable outcome. This law would be about repudiating the Democratic Party, whose political base was in St. Paul. The city was the only municipality in the state that had a segregation policy. It also had the largest concentration of African Americans, the male population of which was now the state's newest voters, indeed, presumably, the newest Republican voters. An antischool-segregation law would be addressing the interests of Republican constituents.

On November 30, 1867, just weeks after the second failed suffrage referendum, the state's leading Democratic newspaper, the St. Paul *Pioneer,* did a curious thing: it published an expose on the dilapidated state of the colored school, a creation of segregation policy overseen by a board of education composed of both Democrats and Republicans. Two years earlier, the Republican *Press* printed a petition from black veterans, but in doing so only reported the grievance, not the reason for the grievance. Now, it was the article in the Democratic *Pioneer* that created the greater impact as it described in dramatic terms the abysmal conditions under which black children were forced to get an education. It had not before shown interest in their welfare and had reported approvingly of the school's establishment; but the November 30 article conveyed sympathy for the plight of African American children. The article in itself could perhaps be viewed as an anomaly but for a series of small events that, when taken together, suggest a different story.

After the 1868 referendum that granted black men the vote, instead of inflaming Democratic voters that the apocalypse was nigh, the *Pioneer* extended what seemed to be a gracious admonition to Minnesota's newest citizens:

But now that we have got [Negro suffrage], we must make the best of it. We advise negroes to read Democratic newspapers, to hear Democratic speakers, to post themselves upon political topics, and to qualify themselves in their minds as they are qualified in law, for the duties of the voter. They should do as a white man should do in Hayti, or Liberia, if the negro governments of those countries should see fit to let the white man vote. They should not be guided by prejudices, nor be beguiled by demagogues, but should ascertain which party will make the best laws, impose the lowest taxes, wipe out the debt, and make the country what it ought to be: then they should vote for the party.[11]

It seemed that things could now settle down. Democratic politicians attended the convention, quietly sitting in the rear of Ingersoll Hall, seeming to take in good humor the chiding remarks of some of the speakers who warned black voters about the falseness of their newfound support.[12] Although the audience clearly enjoyed the ribbing, it seemed that these Democrats saw the benefit of being in attendance in order to convey perhaps expiation of past party sins against the black man, perhaps to demonstrate that they supported or were willing to accept the new political reality, that perhaps in time they could reacquaint themselves with each other to form a new partnership. Even though black speakers took turns attacking the Democrats, the *Pioneer,* in particular, in reporting on the convention, refrained from counterpunching the black leaders: "The colored people filled their part well. They did all things decently and in order. They were temperate, considerate and high-toned, and gave throughout their proceedings, many evidences that they are worthy of the possession of their new rights and franchises." But it referred to the Republican speakers as "white trash," "political hucksters," and "piddling politicians":

There was not a sensible negro in the audience who believed the balderdash of [Ignatius] Donnelly [one of the Republican speakers], that the black race was superior, originally, to the whites. [White speakers] insulted the good sense, and all the ideas of common decency that are cherished by both races, in partisan zeal, smutty jokes, and bad stump oratory.[13]

The paper was telling its readers that the real fools were the Republicans, not the blacks, whose political power was at best negligible, albeit potentially useful. Perhaps in time even these citizens could be brought into the Democratic fold. Until they returned to power, what better way to whittle away at the ties binding this base of new voters to their political patrons than to show how little black men, in the most practical terms—jobs—had benefited from Republican control. The Republicans were hypocrites, in that they had failed to appoint blacks to legislative clerkship positions:

> Not a single colored man has been nominated for any office. The radical party, that has conferred upon the colored people the right to vote, and which demands the votes of the colored people for their candidates, did not give them a single office—not even that of a common messenger or fireman. That is a test of the love of the radicals for colored men. That is the measure of protestations of the white republican politicians, delivered with unction and emphasis at the Negro celebration New Year's Day, in this city. They will be very glad to get the votes of colored citizens, but they have no offices—not even the cheapest and meanest—for the colored voters.[14]

These were seeds Democrats hoped would bear fruit.

However, Jernigan and his fellow members of the Golden Key Literary Society who now composed the Sons of Freedom were not distracted by these gestures. The Republicans, at least for now, were in charge, and it would be on them that Jernigan and his colleagues would focus their efforts. After all, one of the party's strongest voices appeared to have supported a ban on school segregation since 1865, arguing that environment, not heredity, was the cause of any degradation among blacks. In an editorial signed simply "W" that appeared that year in the Mankato *Union*, the organ for Senator Wilkinson, the author wrote: "[Blacks] never have had the advantages of education. They have for centuries been taught their inferiority and stupidity. But the day is dawning when they will show that there is stamped upon their race the image of the same all-wise God."[15] The time now seemed right for the party to act.

On January 10, ten members of the Society who were the core of the Sons of Freedom filed a petition with the state House of Representatives, arguing that the middle-class virtues of industry, intelligence, and sobriety were the "cardinal elements" on which black people could "erect good citizenship"; they added that better education would awaken in blacks "integrity and moral worth" as fine as in the most enlightened and intelligent whites. Literacy, therefore, was inextricably linked with good citizenship.[16] For the remainder of the month, legislators worked on a bill. Then, tragedy struck.

On the morning of February 3, a fire "speedily" consumed the International Hotel with the alarm sounding at two o'clock in the morning. Smoke rapidly filled the entrance and hallways and all two hundred guests poured out from every outlet. According to an eyewitness account by William H. C. Folsom, a hotel guest that night, the International was crowded with boarders, among whom were members of the legislature and their families. The writer occupied a room on the second floor and was among the first to leave. "Hastily seizing my trunk," he recorded, "I hurried down stairs and returned to assist others, but was stopped by a wall of smoke at the entrance." A group of ladies had escaped to the sidewalk, partly clad, some with bare feet. Ladders were placed in the window to save those who had failed to escape through the hallway. Senators C. A. Gillman and Seagraves Smith and their wives were rescued in this manner. Senator Armstrong tried in vain to throw his trunk in the window in which it was wedged fast and was obliged to leave it to the flames. Judge Meeker came out of the hotel carrying his clothes under his arm, having a shawl wrapped around his head, and bemoaning the loss of the maps and charts of his dam. Seagraves Smith tarried too long looking for a Senate bill and narrowly escaped the blaze. Many of the guests escaped in their night clothing and, carrying their clothing with them, completed their toilet standing in the snow in the light of the burning building. Considering the rapidity of the fire and the hour at which it occurred, it seemed miraculous that no lives were lost. The loss was estimated at $125,000. The fire left nothing to be salvaged.[17] Maurice Jernigan lost everything.

Three weeks later, on Saturday, February 27, the House got down to work on the education bill when Representative William H. C. Folsom of Taylors Falls, a survivor of the fire at the International, introduced "a bill to amend section 59, title 1 of chapter 39 of the general statute, regarding education," or Bill No. 198. This bill was intended to deprive school districts "in incorporated towns" of school funds when black children were denied admission because of their race. Despite its statewide purpose, its true purpose was undeniable. In effect, it was intended to ban school segregation. But true to the spirit in most states that deferred to the will of the local board, the bill stopped short of imposing an outright ban of the policy. Rather, it stated only that as long as a district chose to discriminate, it would lose state aid. And since St. Paul was the only "incorporated town" with this policy, it was the bill's intended target. Against token opposition from St. Paul's Democratic representatives, J. L. MacDonald and J. J. Egan, the bill passed in the House by wide margins. Days later it was enacted into law.[18] With this, Minnesota joined the few states that had ended school segregation. The last matter for black equality on the Republican agenda had been fulfilled.

But already there were concerns. The Republican *Daily Press,* perhaps taking the word of school officials, some of whom were Republicans, reported, "[Black children] will have to take their chances with our already-overcrowded schools."[19] This glossed over the real issue—the rejection of school integration by white parents. Democrats claimed that the school district that ran eight school buildings and accommodated nearly four thousand children could not now, because of the new law, absorb anywhere from twenty to forty children: "There is no room for [black students] now, many white pupils having already been refused admission for want to accommodations."[20] The *Pioneer* insisted that in the name of the new law, the education of white children was being sacrificed for the benefit of the blacks. White parents protested, especially when they heard that their young children would share classrooms with much older black youth. The image of "full-grown colored boys" was profoundly unsettling. But this was another pretext for racism, for many whites had themselves received education in the proverbial one-room schoolhouse composed of multiaged pupils. In the colored school, no one complained about the arrangement. For their part, Jernigan and his colleagues had to be thrilled at the passage of the law. Yet the concerns they heard from school officials and white parents were inevitable given the outrage they felt when government intruded on their local affairs, compounded by the depth of racism that many of them felt. But not even one full day had passed since the law was enacted, so it was prudent to be wary. On matters of race, the *Pioneer* had always been provocative; white parents had always been reactive, and school officials had always been duplicitous. And there was one more concern: within the week, most of the Republican friends of black Minnesota, many of whom were their customers, some even friends, would be leaving town. In this context, Jernigan and four other colleagues had to be surprised when on March 23 the county sheriff presented each man with a summons to appear in court.

They had been called to be jurors for a criminal trial, and in so doing they would make history as the first black men in Minnesota to serve in that capacity. It was evident (though possibly not so much to Jernigan and his colleagues at the time) that the summons—indeed, the circumstances leading up to delivering the summons—had been planned for some time, and separate from the drama of the antisegregation law. That jury duty for black men would occur in Democratic St. Paul, just months after black men gained the vote, made the summons that much more noteworthy. If Democratic officials in St. Paul had been pursuing ways to redefine their party as one seeking a new relationship with black voters, the summons would be a powerful gesture. And the press would need time to tell the right story—something dramatic but positive. But it would require a delicate touch. Officials had to know that the white men of St. Paul would not stand for black men being elevated to such a role of responsibility, let alone the prospect of being judged by black men. The key elements had to be just right to mitigate a riot. The facts of the case had to be clear-cut. The trial had to be short. The defendant and his alleged victim had to be black men. And the verdict had to be relatively inconsequential. *State v. Harris* fit the bill.

On December 28, 1869, Willie P. Harris, a twenty-two-year-old unemployed laborer, allegedly entered the boarding room of another black man named Andrew Jackson, and stole from him a sum of money. He was arrested and brought to police court, where his trial was scheduled. Nearly three months after the alleged crime, he had his day in court, and what he saw as he entered the courtroom probably unnerved him. How could such a petty crime warrant such attention? The day was Tuesday, March 23. The answer was not that the crowd in the gallery had come to see him, which might have been unnerving enough, but his jury—five members of the twelve-man jury were black men. The county had gone through considerable effort to get this jury.[21]

Earlier that morning, during the process of jury selection, attorneys grilled thirty-six white men. Only one man, James Pendergast—the only one expressing no racial bias—survived the cut. By noon, when the court adjourned for the morning, Judge William Sprigg Hall directed the sheriff to summon an additional twenty candidates in time for the afternoon session. Because more than 3,500 white voters in Ramsey County were eligible to serve on the jury, it was improbable that five black men—and these men in particular, who probably were not used to being in the limelight—were selected by happenstance. By the time the afternoon session began, reporters from the *Pioneer* and the Minneapolis *Tribune* were present to report the occasion. "The colored citizens looked dignified and anxious; the white folks curious."[22] The men selected were Maurice Jernigan, R. J. Stockton, Thomas Jackson, Henry Moffit, and Robert Hickman, whose church was the site of the founding of the Sons of Freedom.[23] All five men lived in the third ward, densely populated with white native-born and foreign-born neighbors representing every socioeconomic level from unskilled laborer to professional.[24] These were the men the sheriff wanted: the leaders of the black community, the men behind all the changes. "It is a noteworthy fact that the first colored jurymen in the State were summoned by a Democratic sheriff, in a Democratic county and Democratic city, in a court presided over by a Democratic judge, and where the county prosecutor was a Democrat."[25]

Aside from the mere sight of black men seated in the jury box, what made these five jurors objects of curiosity for the white folks had to be how they comported themselves. Perhaps even more important than the verdict they would render, white folks may have wondered: Would these black men break under all the attention or would they act with dignity? Would they puff themselves out like cocksure roosters or show the solemnity that the proceedings required? Would their style inflame or display sober deliberation? And what kind of citizens would they be long after the trial was decided? Perhaps the one white man in the courtroom who considered these and other questions, who studied these men with the scrutiny of a lawman and politician, was the county sheriff.

If any man embodied the Democratic establishment of St. Paul, it was Daniel A. Robertson. He played key roles in the development of the city, territory, and state; but he was also an intellectual force in his party, widely acknowledged to have the largest personal library in the county that included a number of historical documents and first editions.[26] He felt that while the Civil War was just because it ended slavery, extending the vote to black men could only serve to perpetuate racial strife throughout the North and the South. Worse still, he felt, the black voter would be forever indebted to the Republican Party, permitting the party's continued dominance of national and regional power. With such dominance, all accountability would melt away, inviting the most generous of Republican spirits to descend into corrupting absolutism. Prompted by the speeches equating black citizenship with Republicanism at the recent Convention of Colored Citizens, he concluded that such a course could be averted if the Democrats veered away from their tradition of racial exclusion and gave black voters a reason to change parties.[27]

With a résumé including newspaper publisher and former mayor of St. Paul, and so well connected that he could get two judges to testify in his behalf on a land claim, Sheriff Robertson was in a position to modify the face of his party. This was about taking practical steps to shift the balance of power. The question was whether the emerging black leaders were partisan or pragmatic; whether they were men with whom he could work. They surely were not the same black men he thought he knew who had always done a fine job with scissors and razor, and who possessed a pleasing and decidedly deferential manner. These jurors were listening to the evidence in a case against a man who had already been indicted by a Ramsey County grand jury. Although the man's guilt was evident, would these black jurymen see that and opt for good citizenship or would they defer to blind racial loyalty, bias against St. Paul, or both? But a watchful "Colonel" Robertson (as he was sometimes called), truly a man of the world, also probably considered whether these black jurymen as newly anointed race leaders might seek to inflame affairs that were larger than just the fate of young Willie Harris, for the antisegregation law that Robertson viewed as irresponsible was only a week old.

Already events were turning ugly at the schools as white parents harassed black parents trying to enroll their children. The sheriff, who was also the current chair of the board of education, had to be concerned with what the Radical Republican friends of these black jurymen might do to enforce state law against his city, and the added disturbance that it would create. What role would three black barbers and two whitewash laborers play in all this? In that their names had appeared in the press (thanks largely to his friends' own making) as petitioners, convention leaders, and now jurymen, they were the most famous black men in Minnesota; and this gave them certain responsibilities, but to whom? And who said they were "leaders"? The blacks? The whites? Or did they claim that prize for themselves? All of this uncertainty, under this new concept of politics and race in Minnesota, was untested ground and a delicate situation for the city. As part of a plan to appeal to black voters, summoning these men had made sense. But if this was the reasoning of the Democrats, they had misjudged how they should respond to the antisegregation law. Indeed, they had miscalculated any benefit that came from elevating the same African American men who had lobbied for black suffrage and against segregation. Perhaps, on the other hand, and in the end, they had overestimated the compatibility of blacks with the Democratic Party, or even the value of their votes. This was Minnesota, after all, turning whiter by the day with the steady stream of native-born whites and immigrants making homes in the state. In any event, Robertson would have understood that the trial and the issue with the schools were on public display (and in both these black jurymen had played vital roles), and as long as they remained so, the city's ability to move forward diminished. It was better, he would have concluded, for the city to appear reasonable and not reactionary.[28] From the time when the "not guilty" verdict was announced, the response from Democratic opinion makers was markedly restrained. Two weeks after Harris was acquitted, he was charged with larceny for stealing $180 from a store. On April 6, he pleaded guilty and was convicted and sentenced to two years and four months at the Minnesota State Penitentiary at Stillwater. This time the jury, like the victim, was all white. And the account of Harris's troubles was all left to the Republican newspaper to report.[29]

Meanwhile, by the beginning of the spring term in April, only thirteen black children were enrolled in school, owing in some quarters to "a strong deterrent in keeping many negroes away from the schools they were legally entitled to enter."[30] Nonetheless, the board chair listened as school officials interpreted the small number not as a result of intimidation, but for lack of interest of most black parents to have their children in the same classrooms with white children. The superintendent of schools and the *Pioneer* agreed: school integration was a failure because black children did not want to learn with white children. Forcing them to do so was futile and wrongheaded. "The fact stares us in the face, that nearly all of the colored pupils of this city were deprived of the means of obtaining an education through the public schools, by this law. It would seem that such evidence as this would be sufficient as warranted to openly repeal.

[The law] is impertinent and worse than unnecessary in its inception, and is wholly wrong and injurious in the operation. It really deprived the colored people in this city of the opportunity of educating their children and that is sufficient cause to warrant its repeal." The editor of the *Pioneer,* forgetting how he had graphically described the wretched state of the colored school in November 1867, now confabulated those halcyon days: "When the separate school was in existence, fifty to sixty pupils attended. They had good teachers, and made satisfactory progress in their studies. Now, however, under the new law, in substance compelling them to attend public schools with white children, that was all gone."[31]

Segregation was, in a word, good. But if the Republicans were determined to please the blacks, as Democrats surely had reasoned, they must be told that segregation was what the blacks wanted. At the April 19 meeting of the board of education, Mayor James T. Maxfield insisted that black parents preferred separate facilities for their children. Seeing no reason why their desires should be denied, he hoped that the legislature would cooperate in the matter. In the long run, his statement was more pandering than substantive, for he stopped short of calling for a petition or any legislative initiative to start a campaign to repeal the law. Rather, his audience was the board and persons in the audience.[32] Even though the statement seemed hollow, and in time the issue seemed to go dormant, the climate remained such that flare-ups would occur.[33]

The Sons of Freedom watched all of this very closely. Their central concern was getting black children the best education possible, and that was going to be where the white children went to school. But they knew that the mayor was going to please constituents who were adamant in keeping black children out of "white" classrooms. The superintendent worked for a board that, at best, preferred complaisance to the rancor of running a racially diverse school system that stirred up the dust of bias. And the *Pioneer* was uninterested in being true to the facts, even those that it had printed seventeen months earlier. None of these city fathers could be trusted with the welfare of black schoolchildren. And already they were seeing signs that their Republican friends were moving on, satisfied that their work on behalf of African Americans was done.

They remembered hearing Wilkinson say as much at the convention—"*We* [meaning the friends of the African American] *have done our part.*"[34] The attention of their Republican friends was shifting to other matters. The barbers surely overheard their customers talk about rail-road expansion, land acquisition, immigrant labor, politics, trade policies, merging into a single issue that only now was smoldering within the ranks of their power base: the Minnesota farmer. Robertson also knew about their anger as a leader of the newly founded chapter of the Grange that would soon call for a third-party movement.[35] Even Wilkinson, the champion of black rights who was on his way back to Congress, would soon wage war against his own party on behalf of the farmers and the common man.[36] With all this in the offing, the Republicans appeared destined to be too distracted by their own disunity to be concerned about the educational welfare of a handful of black children in St. Paul schools. They had already enacted a law to end school segregation. They had indeed done their part. The "solid rock" that Wilkinson had challenged black Minnesotans to "carve through" would be left to ten fully employed black men whose tools were only scissors and a razor.

The practical challenges of meeting the education objective that faced the Sons of Freedom were immense. Keeping records of school attendance of black students was the only effective way they knew to determine whether black children were getting an opportunity to learn as required by law, and attendance figures were available because St. Paul had routinely kept the data. The data was not always reliable, but it was a start. The problem was going to be collecting statewide data. With an agenda that sought to have a statewide impact, the Sons of Freedom would have to solicit data from many districts, not all of which collected such material, and not all of which had stable, or any, black student enrollment. In any event, nothing compelled districts to even work with the organization, and collecting data would have to be routine in order for trends to be seen.

This work required staff and resources that the Sons of Freedom did not have. The same could be said for the other seemingly unattainable objectives: job training and property acquisition. Indeed, the agenda was an ambitious undertaking that reflected the optimism that had inspired the founders in the wake of the black suffrage vote, but that confronted the community with monumental challenges. To achieve its objectives, the organization needed personnel and a major infusion of capital. But because the founders had decided that no fees were required for membership, there were no funds to support the effort. As a result, the organization had few means to initiate and sustain the massive undertaking. Consequently, it was never able to function effectively.[37]

Nonetheless, organizers did not seek handouts from their white Republican friends, for the abiding principle of the Sons of Freedom was to be self-sufficient even as its goals were ambitious. Only in this manner, the organizers reasoned, could the organization succeed, and all black Minnesotans receive genuine respect. Besides, as monumental as the 1868 vote was, Republicans in Congress were taking black suffrage one significant step further, for they were busy pushing a bill through Congress that would give voting rights federal protection. Meanwhile, the Sons of Freedom would have to make do.

The organization assumed another role in early December when, in the spirit of fostering racial pride, it began to plan for a major celebration to recognize the seventh anniversary of the Emancipation Proclamation, scheduled for January 3, 1870. The previous celebration in 1869 was showcased within the sumptuous setting of Ingersoll Hall, one of the nicest facilities in St. Paul. Railways and stage companies with routes from all over the state charged half price for African Americans coming to St. Paul for the occasion. It was hoped that such generosity would be repeated for the upcoming celebration. "The colored people, now that they are free, should be assisted, prejudice against them destroyed, in right good earnest they should be helped."[38]

Assistance did apparently come. This year the commemoration was to occur in Minneapolis at the prestigious Pence Opera House on Hennepin and Second.[39] Speakers were scheduled to lecture on the emancipation of the slaves and the value of education, citizenship, and the "valor of the negro people at Fort Wagner, Petersburg, and other places. Music was to be provided by the Scotts Band. At the end of the day of celebration, it was judged to have been successful. Between three to four hundred people attended the daylong festivity, including a goodly number of white people who were present as spectators."[40] What they saw was the large number of African Americans who no doubt enjoyed the messages, the racial camaraderie, and what might be the last time many of them could ever afford admission and approval to enter such a spectacular edifice that was normally reserved for white-only audiences.[41]

As successful as the event was, the Sons of Freedom did not appear to benefit from the event as a fund-raiser, although it had long become evident that they needed assistance from white donors. Rather, they seemed more intent on sponsoring an event to promote racial pride and community building. It would have been reasonable to use the event, at least in part, to attract new members and funds by taking the opportunity to showcase the objectives of the organization, the status of its work and of black Minnesotans in general, within the larger theme of the advancement of an emancipated people. But they refrained from doing so, perhaps because what little they had to report paled in contrast to the inspirational messages on the value of education and black heroism on the battlefield.[42]

In any event, this was a time for celebration. To use the occasion to solicit funds, especially from the whites in the audience, would have been poor form. Aside from embarrassing benefactors, some of whom may have facilitated the use of Pence Opera House, it could have been construed to mean that, despite their attendance, their support for black suffrage, and their support for emancipation, these same generous white people had not done enough for African Americans. In 1870 especially, that message would have been unconscionable, for even as they joyfully partook in the seventh anniversary of emancipation, the states of the Union were debating another monumental legislative piece of handiwork by the Radical Republicans—the ratification of the Fifteenth Amendment.

A minimum of twenty-eight out of thirty-six states—two-thirds mandated by the Constitution—was needed and a handful of legislatures already had voted to support the amendment. The reversal of support by the New York legislature, owing to a resurgent Democratic majority that withdrew ratification, caused proponents to worry about ultimate success. Minnesotans watched this closely. The concerned St. Paul *Press* rallied its readers: "There is a strong ground for apprehension that the amendment is in great danger of failing. Minnesota can't come too promptly to the rescue."[43] Finally, on Thursday, January 13, 1870, Minnesota ratified the Fifteenth Amendment "by strict party vote, every Republican voting for it, every Democrat voting against it."[44] Six states quickly followed suit. By February 3, the requisite number of states had voted and the Fifteenth Amendment was ratified.[45]

The Republicans had come through again. They—especially their political and business leaders—could afford to be in a generous mood, for prosperity was the order of the day. Throughout the North the war-inspired boom in industrial profits and investment continued an unrelenting upward trend so that by 1873 the nation's production stood at 73 percent above its 1865 level. The ratio of jobs to workers stimulated immigration into rapidly growing cities. By 1873, the United States was second only to Britain in manufacturing. In the Midwest and West, where farming had been the principal occupation, the economy of states, driven by the vitality of an expanding urban landscape, had catapulted many into the industrial age, and it was the railroads that best characterized the new economic order.[46]

Between 1865 and 1873, thirty-five thousand miles of track were laid, a figure that exceeded the entire rail network up to 1860. Railroad construction helped pull the economy out of the downturn of 1865, and inspired a boom in coal and pig iron production and saw the new Bessemer process for making steel. Railroads opened vast amounts of land to commercial farming and helped cities like Chicago and Kansas City extend their economic sway over agricultural hinterlands.[47]

The same held true in Minnesota. While lumbering and flour milling continued to generate jobs for workers and wealth for owners, the expansion of railroads between 1870 and 1876 had considerable social and economic consequences for the state. With completion of a railroad linking St. Paul to Duluth, the capital city seemed, by voyage through the Great Lakes, to be as near to the Atlantic seaboard as Chicago and gave Minnesota grain and lumber a continuous waterway between the state and New York. By 1872, a number of links radiated out from St. Paul connecting it to all corners of the state and beyond its borders. "At the close of the season in 1872 Minnesota had 1,906 miles of completed railroads, of which seventy per cent had been built in four years."[48] The railway system knitted the commerce of the state together and channeled profits back to the concentrated wealth of St. Paul. Mary Wingerd notes that St. Paul served not only as the base of operations and the financial headquarters, but as the source of capital accumulation in the state that resided in trade and transportation networks.[49] To be the wealthy elite of St. Paul was to also be the elite of Minnesota.

It was from this group that philanthropic efforts came: men who could easily leverage favors from proprietors of the best opera and assembly halls, musicians, and public officials. The emancipated people, most of whom continued to struggle under the yoke of poverty, nonetheless wanted to attend morale-boosting functions that celebrated their race and hoped for a better future, and the elite saw to it—as they had for the Convention in 1869 and the emancipation anniversary of 1871—that railway transportation to such events was available.

Supporting events and celebrations was how the elite chose to direct their philanthropy. In contrast, within months of the 1870 event, the more substantive work initially outlined by the Sons of Freedom in their agenda was virtually nonexistent. For blacks arriving from Minnesota's farmland or from the South, the city was the new promised land; most were headed directly into poverty, where their prospects of gaining trade skills and acquiring property were as cold as a Minnesota winter. As early as 1853, employers in New York City had set up trade schools for women workers in an effort to break the strike of an all-male union. By creating similar trade schools in St. Paul, even for the most altruistic of reasons, St. Paul employers could anticipate opposition from their white workers.[50]

Black leaders knew that to protest was to complain, and to complain was to be un-republican, un-American, unmanly. Indeed, manhood grew from overcoming adversity. All good republican men knew this for, according to their mythology, they had come up from poverty. Poverty was a condition that determined character and a starting point from which one's greatness was measured by how far he individually strove to move up from it, and it was the only measure that mattered. Therefore, as with race and foreign ethnicity, poverty was a condition not to be eradicated but to be overcome by one's own individual effort. According to the mythology of the day, in the long run it was better for African Americans if the Sons of Freedom did not exist.

But another consideration had to be met. The opportunity for economic and vocational advancement for African Americans was not of primary interest to the elite. Indeed, they did not concern themselves much with the impact of the local economy on the poorest of the poor, black or white. Their wealth came from commerce that was derived from the trade and transportation networks they had established. Because of this their enterprise did not rely as heavily on the large local labor force, nor did city politics impinge significantly on their entrepreneurial designs. "Thus, the men who had the capacity to wield the most power and influence in those early years paid scant attention to the internal workings of the local economy or to the imposition of social order." If anything, the St. Paul elite preferred to engage in hometown boosterism, promoting the culture and civility of their fair city, preferring to focus on civic causes. They were particularly interested in building infrastructure—sewers, roads, and other improvements that made their lives more pleasant and increased the value of their property holdings. "Though they made St. Paul the banking center for their myriad of investments and speculated in local property, their business interests primarily operated far to the west and north and only indirectly spurred the local economy."[51] There was no interest in vocational mobility for anyone, let alone St. Paul's African American population. In fact, it ran counter to their desire to present their city in its most positive light, when blacks and whites vied for the same jobs in a competition that would surely result in violence. During a time when other Northern cities struggled with the convulsive realignment of the new postwar labor force, witnessing periodic eruptions of racial strife, St. Paul was cultivating a reputation of harmony. With a population of less than 1 percent of the city's residents, the vast majority of whom were poor, St. Paul's African Americans were easy to overlook.

The St. Paul *Press* did take note of one black Minnesotan, however. On June 3, 1871, it reported a meeting of the Old Settlers Association, a group of some of the state's most prominent figures who had been the earliest Anglo-American presence during Minnesota's preterritorial era. Meeting at the capitol, the *Press* reported, "the only colored member of that organization" in attendance was Jim Thompson, the only black man who lived in the earliest years of the city and who had been invited to join the year before. He was "one of the few living connections between the dim and romantic past of Minnesota . . . and its cultivated, intelligent and prosperous present."[52] Tinted by the reporter's rosy lens was the appearance of Thompson standing among former friends who had become prosperous and revered. Despite his threadbare effort at formal attire, he seemed to be as out of place as the color of his skin, the only man present whose fortunes had not grown since civilization came to Minnesota, and now a common laborer.[53]

The decline of fortune could be seen elsewhere. Almost immediately after the January 1870 celebration adjourned, the Sons of Freedom disappeared from view. No one spoke of it. The strain of an ambitious agenda, minimal resources, and no support from men who could have helped proved to be too much. The organization's work in providing blacks with trade skills, knowledge to acquire property, and in improving the educational welfare of African American schoolchildren would surely be seen as a threat to a much larger white working class growing more surly over the sense that it had been deprived of the American dream, and this threatened social order.

The circumstances of the organizers, many of who were the original members of the Golden Key Literary Society, also changed. Thomas Jackson, finding better opportunity in Duluth, opened a barbershop there and became the first black man to serve on a jury. R. T. Grey returned to Minneapolis. Robert Hickman, a nonmember of the Society who later joined the barbers to work on black suffrage in 1868 and assisted in planning the convention, now focused his energies on building his church.[54] R. J. Stockton took over sole proprietorship of the emporium at the Merchant Hotel and focused more on developing his "Marble Palace." In 1871, after a major infusion of investment into the space, the St. Paul *Press* breathlessly introduced the spectacularly refurbished site to its readers: "As the visitor first enters the main palace, he involuntarily stops and when his eyes have roamed over the large apartment taking in at a glance its magnificent and costly appointments, and the great taste displayed in the arrangement of the rich ornaments of the room, he cannot fail to give vent to his sentiments in terms of unbound admiration and delight, and he will for a time forget that he is in a far western State, and wonder whether this gorgeous palace of beauty is indeed a reality, or only a creation of imagination."[55] This, however, was no longer Maurice Jernigan's establishment. His fortune, three years hence, and in contrast to his former partner, would take an opposite course.

What caused his downturn? As with so much about Maurice Jernigan, one can only speculate. The change could have been economic at a time when men sometimes made quick fortunes and lost them just as quickly. It certainly was not unusual for black barbers to acquire space in one of the prestigious hotels in St. Paul only to leave within the year. But, unlike Grey, Thomas, and (so far) Stockton, Jernigan had impressively navigated the hurdles of demonstrating to customers both skill and compatibility while successfully managing a business that brought him relative longevity at the pinnacle of his profession.

But these were far from ordinary times. He had worked through the unsettling racial tensions in wartime St. Paul, three campaigns for black suffrage, a statewide convention for colored people, a law to end school segregation, and jury service in a St. Paul courtroom, any one of which could have represented a small claim to history, or the end of his career. No black man in Minnesota could claim such service to black equality. None had tested the limits of powerful white men as he had—presumably with a smile that masked inner turmoil. After each victory for black equality, no other black man faced the ever-present contradiction of achieving these ends with means that denied service to his fellow black men. Notwithstanding his principle-driven political activity, if Jernigan was to remain at the Metropolitan, he knew that he must help perpetuate unequal treatment of the black men or lose his white customers.

A similar dynamic prevailed among successful barbers throughout the North:

> The owners of first-class barber shops, found themselves in a quandary. At last they possessed full legal rights so they could pursue their careers as businessmen without restrictions, or more accurately, without infringement of their legal ability to make contracts and settle business disputes in court. They capitalized on their new rights by elevating the first-class barbershop to the highest form, and the investments they made in ever more luxurious shops made these establishments the pinnacle of black business achievement in the late nineteenth century. They also played important roles in the Republican Party. What Reconstruction granted in the political realm, however, it withheld at the social realm. No constitutional amendment or law could force white customers to purchase the services of a black barber in an integrated shop and the freedman generally lacked the disposable income to keep black barbers in business. First-class barbers consequently remained unreconstructed, serving white affluent customers exclusively; a symbol of continuity in a time of changing race relations. For the black barbers who owned these shops, their livelihood and the class status seemed oftentimes to take precedence over their commitment to black equality. However, as before the war, they strove valiantly to reconcile the conflict between these two goals.[56]

Jernigan's story may be of one that demonstrated weariness of the conflict, weary, as W. E. B. DuBois wrote, "of seeking to satisfy two un-reconciled ideals."[57]

On June 27, 1870, the Metropolitan Hotel opened in grand fashion, and within its sumptuous decor was a space that hotel proprietor Gilbert Dutcher offered to the state's most prominent barber, Maurice Jernigan. Dutcher, a friend of Frederick Douglass, saw himself as a supporter of the progress of black people, so he may have considered the barber's work for black equality as a strong expression of his own sense of political purpose. But, as a pragmatic businessman, he would have also seen in Jernigan a special amenity that the hotel could offer guests in his establishment—an accomplished and highly respected barber who offered the additional marquee value of being a genuine historical figure, the first black man to petition for suffrage and serve on a Minnesota jury. After a session in Jernigan's barber chair, customers could boast that they had advanced the progress of black manhood by patronizing a black establishment. Indeed, this opportunity had the potential to become Jernigan's most prosperous venture ever; yet for most African Americans in Minnesota the new age of opportunity was illusory. As he charged top dollar for a trim and a shave, hundreds of miles away in the western part of the state, the prospect of black colonists settling in Todd County was fading, where Lincoln Republicans who had even supported black suffrage in the last election predominated. As he used a powdered brush to whisk shards of clipped hair from the neck and positioned a mirror for the customer to drink in his newly coiffed image, St. Paul school officials continued to omit from reports the enrollment of black students, as if to say that when segregation ended, black children no longer existed. Even as he cheerfully helped the businessman down off his chair, African Americans continued to fill the ranks of St. Paul's underclass. Doing what he could to get unskilled African Americans jobs, Jernigan likely persuaded Dutcher to start what would be a long practice of hiring black men to be porters and staff, so that by the end of the decade the Metropolitan would become the largest employer of African American labor.

Although the laws were vital for black advancement, these jobs at least put food on the table, even though this kind of employment offered no avenue to develop skills that would allow workers to move out of poverty. Most whites in St. Paul were also in the class of the working poor, but Jernigan knew that African Americans were disproportionately frozen in poverty whereas their white, native-born and immigrant counterparts were more able in time to climb out. As David Taylor noted, "Locked into a rigid socioeconomic class structure, black people were generally unable to procure employment above low wage levels."[58] In Lowertown, the section of St. Paul where the largest concentration of poor African Americans lived with other impoverished immigrants, blacks in the coming years would be left behind as their ethnic neighbors advanced into the city's socioeconomic mainstream.[59] This, in the emerging American city of St. Paul, was the beginning of a modern ghetto.[60]

Jernigan would have been consoled to know black laborers at the Metropolitan at least had honest work, working for an honorable man like Gilbert Dutcher. But the condition of most blacks in St. Paul had to be of great disappointment to him, for he believed that the Sons of Freedom could have remedied the problem. He and his colleagues had miscalculated what it would take to get the organization up and running, and their Republican friends had offered no help at all. Everything that the Sons of Freedom sought to do, and that was echoed by the white speakers at the Convention of Colored Citizens of Minnesota in 1869, formed the linchpin for racial progress. The organizers needed help to get started, and Republican assistance was as important for black opportunity as were the ballot, the Homestead Act, and school integration. Yet, Republican patrons proved willing only to support such displays of advancement as the January convention and the suffrage celebration in 1869. Jernigan, who had spent his adulthood studying the ways of the white man, nonetheless may well have been puzzled by the Republicans' selective benevolence.

But he would not have indulged his inclination to think ill of his patrons. Given America's history, given the nature of a state that because of its demography and location appeared least likely to be progressive, the white men of Minnesota had done the unthinkable—they had expanded black rights and included Jernigan in all of the campaigns in a way that affirmed his stature as a leader of his community and gave him the opportunity to be a prosperous and respected businessman. Given all of this, he would have reason to feel profoundly grateful and would have concluded that an emancipated and newly enfranchised people were not in a position to ask for more.

The problems that African Americans continued to face after emancipation, after enfranchisement, after school integration, came from the prejudice of white men acting in defiance of the law, not the law itself, and it must have disquieted Jernigan to see that such defiance occurred with impunity—even by Republicans, even by some of his patrons. How, he must have wondered, could a man with so much reason to be grateful criticize his patrons? How could he ever be fully equal to his patron? The equality of this new age had limits. The issue must have been more clouded by the fact that everything he had acquired in his life—his property, standing, and civil rights, not to mention the protection he had received against envious white workingmen on St. Paul's streets—was because he provided excellent personal service with a smile. There had to be a personal price to be paid for encouraging white men to go beyond their own limits, a price that could only be paid by burying his disquiet deeply within himself.

He would have known that whites saw in him the embodiment of the Republican prescription for black advancement, and he, in turn, absolved them from having to acknowledge that white prejudice—indeed, their own prejudice—trumped constitutional amendments, laws, and wishful Republican thinking that placed overwrought faith in the power of the ballot and hard work. He would have known that equality in the new Republican age had limits even among friends of the two races, and that in his way he enabled it with his congenial manner for the sake of progress, hope for the future, and continued quality of life, with a belief—indeed, a prayer—that they would do the right thing when the time was right. But in absolving them, he became culpable. Thus, their action to do right would become his salvation. He would have needed to believe this in order to continue smiling. It was this imperative to smile that characterized the limit of equality. As DuBois wrote, "It is a peculiar sensation, this double-consciousness, this sense of always looking at one's self through the eyes of others, of measuring one's soul by the tape of a world that looks on in amused contempt and pity. One ever feels his two-ness—an American, a Negro, two souls, two thoughts, two unreconciled strivings, two warring ideals in one dark body, whose dogged strength alone keeps it from being torn asunder."[61] Even in plain view of the Sons of Freedom's agenda lying in wreckage before the "solid rock" of the postwar reality of race relations in Minnesota, Maurice Jernigan would have needed to believe in his white friends, until he could believe no longer, when something happened, the final straw, in the winter of 1873, when he would decide to take his leave.

In January 1873, the Minneapolis *Tribune* proudly announced that "on the evening of February 5th Mr. Frederick Douglass, the distinguished colored orator, [would] deliver his famous lecture on 'Self-Made Man.'"[62] In this speech, which he now frequently delivered, Douglass echoed the sentiment of the Republican age, insisting that the self-made man was one who owed little or nothing to birth, relationship, or friendly surroundings; rather, success could be explained by only one word: *work*. Opportunity was important, but exertion was indispensable. "Give the negro fair play and let him alone. If he lives, well. If he dies, equally well. If he cannot stand up, let him fall down." It was precisely this portion of Douglass's message that would appeal to an audience eager to be vindicated by the credo of the age—*We have done our part.* However, the other portion of his message that recognized the critical value of brotherhood and the interdependence of mankind was often overlooked: "I believe in individuality, but individuals are, to the mass like waves to the ocean. The highest order of genius is as dependent as is the lowest. It, like the loftiest waves of the sea, derives its power and greatness from the grandeur and vastness of the ocean of which it forms a part. We differ as the waves, but are one as the sea."[63] It was this portion of his message that a friendly white audience tended to overlook as they sat rapt in a theater that denied admission to members of the great man's own race. To men like Maurice Jernigan, this paradox showcased a new phase in the struggle for equality, one that required a more relevant articulation of the problem with the ability to persuade white friends to change their ways. This, in other words, was the time for a new style of leadership.

PART II

The

ENTREPRENEURS

5

MR. DOUGLASS AND THE
CIVILIZABLE CHARACTERISTICS
OF THE COLORED RACE

"I recollect, my friends, that you are the only race on the earth that even came in close and intimate contact with the white race, and did not perish before it."

—CONGRESSMAN IGNATIUS DONNELLY,
Convention of Colored Citizens of Minnesota, 1869

At the Convention of Colored Citizens of Minnesota in 1869 Ignatius Donnelly, paying tribute to the African Americans seated before him, grandly pronounced that their race was superior to other racial minorities simply because, unlike the other groups, they had not perished after having a "close and intimate contact with the white race." Neither the Indian nor the Finnic race had these traits, he insisted, "[b]ecause [they did] not have the civilizable characteristics of the colored race."[1] This was a statement about black potential, that with training and education, and a rigorous commitment to industry, sobriety, and good citizenship, the African American deserved a place within proper mainstream society. But it was also evident that he did not feel that most African Americans were ready, not because they were racially inferior, but because they were developmentally impaired as a result of generations of racism. Left unmentioned was whether he felt there were any African Americans seated before him that day who, at that moment, qualified. African American men could now vote and send their children to "white" public schools, but if they could afford a ticket to an opera house or to book a room in a downtown hotel, would they be admitted? Were "civilizable characteristics" dependent on income and class status? If so, were poor blacks, as long as they were poor, "uncivilizable"? The controversial visit from Frederick Douglass in 1873 highlighted discrimination in Minnesota in the area of public accommodations, which primarily benefited a small number of African Americans who could afford a good room in a hotel, a table in a restaurant, a seat at the theater—the black middle class.

When the Republican Party ushered in a new social contract for America that granted black men the same political rights of white men, as monumental as that act was, it did not secure respect for a man's dignity. It is noteworthy that such a potential threat to public order, especially when race was a factor, would go unaddressed at a time when men were fighting and dying for their ideals.

Of course, no policy maker felt that a law could or should control speech or attitudes, nor that prejudice would evaporate with extension of the voting right to black men. Yet little regard was given to the pervasive and persistent nature of racism, especially how it limited what a free man should be able to do. Few whites had genuine friendships with African Americans; they could not really understand the corrosiveness of facing racial slights every day. White men of poverty were also subjects of indignity, but in Minnesota, the paucity of blacks and the many circumstances in which violence could erupt when a black man violated the constraints of racism made black dignity as unattainable as sudden wealth.

On the other hand, policy makers believed in the robust nature of human intercourse. Just because a man had full citizenship did not absolve him of the duty to face challenges and prevail over adversity. Men, if they were to become men, could not be pampered. One had to grab opportunity just as one had to face down all manner of adversity and bend it to his will. Dignity, in other words, had to be earned. Few black men now seemed to deserve it, but that was the challenge the black man was expected to face. As Donnelly had said in 1869 at the Convention of Colored Citizens, "Your race is on trial." And trials required adversity.

However, in this new era of reconstruction, none of the policy makers anticipated that a white man's rights might outstrip a black man's dignity—a white man's right to discriminate against a black man's desire to be served. Policy makers knew that many white men would feel this way, including white men in Minnesota, even Republican white men who were the black man's friends. As long as there was peace—and peace was possible since the black population was very small and seldom had any of them broken the fragile calm—the problem of visible and volatile racial tension would not arise. In its absence, whites could allow themselves to think that there was no racial problem.

But because St. Paul was connected to the rest of the North and a part of the circuit where speakers of national repute often visited, it was a matter of time before the most visible black man in the nation—the only black man whose dignity they respected—would be coming to town. What made this situation especially complicated—the central trait of the black–white relationship during this era in Minnesota—was that the white and powerful friends of black people, who had contributed so much to the cultural enrichment and enjoyment of the African American communities in St. Paul and Minneapolis, who were even outraged at antiblack sentiment and to whom gratitude was owed, nonetheless participated in racial discrimination within their own places of business and recreation.

On February 7, 1873, the St. Paul Library Association sponsored Frederick Douglass to speak at the Opera House before a select crowd. By now well-known as an adviser to President Lincoln and the first black man nominated to serve as president of the Electoral College, his growing array of distinctions cast him as a figure of great pride for a generation who had fought four long years of war in the name of universal freedom. Douglass's speech, initially titled "The Composite Nation," was supposed to be on the nature of black progress within the new America. But standing outside the Opera House, a small group of white men heckled and catcalled, disturbing those in attendance and the great man whom they had come to hear. Because of "the boisterous constitution of the atmosphere outside," Douglass instead reminisced about the abolition movement. Douglass concluded his long speech by referring to his experience as a slave and "to

Frederick Douglass, circa early 1870s. Collection of the New-York Historical Society (negative number 35765).

his feelings when he found that white men could sympathize with him." "Throughout," one reporter noted, "the lecture abounded with thrilling interest, and was enthusiastically applauded."[2]

When Douglass ended his speech, Colonel Gilbert Dutcher, proprietor of the Metropolitan Hotel and longtime friend of Douglass, invited him to be his guest for the night. However, later that evening, when Douglass tried to book a room at the hotel, the clerk refused to admit him. The Merchant Hotel likewise refused him service. Upon learning of the affront, Dutcher extended his apologies "for the unauthorized insult offered [to Douglass] by the clerk," and gave a banquet in honor of his distinguished guest.[3]

The episode captured the conflicting nature of the black–white experience in postwar Minnesota. First, a hostile crowd had assembled outside the Opera House to heckle Douglass throughout his speech. That it would happen to Frederick Douglass—a figurehead of the abolition movement and loyalist to the Grand Old Party, the same party that dominated Minnesota politics, and who now stood before a supportive, largely Republican crowd and civic leaders—made it that much more poignant for it highlighted the sharp division that existed in the city over the issue of race. Douglass, who rose from a lowly slave to become a freeman of great renown, embodied the full scope of America's shame and redemption, and his speech was intended to mark both that remarkable achievement and the significant leadership of "white men (and white women as well) who sympathized with him."

But his appearance on this St. Paul stage exposed a community not so much divided as it reflected in broadly theatrical display the double-faced head of Janus—the crowd inside swept away by throaty admiration while the other outside foamed with derision; one placing him on a high pedestal, the other belittling him through boisterous denigration and insult. Yet, neither group attacked nor even reproached the other. Rather, in a strange way, both groups—the Opera House crowd and the street crowd—brought together by the singular visage of Frederick Douglass, were groups composed of men who shared a common past as veterans of the same struggle, having fought under the same flag during the war for national unity. The Opera House crowd did not shout in protest or issue calls for the police. Rather, to them, it seemed, the rancor outside was noisy but harmless, more a nuisance than a symptom of a deeper problem, more a moment of embarrassment than the societal stain of racism that was yet to be addressed. Only Douglass appeared truly threatened.

To the Opera House crowd, Douglass symbolized the end to slavery that now allowed America to take its rightful place in the pantheon of great civilizations. To the street crowd, Douglass symbolized all the black men down South who were now free to flood the North with their cheap labor and threaten the survival of white workingmen for jobs. Absent was any discussion of how America was going to create a new national economy with a stable, realigned, integrated labor force. But this was a complicated message to address off the cuff and one that many in the audience might not have wanted to hear. The two crowds represented two socioeconomic classes. One possessed the disposable income to attend a speech; the other was not likely to be able to afford tickets for admission and characterized with the profane and reeking coarseness of "hardhanded" labor. One, the employer, would profit from an infusion of competing cheap labor while the other was white workingmen, enraged from an already-stoked grievance that transcended race. All in the name of *Douglass.*

Another example of how the evening reflected the complicated nature of black–white relations was the topic to which Douglass switched when jeers from the outside seeped into the hall. He had prepared a message of uplift, one that showed the felicity of interracial cooperation, mutual respect, mutual benefit, of how America, when it freed the slave, freed itself from its own chains of infamy. But the crowd outside made the words sound hollow. From the omniscient vantage of hindsight, one wonders why he did not say that while much had been accomplished, much more (noting the crowd outside) needed to be done. He could have issued a clarion call for national dialogue on how America was going to create a *reconstructed* national economy with a new labor force that was at once realigned and stable, integrated, industrious. However, even the call for such a dialogue would have been a complicated message for an audience that was likely filled with skeptics. In fact, by 1873 many Republicans—liberals and conservatives alike—had already grown weary of hearing about the woes of African Americans. For some, the easily misconstrued call to give more aid to black men who, after having received so many political and civil benefits, remained stymied by racism seemed highly questionable. It would no doubt confuse those "friends of the black man" who also revered the self-made laissez-faire doctrine of social Darwinism, even prompting some to question whether Southerners had it right all along, that black men were too weak in their constitution and character to deserve full equality.

In the end, the message was too large for the moment, and possibly for even the grand old man himself. Instead, Douglass, ever the fighter, defiantly, reflexively, and tactfully went with a message that for all of his life defined him to his core. In talking about the abolition movement, he was proclaiming to those in the street, *I have a right to be here to speak my mind, and my bono fides rest solidly within that struggle to be free!* The chief spokesman for the African American cause—indeed, the *only* spokesman for now—was at a loss for words to adequately explain a new agenda for equality.

Douglass could not have prepared for this moment. He had spent the previous year defending his party against the insurgency of the Liberal Republicans and in doing so refrained from criticizing the party for being ineffective in bringing economic opportunity to African Americans in the North.[4] But this is why the moment was a uniquely Minnesota story. He had every reason to assume that St. Paul would be a friendly venue. The city had been the staging ground for the first Northern volunteers to join the Union army in 1861. It sent a regiment of heroes who gave their last full measure on a hill at Gettysburg, who saw their numbers drop on the second day of battle from 247 men to 46. Just blocks away at Ingersoll Hall, in 1868, the state's political elite celebrated with Minnesota's newly minted black citizenry in a referendum in which the majority of voters—white men all—extended the right to vote to black men, the first electoral act of its kind anywhere in the nation. On that proud day, his own likeness was prominently displayed on a large banner along with those of Lincoln, Grant, Sheridan, and Garrison. Just months later, the state legislature, housed blocks away, passed a law that effectively banned school segregation. And it was in this city that the first black men in Minnesota history served as jurymen.

Dred Scott sued for his freedom after residing in Minnesota and the court decision sparked the Civil War. This was indeed the North Star State, named with appropriate coincidence for the celestial orientation that had guided runaway slaves during their nighttime escape to freedom. Although Minnesota was never a prominent terminus for the Underground Railroad, it nonetheless was a place for safe harbor for those coming up from Galena, finding sanctuary with a black barber named William Taylor. The slave woman Eliza Winston was emancipated in a Minneapolis courtroom in the fall of 1860. Yet, thirteen years later, the events that followed Douglass's speech would provide a different aspect of race relations during the postwar era.

After his speech, and needing a place to rest, Douglass accepted an invitation from proprietor Gilbert Dutcher to stay at the Metropolitan Hotel, one of the city's most prestigious establishments and where prominent businessmen, out-of-town movers and shakers, many of the state's legislators, and its leading politicians frequently met to discuss business and politics. It was also the largest employer of black labor. The Metropolitan seemed a fitting place for the iconic Frederick Douglass to spend his evening, and Dutcher was a longtime acquaintance.

But, as we have seen, the night clerk had not received his orders to give the great man a room. The nearby Merchant Hotel likewise refused Douglass service. Finally, Dutcher, upon learning of what had happened at his hotel, and obviously embarrassed, interceded. This was not the first time he had to do so. Years earlier, he had to intercede to allow Douglass to register as a guest at the Capitol House in Madison, Wisconsin, where his policy "on distinction of color" was also enforced.

The two St. Paul hotels insisted that their refusals in no way reflected animus against Douglass personally, for had they known who the old black man really was, "there would have been no objection offered and he would have received the best the house could offer on the same terms as the other guests." As for the Metropolitan, it was the "stupid" night clerk who was to blame.[5] Others asserted that the slight at the Metropolitan was simply a matter of the clerk not having been authorized by Dutcher to admit Douglass "as an ordinary guest." In any event, but for Dutcher's intercession, the fifty-five-year-old Douglass might not have found a decent place in which to sleep on that cold Friday night in 1873.[6]

The banquet Dutcher proposed was compensation for the indignity Douglass had suffered at the hands of the hotel clerk, who was enforcing Dutcher's discrimination policy. The paradox was that Dutcher had come to the rescue. For this, the courtly Douglass had to feel a bit of relief at having a warm room and a soft bed to sleep in; but relief came in a hotel that discriminated against men like him.

In the context of this complicated relationship, people of goodwill lost sight of perspective. Dutcher, with his large black workforce, probably felt he was doing his share to uplift the black race. Yet, he also likely shared the conventional Republican view that hiring the kind of white rabble who heckled Douglass earlier that evening only courted trouble. It was a better investment to hire black labor that desperately needed the work. However, this was not the kind of work that translated into marketable skills. The wages would never be sufficient for workers to purchase a farm or a house. And, remarkably, even if they had the time and money to treat themselves to the finer things of life, they were not welcomed as guests of this hotel or as patrons at the Opera House, even to hear Frederick Douglass speak on the advancement of the race or the antislavery movement.

Still, this was not the South. Throughout the North, including the North Star State, black men could vote but they could never create enough of a voting bloc to affect public policy or hold powerful white men accountable. To place demands on political patrons would seem inappropriate, for the Republicans who had made Minnesota relatively accommodating to African Americans knew what was best for the country, the legacy of their political party, and, just as important, the maintenance of their political dominance. To accomplish this, they needed to show a proper balance between principle and expediency.

Yet some members of the Republican establishment were sensitive to how badly the whole incident reflected upon them. The editorial voice of the Republican Party, the St. Paul *Press,* understood this. Democrats called the *Press*'s account a "tempest in a teapot," that there had been no harm other than the *Press*'s histrionics. The Democratic *Pioneer* never even questioned the integrity of the whites-only policy of the hotels. "[I]n this instance," it editorialized, "an evident attempt was made to create a little cheap notoriety at Mr. Douglass' expense, and the *Press* seized the opportunity to make the most of it, and the sovereign State of Minnesota. In its legislative capacity, through one of the members of the House from Ramsey County, [the *Press*] belittled itself by taking cognizance of this trifling matter."[7] *This trifling matter* for the Democrats, therefore, was the small bump in the road that ultimately led Douglass to lodging. For the Republicans, it meant something altogether different.

Representative Henry A. Castle, a thirty-one-year-old merchant and lawyer from St. Paul, had offered a resolution to instruct the House Judiciary Committee to examine the viability of a bill that would punish landlords and innkeepers who denied service to people solely on the basis of their race.[8] The resolution stimulated "pretty warm expressions of indignation" among House Republicans upon hearing how Douglass had been treated at the hotels. Representatives Simeon P. Childs and Charles H. Clark were so incensed that they proposed punishing the city of St. Paul as a whole by "the immediate removal of the Capitol."[9] Nothing came of either proposal. St. Paul remained the state capital and nothing more was mentioned of an antidiscrimination law.

When discrimination was exposed by their own newspaper—no black Minnesotan could have garnered this kind of attention—Minnesota Republicans considered advancing black equality by allowing African Americans to lodge at any hotel in the state. That certainly would have addressed the highly visible and embarrassing incident that had sullied their image as guardians of racial progress. But, in the final analysis, its effects would have been minimal for it would not have stimulated job training, improved education for black children, or promoted property ownership. What mattered more to them was using legislation to restore their image when it came to black equality.

Pragmatically, the new law would not threaten the vast number of white Minnesotans who, like many other Northerners during the period, saw the African American as a threat to their interests. But few of these Minnesotans could afford to attend opera halls, stay at pricey hotels, or even travel frequently by railroad. In contrast, the objectives of the Sons of Freedom would surely threaten them: a well-trained black labor force, black owners of prime farmland, black children who could educationally compete with white children. National Republican leaders also understood this about their own constituents. In Congress two years later, lawmakers would later strip the provision to desegregate public schools from the bill that would become the Civil Rights Act of 1875. Even some of the framers of the Fourteenth Amendment would argue that it was not intended to desegregate public schools.[10] Rather, the resolution would have presented Minnesotans with the opportunity to laud the advancement of a freed people who had ascended to the ranks and sensibilities of a cultured middle class, those freedmen and -women who had developed sensible tastes for the best things of life. The *Press,* in 1873, made the case for reform.

In March, the newspaper reported that Frederick Douglass had been refused entrance to a hotel in Trenton, New Jersey, "on account of his color," an outrage that apparently "made an impression on the [state] legislature."[11] As a result, a bill was introduced, "which, by several penalties, prohibited any discrimination between whites and blacks by common carriers, hotel keepers, theatre managers, and in school . . . whose support is derived by public funds." The *Press* editorialized that if passed, the new law would be "an amazing step in advance for New Jersey to take."[12]

The paper argued that racism flowed wide and deep in Minnesota's capital city. Discrimination against impoverished blacks clearly existed among the city's poor, native-born whites and ethnic groups, but now opinion makers seemed ready to take note of the discrimination against black middle-class Minnesotans who attempted to enjoy the privileges of the white middle class. The presumed middle-class status of the aggrieved

African Americans seemed to matter more than race, which in the eyes of white opinion makers made discrimination more egregious.

In 1871, a massive picnic was held in Minneapolis's Minnehaha Park, by the black residents of St. Paul and Minneapolis. The Milwaukee and St. Paul Railroad provided transportation at reduced rates for those who desired to attend the picnic. Henry Robinson and his wife, who had purchased their "picnic" tickets, boarded the train in St. Paul and attempted to take their seats in the ladies' car. The conductor barred them from doing so. Robinson alleged that the railroad had violated his civil rights, and brought suit to recover $1,800 in damages. An all-white jury, after hearing the facts, could not agree. Robinson filed suit a second time, and again a separate all-white jury failed to agree. In 1873, after Robinson had filed a third time, the jury of twelve (again all-white) reached a verdict after three ballots, finding for the railroad. The final verdict came one month after the Trenton article appeared in the *Press*.[13]

Without access to the evidence presented, it is difficult to know whether the jury rendered a just decision. The railroad may have issued tickets that limited all holders, regardless of race, to certain places on the train, in which case, no racial discrimination occurred. In any event, Robinson had his day in court three times, before three different juries. The lesson of the case is not just about persistence but about the fact it was undertaken in the first place and that a public record of the dispute was made. It was an urban matter covered by one of the state's most prominent newspapers.

In four years since Morton Wilkinson and Ignatius Donnelly said that character and manliness were built by tilling the soil—a livelihood that was proving to be untenable for thousands of white homesteaders whose farms were infested by grasshoppers—character and manliness were now being defined in the city by achieving middle-class status.[14] "Hardhandedness" was being replaced by "hardheadedness" when one's dignity was threatened. The middle-class black man who had attained his station by industry and attempted to avail himself of public entertainments that bigots denied to him was a more sympathetic character.

There were vocal opponents. Democratic opinion makers insisted that a black man who received such gratuities as a ticket to ride a train needed to be grateful. Robinson should have let the matter drop after the first verdict. The conservative editor of the *Daily Pioneer* wrote: "There is all together too much disposition on the part of some of our colored citizens to bring this class of action. It is to be hoped that they will take warning by this verdict."[15] However, the *Press* argued that St. Paul jurors could not resist the same discriminatory impulses as their white neighbors. Segregation on certain conveyances in Philadelphia, San Francisco, and Chicago had been found to be unlawful.[16] In contrast, St. Paul could not be trusted to dispense justice to its own black citizens. If justice for all was to be secured, it would have to come by the enforcement of federal or state law.

By 1873, liberal-minded Republicans had reason for hope. The U.S. Supreme Court made its first antisegregation ruling in a railroad case, holding that a black woman could not be forced to leave the car reserved for white passengers to ride in a car reserved for blacks.[17] New York and other states joined New Jersey in enacting state public accommodations laws.[18] The state legislature of Delaware passed a resolution supporting Massachusetts's Charles Sumner's civil-rights bill before the U.S. Senate.[19]

Two years later, Sumner's bill would pass both houses of Congress as the Civil Rights Act of 1875. It asserted that all people, regardless of race and color, were guaranteed "the full and equal enjoyment of the accommodations . . . of inns, public conveyances on land and water, theatres and other places of public amusement."[20] It extended "certain social rights" to the African American and empowered him to bypass municipal juries and instead seek redress in federal court, an "unprecedented exercise of national authority."[21]

In the real world, however, few black porters and laborers could afford to attend the theater or eat at a restaurant patronized by whites, pay attorneys' and court fees, have the luxury of time to wait for the case to be argued and decided, and withstand reprisal from a white employer. The application of the new act was better suited for middle-class litigants.

Few African Americans challenged discrimination in the federal courts. "It was easier," wrote one historian, "to avoid painful rebuff or insult by refraining from the test of rights. Negroes rarely intruded upon hotels or restaurants where they were unwelcome."[22] Blacks would not invoke the Civil Rights Act "to make themselves obnoxious" because they "had too much self-respect to go where they were not wanted . . . [S]uch actions would end only on disturbances" and "colored people wanted peace and as little agitation as possible."[23] Black businessmen in particular feared losing white clientele, while others viewed the prospect of equal but separate facilities as an improvement."[24]

The few blacks who did sue found the enforcement of the law burdensome, for the act was more a broad assertion of principle than a blueprint for corrective action by the federal government. It required black litigants to launch the case at their own expense in a federal court system that was already overburdened by civil and criminal cases.[25]

Nationally, only a handful of blacks filed suits and the number of filed cases dropped further by 1880. By then a class action had come to the Supreme Court, where the case stalled for three years. Federal officials, preoccupied by how the Court would decide, discouraged blacks from filing, leading to an even sharper decline in lawsuits. Indiana held up cases in 1879, pending the Court's decision. The delay encouraged whites to disrespect the law and flagrantly discriminate against blacks.[26]

Despite passage of the Civil Rights Act, America displayed no interest in defending the rights of African Americans. Republicans—even those who ultimately voted for it—were divided as to whether the law was constitutional.[27] More pointedly, the *Nation,* the nationally recognized newspaper founded in 1865 by crusading antislave advocates, stated: "We ought not to have attempted the insane task of making the newly emancipated field hands led by barbers and barkeepers, fancy they knew as much about government, and were as capable of administering it, as the whites."[28]

One year later, in 1877, the St. Paul *Dispatch,* which since the demise of the *Western Appeal,* a black newspaper, had assumed the role of defining the interests of African Americans for African Americans, reminded its readers that as early as 1873 abolitionists had already declared that the great struggle for equality had ended.[29]

A month after the *Dispatch* article, newly elected President Rutherford B. Hayes ended federal oversight of Reconstruction and with it the protection of Southern African Americans. The new president seemed nevertheless to be respectful of Frederick Douglass, whose personal stature and dignity were unimpeachable. Douglass in turn seemed comfortable with the man for whom he had campaigned in the recent tight election against Democrat Samuel Tilden, and was now "almost totally oblivious to the concessions to white supremacists in the South that [had] betrayed their own candidate to put him into office."[30]

In matters of race, Frederick Douglass was the favorite of the Republican Party. In the following years he traveled ceaselessly, speaking to enthusiastic crowds who reveled in his reminiscences of the antislavery movement. But he was less authoritative in his prescription for the challenges that faced his people. As in St. Paul in 1873, rather than take the opportunity to expose the discriminatory society that Northern Republicans had contributed to making, he held up a mirror in which he and his audience could admire themselves while resting on their laurels. It was the only message he knew and one that Northern Republicans never tired of hearing. As he would later acknowledge in his memoirs, "My great and exceeding joy over . . . the abolition of slavery was slightly tinged with a feeling of sadness. I felt I had reached the end of the noblest and best part of my life."[31]

He was a man from a bygone era. Years earlier he had argued with William Lloyd Garrison, contending that once the nation had ended slavery, the ex-slaves would make their way, unassisted, in the world of their former slave master. But now he seemed not to comprehend the desperate fate that had befallen so many freedmen and -women. When they needed him most to articulate a fundamentally new agenda for equality, he seemed to chastise them for not following his personal example. To him, they were like immigrants just off the boat, whose arrival would "cast upon the people of Kansas and other Northern states a multitude of deluded, hungry, homeless, naked and destitute people." In this black migration that he opposed he saw "a tendency to convert colored laboring men into traveling camps."[32]

To Northern Republicans, his powerful voice gave succor to their fears of massive black migration. By the end of the decade, the most prominent black man in America and a favorite speaker of Republicans found himself for the first time in his life hissed and shouted down by black audiences.[33] Black Minnesota—indeed, black America—entered the next decade without a champion.

Eric Foner noted: "While many blacks in Northern cities fared relatively well during the boom years of the Reconstruction Era ascending in many cases to the middle class, the bulk of the population remained trapped in urban poverty and confined in inferior housing and menial and unskilled jobs and even here their foothold, challenged by the continuing influx of European immigrants and discrimination by employers and unions alike, became increasingly precarious."[34] In St. Paul the story was the same, and the lines of demarcation among the groups, especially as they related to the African American community, were quite rigid and were reflected in the residential patterns of the city. A sign posted on a house in a German neighborhood in the fourth ward stated that "nigger tenants" were not wanted. As David Taylor noted, the physical growth of the emerging black neighborhood was to a great extent limited by the ethnicity of the residential neighborhoods surrounding the commercial district where most poor blacks lived. On all sides of the commercial district, ethnic groups zealously guarded neighborhoods almost as if they were sovereign territories.[35]

Despite these residential cleavages between blacks and immigrant groups and the desperation of the underclass, it took the effrontery of a St. Paul street crowd and a hotel clerk carrying out his employer's long-term discrimination policy against America's most famous "civilizable" black man to finally capture the attention of the state's opinion makers. The event underscored the pervasive bias in the state's psyche that no doubt instilled within Black Minnesotans the belief that survival depended on staying out of trouble and among their own kind.

On a Friday night in June 1869, a black man named Taylor Combs, son of Fielding and Adeline Combs, who were two of the original Pilgrims who had followed Robert Hickman to St. Paul in 1863, was accused by three witnesses of raping a nineteen-year-old Swedish immigrant woman in a ravine alongside the Stillwater road. The next night, while he was being held in jail, "about two hundred Swedes" assembled with the intention of lynching him. The jailor fended off the assault, and when he threatened to shoot them they dispersed, shouting that they would return. The Democratic *Pioneer* saw it necessary to report that while the mob banged on the door, "a little negro who was in the jail for some minor offense" became frightened that the crowd would get in and "get hold of the wrong nigger." He accordingly begged to be locked up in the "safe." Combs was placed on trial, found guilty, and sentenced to twenty years in the state penitentiary at Stillwater. In 1872, Governor Horace Austin pardoned him, but no sooner had he been set free than he committed another rape, for which he was sentenced to five years and released in the spring of 1877.[36]

On Sunday, June 10, 1877, Combs allegedly raped the thirteen-year-old daughter of Samuel Frick in the town of Point Douglas, Washington County, "inflict[ing] injuries which are expected to cause the child's death," and fled the area soon afterwards. For four days he eluded capture. Authorities learned that he was at the home of a black man who resided near Point Douglas. The man told them that Combs was on his way to St. Paul. A widespread manhunt ensued. The *Pioneer Press* reported: "Among the officers in search there [was] a general feeling that the fugitive should be caught, and it does not make any special difference whether he is dead or alive." To aid in Combs's capture, the paper published the following description: "Taylor Combs is an African of exceedingly 'black' complexion; he is 28 to 30 years of age and about 5 feet 7 inches in height, with a large mouth, smooth face, and weighs about 150 pounds. On Sunday he wore a dark coat, gray pantaloons, a slouched cap, and a pair of fine shoes, which the officers mentioned as 'fancy.'" There were no arrests, perhaps because most African American young men in the city fit this description. Four days after the assault, Combs was arrested in St. Paul by Stillwater Police Detective John Brissette and taken to Hastings en route to Point Douglas. The plan was for Combs to be identified by the alleged victim and then returned to Stillwater where he would await action by a grand jury. However, an incident occurred in Hastings.[37]

At the Tremont House where Combs was being held, "a crowd of forty or fifty" shouted out threats of lynching the man. Brissette quickly spirited Combs to a ferry on the river, where they passed over to Point Douglas. There they met with Justice of the Peace T. E. Wright and went to the residence of Samuel Frick where Combs was identified by his daughter "as the party attempting violation of her person." Combs was then returned to Wright's office.[38]

In the meantime, people had begun to assemble outside after arriving from Hastings and Prescott and the surrounding countryside, each trip of the ferryboat swelling the number until it was estimated that fully two hundred stood in front of the justice of the peace's office. Twice the mob advanced toward the office; twice Detective Brissette brandished his revolver, threatening to shoot. At about this time the town constable arrived with a carriage to whisk Combs and Brissette away and the mob made another rush. "For God's sake," pleaded Combs, "protect me and take me to a working prison" (meaning the penitentiary).[39]

Someone in the mob threw a noose that lodged just above Combs's eyes, but Brissette knocked the rope off and aimed his revolver at the man who had tossed the noose, which again repelled the mob long enough for the carriage to pull away. At three o'clock, when they arrived at Stillwater twenty-four miles away, they were met by the chief of police, who warned them to rush to the jail "as there was danger of lynching." "The key was hardly turned in the door [of the cell] before Combs rushed in, and then for the first time since leaving Hastings, he seemed to breathe easy." Combs "was very profuse in his thanks to Brissette for, as he declared, saving his life."[40]

To be sure, the Combs incident was unique: till then, black men had not been accused of crimes or attacked in rural Minnesota during this era. Still, for black residents of St. Paul who had come from the South to escape the terrorism of white supremacy, the incident may have triggered reminders of how tragically suddenly a black man could become a victim of the lynch mob, especially in retaliation for an alleged rape of a white girl or woman. The slight of Frederick Douglass by a white innkeeper in St. Paul paled in contrast. To date, no civil-rights suit was filed challenging discrimination. But those African Americans most likely to sue, those who had the disposable income to enjoy places covered by the law, appeared to content themselves in numerous celebrations of racial and cultural pride and institutional development.[41] It would be the newly arrived Thomas Lyles, a black barber from Maryland, who personified the efforts of a small number of African Americans who would cultivate their civilizable traits.

A thirty-one-year-old black man who arrived in St. Paul in 1874, Thomas Lyles was very much in the mold of the black barbers at the beginning of the decade. Although it had been less than four years since Jernigan and Stockton prominently stood on stage with the state's political leaders, they had fallen from view, vacating the leadership role that would go unfilled until Lyles. He would come to personify the new social, economic, and political leadership who also understood and spoke the language of soon-to-be patrons. Lyles arrived in the capital city from Maryland, where he had learned the skills of barbering and qualities necessary to attract an affluent white clientele. Soon after his arrival, he opened a shop in the

American House, a popular hotel located at Fourth and Wabasha. But he distinguished himself by using his contacts to acquire enough capital to buy and sell real estate. By the late 1880s, he would be listed as having assets ranging up to a hundred thousand dollars.[42]

Through his influence and largesse, Lyles was able to persuade officials to open the police and fire departments to blacks, and helped many black men get employment. He was one of the men who started the *Western Appeal,* Minnesota's first, though short-lived, black newspaper, and was part owner. As the black community grew, he sought out and succeeded in attracting the first black lawyer and the first black medical doctor to St. Paul, from which grew a small and cohesive leadership, later augmented by an influential black professional class recruited to serve the needs of the Twin Cities black community.[43]

During the 1870s, Minnesota's black population increased from 759 to 1,564, and in St. Paul from 207 to 600. As their numbers grew, black citizens began to form many kinds of organizations. Like the Swedish and Irish immigrants, black St. Paul residents formed their own churches, lodges, musical groups, literary societies, and other clubs. All of this reflected the emergence of a class of black citizens with resources and leisure time. It is they who became St. Paul's black elite; and it was they who had the necessary influence with the city and state elite to sustain their endeavors. These connections supported black activities and even preserved, through a form of commemoration, a bit of their history.[44]

Indeed, during this period black Minnesotans held many social, religious, and political gatherings where it was not unusual to see white citizens in attendance. For years they celebrated on August 15, as blacks in other Northern cities did, to commemorate the freeing of slaves in the West Indies by Great Britain. The first such celebration took place in Minnesota in 1868; in later years it would be joined with an observance of the Emancipation Proclamation. This affair usually lasted the entire day with a picnic, speeches, a band concert, and other festivities. In 1875, the celebration held in a St. Paul park was attended by 500 people, including approximately 200 from Minneapolis and 60 from Stillwater. Trains and stage lines often provided transportation to such events at reduced rates. Whites also contributed money to events that celebrated the advancement of black America, as in their sponsorship of three lectures by Frederick Douglass in St. Paul.[45]

To advance the social and cultural enrichment of his people Lyles launched and presided over the Robert Banks Literary Society, among other organizations, and raised money to support them.[46] His wealth reflected a time in Minnesota that was, as historian David Taylor observed, "[t]he beginning of a period of unparalleled industrial expansion and commercial growth for St. Paul."[47] During the 1870s, black women participated in political, social, and cultural activities, and in some instances held leadership positions. For example, they played a key role in the Robert Banks Literary Society founded in 1875 and named for a respected black St. Paul leader, barber, and orator who had presided over the conventions in 1869 and 1870.[48] Amanda Lyles, soon to a leader in St. Paul's black society, taught music and later became proprietor of a ladies salon in the Opera House block where her husband's barbershop thrived.[49]

In contrast, the only other literary society that existed in black Minnesota in the mid-1860s—the Golden Key Literary Society—was expressly established for the cultural and intellectual development of the black men of St. Paul. Within a period of one month its membership grew to forty, making it one of the largest reading and debating societies in the city.[50] It was affiliated with Pilgrim Baptist Church, where, as was typical across the nation, women formed the backbone of the black church. The black church not only became the locus of community life but was an important agent for social control. It attempted to curtail sexual promiscuity and encouraged monogamy and marriage. It also gave support to the family and sustained the male's image as family patriarch.[51]

In St. Paul, the churchgoing portion of the black population was small in proportion to the overall population. Married couples and single women constituted the bulk of congregations in a population where the majority were young males. In terms of social relationships between the sexes, the church tended to be conservative. Between 1871 and 1876, Pilgrim Baptist Church remained the only black congregation in St. Paul, growing from thirty to seventy-five members.[52] Although it was a moral presence in St. Paul's black community, ministers did not enjoy the same level of influence in the larger community:

> More often than not these ministers were men of limited vision and ability who shared power with the laity rather than dictating to them ... Because of the rapid turnover in ministers, the secular community

leaders were better known and respected. As race leaders they were recognized and given at least token respect by the white community. As such the secular leadership wielded more influence causing the center of economic and political power to be concentrated outside of the church rather than within.[53]

Thus, the rudder of social custom was more likely to come from the patronage of a secular leader such as Thomas Lyles rather than his pastor Robert Hickman.

Unlike Jernigan, Stockton, Hickman, and the rest of the Sons of Freedom whose focus had been on job and property acquisition, training, and the education of children, Lyles's emphasis was on community building and cultural and social efforts to promote middle-class values and racial pride. Of course, the times had changed by the time Lyles entered the scene. The Sons of Freedom, now at best a memory for only a few, had a statewide agenda that was overextended and sought to uplift a part of the black community: the poorest and least respected, a population with few champions, black or white. Lyles's vision for black St. Paul attracted willing black constituents who agreed that taking on middle-class trappings was the best way to secure "civilizable traits." His agenda did not seek to breach the barricade of white dominance in the traditional "hard-handed" areas of homesteading and the trades, nor to assault the gate that barred social equality, for cultural enrichment provided more succor than forcing oneself into white opera houses, hotels, and restaurants. Social equality was not a priority for Lyles, but before long, African Americans participating in his activities would feel that discrimination defamed their dignity and would seek to confront it—though not on behalf of all African Americans. A burgeoning black middle class increasingly wanted to distance itself from impoverished brethren whom they feared reinforced white stereotypes and that this would be held against those who had earned a seat in the hall, a place at the table, or a room in the hotel. Nonetheless, for the time being, their grievance was stillborn.

For now, this was a time for celebrating themselves as a proud cultured people. White opinion makers had the impression that black Minnesotans on the whole were doing better in their present quality of life, were better off than their Southern cousins, and were pleased with being the newest members of the state's great cultural melting pot.

By July 1875, just five months after the enactment of the Civil Rights Act of 1875, there was a different display of community. Even though this would seem to be a time when African Americans would renew their loyalty to the Republican Party, a growing number were wary of the party's sincerity as they took note of the fact that some of its most prominent members were expressing less interest in the welfare of Southern blacks. Some of the owners of places of entertainment that discriminated against them were Republicans, and their caucus in the 1873 legislative session ultimately did nothing to ban discrimination in hotels. Local Democrats saw an opening to attract black voters.

As the minority party seeking to come back into power, Democrats had sought to strike alliances with insurgent groups traditionally affiliated with the Republican Party such as disgruntled farmers who belonged to the Grange and the Susan B. Anthony–Elizabeth Cady Stanton wing of the suffrage movement. As early as 1869, local Democrats were planting seeds, attending the Convention of Colored Citizens, and good-naturedly facing derision from Republican speakers, and months later appointed the state's first black jurymen. Now, six years later, it seemed to be the right time for Democrats to build on what they had begun.

African Americans enjoyed displays of racial unity and traveled by road and rail to St. Paul, where Freedom Day was typically celebrated. In July 1875, more than sixty visitors from Stillwater joined two hundred from Minneapolis to participate in the annual festival commemorating Britain's emancipation of Haitian slaves in 1833. Including those from St. Paul, more than five hundred African Americans were estimated to have attended.

John X. Davidson, St. Paul legislator and owner of the old St. Paul *Pioneer,* the newspaper that had been the voice of the city's Democratic Party, improbably hosted "a grand barbecue and dance" on his "spacious home and grounds" on the shore of Lake Como. Before midday, more than five hundred African Americans were present and a program recognizing the purpose of the gathering commenced. Thomas Lyles, selected President of the Day, presented a "very neat speech" and Reverend Hickman served as the chaplain who delivered a "fervent prayer," followed by the choir of Pilgrim Baptist who sang "Before Jehovah's Awful Throne." The guest speaker, a Professor Bowser of Kansas City, delivered an eloquent speech recalling the circumstances of the abolition of slavery in the West Indies and the United States and drawing from there many valuable and instructive lessons for his hearers.[54]

A week later, on August 6, in the city in which black equality had faced considerable opposition, particularly from St. Paul's Irish Catholic community, and where Donnelly first attributed the concept "civilizable characteristics" to black people, organizers of a celebration to honor Daniel O'Connor, the great Irish leader and proponent of slave abolition, invited leaders of St. Paul's black community to participate. The Minneapolis *Tribune* reported: "One fact in connection with this event worthy of mention is an evidence that a common and unjust prejudice is no longer entertained by the intelligent countrymen of the great commoner, Daniel O'Connell. Mr. [Robert] Banks, a very intelligent and worthy colored citizen of St. Paul, was invited to address the meeting of Irishmen . . . The Robert Banks Literary Society (colored) was in the parade."[55] Because Thomas Lyles was a founder of the Literary Society and by now was securing his footing within the St. Paul scene, he very likely was instrumental in arranging this event along with the barbecue at Davidson's estate. His stature grew during this period, and he would leverage it in 1876 for Minnesota's first black newspaper, the *Western Appeal*. On September 23, the *Dispatch* reported: "An intelligent and enterprising colored citizen in St. Paul has commenced the publication of a paper called the *Western Appeal*."[56] For the time being, he sat politically in the catbird seat. Three days later, the latest incarnation of Davidson's old newspaper, the *Pioneer Press*, published a succinct notice on the foolish nature of racial discrimination: "A vacant house in the Fourth Ward bears the sign, 'To rent, but not to niggers.' Landlords should read up on the civil rights bill."[57]

For the remainder of the decade, for every story like Combs's or the "colored skirmish on Nicollet Island" between a black husband fighting the black lover of his white wife,[58] the major newspapers of the Twin Cities published several articles on concerts, celebrations, recitals, ball games, church socials, debate competitions, and a longer piece on Mrs. Amanda Lyles's flag dedication at Pilgrim Baptist Church to the Robert Banks Literary Society. "In presenting your society with its first flag, we are not unmindful, that our race is the latest of races of mankind, baptized and regenerated in the fountain of American freedom . . ."[59] On the surface, it seemed that Minnesota's black community was thriving, even within a context of limited opportunities that were available to most of them. The only face of the community that white Minnesota routinely saw was the one that appeared in white newspapers. Lyles's first effort to establish a black newspaper had long ended. And publishers, like black notables who benefited from the image of a thriving black community under their leadership, seemed to believe that there was substance to the gloss.

In 1879, the *Pioneer Press,* by now the state's most prominent Republican newspaper, gave tribute to yet another grand display of civic activity. In doing so, however, it laid bare the fallacy that Frederick Douglass, the black hero of the Republican establishment, was the spokesman for black America, and it exposed the true consequences of the new Republican policy of regional reconciliation. Douglass had criticized black refugees who fled the South, and much was made of his gesture of forgiveness to his former master. Yet, the *Pioneer Press* article stated: "The weather was not favorable, but in spite of the rain quite a respectable representation of the colored population of St. Paul were in attendance." This event was different, however, for blacks now had assembled "to consider the remarkable exodus of field hands from the States bordering on the lower Mississippi."

The speaker, the Reverend H. Simons, commended the exodus as deserving of sympathy, cooperation, and material aid. Hundreds of colored refugees were now fleeing from the South, "fleeing from a second slavery." "Their struggle to make their way to the free West should receive the attention of liberty-loving men and women everywhere; and we appeal to the citizens of St. Paul for help in furnishing means to assist them in finding new homes. They have started for Kansas because they have heard they would be free there and could dwell in peace, and because it is impossible for them to live longer in their old homes."[60] The article, written as a tribute to the organizers of the event, instead shed light on the horror of Republican policy of regional conciliation at the expense of black Southerners. The next day, the newly formed St. Paul *Daily Globe,* the Democratic counterpart to the *Dispatch,* reported that "the colored emigration committee [was] now permanently organized." Reverend Simons was the president and James Hilyard, business partner of Thomas Lyles, was made treasurer.[61] Throughout the spring, the emigration movement spread to Minneapolis and Stillwater.[62]

In June 1881, in an effort to disassociate themselves from the Democratic white supremacists in the South, St. Paul Democrats took another step toward connecting with the city's African American community when Democratic Mayor Edmund Rice appointed Louis R. Thomas to be the first black man to serve in the St. Paul Police Department. "In making this appointment Mayor Rice was guided by the consideration that in a city where the colored population is so large, one of their own numbers could best cope with the peculiar social qualities of the race."[63] In a twenty-year period, the black population had grown, though not as dramatically as the white population. From a total of 259 African Americans in the state in 1860, the number rose to 759 in 1870, and to 1,564 in 1880. Ramsey County continued to have the greatest concentration, going from 198 African American residents in 1870 to 491 in 1880. The state population in 1870 was 439,706 and 766,773 in 1880. In St. Paul, the population jumped from 20,030 to 41,473. The mayor of the smaller twin city, Minneapolis, followed suit by appointing a black man to the city police force. In 1895, Company No. 9 of the St. Paul Fire Department was organized as an all-black company. "The pride taken by Negroes in this accomplishment," Spangler notes, "was evident in many current papers."[64] Outwardly it seemed that Minnesota had not just avoided racial problems experienced in all the other states but had solved them. By the end of the decade, during a period of considerable social, civic, educational, and cultural activity, there was as yet no suit filed to challenge discrimination. The only source describing the quality of life of Minnesota's African Americans was the white-owned press. Frederick Douglass was not in the city to test the patronage of white establishments.

Across the country, white proprietors continued to discriminate against blacks despite the Civil Rights Act of 1875.[65] More than a hundred test cases from various parts of the country were making their way through the courts. Finally, during the 1882–83 term, the Supreme Court selected five cases to hear, lumping them together in a class action that would be called the *Civil Rights Cases.*[66] Those in favor of civil rights had reason to feel hopeful that the Court would uphold the law. Of the five most recent court appointees, most were from the North and West, appointed by Lincoln, and all were presumed to be friendly, to some extent, to the intent of the Reconstruction amendments. In October, the decision was handed down Justice Joseph P. Bradley, who had run for Congress in New Jersey as a Lincoln Republican, ruled that where a law steps into local jurisprudence and lays down rules for the conduct of individuals in society toward each other, without referring in any manner to any supposed action of the state, or its authorities, it exceeds the scope of Congress's power because the wrongful act of an individual, unsupported by any such authority, is simply a private wrong, or a crime by that person. Congress, he argued, had no constitutional authority to prohibit private conduct: "It would be running the slavery argument into the ground to make it apply to every act of discrimination which a person may see fit to make as to the guests he will entertain, or as to the people he will admit into his coach, or cab or car, or admit into his concert or theatre, or deal with other matters." The excluded African Americans had suffered public wrongs to "social rights," not the invasion of their political or civil rights by the state or under state authority. Essentially, Justice Bradley, whose vote on the Electoral Commission had made Hayes president in 1877, had determined that African Americans "must cease to be the special favorite of the laws." Thus, the Civil Rights Act of 1875 was unconstitutional.[67] As the decision related to Minnesota, congressional action could not penalize Gilbert Dutcher or the owner of the Merchant Hotel if they denied service to black men because Castle's resolution had never become law. "Civilizable characteristics" did not qualify the African American to sit next to a white patron as an equal in the same social and public setting. Although "civilizable traits" remained attainable—for blacks could acquire middle-class trappings—Republican policy makers, in upholding discrimination practices, rendered such traits as meaningless. All blacks, despite the strivings of the few—middle-class and poor, educated and illiterate, Northern-born and Southern—carried the same stigma of their race.

The same year that the *Civil Rights Cases* was decided, the fortunes of St. Paul's onetime premier barber Maurice Jernigan were in evident decline since his leaving the Metropolitan, for he now worked out of a humble storefront in a working-class neighborhood on Fourth Street that doubled as his residence.[68]

That same year, not far from Jernigan's barbershop, the "emaciated form" of aged Jim Thompson lay ill on the couch of his daughter's living room in West St. Paul. In stark contrast to his once "stout, healthy person, turning the scales about two hundred," sickness and old age had conspired to leave but a semblance of what was once a hale and vigorous presence.[69] Now, the old man and his wife Mary made plans to move near his son

George who lived on the Santee Dakota Reservation in northeastern Nebraska. That June at the Old Settlers' meeting in Minneapolis, the men assembled (many of whom possessed prominent names in Minnesota history) took up a collection of $17.65 for the ailing octogenarian—"the only colored . . . member of the association"—to help their indigent friend who had fallen on hard times.[70]

In fall 1884, the man many considered to be the "the oldest settler of [Minnesota]" died on the reservation four days after his wife Mary had passed on, far from the city he had helped to build, far from the stigma of being black, far from the kind of society that St. Paul had become.

6

Senate Bill No. 181

"In the name of humanity don't hamper our progress with measures as bright as gold but as hollow as a gourd."

—*Western Appeal*, July 4, 1885

It was a peculiar thing. Many Republicans in the North were never happy with the Civil Rights Act of 1875. Since 1870, when Massachusetts Senator Charles Sumner first introduced the bill, his Republican colleagues viewed the measure as a political liability. Their white constituents would never countenance a federal law that affronted their racial sensibilities by requiring them to serve blacks demanding service in a white-owned restaurant or a seat next to white customers. By the mid-1870s, as national discontent with President Grant mounted to such a level that Republican power over the federal government was threatened, they wanted little to do with measures that would further alienate much of their base. In 1875, when the unpopular bill was enacted into federal law, it had been watered down and approved more in tribute to their recently deceased and highly revered colleague—Sumner had just died—than out of genuine support for the bill. Justice Bradley's opinion summed up what many Republicans throughout the North and West felt. In 1885, two years after his decision, the Minnesota legislature enacted a public accommodations bill, righting a wrong by fulfilling the vision of Henry Castle's 1873 resolution. But what was the "wrong"? The absence of an antidiscrimination law from the statutes of a Republican-dominated state government?

The belief that African Americans were inferior to white people? This was the paradox. Describing an earlier generation in terms that applied in the mid-1880s, V. Jacque Voegeli observed: "[M]any of the most dedicated advocates of equal rights and advancement [in the Midwest] wanted equality for Negroes, not because they believed the Negro race to be biologically or intellectually equal to the white, not because they had any intention in accepting them as their own social equals, but because they felt all men ought to be equal before the law."[1] In other words, it was fine to grant the ballot, but not an opera ticket or a receipt authorizing occupancy of a hotel room. Republican legislators set to threading the needle by drafting just such a law for equality without including terms that could make it enforceable.

It was the morning of Tuesday, January 27, 1885, nearly two weeks after the Minnesota legislature had convened, and it was to be C. D. Gilfillan's last term in the state senate. Soon he would move to his vast landholdings in Redwood County where he would live out the remainder of the century as a gentleman farmer. But first there were bills to pass. About the work at hand, the Minneapolis *Tribune* later reported, "It can well be anticipated that the issues of the season, the great question of paramount importance, preceding all others, was the regulation of railroads and elevators, and to this all efforts were directed."[2] In addition to these matters, and with far less prominence, Gilfillan was to introduce Senate Bill No. 181, which would protect the civil and legal rights of all citizens.[3] At three hundred pounds and fifty-three years of age, the short, bearded, corpulent figure of state senator Gilfillan, a wealthy Republican capitalist, banker, and lawyer who represented St. Paul, had long played a major role in the development of the city he had represented in both legislative houses. Charles Duncan Gilfillan was indeed a man for whom the title "Honorable" was intended, the sort of man who characterized the Republican elite.

A man of considerable financial and political stature in St. Paul, he had come from New York to Minnesota in 1851 as a man of humble means. At first he settled in Stillwater, where he taught school. Afterwards, he studied law and then practiced in Stillwater before moving to the capital city in 1854. A year later, he joined others in founding the Minnesota Republican Party, later serving for three years as chairman of the central committee.

By 1862, with the defeat of the Dakota Indians and their removal from the region, Gilfillan had acquired vast acreages of land in the southwestern county of Redwood. In 1864, he launched an enterprise for which he would later be best known: St. Paul Water Works, a "monument to his genius," which transformed the still-frontier community into a civilized city because its buildings and houses soon had running indoor water.

He eventually sold the company to the city for more than half a million dollars, and then engaged in banking, farming, and construction. A piece of commercial property in St. Paul was named for him, the Gilfillan Block, occupied by a six-story, fireproof office building noted for "its massive solidity and architectural beauty." He invested well, involved himself in several commercial interests, and enjoyed a successful political career as a Republican whose Gaelic name befitted the heritage of his St. Paul constituents. He represented the city for three terms in the state House of Representatives and four terms in the state Senate, where he served as leader.[4] His political standing alone assured passage of Senate Bill No. 181. He was in virtually every way a paragon of the age of social Darwinism. He was a friend of big business, which included establishments that would be impacted by the new law—his own hotel, the Merchant, included—and on matters of race, instead of being a vocal friend of African Americans, he was better suited for the conventional Republican passivity. He was the best person to sponsor the bill. The weight of his political stature alone would smooth out controversy that the bill might have sparked.

Formally drafted as "a bill to protect all citizens in their civil and legal rights, to prevent discrimination on railroads, in theatres, and all places of amusement or public conveniences, as to race, religion, or color under penalty of $500 fine or a year's imprisonment," Bill No. 181 was submitted "in the interest of the colored people of Minnesota" and, as if to assure legislators that it was not radical, it was described as "an exact copy of the Ohio law on the same subject." On March 6, the House voted 56 to 6 to approve the bill and the Senate approved it 27 to 10.[5] On March 7, ten days after the bill was introduced, and with little fanfare, Senate Bill No. 181 became chapter 225 of the General Laws of Minnesota for 1885:

> Whereas, It is essential to just government that we recognize the equality of all men before the law, and hold that it is the duty of government in its dealings with the people to mete out equal and exact justice to all,

of whatever nativity, race, color, or persuasion, religious or political, and it being the appropriate object of legislation to enact great fundamental principles of law, therefore be it enacted by the Legislature of the State of Minnesota.[6]

It indeed appeared that Minnesota had committed itself to prohibiting operators from segregating or excluding African Americans.

Two years earlier the U.S. Supreme Court declared the Civil Rights Act of 1875 unconstitutional,[7] thereby leaving any enforcement of legal redress for acts of racial discrimination to the states, if they wanted to assume the authority.[8] The political landscape had changed from 1875 when Republicans reluctantly enacted the Civil Rights Act in the face of Democratic insurgence to take the House, to now, 1883, when Democrats had found a presidential candidate blacks could like. Upset from the decision in *Civil Rights Cases,* black voters in a number of Northern and Eastern states looked to the Democratic Party to respond. Until the end of the nineteenth century, the voting blocs of Northern blacks remained relatively small; but, despite their numbers, their votes could turn an election against the Republicans because party policies were also alienating many white voters. The party needed to hold its base among increasingly restless African Americans they now needed. Thus, Republican-dominated legislatures across the North and West filled the breach left by the Supreme Court's ruling. Within the year, a series of state legislatures adopted laws modeled on the federal statute. In 1884, four states took the lead—Connecticut, Iowa, New Jersey, and Ohio.[9] In 1885, Colorado, Illinois, Indiana, Michigan, Nebraska, and Rhode Island adopted public accommodations laws. Minnesota joined this group soon thereafter. Pennsylvania adopted this law in 1887; Washington in 1890; Wisconsin in 1895; and California in 1897. By 1900, eighteen Northern, Eastern, and Western states had adopted a public policy against discrimination based on race or color in places of public accommodation.[10]

The wording of all the early statutes was essentially the same: "all persons within a jurisdiction of the state, regardless of race, color or previous condition of servitude, are entitled to the full and equal advantages, facilities, and privileges of the various places of public accommodation, resort or listed amusement." Persons who defied the law were subject to fine or imprisonment (criminal sanction), or were responsible in damages to the party aggrieved (civil sanction). In some states, both remedies were available, but an action for one barred an action for the other. Each statute listed places were the law was to be enforced.[11] Structurally, Minnesota's law was no different.

The new public accommodations statute embodied divergent themes. While it provided for black Minnesotans the right to attend most private establishments that catered to the public where whites assembled, it empowered state government to dictate to citizens in private businesses that they must serve people they wanted otherwise to exclude. However, the theme that granted social equality as defined in chapter 224 expressly denied whites the privilege to discriminate. In the age of laissez-faire, which held that the marketplace had to be free from government intrusion, the law seemed to deny white citizens the right to run their businesses as they saw fit. In other words, in promoting a right for one class of citizens, it infringed on a right of another class. This divided the Minnesota Republican delegation—one of the few issues to do so during this period.[12] Indeed, while the majority of senators who voted for the bill were Republicans, half of those opposing the bill were also Republicans.[13] Still, even though the bill embraced the controversial issue of social equality, it nonetheless pricked the conscience of those still holding true to the legacy of their party. In other words, the bill was intended to free black Minnesotans from a "previous condition of servitude."[14] When discrimination was defined as a vestige of slavery, the majority of Republicans felt compelled to support the bill.

However high-minded they were, Minnesota Republicans waited two years after the *Civil Rights Cases* before passing the law, becoming the tenth state to do so and reflecting as much an act of sectional loyalty as principle. In the ten years since the Civil Rights Act was ratified, no black Minnesotan had filed a lawsuit. With no complaints reported in newspapers—the only measure policy makers had about matters of race—it seemed that all was well in that community. Even the two failed black-owned newspapers had focused attention on the abuses of Southern white supremacists and criticized Republicans for failing to protect Southern blacks.[15] The political influence of black voters, however significant symbolically, remained politically ineffectual.[16] Minnesota's relative lack of urgency was measured against the apparent absence of a grievance against discrimination and was not, even when the bill was proposed, foremost on the minds of the legislators and opinion makers. For all its moral importance, they had other priorities. As the Minneapolis *Tribune* reported at the close of the session, "the great question of paramount importance, preceding all others, was the regulation of railroads and elevators, and to this all efforts were directed."[17]

The bill moved through the legislative procedure without controversy or comment, and no debate ensued when it came up for a final vote. In what seemed to be a gentleman's agreement, all understood that any debate would call unwanted attention to the measure. The St. Paul *Dispatch*, wrote a simple, race-neutral, and rather innocuous line: "(An Act) to secure to citizens civil and legal rights."[18] The St. Paul and Minneapolis *Pioneer Press* reported similarly: "To secure to citizens of Minnesota their civil rights." Editors overshadowed the new law with other accomplishments. The St. Paul and Minneapolis *Pioneer Press*, which had bought out the *Pioneer* to become the Republican organ, reported that "This has been one of the most generous legislatures ever known," mentioning that almost "every positive claim" was met with appropriations. All road and bridge bills were consolidated in an omnibus bill. There was also "a bill to prevent deception" in dairy products that exacted heavy penalties against sales of "oleomargarine, butterine and other adulterated products." Finally, the paper reported, "The most interesting 'purely local bill' was that increasing the limits of St. Paul, making her western boundary coterminous with the eastern boundary of Minneapolis."[19]

Even commentary describing Senator Gilfillan as "herculean" attributed none of the accolade to his shepherding of Senate Bill No. 181 through the legislature.[20] What enthusiasm he had for the bill—the only connection he had with Minnesota's civil-rights history—seemed to be overshadowed by his other legislative accomplishments. The law that it became was the price the state paid to maintain, without fanfare, its membership in the fraternity of enlightened states.

Minnesota had satisfied a moral imperative by filling the breach that was left when the *Civil Rights Cases* had left the whole issue of social equality to the states. Twelve years had passed since the incident when the Metropolitan and Merchant hotels had refused Frederick Douglass a room. The onus on Minnesota to rectify this embarrassment was mitigated by Sumner's bill working its way to a final vote; and for the eight years that followed, with no litigation in Minnesota, and no racial conflict (notwithstanding the Combs incident), it was as if the whole issue of discrimination had become insignificant, except in states that had not yet enacted civil rights laws. Now that Minnesota had its own law, lawmakers were confronted with conflicting interests. On the one hand, and of foremost concern to many, the law promoting social equality would necessarily infringe on the right of proprietors to deny service on the basis of race, and in so doing government was granting more rights to blacks than to whites. Critics felt the law threatened business for it required an unwilling white clientele to associate with blacks. And social equality meant imposing blacks, who owing to prejudice against their race bore the indelible brand of stigma, on gatherings of refined white people. On the other hand, a state with the racial legacy that Minnesota had simply could not have a policy that allowed proprietors to deny a room to the likes of Frederick Douglass. Granted, most black men—indeed, many white men as well—were not his social and intellectual equal. But if "the law is the witness and external deposit of our moral life," as Oliver Wendell Holmes wrote, then every black man needed to be legally treated as if he was the great Negro abolitionist, himself.[21] In any event, a law like this necessitated a collision between principle and expediency. However, expediency won out.

Minnesota's new public accommodations law did not require government to aggressively seek out discrimination in the private sector. Moreover, although the law was a statement of principle, it left the initiative for enforcement primarily with black litigants who had to sue for their rights in already overburdened state courts. Whether the injured black sought a civil remedy or pursued it as a crime, thereby requiring the state to be the plaintiff, the outcome nonetheless rested in the hands of a jury. which would most likely be all-white.[22] Consequently, the determination of fact was not left with government but with other private citizens. The law not only held government in check, but empowered citizens as jurors to reject "frivolous" claims. Thus there was no need for whites to feel outrage. Their peers had the final word on all such disputes.

Essentially, the law reflected Minnesota's commitment to civil and political equality for blacks while continuing to demonstrate its ambivalence to social equality. In the end, most Minnesotans—or at least the opinion makers—were neither jubilant nor outraged, but oblivious. Not even Minnesota's black community appeared to be jubilant. There were no toasts, speeches, or comments in the newspapers, and the earliest issue of the *Western Appeal,* the third black-owned newspaper established in St. Paul just three months after passage of chapter 224, made no mention of the civil-rights statute. The years of unaddressed discrimination experienced by black Minnesotans seemed to temper any sense of gratitude that some Republican policy makers might have expected. What jubilation may have been felt in March by the black community had turned by June to an attitude of wait and see. It took only that long for an act of legal redress against blatant discrimination in public accommodation to test the new law.

In late June, two black men went into Donnelly's Saloon on Wabasha Street and ordered drinks. The bartender refused to serve them and told them they could get nothing there. The black men were indignant and threatened criminal proceedings. The incident was an opportunity to test the new state law to "see what virtue there is in it." John Adams, the editor of the *Western Appeal,* commented:

> [N]ow if ignorant contemptible saloonkeepers are to be allowed to insult respectable colored men simply because they wish to purchase of them the same as any other person, we would respectfully ask the lawmakers of this state to erase the farce from the statute books, and herald the news that Minnesota, once the home of the free and brave, is now the sheltering abode of the weak-kneed nabob. Give us a full and fair test of the law, Mr. [County Attorney] Egan, and let us see how much of it was meant, when it was placed upon the statutes.[23]

They called upon County Attorney Egan, who sent them to U.S. District Attorney Congdon, who sent them back to Egan. The county attorney examined the law and determined that there was no provision that could be construed to apply to a saloon: section 1 of chapter 224 read: "That all persons shall be entitled to the full and equal enjoyment, privileges ... of inns, public conveyances, theatres, and places of public amusement, restaurants and barber shops." Saloons were not mentioned in the list of places where the law prohibited discrimination. Egan informed the men that he could do nothing for them.[24]

Adams wrote a scathing criticism, not of the county attorney's decision but against the St. Paul Daily *Pioneer Press* for having placed a spotlight on saloons as a "loophole" in the law, undermining the spirit of the law and abetting discrimination:

> The *Pioneer Press* of June 30 informs its readers that the Civil Rights Bill passed by the republican legislature last winter, was a farce. We know the *Press* is glad that a flaw or loop-hole has been found, where it is made possible for all offenders of the law and insulters of colored men, (when exercising their rights as men and citizens) to escape punishment. Had the *Press* with true spirit of republicanism, when this bill was first proposed, taken the proper course in its criticism and showed where the faults were, without holding the measure up to ridicule, perhaps some of our leading representatives, (who at election time can always know you and cause you to be treated as a man for the time being) would not have taken the bill and passed it from one to the other until it was passed out of existence.[25]

Adams had a point. In a city that had more saloons than theaters, hotels, and railways combined, it was noteworthy that the legislature had failed to include this place of public accommodation in the statute. The omission may have been intentional, but because the language of the act was taken directly from Ohio's law, it was more likely that little consideration was given to drafting legislation that addressed the realities of life in Minnesota's cities. Legislators—Gilfillan, in particular—had other legislative priorities.

However, it is just as possible that legislators were fully cognizant of omitting the word *saloon* from the statute, and did so to avoid enacting a law that was not likely to be practicable. On the one hand, hotels, theaters, and railways tended to be large enterprises owned by important men who did business with the Republican leaders of the state. Owners of these sorts of places—Gilbert Dutcher, the owner of Ingersoll Hall where the Convention of Colored Citizens had been held, the owners of the St. Paul railroad, who had provided free transit to blacks—were likelier to be much more reasonable. On the other hand, saloons were quite numerous and were likeliest to be owned and operated and patronized by some of the less "enlightened" citizens of St. Paul.

Adams insisted that Republicans wanted it both ways: they wanted to appear to be advancing civil rights while expecting blacks to be placated.

"Now this is the way the Republicans have been treating us ever since we have ceased to have a champion in the halls of Congress. With Wendell Phillips, the last of that school of great advocates, passed away, we have had none who dared step out from the throng and say or advise what should be open for our further benefit; no, but like the *Pioneer Press* they, as the representatives of republicanism in this section, declare that we are doing well enough, and we are always wanting something. Yes, we are always wanting something, and will continue to call on advocates of rights and liberty, until we get what we want and can care for ourselves."[26]

As long as the state's Republicans passed laws without meaningful enforcement, the laws were empty measures, and the party would be held accountable to black voters:

> [B]ut in the name of humanity don't hamper our progress with measures as bright as gold but as hollow as a gourd, and to be frank, if the republican party of this state, or any other party, expect the support of the Negro in the future, it must bring forward some measure that will benefit them and not do them more harm than good, as this contemptible act that is a disgrace to the statutes of any state claiming the record that this state claims for dealing squarely and rightfully with all men.[27]

It seemed that the civil-rights history of Minnesota had entered a new phase with an uncharacteristic voice being heard, a voice of grievance and demand that only a black newspaper could issue, one that had the courage and singular focus to report that within the liberal state of Minnesota, a small businessman was driven from prime land across the street of the newly opened Ryan Hotel simply because he was black.[28] It seemed to be a new phase in which the reflexive gratitude of African Americans would no longer be given easily.

In many ways, John Quincy Adams was a man of the times and just the man the black community of St. Paul needed. As editor of the revived *Western Appeal,* he gave voice to black impatience with Republican apathy to the welfare of Southern African Americans, and he knew how to strengthen the standing of his newspaper well enough to make it a going concern, politically astute knowing how far he could tweak the noses of

John Q. Adams, circa 1892. Courtesy of the Minnesota Historical Society.

his Republican patrons, while delicately creating a tie with a resurgent Democratic Party. Most important, he wrote about discrimination that existed in the Twin Cities, unafraid to criticize the weakness of the law, while tactfully avoiding a frontal assault on the politicians in municipal government. He combined the self-help principles of the day, which would later be amplified by Booker T. Washington, while raging against racism and hypocrisy that stacked the decks against opportunity. He was, indeed, in his words, quite "touchy." The *Western Appeal* reflected a time when the black community nationally was beginning to gain its own voice through an emerging black press. But he understood that his paper could only be a successful business venture if his paper was viable. He needed to attract two audiences—the black audience that desperately wanted to see its experiences recorded, and a white audience that would pay to read them—and he knew that the stories they wanted were not necessarily the same. To add to this, the times were changing.

The Republicans, whose banner was now stained with corruption, had lost the White House in 1884 to a Democrat. And in the Democratic stronghold of St. Paul, the streets—if not the banks, corporate board-rooms, and editorial desks of the established newspapers—belonged to the Democrats. Adams represented a new black leadership, which now included Lyles and the young attorney J. H. Loomis, who recognized that the interests of their community could only be advanced by striking that delicate balance of reaffirming their allegiance to the party of Lincoln while developing ties to local Democrats, as Lyles had begun to do with St. Paul *Pioneer* editor Davidson and the Daniel O'Connell Club. Although he did not sever his ties to the Republican Party, he would fault it for being complaisant to the persistence of discrimination perpetrated by men typically affiliated with the Democratic Party. But in a larger context, he was a man on a tightrope on a windy day. Eventually, the only money he could expect to attract to maintain his work would come from the Republicans. Attempting to play both sides, Adams faulted the Republicans for the persistence of discrimination, which at the time seemed to suit bosses of both parties.

In the effort to provide African Americans legal protections, Minnesota's public accommodations law exposed discrimination and racism in St. Paul and Minneapolis, as well as how flimsy the law was in providing significant legal redress. Presented through the pages of the *Western Appeal,* the insults and indignities to black Minnesotans revealed a reality of race relations that undercut images of placid civility depicted by the leading white newspapers. These stories, commentaries, and editorials revealed black discontent with the world Republicans either made or tolerated. In this they felt similarly to their brethren across the country.

The 1880s were a time of great disappointment with national Republican leaders for African Americans. They had known disappointment throughout much of the 1870s, but the 1880s were significantly different. Discontent had never been as vocal and documented as it was now. Black newspapers proliferated nationwide, sponsored initially by black churches, the only institution that African Americans controlled, but eventually and increasingly as self-supporting ventures. By 1881, some thirty black newspapers existed. Editors who wrote on politics and civil-rights matters, articulated, amplified, and validated grievances that had largely gone unacknowledged. They thereby made visible a community that had been invisible. The printed word publicly measured and judged the actions of governmental leaders, comparing a politician's rhetoric to his action, and chiseled an identity into the consciousness of a community. As a result, the reader gained an otherwise unrealized sense of empowerment. These were the elements that combined to form the new leadership, selected by the black community that purchased their newspapers.

When Vice President Chester Arthur became president following the assassination of James Garfield, whose sincerity had offered black America a glimmer of hope, Arthur chose not to appoint African Americans to administrative posts as Garfield had, favoring instead Southern segregationists. An outraged T. Thomas Fortune, the fiery and able editor of the New York *Globe,* and soon to be considered the dean of black journalism, charged that "the Republican Party has eliminated the black man from politics . . . It has left the black man to fight his own battles." The black-owned Huntsville *Gazette* fumed: "Spit upon the house of his friends, despised and ignored at feast times, and reorganized when and only when his services are needed—is the lot of the Negro." The Washington *Bee* and other newspapers expressed similar views. When Arthur ignored the civil-rights infringements of Southerners, Frederick Douglass, whose loyalty to the Republican Party had outlasted that of many African Americans, criticized it for failing to protect the civil rights of African Americans at the National Convention of Colored People in Louisville in September 1883. The convention refused to endorse the Arthur administration, and the growing repudiation of Arthur even prompted a call to form an independent party.[29]

Black editors were deeply critical of the decision in the *Civil Rights Cases.* The black-owned Cleveland *Gazette* derisively referred to "the

Republican court," a term normally used by the Democratic press. Fortune observed that "The black man had been baptized in ice water" and that "The Republican Party has carried the war into Africa, and Africa accordingly is stirred to its centre." A packed audience at the fashionable black Fifteenth Street Presbyterian Church in Washington, D.C., heard John Langston call the decision a "stab in the back." Arthur was blamed. And in the face of a mounting black revolt, Arthur continued to say nothing in response. Despite the prevailing view among Democrats that African Americans merited second-class citizenship, African Americans were for the first time willing to vote against a Republican candidate for president. White voters who had supported the party were also alienated, but for another reason: corruption. Voters took note when the party selected James Blaine and John Logan to be its standard-bearers— two men who benefited from shady business connections. Heather Cox Richardson observed that "Under the Republican Party vast corporations had come to control politics, and rather than cleaning up Washington, party hacks had nominated for president men closely associated with corporate bribery."[30]

When the Democrats nominated reformer Grover Cleveland, independent Republicans hinted that they intended to support him. Black voters were also attracted to the candidate, who stated his commitment to racial harmony. In his inaugural address, he declared his intention to protect black rights and to demand improvements for African Americans: "The fact that they are citizens entitles them to all the rights due to that relation and charges them with all the duties, obligations, and responsibilities." William Gross, an African American from New York, wrote Cleveland that his references to his race had been "well received." A Thomas Nast cartoon on the cover of *Harper's Weekly* showed two mainstream men, one black, the other white, shaking hands in front of the new president. What Cleveland promised was balm to the soul of black Americans. Northern black voters who rejected Republican policy had contributed to this first Democratic success since the Civil War. In the end, the platforms of both parties were largely the same, for Cleveland, as the Republicans had done for the previous two decades, endorsed the mainstream ideal of success through hard work rather than legislation, refusing to acknowledge that racial discrimination made success illusory for many hardworking African Americans:

It is evident that as long as the South was unmolested, the nation had arrived at a dead center with respect to the Negro. It made little difference whether a Republican or a Democrat—at least a Northern Democrat—was President. Party platforms were frankly hypocritical on the constitutional rights of Negroes. Presidents of both parties uttered pious platitudes, but said nothing, and did nothing, except to give a few jobs to professional Negro officeholders.[31]

Fortune did not seek or receive a presidential appointment, even though he vigorously appealed to black voters to support Cleveland. A strong advocate for black rights, he would come to clearly see the truth of Cleveland's commitment, and reject the party. The revival of Republican interest in the Southern African American was in large measure owing to Cleveland's victory in 1884. Fortune could claim some credit for this, for he contributed to what happened when Republicans took the black vote for granted. This was an inspiring message to African Americans, and for the moment to Republican leaders. But, as Fortune became better known, he didn't make much money, unlike Adams in Minnesota. It did not go unnoticed that in 1884 Minnesota had remained firmly Republican, casting nearly 59 percent of the vote for Blaine and 37 percent for Cleveland. In a state whose population was nearly 1,300,000, more than 3,600 were African American.[32] By 1887, the question Adams had to answer was how vigorously should he wag his finger at Minnesota Republicans.

On May 5, 1887, the *Western Appeal* ran an editorial that applauded the *Pioneer Press*, considered the "leading Republican organ of the Northwest," for issuing a momentous forty-page paper. But it cautioned the white newspaper that black Minnesotans, the majority of whom were "tried and true members" of the same party the *Pioneer Press* championed, expected the paper to print articles that were more respectful of black people and more constructive than those being published by other papers. The *Western Appeal* would be watching it closely. "We are very touchy," the editor wrote, "and take exceptions very much more readily to sentiments expressed, or treatment received from those we consider our friends, than those who are known to be opposed to our general advancement."[33] The *Western Appeal* was indeed "touchy" and showed it by chastising its Republican friends who gave words of support for the paper without subscribing to it:

Now let our Republican friends who wish to see us succeed, and who desire to show us that they appreciate the effort we have put forth in the past, to aid them to succeed in their many triumphs, subscribe for the paper, give it a boom among their friends, advertise with us, and demonstrate to the public that your desire for success is from the heart and well intended.[34]

Blunt notices to readers to pay up their subscriptions and patronize black and white businesses that bought advertising space appeared prominently on the front page.[35] Bona fide members of the middle class were, above all, consumers. The *Western Appeal* was just as quick to criticize even its journalistic ally, the *Pioneer Press,* when the paper referred to a black thief as a "black gentleman." "We beg to differ, Colored gentlemen are never burglars."[36] The paper raged against hypocrisy as one issue attacked white Christians who "send missionaries to Africa to prepare [African] souls for heaven" but did nothing to "christianize the white heathen of America at the same time."[37]

The *Western Appeal* could be critical of the state Republican Party, as in an editorial demanding better political appointments and elective opportunities: "We wish to have a hand in home affairs, and a share in the honors and emoluments at home . . . We have men capable of filling any office in the county and we wish to see some of them placed in positions of honor and trust not only by appointment but by election."[38] Claiming that the only Republican appointments were janitorial or police and fire positions (which it noted was not remarkable since "[t]his was true of most cities under Democratic rule"), the paper demanded "something higher." What was at stake was the continued loyalty of black voters:

We hold the balance of power in this county, as the recent elections prove, and, it is an open question if under certain circumstances we would not do so in National politics. We are cheerfully disposed to be in and of the Republican Party, and while we ask for nothing because we are colored, *we do not wish to be so glaringly ignored because we are colored, which undoubtedly is and has been the case, heretofore.* We do not propose longer to be catapaws, and we intend to demand our just recognition from the powers that be in the Republican Party.[39]

The *Western Appeal* was stating quite clearly that Republicans had been taking blacks for granted and that the party would be held accountable. Although black voters were not likely to bolt to the Democrats, the paper argued that they would go to any other party that advanced their interests. "We are for ourselves first, parties afterwards; the Republican Party has done better by us than any other party, and we will stick by our *friends until greater friends arise.*"[40]

Not even black people were spared. When readers in Minneapolis complained that the *Western Appeal* did not publish local news of that city, the editor replied "the fault, to a great extent, lies with the people. Our columns are open, and any person who feels enough interest in getting the news of his vicinity before our readers, as to write us letters, they will be published."[41] Exasperated with the continued victimization of black men in the South, the paper stated that "colored men who remain in the South . . . deserve no more sympathy than the foolish men who are killed."[42] It called for more stringent enforcement of the vagrancy law against black idlers: "[I]t is sad but true that there are men in this city who have not done an honest day's work for years and yet they are allowed to loaf around and remain idle, creating mischief, and corrupting the good standing of the race. The time has come for action and we insist on it."[43] In February 1887, the paper criticized "the short-sighted colored teachers" of Cincinnati, Ohio, for assisting white board members who sought to contravene the legislature's recent enactment to desegregate city schools.[44]

The newspaper was especially critical of blacks for not being more financially astute or racially united:

> While everyone seems to be going wild and growing rich through real estate in this part of the woods, it seems a little singular that colored men generally, do not "catch on." They seem to be splendid imitators of the fashionable foibles, vices and follies of their fairer-hued and straight-haired brothers, and in everything but financial undertakings, "you can't lose them." But when it comes to business enterprises, where confidence in one another, and co-operation, are essential elements of success, they seem to be at sea. One of the greatest drawbacks is the lack of confidence in each other, and just so long as this prevails, there will be little general progress.[45]

Its view of hopefulness was laced with a bitter critique of black lethargy:

> To sit in idleness and brood over the misfortunes of the past is both foolish and unwise. The past is beyond recall. As well you might try to restore the dried up mummy to life and beauty, as to live over the past, and correct the mistakes committed; it is gone, buried beyond resurrection, and is worthless as a dream, except as an example for the present and future.[46]

Too often, it argued, black people rely on demagogues and charlatans to lead them, and it insisted that there were no race leaders.[47] It was not even above an intemperate call for self-defense, meeting Southern white supremacist force with force:

> Isn't it about time for the Colored people of the South to take in their own hands and meet these hellish heathens halfway? Blood for blood. If a Colored man is lynched who is guilty of no crime, whose life is safe? Every Colored man should go armed and sell his life as dearly as possible. Blood for blood.[48]

In the same issue, an editorial seemed to be warning the nation about the consequences of failing to end mob violence: "Eight millions of people driven to desperation could make much trouble in these United States."[49] Above all, however, the *Western Appeal,* for all its truculent tone, espoused race unity and love. For black people who lived within a predominately white community, a paper that articulated racial pride and love was essential to affirming self-worth. "Labor to be proud of [yourself]. A proper self-respect is expected of races as of [your]self. We need more self-love. The tie of race-hood should bind us as the tie of brotherhood."[50] The history of the *Western Appeal* began three months after chapter 224 was enacted when Samuel E. Hardy and John T. Burgett, two Civil War veterans who had served in the U.S. Colored Infantry, wrote a six-column folio. Within seven years, this folio, which they named the *Western Appeal,* would achieve a position of importance that it retained until the end of the nineteenth century. Later it billed itself "A National Afro-American Newspaper" and promoted itself as "the people's paper," according recognition for personal achievement regardless of social standing while providing "for black businessmen a medium for advertisements, the black politician a forum, and the black writer and artist an audience."[51]

But this paper was much more. What most whites knew about Minnesota's black community came from the main newspapers of St. Paul and Minneapolis, which printed articles that tended to portray blacks as either grateful and unfailingly content people who held picnics and benign cultural activities or criminals. But in 1885, under the leadership of Burgett and Frederick Douglass Parker, the *Western Appeal* was as provocative as it was progressive, embracing such anti-Republican themes as the rights of laborers and antimonopolyism, as well as the right of women to be lawyers.[52] Under the editorial guidance of John Adams the paper's voice would grow more moderate, as overt acts of discrimination tended to be Southern occurrences. Rarer still would be stories of discrimination in Minnesota. Under Adams, the image was clear: Minnesota was the promised land and black people knew it.

In contrast to later iterations, the *Western Appeal* of 1885 "printed what a spiritually, politically, economically, and socially oppressed people wanted to read. It dared to say what thousands of black men and women kept to themselves."[53] The public could read about a black man named C. W. Baptist, who was ordered by unnamed persons to move his business because it was situated across from the prestigious Ryan Hotel "or they would find some way to make him"—a story that never appeared in any of the bigger newspapers.[54]

The bigoted slights of white men followed by the humiliating actions of white policemen, as illustrated in the case of Mrs. J. J. Wiley, went virtually unseen by proper society. Mrs. Wiley and friends were in a crowd that had gathered to see President Grover Cleveland when he visited St. Paul in October 1887. Jammed in next to "some big burly white men," Mrs. Wiley grew impatient after the men continued to insult them. A policeman worked his way to the commotion and, "seeing Mrs. Wiley was colored," at once arrested her for being drunk and disorderly; the men were allowed to go free. Wiley retained J. H. Loomis, for whom this was his first case before the Minnesota bar; he succeeded in getting Mrs. Wiley discharged once it was clearly proven that the charges were false.[55] The St. Paul police were always biased against black people:

It is worthy of notice that the policemen of this city are very eager to arrest Colored People, whom they in their intelligent (?) minds have a shadow of suspicion of, and often, with no other reason than they are Colored. This thing must be stopped. We wish all criminals, black or white, to be punished, but we do not wish to be subjected to these outrages at the hands of these ignorant boors, whose prejudices outweigh all sense of justice and right.[56]

One could imagine a black reader who had experienced a similar encounter nodding with recognition and approval of the newspaper's outrage. Such reports, rarely published in the Republican press, affirmed the legitimacy of black frustration and demands for justice. The *Western Appeal* articulated the distinction between social equality and civil rights.

It was not social equality that colored people desire ... but they do wish to have civil rights. Men meet each other in the business world day after day and become very intimate, but they do not have to mingle in the social world together unless they choose to do so. The sensible portion of the colored people are as averse to going where they are not invited, when invitations are a necessary passport, as any people on earth, but when the Almighty dollar is the only necessary passport, they wish it to be as serviceable to them as to all others. Is there any social equality in that? That's all the colored people wish in either the South or the North.[57]

Under the fiery leadership of John Adams, the *Western Appeal* criticized white America for its hypocritical treatment of its black neighbors, defended blacks against malicious racial propaganda, and condemned the disenfranchisement and discrimination they faced.[58] Yet, despite sentiments that may have left some white and black conservative readers ill at ease, from its inception until it closed in 1924, the *Western Appeal* remained decidedly pro-establishment. While Adams espoused property ownership, entrepreneurialism, and education, he also championed prohibition and, at least passively, supported women's suffrage:

Within the last few days, over one thousand of the leading women of Leavenworth, Kansas, have registered, and will vote under the recent law granting municipal suffrage to women, and it is safe to bet that the officers elected will be of a better quality than heretofore.[59]

Although the newspaper mainly addressed matters of interest to black Minnesotans, Adams clearly wanted to appeal to a broader readership. In addition to printing stories on gardening, cooking, housework, and social events, a column titled "The Old World" routinely reported news items from Ireland, Germany, Great Britain, and other European countries. When the legislature was in session, the paper covered state and federal matters.[60] Adams also wanted to broaden the awareness of the black community and publicized classes that blacks could take to learn the German language.[61] The *Western Appeal* published an article encouraging Southern blacks to relocate to Minnesota "with miles of lands to be had by the mere occupying," and another article that touted the benefits of farming in Minnesota on "the millions of acres of land of unsurpassed fertility." Neither mentioned the issues of farm politics that had led to Grange activities in the 1870s and the Farmers' Alliance of the 1880s.[62] But, most important, the newspaper regarded the everyday experiences of black people as significant enough to be recorded for time immemorial.

The *Western Appeal* became decidedly Republican. Despite its earlier claim to nonpartisanship, the cost of independence was too high to maintain without the support of friends within the political establishment. The relationship between the *Western Appeal* and the Republican Party was not unusual, for many black newspapers during the post-Reconstruction era survived because of similar relationships, a unique phenomenon of the Northern experience. In the South, few black newspapers existed because of the region's high degree of black illiteracy, whereas "race journals," as they were often called, proliferated in the North because of higher literacy, a more urbanized and therefore accessible body of subscribers, greater per capita income, and generous subsidies from the Republican Party. "More often than not, partisan politics was the greatest consideration in the establishment and survival of northern race journals."[63]

Adams, a man of moderate temperament and reserved courtliness, who could occasionally write with bombast, was decidedly not militant, but he was politically astute, which was particularly evident in the years preceding his arrival in St. Paul. Born in 1848 in Louisville, Kentucky, he was raised in comfortable circumstances in which education and political activity were prized. He left home in 1870 and sought his political fortune in Arkansas. As a teacher in Little Rock, he soon advanced to the position of superintendent of public instruction for the Republican-controlled state.

"In time," observed David Taylor, "Adams became even more enmeshed in party politics, serving twice as secretary to the state conventions." In 1872, he ran on the same ticket with Ulysses S. Grant and was elected justice of the peace. Before the Democrats regained power in 1876, he served as engrossing clerk to the state senate and as deputy commissioner of public works. (As a bill works its way through the legislative process, language or provisions in the original bill are added or deleted. An engrossing clerk is one who prepares the bill in a manner to show the changes as the bill works its way to a final vote.) After his return to Louisville, he advanced in the inner councils of the local Republican Party, eventually serving on both the party's city and state executive committees.

For his partisan activity Adams was appointed delegate to the National Republican Convention of 1880 that nominated James Garfield for president and Chester Arthur for vice president. Following the election, he was rewarded with an appointment to the U.S. Revenue Service as granger and storekeeper in Kentucky's fifth district. "The election of [Democrat] Grover Cleveland as president of 1884," wrote Taylor, "brought an abrupt end to Adams' second political ascent."[64]

As editor of the *Western Appeal,* Adams proudly continued his "uncompromising allegiance to the Republican Party," a stance that Taylor called "a salient flaw in [his] approach to civil rights." By now, in issue after issue, Adams had made clear his loyalty to the Republican Party. At times when the party was complaisant in the face of constant discrimination against poor blacks in Minnesota, Adams remained silent. In election years, the newspaper swelled from its normal four-page size to eight pages, most of it filled with Republican propaganda, pictures, engravings of candidates, images of the flag, and frequent exhortations to vote straight Republican.[65]

Taylor noted that it remained a matter of conjecture as to whether Adams's newspaper was subsidized by the Republicans, especially during election years. It is known that during the presidential election of 1900, Republican Senator Marcus A. Hanna of Ohio used the *Western Appeal* to promote the candidacy of William McKinley among blacks. Afterwards, Hanna appointed Adams's brother Cyrus, who was then editor of the

Chicago edition of the *Western Appeal,* to the Republican National Advisory Committee.

In years to come, as the party appeared oblivious to black interests in both the North and the South, and black leaders began to criticize Adams for his continued allegiance, the editor remained steadfast. Even when he became disillusioned with Northern Republican leaders, Adams's loyalty to Republican principles remained firm.[66] Republican largesse at least allowed him to continue to speak out on issues in the only way available.

Yet, despite this history, it would be unfair to characterize Adams as a dupe for the Republican Party, especially during the early years of his newspaper, for he was a practical man, concerned about practical solutions to problems facing his community, and St. Paul was a Democratic city and the president was a Democrat. Accordingly, he joined black Republican businessman Thomas Lyles and black attorney J. H. Loomis and their wives, who participated in a reception at the Ryan Hotel for the Democratic President Glover Cleveland when he visited the city in October 1887. "It is gratifying to note the recognition accorded to the Colored Citizens . . . [This] tardy reception leads us to conclude that we are being more important in their eyes, as we become more intelligent, and cannot be overlooked with impunity, any more than the Germans, the Irish, and the Scandinavians, or any other class of our citizens."[67]

This was the event at which Mrs. Wiley was arrested. This flirtation with the Democrats, however, did not affect Adams's view that unless another party came along that better served the interests of black people, he would stay with the Republicans. "No other state in the Union offers more opportunities for the progress of the Colored People than our thriving state," he wrote, "[a]nd no other state has so few of the worst and so many of the best elements as Minnesota."[68]

7

A Certain Class of Citizens

"Let us organize and prosecute. In union there is strength."

—*Western Appeal,* October 15, 1887

It is not known what Republican leaders thought of the flirtations of Adams, Lyles, and Loomis. But they could afford to be tolerant, considering the returns in 1884 that went overwhelmingly for their party. The black population had grown, but not so much that their demands would be a significant concern, for they were hardly sizable enough to turn an election. The Republicans did have concerns, not because Grover Cleveland was president but about third-party politics, which had nipped at the party's heels throughout the 1870s. Throughout the 1880s, disgruntled farmers were re-formng into a more intense effort in the incarnation of the Populist Party. This was a threat from the farmland whose produce created the foundation of much of their profits. And the increasing immigrant population, particularly the Germans and Scandinavians, cast ballots that the party needed. The leverage Adams sought paled in comparison. His paper had few subscribers and even fewer resources. The Republicans still held all the cards. When he wagged his finger, they could afford to be magnanimous—but within limits. It behooved Adams and his colleagues to know just what those limits were.

The biggest employer of black men in 1880 was the Metropolitan Hotel, where they worked as cooks, porters, dining-room waiters, bellhops, messengers, and janitors.[1] In 1885, the Metropolitan was eclipsed with the opening of the Hotel Ryan. Initially, all of Ryan's employees were white. That summer H. C. Reeves, the headwaiter, and a crew of twenty-five men arrived from New York to work there. Within a year of its opening, most of Ryan's white employees had been replaced by black men as the hotel fast became the preferred destination of the white middle and upper class.[2] Just as it had been fashionable for affluent whites to be served by elite black barbers, so it increasingly was to be served by black waiters at elite hotels during the late nineteenth century. A porter, however, could not leverage his value to the hotel to his financial benefit. Moreover, although black workers in the hotel industry filled most of the menial and service-related jobs, they did not represent a collective bargaining force. Marginally employed or underemployed and fearful of losing jobs in an artificially constricted labor market for unskilled blacks, most black hotel workers were manipulated and easily victimized by unscrupulous employers.[3] This motivated Adams to criticize the values of his political friends and patrons, and the local monopolies for the manner in which they treated workers:

> The injustice practiced by monopolies toward the laboring man is mak-
> ing itself felt all over this western country, at this time, and the laboring
> man has stood the imposition until patience has ceased to be a virtue.
> While we do not advocate strikes or any kind of labor strife, because
> more harm generally results in place of the good that is intended, but
> aristocratic nabobs must be given to understand that laborers have
> rights that are to be respected, and wants that must be met.[4]

The fact that more blacks in Minnesota worked as laborers than as farmers made employment conditions and personal dignity a matter for the black community. Unskilled laborers were disposable and therefore the least respected. By 1889, Adams's tone intensified as he leveled his rhetorical guns on the Pullman Palace Car Company, whose wage cuts fell dispro-portionately on blacks working as sleeping-car porters:

> [P]orters at $15 and conductors at $75 doesn't look fair, and it robs the
> poor porters of considerable of their manhood to have to stand for all

sorts of insults from country boors and ill-bred people for fear of losing a "tip". For a corporation which at last accounts had $10,000,000 over what the law allowed it to pay out in dividends, to refuse to pay the very men who do most toward making the sleeping car system a success, decent wage is a burning shame.[5]

In one year, another man who later would be internationally known as a champion for civil rights would have an experience prompting him to lend his voice to a similar appeal.

In 1888, a twenty-year-old black man who had graduated from a Southern university and prepared to attend Harvard University that fall came to Minnesota to work for the summer at a hotel on Lake Minnetonka. Ten years earlier, Major Thomas A. Harrow, the hotel proprietor, was lauded for bringing fifty colored servants from the South to be employed at his hotel, and it was a practice he continued.[6] Although the twenty-year-old servant from Nashville, William Edward Burghardt DuBois, had no experience waiting on tables, he wrote that his friend Fortson, who had told him of the job, said, "Never mind . . . you can stand around the dining room during meals and carry out the big wooden trays of dirty dishes. Thus you can pickup knowledge of waiting and earn good tips and get free board." In his book *Darkwater: Voices from within the Veil*, DuBois described himself as being skeptical, but he agreed nonetheless to go along. He described the hotel as "broad and blatant . . . with distinct forebodings . . . The flamboyant architecture, the great verandas, rich furniture, and richer dresses awed us mightily. The long loft reserved for us, with its clean little cots, was reassuring; the work was not difficult." But the food they were required to eat was bad:

> [T]he meals! There were no meals. At first, before the guests ate, a dirty table in the kitchen was hastily strewn with uneatable scraps. We novices were the only ones who came to eat, while the guest's dining room, with its savors and sights, set our appetites on edge. After a while even the pretense of food for us was dropped.

He feared that he and the other waiters would starve until he learned that stealing food was common practice among waiters at this hotel, and the experience pressed them into a corrupting and bestial state:

We gulped and hesitated. Then we stole, too . . . and we all fattened, for the dainties were marvelous. You slipped a bit here and hid it there; you cut off extra portions and gave false orders; you dashed off into darkness and hid in corners and ate and ate. It was nasty business. I hated it. I was too cowardly to steal much myself, and not coward enough to refuse what others stole.

He [DuBois] described his job as demeaning and one tending to reduce a noble spirit to ash.

Our work was easy, but insipid. We stood about and watched overdressed people gorge. For the most part, we were treated like furniture and were supposed to act the wooden part. I watched the waiters even more than the guests. I saw that it paid to amuse and to cringe. One particular black man set me crazy. He was intelligent and deft, but one day I caught sight of his face as he served a crowd of men; he was playing the clown—crouching, grinning, assuming a broad dialect when he usually spoke good English—ah! it was a heartbreaking sight, and he made more money than any waiter in the dining room.

Although he did not mind the actual work or the kind of work he was hired to do, he despised how the job compelled success to be obtained by dishonesty and deception, by flattery and cajolery, by "the unnatural assumption that worker and diner had no common humanity . . . It was inherently and fundamentally wrong." The end of his service came in one disgusting moment:

I stood staring and thinking, while the other boys hustled about. Then I noticed one fat hog, feeding at the heavily gilded trough, who could not find his waiter. He beckoned me. It was not his voice, for his mouth was too full. It was his way, his air, his assumption. Thus Caesar ordered his legionaires or Cleopatra her slaves. Dogs recognized the gesture. I did not. He may be beckoning yet for all I know, something froze within me. I did not look his way again. Then and there I disowned menial service for me and my people.[7]

Near the end of the summer, DuBois described how his friend Fortson asked him to help write a letter to the absentee proprietor about the activities of some of the guests, "telling of the wild and gay doings of midnights in the rooms and corridors among 'tired' business men and their prostitutes." The proprietor neither thanked them nor answered the letter. They simply did not understand that the proprietor probably intended the hotel on the wooded shoreline of Lake Minnetonka to provide the business and political elite with a respite—a morning's ride from the Victorian confines of Twin Cities society.[8] "When I finally walked out of that hotel and out of menial service forever, I felt as though, in a field of flowers, my nose had been held unpleasantly long to the worms and manure at their roots."[9]

Adams and DuBois both understood the desperate quality of life experienced by the black laborer; but while DuBois's reminiscence would germinate into a career of confronting the established order, both white and black, Adams's would increasingly become more tempered.

Two years passed after the Donnelly Saloon incident before leaders in St. Paul's black community initiated what was intended to be a test of the new law as well as the sentiment of the white community.[10] On May 17, 1887, William A. Hazel, a black architect from Massachusetts, attempted to get a room for the night at both the Astoria and Clarendon hotels in St. Paul but was refused because of his color. When the clerk, who acknowledged the existence of a state law prohibiting discriminatory acts in public facilities, refused him lodging, Hazel demanded to speak to the proprietor.

The proprietor likewise refused him lodging and verbally abused him. Hazel protested his treatment but was arrested, charged with drunken disorderliness despite his obvious sobriety, and forced to spend the night in the city jail. Encouraged by *Western Appeal* editor John Adams, Hazel sued the Clarendon Hotel for discriminatory practices under chapter 224. Adams explained:

> [Black citizens] do not intend to sit supinely and mourn over the state of affairs, but propose to learn if there is civil justice to be obtained for a human being upon whom God has seen it fit to place a dusky skin. There is a civil rights law upon the statute books of the State of Minnesota, and it is the intent of Mr. Hazel to bring a suit under the same; not alone to punish these prejudiced landlords, by forcing them to pay

heavy damages for the outrage perpetuated, but to establish the principle that we are citizens of this commonwealth, and we do not intend to be debarred from our privileges . . . We speak for every colored citizen in this city, and we intend to test the law and the sentiment of the people, and we intend to fight it out on this line if it takes all summer.[11]

St. Paul, the capital of black Minnesota as well as the center of white bigotry, would be the battleground for social justice.

On June 20, Hazel filed suit against Michael E. Foley and Thomas J. Foley, proprietors of the Clarendon, in the Second Judicial District Court in St. Paul. However, rather than sue under chapter 224, which had a damages cap of five hundred dollars, he brought a common-law action seeking two thousand dollars in damages, transforming the suit into a conceptual, rather than an actual, challenge under chapter 224. The case was tried on October 17. Three days earlier, when he came from Minneapolis to attend the hearing, Hazel was yet again "the victim of bad luck."[12]

William A. Hazel, whose portrait adorns this page, is the latest contribution of the race to the professional and business ranks of St. Paul having come to this city from Minneapolis at the beginning of the year. By profession Mr. Hazel is an architect and decorative artist, and as such fills the position of designer, in addition to that of manager of the St. Paul branch of Brown & Haywood's stained glass works; the main house being in Minneapolis.

William Hazel, profiled in the *Appeal*, February 8, 1890.

He went to McVeigh's bakery and lunchroom on Third Street and placed an order for wheat cakes and coffee. But when the order came and he tasted it, he found that it had been spiked with salt. Hazel complained to McVeigh, but the proprietor refused to remedy the problem. "It is very plain," the *Western Appeal* reported, "why this outrage was perpetrated." The newspaper then, for the first time, called for an organization to monitor and prosecute civil-rights offenses. This was to be the first time that blacks planned to rely not on Republican patrons but on themselves:

How long will the Colored citizens of St. Paul submit to these outrages? If there is any place where a Civil Rights League is needed this seems to be the place. Let us organize and prosecute these men who heap insults and injuries on us. In union there is strength. A Civil Rights League has been formed in Cincinnati, which had prosecuted several cases and never lost one. We can do the same.[13]

After the evidence was presented, the jury decided in favor of Hazel, but he was awarded only a token twenty-five dollars in damages plus nineteen dollars in costs.[14] Even though chapter 224 was not actually tested, black leaders concluded that the sentiment of the white community in fact had been tested and that it had failed, as indicated by the meager award.[15]

Hazel's award was far from sufficient to cover the expenses incurred, and the *Western Appeal* resorted to soliciting funds from the black community, "in whose behalf the suit was filed," to help defray his expenses. Adams argued that the cost of bringing a civil suit was prohibitive for the average black man.

If two thousand dollars for attorney fees for a one-day trial was a reasonable amount, and this amount was prohibitive to the average black Minnesotan likeliest to file a suit of this nature, then the statutory cap of a mere five hundred dollars was yet another reason why chapter 224 needed to be criticized. However, the *Western Appeal* did not find fault with Hazel's white attorney, the white judge, or the all-white jury:

> Thanks to Mr. Henry Johns, the able young lawyer, in his management of the case; thanks to the honorable men who formed the majority of the jury, and, last but not least, to the upright Judge Kelly, for his impartial, unbiased decisions, and for his admirable charge to the jury, which was so clear and succinct that there was no chance for the most ignorant to go astray, thanks are due to all of these for the victory we have won.[16]

At the same time that the Hazel case was being litigated, a case in Minneapolis was being tried involving a black man named Hamilton who had assaulted a white man for besmirching the honor of his wife. Hamilton was acquitted by a jury of white men. The *Western Appeal* proudly commented, "These two cases are the most important ones which have occurred in the history of the twin cities in years, and we have won both, thank God!" However, the expenses of that case, as with *Hazel*, remained unpaid, a burden the paper felt the entire community should help to bear. Despite the sense of justice that some whites were capable of exhibiting as jurors, discrimination would primarily be fought in a broader context: "Other [cases] of equal importance may arise in the future . . . and it will be well for us in time to prepare for war." The *Western Appeal* was not interested in lobbying the legislature to modify the statute, so the fight had to be waged by Minnesotans committed to civil rights. Again, the paper called for action, this time on a statewide level: "We should form a protective league to take charge of all cases where our rights as citizens of the United States are abridged or denied and fight them to the bitter end."[17]

On December 3, 1887, the *Western Appeal* announced the presence of "a certain class of citizens of Minnesota" who were pooling resources to help each other pay for lawsuits against discrimination and the "damnable prejudice of which exists in the bosoms of other classes of citizens in the commonwealth."[18] Simply put, in the wake of a series of discriminatory acts against middle-class blacks of St. Paul, no doubts remained that they could not depend on the Republican elite to deliver justice. Even if an all-white jury found for a black plaintiff, judging by *Hazel* and *Hamilton,* the plaintiff could not expect his expenses to be covered by a jury award. Therefore, if the burden of protecting the right to public accommodations rested in the ability to cover attorneys' fees and if a plaintiff was unable to do so, his rights were virtually nonexistent. All blacks—poor and middle-class—were vulnerable.

Men such as *Western Appeal* editor John Adams believed that a state civil-rights league should be organized to keep vigilance against acts of discrimination and to raise funds to prosecute lawsuits. The convention that Adams called for in an apparent effort to assuage Republican leaders' concerns that this might be a seedling for a third party was decidedly not political: "The sole object of the convention is to form a state league for the purpose of protecting the Colored citizens of Minnesota in their civil rights and to draft a constitution and set of by-laws for the government of the same, and for no other purpose whatever, either directly or indirectly."[19]

The organization's success rested on race unity, and the call for a statewide convention was to be held on December 5, 1887. "Remember the sentiment of the call," announced the *Western Appeal* on November 19, 1887. "In union there is strength; and let us in this moment work together as one man. What benefits one man, benefits all; what injures one, injures all."[20]

In a spirit of cooperation, or co-optation, the Republican political establishment made a grand gesture of support by providing use of the courthouse for convention planning and the hall of the House of Representatives in the state capitol for the convention itself.[21] On the heels of the convention, the Protective and Industrial League had transformed from a civil-rights legal defense organization to something more ambitious.[22]

The league's manifesto sought to improve the social and economic circumstances of black Minnesotans. F. D. Parker, chairman of the executive committee and Adams's predecessor as editor of the *Western Appeal,* said that "the league was not designed to become a political machine, but it will earnestly seek to promote the material interest of the race as well as to protect them in their political rights."[23] During this time in Minnesota when third parties were taking shape to voice the discontent of farmers and laborers, the league was not going to be a competitor for black votes with the Republican Party. Rather, it sought to expand avenues of advancement for blacks and give them material assistance.[24]

Membership was open to all, regardless of sex, creed, or color. Participants paid a membership fee of fifty cents and monthly dues of twenty-five cents. The league was organized into local committees that were to keep records of acts construed as an abridgment or denial of black rights, and to promote projects designed to improve the quality of black life in Minnesota. For example, one program intended to help build inexpensive homes for small monthly payments, with the belief that home ownership facilitated community stability, prosperity, and general well-being. The league also set up a bureau that would pursue an even more ambitious plan of attracting Southern blacks to settle in Minnesota. Fifty thousand acres of fertile farmland were to be acquired from public land officials and railroad interests and made available to form colonies of black settlers.[25]

Black settlers could rely on the league to provide resources to purchase farmland. Only a special breed of black settler was desired, one that befitted the racial legacy that Adams and his colleagues were trying to establish. Bureau secretary James M. Hilyard, a Pennsylvanian who had worked on steamboats before settling in St. Paul, where he opened a clothing store and tailor shop, wrote: "Minnesota being so remote from the South, will escape the incoming drifters and be blessed with only the hardier and bolder representatives of the race. What we want are thoughtful men, men who deliberate first, men who having once begun will not back down."[26] The *Western Appeal* echoed his optimism:

> No doubt the words of [bureau secretary James Hilyard] will sound somewhat utopian to many of our readers, yet calm and careful consideration reveals the feasibility of all he claims. Much more stupendous undertakings have been successfully carried out, right before our eyes, in this state during the last ten years. While some of us here have found it all we could do to make a living and buy us a little home, others of the white race, have started in without a cent and are now worth a million, they have not worked any harder than we have, but we have had the grit to enter into big enterprises and have had the ability to succeed . . . We do not doubt that there are men of our race in this state who have the ability to accomplish all the secretary suggests. Now is the time for strong men to come to the front.[27]

The optimism, however, reflected a lack of awareness of the reality of farming in Minnesota during the last decade of the nineteenth century. The best farmland had long been owned and under cultivation and the lives of smaller farmers had grown increasingly desperate. The one-crop system of wheat farming, in which most farmers participated, overexpansion in boom times, then hard times and low prices, and worldwide competition all contributed to the distress of Minnesota farmers. Farm grievances abounded with the imposition of warehouse and commission merchants, inequitable railroad rates, and unregulated grading practices. Throughout the 1870s and 1880s, farmers were organizing to achieve economic parity.

By the mid-1870s, the Grange had lost ground during the hard times after the Panic of 1873 when railroad bankruptcies were frequent and various granger laws were repealed. In 1880, there were only four thousand Grange chapters nationally, compared to twenty thousand in 1874. "But farmers," wrote Theodore Blegen, "had on their palates the taste of organization to advance their social and political interests." The Farmers' Alliance, started in Chicago in 1880, spread widely in the West and South. By the end of 1881, Minnesota had more than eighty local alliances and a state convention. By the end of the decade, the passion of disgruntled farmers had begun planting the seeds for a third party.[28] The aspirations of the Protective and Industrial League, while well intended and ambitious, were out of step with the times.

One can only speculate as to why the agenda of the league grew to such a large scale by going beyond the establishment in its pursuit of political and civil rights. It was now seeking, as Hilyard wrote, "material and practical good for the race," never before initiated by black Minnesotans.[29] Adams continued to encourage his readers to participate in property ownership and real-estate investment. Thomas Lyles and James Hilyard made their fortunes in these activities. They epitomized the potential that existed for industrious black men and women, "a certain class of citizens," and may well have stimulated the expansion of the league's agenda.

Yet, while the league may have expected help from the Republican establishment to support its aspirations, nowhere in Adams's articles preceding the convention was financial support mentioned, let alone the plan to facilitate massive migration of black people to Minnesota. The league's agenda nevertheless reflected a new attitude. As Taylor noted, "The emergence of the Protective and Industrial League in 1887 was a significant milestone in the development of Black vigilance in Minnesota."[30]

Because of a lack of resources, the skills needed to mobilize a statewide organization, and, perhaps, the inability to marshal the small numbers of blacks residing in rural Minnesota counties, the league's plans did not materialize. The fire of vigilance burned brightest in the city where the kindling of outrage was concentrated. The league welcomed all who were committed to advancing black interests and civil rights, and civil rights had become synonymous with black rights, just as it was in the congressional effort to pass the Civil Rights Act of 1875, Minnesota's chapter 224, and the creation of the League. Only an organization whose purpose was to oppose antiblack discrimination could be relied upon to do so.

Adams's *Western Appeal* became the mouthpiece for this effort. It soon gained a national readership and was being published in several cities after changing its name to simply the *Appeal* in order "[t]o lessen its identification exclusively with the Midwest."[31] Adams used his newspaper to connect black Minnesota with black communities throughout the North and provided a forum for race leaders to communicate with his readers.

Timothy Thomas Fortune, now editor of the *Freeman*, a black newspaper, had become a leading ciritic of the rising tide of white supremacy and the neglect of the Republican Party for the welfare of Southern

Timothy Thomas Fortune, circa late 1890s, from *The Negro Problem* (James Pott and Company, 1903).

blacks. Adams periodically reported Fortune's speeches and activities in the *Appeal*. In summer 1887, Adams published a call by Fortune for black people across the country to form local and state leagues that would act in concert to force politicians to review the grievances of blacks. A National Afro-American League later would challenge the national parties to have respect for the black electorate and fight local acts of discrimination.[32]

The issue of legal fees raised by the *Hazel, Wiley,* and *Hamilton* cases prompted Adams to plan for a statewide league in response to Fortune's call. The National Afro-American League was formed. Adams shared many of Fortune's ideas—both men condemned the denial of accommodations to blacks and felt that a national league should provide funds to aggrieved blacks initiating lawsuits—but Adams modified the concept to fit the parameters of the agenda of black Minnesota.[33]

Adams and other black Minnesota leaders rejected a central tenet of Fortune's plan—an organization ostensibly formed to pressure the body politic—and in doing so, illustrated a key difference with the national black experience. Despite their reasons for criticizing Republican complaisance, the exploitation of unskilled black labor, and discrimination faced by the black middle class, the Minnesotans lived in a comparatively benevolent society compared to other states, North and South, and enjoyed relatively benign relationships with the state's Republican power elite. To put it coarsely, Republicans helped pay the bills. Meanwhile, organizations to oppose discrimination were formed in other states.[34] By 1889, Fortune began to plant seeds for a national organization, prompting Adams and others to resurrect a statewide organization. On October 25, 1889, Adams and others met in the law office of Fredrick L. McGhee to plan for a new organization for black men that would convene in Chicago.[35]

By the last decade of the nineteenth century, Minnesota was attracting an expanding number of professional men who also became leaders in many local and national Negro organizations: Fredrick McGhee was one. In fact, a flamboyant McGhee illustrated one more reason for the change in character of black vigilance in Minnesota—its connection to national efforts, and a high quality of leadership skills.

In a sense, these efforts retraced the steps of the Sons of Freedom, who in 1870 had attempted to create a statewide organization to deal with jobs training, help African Americans to acquire property, and track the educational status of black children. It was an ambitious agenda, very much in line with the challenges of Morton Wilkinson, Ignatius Donnelly, and other prominent Republican black suffrage advocates. Their objectives required considerable administrative and financial resources in order to demonstrate the genuine desire of the state's newest citizens to grasp the opportunities that had been granted them in 1868, to vindicate the faith that white Republicans had in them, and to advance both the black race and the enlightened civilization of Minnesota. Now Adams, McGhee, and their colleagues sought a similar agenda, and just as the Sons of Freedom failed because of a lack of resources, so too would the league. In the spirit of racial self-sufficiency, they tried to raise the funds from a community that was mostly poor, for their work was not a priority for Republican leaders. In hopes of gaining resources, the league entered into an alliance with the fiery Timothy Thomas Fortune of New York, whose national agenda included a third-party organization that the Republican establishment condemned. This was the test: who—the African American or the white Republican—should control the agenda for equality? Could there be middle ground?

Anticipating that Fortune would issue a call for a national convention, the Minnesota leaders worked to get their state league organized. At a meeting in McGhee's office they decided to hold a mass meeting on October 31 at Market Hall on the corner of Seventh and St. Peter streets, where they founded the Afro-American League of St. Paul, Minnesota, No.1 (St. Paul League). John Adams chaired the first organizational meeting, and explained the objectives of the league and a proposed constitution that was modeled after a plan developed by Fortune and reflected growing frustration with Republican policies. Fortune's plan declared that the goal of such leagues should be achieved "by the creation of a healthy public opinion through the medium of the press and the pulpit, public meetings and addresses, and by appealing to the courts of law for redress of all denial of civil rights," as stated in section 4 of the new constitution:

> The object of this League shall be conserved by the creation of a healthy public opinion, through the medium of public meetings and addresses, and by appealing to the courts of law for redress of all denial of legal and [U.S.] Constitutional rights; the purpose of this league being to secure the ends desired through peaceable and lawful methods.[36]

As with the Protective and Industrial League, the St. Paul League was to be open to all people over the age of eighteen, regardless of race, creed, or sex. The organization was to be nonpartisan, meaning that "no man shall be debarred from membership therein because of his political opinions." Theoretically, therefore, even an active Democrat could be a member in good standing, provided he "subscrib[ed] to [the league's] constitution and bylaws and payment of fifty cents membership fee, and monthly assessment of twenty-five cents." The constitution contained provisions that had never before been considered for African Americans in the North Star State, including that the league would protest against taxation without representation, the inequitable distribution of school funds, unfair and partial judges and juries, and demand protection against mob violence, as well as arrest and punishment of violators of black legal rights. Some of these provisions may not have been in response to problems faced by black Minnesotans so much as transferred from other states, much the way chapter 224 had been patterned on the Ohio public accommodations statute. Fredrick McGhee, a Mississippi native, had surely known the horror of lynch law. Adams, likewise, whose newspaper was being circulated in other cities, knew firsthand of the sorts of injustices that the provisions were designed to address. And the "no taxation without representation" provision addressed the voting infringements that were now the official policy of every Southern state and effectively invalidated the Fifteenth Amendment. Still, some of these provisions revealed elements of the black Minnesota experience that were far worse than formerly imagined by white society. Despite the ban on school segregation in 1869, most black students in Minnesota were no better positioned to enter as adults into skilled or professional positions. (For now, in most cases, members of the black middle class were recent arrivals to the state and not longtime residents.) Blacks were being found guilty and incarcerated disproportionately. Lynch law (the Combs incident) was an ever-present threat in both the countryside and the city. The league also included a provision that sought "to prosecute all corporations and their employees in State and federal courts" for "violent and insulting conduct" that sought to deny services to black citizens. It was an ugly portrait of the promised land.

This constitution, like that of other leagues, condemned the country's penal system for its "barbarous, cruel and unchristian treatment of convicts," and revived the plan to help Southern blacks migrate "from terror-ridden sections to other and more law-abiding sections." In the revised constitution adopted on December 10, the league further intended "to promote the industrial and moral welfare of the Colored citizens of our city, and to seek for worthy and competent persons, access to the various industrial enterprises, to encourage labor, frugality and honesty." In an effort to fuel the coffers of the national league, each member was expected to contribute one dollar annually for the purpose of financing the group's work. Despite efforts to increase membership, the numbers were apparently low, considering that only nine members constituted a quorum for the transaction of business. Robert F. Anderson was chosen the league's first president, the *Western Appeal* was designated its official organ, and McGhee, Adams, Hilyard, Lyles, and Allen French were elected to the executive committee.[37]

On November 4, 1889, Fortune issued the call for a national convention to create the Afro-American League, and the following January the Minnesota league elected Adams and McGhee as delegates to the Chicago convention.[38] In stark contrast to two years earlier when Republicans opened the doors of the capitol to Minnesota's black delegates of the Protective and Industrial League, the St. Paul League members found it difficult to defray the cost of sending delegates to Chicago, let alone to find a place to hold its meeting on December 30.[39] The Minnesota Republican elite defeated their effort by simply ignoring it.

On January 15, 1890, 141 delegates from twenty-three states assembled in Chicago to form a permanent national organization. Although the largest number of delegates came from the states in the Midwest, seven persons from Georgia attended, as well as delegates from South Carolina, North Carolina, Texas, Tennessee, and Virginia. Only black men were present. No effort had been made to invite interested women or white men even if they were dues-paying members. A few whites, among them Albion W. Tourgee, who would argue for the petitioner in *Plessy v. Ferguson,* sent messages of goodwill, but even such expressions were viewed with suspicion by some delegates who were convinced that white men took an interest in the affairs of black men only to dominate them.[40]

The St. Paul *Daily Pioneer Press* and the Minneapolis *Tribune* reported that Judge Tourgee suggested that the league might be a secret organization "in order that members might not be in danger of murder and outrage in the South." In response, the *Daily Pioneer Press* reported that several delegates opposed Tourgee's suggestion, saying "it was time for the Negroes to show that they could get along without any help from white men."[41] Although they were undoubtedly impressed with the gathering, Adams and McGhee, representing the St. Paul League, who already had strained relations with their white Republican friends because of their association with Fortune, may have felt uncomfortable at the antiwhite atmosphere of the convention. Earl Spangler noted that "The Minnesota group was much less demanding and more fraternal than the national leadership declaration indicated."[42]

As temporary chairman of the convention, Fortune delivered an impassioned speech in which he threw down the gauntlet: "We have been patient so long that many believe that we are incapable of resenting insult, outrage, and wrong; we have so long accepted uncomplainingly all the injustice and cowardice and insolence heaped upon us, that many imagine that we were compelled to submit and have not the manhood necessary to resent such conduct."[43] He ended on a solemn note:

> As the agitation which culminated in the abolition of African slavery in this country covered a period of fifty years, so may we expect that before the rights conferred upon us by the war amendments are fully conceded, a full century will have passed away. We have undertaken no child's play. We have undertaken serious work which will tax and exhaust the best intelligence of the race for the next century.

The convention's constitution built on Fortune's ideas to arouse public opinion against discrimination as well as to initiate lawsuits. The league was to be nonpartisan, and any officer of the organization who was elected or appointed to a political post had to resign his league position. Fortune believed it was imperative to refrain from Republican affiliation in order to prevent the league from being co-opted by either party, as most other black organizations had been. Historian Emma Lou Thornbrough noted: "[Fortune's] insistence upon this point undoubtedly was the reason that few prominent Negro politicians supported the League and one of the reasons why the League did not attract a greater following."[44]

Much of the Northern press pilloried the convention. The Chicago *Tribune,* for example, called Fortune's speech an "oily harangue" and characterized him as "a tricky New York coon" who was playing the part of "a Democratic decoy duck." The *Nation* accused the convention of seeking "class legislation" and said that gatherings like the one in Chicago only strengthened the growing resentment against black people.[45] In St. Paul, however, the *Dispatch* was less harsh in its criticism of the speech. Under the headline "Loud but Not Sensible," the editor wrote: "The opening address by T. Thomas Fortune does not indicate that any substantial gain to the colored race is likely to result from the gathering."[46]

Some delegates took the criticisms to heart. Apparently troubled by the league's militant tone, the more moderate delegates persuaded the convention to bypass Fortune as president, choosing instead a Southerner named Joseph C. Price, president of Livingston College in North Carolina. William Pledger of Georgia became vice president, and Fortune, perhaps as consolation, was elected secretary. The National Afro-American League, at least initially, would be led by moderates. Adams and McGhee shared the moderate view and were placed on the executive committee.[47] Back in St. Paul, the local chapter began a membership drive attempting to draw the entire black community of the city into the organization. As the St. Paul League's official organ, the *Appeal* published notices of its meetings and gave detailed coverage of its activities. Attendance and membership were low, making the league more an organized expression of vigilance by St. Paul's black elite than a manifestation of a fully engaged community. In time, leagues were also formed in Minneapolis, Stillwater, Duluth, Faribault, Anoka, and certain counties, but the local leagues were destined to fade owing to the exceedingly small numbers of members in outstate areas. Before these local chapters began to fade, however, one state convention was held in Minneapolis, in May 1891.[48]

Meanwhile, the national organization was showing signs of decline, failing to attract mass support, exhibiting growing tensions in the ranks. When a second national convention was scheduled to meet in Knoxville, Tennessee, that summer, the St. Paul League submitted a formal petition to the national body protesting against meeting in that city because of Tennessee's adoption of the discriminatory "separate coach" act. Despite this protest, the Knoxville convention and the St. Paul delegation were forced to accept Jim Crow accommodations on a Tennessee railroad. Attendance was sparse. Those who came paid their own expenses because the local leagues lacked funds. Fortune was elected president but he was unable to carry out any part of the program he first proposed for the still black-only league.[49]

Relaxing the rules, guidelines for the convention were amended to allow the league to take political action "which was regarded as being for the good of the race."[50] This provision was probably intended to allow the organization to appeal to and advocate for established parties, mainly the Republicans. The ban on holding political office by league officers was also dropped.[51] In addition to a debilitating lack of funds, another critical problem facing the league was its inability to attract the support of black political leaders across the country who could lend credibility to its efforts. At this point, survival made for strange bedfellows. Clearly, these two amendments were not enough to rejuvenate the league. Fortune needed something more.

He decided that nothing but a righteous crusade could galvanize support and that would be a major test case against discrimination, not one that sought remedy for an isolated discriminatory act violating state law but one that challenged a discriminatory state law itself. But Fortune's efforts eventually were frustrated. Serious consideration was given to instituting a case after a member of the Afro-American League, who was traveling by railroad in Tennessee, was compelled to leave a Pullman car and ride in the Jim Crow coach.

St. Paul League member Samuel Hardy had purchased a first-class ticket to Knoxville where the national league convention was convening. After the train crossed into Tennessee, the conductor ordered him to move to the "black" car in compliance with a four-month-old statute requiring segregated passenger cars. Conductors and railroads that did not enforce the new law were subject to fines. Unfortunately, the league treasury was empty. Back in St. Paul, league members sought to remedy the shortage of funds. As Adams reported in the *Appeal*:

> The separate car bill which was recently enacted in Tennessee has raised a storm of indignation throughout the country in which both the Colored and fair-minded white people join. The Afro-American citizens of Minnesota have taken the lead in starting a fund to test the law and in holding a mass meeting to express their condemnation and indignation.[52]

A meeting of St. Paul blacks was held on August 25, 1891, at Pilgrim Baptist Church. Out of it was born the Minnesota Civil Rights Committee, whose purpose was to assist the local league in raising funds to test the legality of Tennessee's "separate coach" act. But by September it was clear that the St. Paul chapter's efforts were insufficient to help the national league challenge the Tennessee law. A discouraged Fortune pointed out that it was "tomfoolery" for a group without funds to try to sue a railroad.[53] But he was able to reach a settlement with the Pullman Company. At an informal meeting with Fortune, Reverend W. H. Heard, Hardy (another

St. Paul delegate), and representatives of the Pullman Company agreed to discharge the offending Pullman conductor and reimburse Heard for the price of his ticket.[54] It was an empty victory. Nothing of significance was changed except that a conductor lost his job for following state law. Hardy and the St. Paul League wanted to pursue the case on principle.

On November 17, 1891, the St. Paul League held a mass meeting to raise funds, enough to file papers and defray some of McGhee's costs, but it could not pay for long-distance litigation. McGhee did not base his complaint on constitutional grounds—a legal theory that probably would have been rejected by the U.S. Supreme Court, which would soon decide that separate but equal was constitutional. Instead, he used the breach-of-contract theory that had been relatively successful in similar cases. According to that theory, by selling Hardy a first-class ticket, the railroad agreed to grant Hardy a first-class seat.[55]

However, the case stood no chance of succeeding. As Paul Nelson noted, "No plaintiff's case can survive for witness fees, travel expenses, secretarial work, stenographer's costs, not to mention a dollar here and there for the lawyer."[56] On November 16, 1892, one year to the day of the mass fund-raiser in St. Paul, the federal district court in Chattanooga was finally ready to hear *Hardy v. East Tennessee, Georgia, and Virginia Railway Company;* neither plaintiff Hardy nor his counsel, Fredrick McGhee, was present. The judge dismissed the case.[57]

The St. Paul League and the Civil Rights Committee shifted their fund-raising efforts to a similar test case in Oklahoma, but the effort was likewise futile. Attempting to challenge "separate coach" laws around the country became the St. Paul League's last major legal undertaking for many years and the effort was met with mounting frustration as a growing number of cases were lost in court. Disillusionment set in when league members saw racism become institutionalized and the national organization remained impotent. By 1893, the St. Paul League and the Civil Rights Committee both began to fade. In August of that year, Fortune announced that the league was defunct because of lack of funds, lack of mass support, and lack of support from race leaders. He declared himself thoroughly discouraged and disillusioned, and concluded that the attempt to organize the league had been premature.[58]

Whether "prematurity" explained the failure of the national league is subject to debate. Here, for the first time, black men from around the country met to deliberate over the best means to secure the civil rights of black America, and they did it without sustainable resources, which meant the endorsement and participation of white men of means. Certainly, the low attendance and diminishing membership among black men from across the country crippled the organization's prospect of vitality, but the problem was twofold: there was little support from black America, to be sure, but its leadership was also unacceptable to the nation's establishment. Neither black nor white America was prepared to listen to the militant voice of Thomas Fortune.[59]

The St. Paul delegation itself, though sympathetic to many of Fortune's views and sincere in its support of the national leader, recognized the need to tread cautiously on the political landscape in their state. McGhee and Adams were now both active members of the Republican Party.[60] To them, the league, at least as far as the St. Paul chapter was concerned, was to be nonpolitical. In other words, the convention that was expected to attract black community leaders from across the nation would not become a springboard for a third party for black voters. Indeed, those facilitating the convention were as respectable and as loyal as St. Paul's own delegates. On January 11, 1890, to mollify his black and white readers, Adams stated:

> It is personally understood that the [national league] meeting has *no political significance,* and politics has no part therein. This is a movement inaugurated by the younger and more progressive elements of the Colored people, and the convention will be composed mainly from the men of this class.[61]

The *Appeal* was telling the Republican establishment that it did not need to worry. It was denying a national political agenda. But the reverberation of Fortune's fiery speech spoke louder than Adams's assurances to the contrary and provoked the more combative elements of the national press to let free their fury. This time the response of the Republican establishment would be punishing.

When the league was not being pilloried for being too outrageous and too exclusionary (because of its alleged lack of Southern delegates), it was being trivialized in the white press. The St. Paul *Daily Pioneer Press,* after mentioning that St. Paul's J. Q. Adams was one of the league's vice presidents, rebuked the black delegates for rejecting the "help" offered by white men and chided the New York delegate who proposed a sarcastic resolution opposing U.S. Senator M. C. Butler's well-publicized migration bill to send blacks to Africa.[62] The resolution, which the delegates unanimously adopted in the spirit intended, called on Congress to provide aid to help Southern white men who did not want to live near Southern blacks migrate.[63] The actual goals of the league seemed less newsworthy to the *Pioneer Press,* for they were printed on page 9 without editorial comment, in contrast to the criticism of the delegates that appeared on the front page.[64] Ultimately, the delegates' failure to convert the true spirit of the convention into a sustainable organization stemmed in part not from "prematurity" but from these reports. After three days of meetings, a constitution, a called rebuke of benevolent white men, and a resolution to request Congress to appropriate $100 million to help unhappy white citizens of three states settle where no blacks lived were all that the delegates reportedly achieved, according to the only source available— the white newspapers.[65]

To readers of those newspapers, the accomplishments of black men hardly seemed substantive. It fell to the *Appeal* to provide a more complete picture of the events, but even here there was a problem. In an apparent fund-raising effort, the National Afro-American League leaders compiled a complete record of the convention to be sold to interested persons across the country.[66] The *Appeal* could not afford to purchase the record and did not choose to report the event. Readers of the *Appeal* did, however, learn of squabbling among black delegates.[67] Indeed, the *Appeal* itself reflected the weakening of the organization. It had lost too much money on league adventures and Adams was determined to recoup the losses by printing what subscribers really wanted to pay for: stories about themselves.

In issues appearing throughout 1890, the National Afro-American League was hardly mentioned by the *Appeal*. Increasingly, pages were filled with social news from Minneapolis, Chicago, St. Louis, and St. Paul. Prominently displayed on its front pages during the fall and winter months was a contest inviting readers to vote for the best preacher in America. Newly arrived black professionals setting up offices in St. Paul were profiled. Now, one page was dedicated to the vanity of persons who bought space to announce weddings, interments, travels, vacations, and graduations. The first page of each issue was reserved for reports on black colleges in the South. A Jewish feast was planned at St. James African Methodist Episcopal church.[68] A feature appeared on the Dakota people.[69] In May, the following article appeared:

> W. E. B. Dubois, a young colored man recently won the Boylston prize for declamation at Harvard College. About the same time Godfrey the Colored pugilist of Boston knocked out Patsey Cardiff of Minneapolis in 16 rounds. Muscle and mind, brain and brawn or science and sense seem to be a somewhat characteristic of the Afro-American lately. Did you notice it?[70]

Throughout 1890, crammed into an innocuous box on a crowded page filled with yet more social news, an article on lynching appeared.[71] In another article, black waiters in St. Paul restaurants enjoyed the results of a successful strike for higher wages as they saw their pay increase from $7.50 to $10 a week.[72] In November, the *Appeal* reported in disbelief that Mississippi would actually amend its state constitution in a way that would disenfranchise black voters.[73] And in a letter printed in the November 22 issue, the writer wanted "to see new life put into the Afro-American League of St. Paul." A meeting was held within the week, and plans to reflect this "new life" were announced.[74] For the most part, however, society news of the black middle class dominated the pages, for it was they rather than poorer blacks who were likelier to be subscribers: people loved to read about themselves.

During the same period, the Blair bill in Congress for federal aid to public education and the Lodge bill for the supervision of federal elections were defeated. In the South, Mississippi led the way calling for a state constitutional convention to pass a new suffrage law for the avowed purpose of disenfranchising black voters, in direct contravention of the original intent of the drafters of the Fourteenth and Fifteenth Amendments. A result of its new suffrage law was that 123,000 Mississippi black voters lost their right to vote practically overnight.

In quick succession South Carolina, Louisiana, and North Carolina followed suit, installing such infamous procedures as restrictive property and educational requirements, the poll tax, and the grandfather clause.

Within four years, the number of registered black voters in Louisiana dropped from 130,344 to 5,320. Lynchings increased. In the twenty years following the U.S. Supreme Court's decision in the *Civil Rights Cases*, three thousand lynchings occurred. "Almost certainly," wrote Richard Kluger, "many others went unreported. Because they were carried out with impunity . . . no black man anywhere any time could feel secure. He always had to be on his mettle or risk providing the kindling for the quickly stirred mob's Saturday night spectacle."[75] And in Minnesota, where these offenses were not happening, discrimination nonetheless persisted: "Colored men and women in St. Paul, habitually avoid places of accommodations of the public. Young men engaged in business, seek Colored boarding houses often at the expense of time and great inconvenience. Why? [It is] not always from choice, but because prudence dictates such a course unless they are willing to 'pocket' insults or have recourse to the law."[76]

In short, the St. Paul League had an ample number of initiatives to pursue. However, following its practice of reserving most of the first two pages of the *Appeal* for society news, an announcement was placed for a celebration to commemorate the anniversary of the Emancipation Proclamation to be held on January 1 at the St. Paul Armory, for which admission was charged.[77] The *Appeal* and the St. Paul League, it appeared, were out of step with the needs of most black Minnesotans. "At the appointed hour [of the celebration of the Emancipation Proclamation]," reported Adams, "the Armory contained a fair representation of the most intelligent portion of the Colored citizens of St. Paul and a small sprinkling of the right sort of white ones who had gathered to show their appreciation of God's work in freeing 3,000,000 slaves and by their presence and words attesting thereto." Many of the state's political leadership were invited, including Governor W. R. Merriam and Ignatius Donnelly. Although none attended, they did send letters of regret.

In the absence of state leaders, the men who spoke applauded efforts of the country to end slavery, supported interracial marriage, and expressed concern over the rising militancy of farmer activists. In the last "very sensible speech" delivered before a rally committed to public accommodations, the Reverend D. P. Brown proudly stated that he was not ashamed to be a colored man and therefore would never ask to be admitted to the homes of whites unless they wanted him under equal terms, seemingly taking a position that he was opposed to social equality. He urged black people to acquire homes and improve cultural opportunities, and not to impose themselves upon anyone, but to act like honest people who have self-pride.[78]

The *Appeal* expressed satisfaction with the proceedings: "After the foregoing exercises were concluded, [St. Paul League] President Hardy thanked the audience and speakers, and invited them to the banquet, which was served in the arsenal. After the appetites of the people had been satisfied, dancing was indulged in for a couple of hours, and then all adjourned to their homes and the celebration was numbered among the things of the past."[79] Only two of the four St. Paul dailies covered the celebration; Minneapolis papers ignored it altogether. "Overall," commented Paul Nelson, "the rally did not seem to have the desired effect of provoking public debate on race or inciting greater interest in the Afro-American League."[80]

Throughout 1890, league leaders returned to the political fold. As the St. Paul chapter languished in inactivity, leaders stepped up their participation in the Republican Party. The *Appeal* reported on the activities of chapter leaders Lyles, McGhee, and Adams at Ramsey County party caucus meetings, as if showcasing important connections they were cultivating.[81] These activities contravened one of the tenets of the national league that expressly rejected party affiliation, yet the St. Paul leaguers assiduously courted party officials both to regain Republican favor and to gain access to the resources the party controlled. As the November 1890 elections approached, black endorsements for Republican candidates began to appear with greater frequency in the *Appeal*. The recently formed Afro-American Republican Club (AARC), meeting in the County Caucus Rooms in the stately Endicott Building, adopted as an organizational objective "to forward the interests and diffuse the principles of Republicanism" and endorsed the reelection of Governor William Merriam and the entire Republican ticket. A list of club members contained the name of every active St. Paul League member. At the same time, another organization, called the Colored Citizens' Union, many of whose members belonged to the AARC, also endorsed Governor Merriam and the Republican ticket.[82]

For their loyalty, the party made sure that its luminaries would be available for the next major celebration—the state Afro-American League convention to be held in Minneapolis on May 27, 1891. This time, unlike the St. Paul League's celebration on January 1, the governor attended the convention, accompanied by U.S. Senator Cushman Davis, the Honorable

Charles A. Pillsbury, Minneapolis mayor P. B. Winston, and John Good-man, president of the state Republican Club. McGhee, Lyles, and F. H. Shelton of Duluth were scheduled to speak. The *Appeal* heralded the event: "This will be the greatest social gathering of Afro-Americans citizens ever held in this state."[83] In late June, the league planned to circulate a petition against the Tennessee separate car law, and Republican political leaders made the caucus room at the capitol available for the meeting.[84] But a space in which to confer was all they offered. Because the league had no resources with which to launch a significant campaign, by July the petition effort was abandoned.[85]

Essentially, the league was incapable of functioning. Its leaders knew the state's political and religious movers and shakers, but their influence went no further than mere acquaintance. St. Paul League coffers were as empty as the national league's. The league's dormancy following the national league convention in Chicago and the insolvency of the St. Paul League reflected a serious lack of organizational skills. Having worked together so intimately, its leaders had formed a clique and become isolated from the community outside their own social class. Thus, they could not galvanize the black population by pursuing an agenda that the local population could support. Sending their hard-earned dollars to pay for a lawsuit in Tennessee did not seem practical. And issues that were meaningful to local blacks fell into disfavor with the Republican establishment. The league was stuck in impotency. It hosted more festivals that celebrated itself and white Republicans who provided spaces for the group to meet.

Since the *Hazel* case, which launched the organization with a goal of aiding in the prosecution of civil-rights cases, the league had done nothing to address persisting discrimination against St. Paul's black citizens. As one critic bitterly stated in a letter to the editor, "One of the most precious pieces of humbuggery to which long-suffering people have been subjected to, is that monumental sham known as the National Afro-American League; and of all its gaseous offspring, the St. Paul League heads the list for bombast and absolute vacuity."[86] The author attacked the two key black speakers at the Emancipation Proclamation celebration—the Reverend D. P. Brown and attorney Fredrick McGhee. By virtue of inviting to the dais a speaker who condemned social equality, the St. Paul League was out of step with the realities of black Minnesota. The letter writer attacked McGhee first: "[McGhee said,] 'The sun of our perfect freedom is rising in the Northwest. Education on the question is flowing from here and we are creating a sentiment which will spread throughout the country.' How much of this did the orator believe? How much did his audience believe? How much of it was true?"

Why, he asked, did an organization ostensibly created to fight the denial of social equality invite Reverend Brown to speak when he did not believe in the principle? Was the league, in fact, guilty of lethargy, or betrayal? "There is not a colored man—the writer cares not who he may be—who dares take his wife or daughter into a respectable eating house in this city with any assurance that he or they will not be liable to the insult of refusal, which he must 'pocket' or fight. Local leagues have remained quiescent while wrongs they were designed to confront have been perpet-uated under their very eyes. It wakes to life only when there is an occasion for feasting or a chance for a few individuals to emerge from their native obscurity, pose for a moment in the public's gaze, and indulge in sounding declamation which deceives no one—not even themselves."

The writer attacked black reliance on the white Republican patron: "Freedom and citizenship were gifts from a race that still had the power to withhold, yet with all compelling freedom and citizenship within its grasp, the race is quite content to sit quietly by until its civil rights drop into its lap—like overripe fruit without even lifting up a hand to shake the tree.[87] He then attacked the *Appeal:* "Our newspapers are dumb, or at best dole out perfunctory half column of stock indignation so lacking in spirit that it fails to stir a single impulse."[88]

Finally, he attacked the league leadership: "Meanwhile one last word for the League, that organization owes it to the citizens of St. Paul that it should shut up and do something worthy of its name; let the officers who are alleged to be running it, step down and out, and give someone a chance who has some other purpose to serve than to gain a little cheap notoriety. A league that has never had a dollar in its treasury, is worse than powerless, it is a delusion and a snare, and is worthy only of contempt. Get down, 'Gentlemen,' and if there are any men in St. Paul, give them a chance."[89]

The critic signed his name "W. A. Hazel."

8

PROFESSOR WASHINGTON, LEADER OF THE RACE

"You can be sure of the future, as in the past, that you and your families will be surrounded by the most patient, faithful, law-abiding, and unresentful people that the world has seen."

—BOOKER T. WASHINGTON, Atlanta Cotton States and International Exposition, 1895

William Hazel's fundamental complaint against the league was the lack of sound leadership. It did not aggressively confront discrimination in St. Paul. Instead, it frittered away the meager funds that humble people donated on hopeless lawsuits in other states where the law was stacked against a positive ruling. That money could have been spent in St. Paul. The league's goals were good, but its methods were bankrupt, and because its members talked and socialized with each other, they were insular and stale, preferring their self-satisfied status of "community leader" without a community larger than themselves. They relied unhealthily on white Republican patrons who supported their businesses and social activities, but not the right of the league to think for itself. Worse, the league allowed white men to select the "leader of the race," a person who suited their own agenda.

The St. Paul *Dispatch* was especially critical of Fortune's speech at the national league convention, describing it as "incendiary" and condemning him as disingenuous: "Given the expression to incite, as it has been, by a gentleman whose individual, social and political rights are about as secure as they can well be, and whose personal experience is probably confined entirely to northern communities, it possesses force and significance in an inverse ratio to vehemence." The editor was particularly incensed when Fortune reportedly said, "We have been robbed of honest wages for our toil; we have been robbed of the substance of our citizenship by murder and intimidation; we have been outraged by our enemies and deserted by our friends."[1]

"Who has been robbed, and by whom?" the *Dispatch* asked. The savagery of Southern white supremacy paled in contrast to Fortune's lack of gratitude. To the *Dispatch*, Fortune was a Northern black man who enjoyed voting rights, financial security from his successful business, and nationwide respect. Indeed, by virtue of being from the North, the editor seemed to say, this middle-class black man—the sort of person likeliest to be a league delegate—had nothing to complain about. In fact, Northern blacks were not qualified to criticize America's race problem:

> The delegates of the convention at Chicago were entirely from the northern communities. There are none, we are informed, from the Southern states. Mr. Fortune and his fellow Afro-American delegates are all reasonably secure in their social and political rights. They ought to speak for themselves. Mere similarity of race does not entitle them to speak for those Americans citizens whose civil rights are said to be invaded by the Southern white man. The country does not want to hear from Mr. Fortune. It wants to hear, if at all, from those who have cause of complaint.[2]

In fact, Fortune was Southern-born. Although he had made his reputation in the North, he knew from personal experience what it was to be a black man in the Deep South. Born a slave in 1856 and growing up in Marianna, Florida, he saw the Ku Klux Klan in action perpetrating some of the worst outrages imaginable. Joseph Price, the first president of the national league, and his vice president, William Pledger, were both from the Deep South. Many of the delegates, while coming from Northern states, had roots in the South, where many of their family members continued to live, something the *Dispatch* conveniently overlooked.

The expense of traveling to the distant northern city of Chicago from anywhere in the Deep South for a three-day convention was prohibitive for most black men, but it was the personal risk of being identified as a race man to white supremacists who lived in their community that made such a trip, as well as returning home, life-threatening. None of this mattered to the *Dispatch*. Misinformed and ill-tempered, the *Dispatch* nonetheless reflected a part of white America that was only willing to listen to race leaders they chose rather than those chosen by black America:

> There are teachers and ministers and editors in the South among the blacks, as well as men engaged in the productive industries. Why can they not be heard from as well as the politicians? The Southern white has had the floor for a long time on the subject. Let us hear authoritatively from the southern black, and let his spokesman not be chosen from among those we are hunting for federal offices. Mr. Fortune's convention does not fill the bill.[3]

It was not that the *Dispatch* sought a Southern black to speak, for there were several at the convention; the *Dispatch* wanted a *certain* Southern black to speak. Not until 1895 would a black man the *Dispatch* could support be introduced to the nation as the officially sanctioned "leader of his race."[4]

Booker T. Washington, anointed by organizers of the Atlanta Cotton States and International Exposition as "representative of the Negro race," left his home in Tuskegee, Alabama, with his wife and three children to meet his destiny in the most cosmopolitan city in the Deep South, Atlanta, Georgia. There he would deliver a five-minute speech that would be heard and hailed throughout the nation. The year was 1895. "I felt," he wrote, "a good deal as I suppose a man feels when he is on his way to the gallows." In passing through Tuskegee, he met a white farmer who said to him, in a jesting manner, "Washington, you have spoken before the Northern white people, the Negroes in the South, and to us country white people in the South; but in Atlanta, to-morrow, you will have spoken before the Northern whites, the southern whites, and the Negroes all together.

Booker T. Washington, circa 1890s. Library of Congress Prints and Photographs Division.

I am afraid that you have got yourself into a tight place." Washington commented, "This farmer diagnosed the situation correctly, but his frank words did not add anything to my comfort."[5]

The Atlanta address was only the third major speech that Washington delivered on the larger issue of race relations. Although he had indeed spoken on several occasions to raise money for Tuskegee, rarely did he venture into the quagmire of one of America's most painful matters. His first effort to do so occurred in Madison, Wisconsin, two years earlier before the National Education Association. In that speech he stressed the importance of bringing the races together "by every honorable means" available "instead of doing that which would embitter" (118–19).

"I further contended that, in relation to his vote, the Negro should more and more consider the interests of the community in which he lived, rather than seek alone to please someone who lived a thousand miles away from him, and from his interests." Evidently, asserting one's rights by electing candidates to advance civil rights was not in the immediate interest of Southern blacks as much as it was in the interest of others from outside the region. In the Madison address, Washington pressed a theme that he would develop more fully in Atlanta: the future of the Negro race "rested largely on the question as to whether or not he should make himself, through his skill, intelligence, and character, of such undeniable value to the community in which he lived that the community could not dispense with his presence" (118).

He said that "any individual who learned to do something better than anybody else—learned to do a common thing in an uncommon manner—had solved his problem, regardless of the color of his skin," and that respect for the Negro would correspond in the same proportion to his ability to produce what other people wanted. He told of how one of his graduates produced 266 bushels of sweet potatoes from one acre in a community where the average production was forty-nine bushels to the acre, and that white farmers respected him and came to him for ideas about the reason for his success. He said that these white farmers honored and respected him for his skill and knowledge, and he had "added something to the wealth and the comfort of the community in which he lived" (ibid.).

Washington believed that his theory of education for the Negro would not confine him to work on the farm forever, "but that if he succeeded in this line of industry he could lay the foundations upon which his children and grandchildren could grow to higher and more important things in life." "Since that time," he wrote, "I have not found any reason for changing my views on any important point," and it would be these views that formed the basis of his more notable speech to be delivered at the Atlanta Exposition two years later (ibid.).

Black and white people alike flocked to Washington's train as it made its way from Tuskegee to Atlanta, standing alongside the tracks, pointing out Washington, and talking hopefully about what was to happen the next day. Washington reported later hearing an Atlanta black man say, "Dat's de man of my race what's gwine to make a speech at the exposition tomorrow. I'se sho gwine to hear him." Washington found the city of Atlanta to be crowded with people from all parts of the country and with representatives from foreign governments present to assess whether the new South had indeed—as advertised—solved its Negro Problem. Civic and military organizations were also present, and the afternoon newspapers all printed anticipatory articles of the proceedings to occur the next day. Washington noted:

> All this tended to add to my burden. I did not sleep much that night. The next morning, before day, I went carefully over what I intended to say. I also kneeled down and asked God's blessing upon my effort. Right here, perhaps, I ought to add that I make it a rule never to go before an audience, on any occasion, without asking the blessing of God upon what I want to say.

The next day a committee came to escort Washington to his place in the procession that would march to the exposition grounds. In this procession were several Negro military units and prominent black residents of Atlanta, all riding in carriages that followed Washington's, in deference to the station to which he had been anointed. "I noted that the Exposition officials seemed to go out of their way to see that all of the colored people in the procession were properly placed and properly treated." It took three hours to reach the grounds, under a scorching Georgia sun, which, compounded by anxiety, made him feel ready to collapse in fear that his address was not going to be a success. He was stunned by what he saw inside the hall (125–26).

The auditorium was packed "with humanity from bottom to top," and there were thousands of people standing outside unable to get in. When he entered the room, the blacks in the audience erupted in cheers while the whites responded in a more subdued manner. Earlier, he had been told that while many white people were going to be present to hear him speak, simply out of curiosity, many would be there out of genuine sympathy for him and his people. But there was "a larger element in the audience" consisting of those who were going to be present for the purpose of hearing Washington make a fool of himself, or at least "say some foolish thing so that they could say to the officials who had invited him to speak, 'I told you so'" (126–27).

He nonetheless desired "to say something that would cement the friendship of the races and bring about hearty cooperation between them."

At last it was Washington's turn to speak. He was introduced by former Georgia Governor Rufus Bullock: "We have with us today a representative of negro enterprise and Negro civilization." As he approached the microphone, Washington "saw thousands looking intently into his face." Meanwhile, William H. Baldwin, a personal friend and trustee of the Tuskegee Institute as well as general manager of the Southern Railroad, was in Atlanta at the time but he was too nervous to go inside to hear his friend speak, and chose instead to pace back and forth on the grounds outside (126).

The organizers could not have known that Washington's appearance was the drama of the exposition. Instead, they were focused on showing to the world how the feudalistic Old Confederacy had been transformed into a modern commercial and (if they were successful) international center. In 1895, Atlanta symbolized the politically restored and economically reviving South. In the thirty years since Union General William Sherman had ordered his troops to put the torch to the city, it had been entirely rebuilt. Atlanta was turning into the rail and industrial hub of the burgeoning Southeast as the whole region began to attract such titans of industry as Mellon, Rockefeller, and J. P. Morgan, who had just organized the Southern Railway system.[6]

To celebrate Atlanta's success, city leaders decided to organize the closest thing to a world's fair the South had ever seen, immodestly called the Atlanta Cotton States and International Exposition. The organizers were some of the most progressive thinkers in the region, and they wanted to include a pavilion recognizing the progress achieved by Southern blacks since acquiring their freedom, in order to assure outside investors that the South, despite the proliferation of national and international headlines of lynchings and racial strife, "was kindly disposed to its black population" and coping well with the so-called Negro Problem. In Minnesota, the editor of the St. Paul *Pioneer Press* was impressed.[7]

"Washington felt that the Atlanta Exposition would present an opportunity for both races to show what advances they had made since freedom, and would at the same time afford encouragement to them to make still greater progress."[8] To underscore the point, they looked to "a beautifully mannered ex-slave" who had done ennobling work to uplift his people at the school he ran in Tuskegee, Alabama.[9]

The organizers had heard of Washington's abilities from a widening circle of influential friends he made while traveling throughout the North to raise money for Tuskegee. In 1895, he was asked to accompany a delegation of Atlanta businessmen going to Congress to seek federal money to hold their exposition. Although Washington was the last man to speak before the congressional committee, he undoubtedly contributed to the success of the mission, emphasizing the need to assist the intellectual and material growth of *both* races.[10]

Rather than promote the exposition per se, Washington spoke more broadly of the need for racial and sectional reconciliation. He insisted that the Negro should not be robbed of his vote "by unfair means" and argued that political agitation alone would not advance his cause. In other words, he condemned any organized black political initiative, the likes of which had appeared during the earliest stages of the Populist movement, that threatened the established Republican and Democratic leaderships alike. The suffrage movement must rest upon property, industry, skill, economy, intelligence, and character.[11]

Here at last, the nation's leaders must have reasoned, was an impressive black leader who truly understood the needs of his people, his region, and his nation. Here was a man who could relieve them of the burden of shame. "Within a few moments after Washington had concluded his remarks," wrote historian Rayford Logan, "the committee unanimously agreed to recommend the requested appropriation." Washington's comments also "opened the eyes of Atlanta leaders to [his] remarkable powers of persuasion."[12] On September 18, in a five-minute speech, Booker T. Washington secured his place in history.

The opening lines struck a key point of his address. He reminded the audience that one-third of the Southern population was of the black race, and that "no enterprise seeking material, civil, or moral welfare of this section can disregard this element of our population and reach the highest success." What was good for black people was good for the region, and vice versa. He praised the managers of the exposition for including his people in the festivities, and characterized the gesture as "recognition that they will do more to cement the friendship of the two races than any occurrence since the dawn of our freedom." He then ridiculed members of his own race for striving to begin "at the top instead of at the bottom; that a seat in Congress or the state legislature was more sought than real estate or industrial skill, and that the political convention or stump speaking had more attraction than starting a dairy farm or truck garden."[13]

To his black listeners he told the story of a ship lost at sea that, after many days, sighted "a friendly vessel." "Water, water," called sailors on the lost ship, "we die of thirst!" The answer from the friendly vessel came back: "Cast down your bucket where you are." The lost ship again called out, "Water, water, we die of thirst!" Again, the friendly vessel responded, "Cast down your bucket where you are." And so it went, one more time: the lost ship calling for water—*we die of thirst!*—and again, in the nautical wisdom of a landlubber, Washington repeated that the friendly vessel called back to the lost crew to quench their thirst on seawater. To the president of Tuskegee, this allegory bespoke an inner truth for those of his race who depended on bettering their condition "in a foreign land"— namely, the American South—or who underestimated the importance of cultivating friendly relations with the Southern white man, "who is their next door neighbor." "I would say, 'Cast down your bucket where you are'—cast it down in making friends in every manly way of the people of all races by whom we are surrounded" (128).

Washington further challenged blacks "to cast it down" in agriculture, mechanics, commerce, and domestic service, as well as the professions; in this context, he argued, "it is in the South, that the Negro is given a man's chance in the commercial world, and in nothing is this Exposition more eloquent than in emphasizing this chance." Then he stated "our greatest danger":

> Our greatest danger is that in the great leap from slavery to freedom we may overlook the fact that the masses of us are to live by the productions of our hands, and fail to keep in mind that we shall prosper in proportion as we learn to dignify and glorify common labor and put brains and skill into the common occupations of life; shall prosper in proportion as we learn to draw the line between the superficial and the substantial, the ornamental gee-gaws of life and the useful. No race can prosper till it learns that there is as much dignity in tilling a field as in writing a poem. It is at the bottom of life we must begin, and not at the top. Nor shall we permit our grievances to overshadow our opportunities. (128–29)

To whites who were mindful of the increasing arrival of immigrants with "strange tongue and habits" to American shores, Washington proclaimed

his race to be loyal to Southern values and more grateful to Southern benef-
icence in a way the foreigners could never be, loyal to employers, landown-
ers, and investors, and therefore more worthy of their high regard. Here he
repeated the refrain: he told them where they could put their bucket:

> Cast down your bucket where you are. Cast it down among the eight
> millions of Negroes whose habits you know, whose fidelity and love
> you have tested in days when to have proved treacherous meant the
> ruin of your firesides. Cast down your bucket among these people who
> have, without strikes and labor wars, tilled your fields, cleared your for-
> ests, built your railroads and cities, and brought forth treasures from the
> bowels of the earth, and helped make possible this magnificent repre-
> sentation of the progress of the South. (129)

"Help me educate my people, head, hand, and heart," he said, and they
will use that education to buy "surplus land" (farmland that no one else
wanted), "make blossom the waste places in your fields, and run your fac-
tories." In casting down the bucket, in Washington's sentimental world,
past loyalties would beget future loyalties:

> [Y]ou could be sure in the future, as in the past, that you and your
> families will be surrounded by the most patient, faithful, law-abiding,
> and unresentful people that the world has seen. As we have proved our
> loyalty to you in the past, in nursing your children, watching by the
> sick-bed of your mothers and fathers, and often following them with
> tear-dimmed eyes to their graves, so in the future, in our humble way,
> we shall stay by you with a devotion that no foreigner can approach,
> ready to lay down our lives, if need be, in defense of yours, interlacing
> our industrial, commercial, civil, and religious life with yours in a way
> that shall make the interests of both races one. (Ibid.)

He then assuaged any concern that the audience might have had about
his views on integration: "In all things that are purely social, we can be as
separate as the fingers, yet one as the hand in all things essential to mutual
progress" (ibid.).

He again praised the organizers of the exposition for exhibiting
Southern black progress, but quickly asserted that little of this progress

could have occurred without the aid and support "not only from Southern states, but especially from Northern philanthropists, who have made their gifts a constant stream of blessing and encouragement." Accordingly, "the wisest among my race understand that the agitation of questions of social equality is the extremest folly, and that progress in the enjoyment of all privileges that will come to us must be the result of severe and constant struggle rather than artificial forcing" (131).

In other words, it was wrong for blacks to believe that they should compel whites to view blacks as their equals until blacks had proven themselves worthy. "It is important and right that all privileges of the law be ours, but it is vastly more important that we be prepared for the exercises of these privileges." Blacks must be sober and modest in demeanor and in their aspirations, not pretentious and frivolous. "The opportunity to earn a dollar in a factory just now is worth infinitely more than the opportunity to spend a dollar in an opera house":

> In conclusion, may I repeat that nothing in thirty years has given us more hope and encouragement, and drawn us so near to you of the white race, as this opportunity offered by the Exposition; and her bending, as it were, over the altar that represents the results of the struggles of your race and mine, both starting practically empty-handed three decades ago. I pledge that in your effort to work out the great and intricate problem which God has laid at the doors of the South, you shall have at all times the patient, sympathetic help of my race; only let this constantly stay in mind, that, while from representations in these buildings of the product of field, of forest, of mine, of factory, letters, and art, much good will come, yet far above and beyond material benefits will be that higher good, that, let us pray God, will come, in a blotting out sectional differences and racial animosities and suspicions, in a determination to administer absolute justice, in a willing obedience among all classes to the mandates of law. This, this, coupled with our material prosperity, will bring into our beloved South a new heaven and a new earth. (Ibid.)

When he finished, black and white listeners alike erupted in applause. In a breach of Southern etiquette, former governor Bullock rushed across the stage to shake his hand. The volume of applause from the white people had hardly been witnessed before in the South. Congratulatory telegrams began to pour in from all parts of the nation. Washington was mobbed on the streets of Atlanta, and, after arriving home in Tuskegee, he could scarcely walk the streets without well-wishers approaching him. For days, newspapers across the nation rhapsodized about the brilliance of his speech and how it was the most significant step toward racial and sectional reconciliation. Requests to speak arrived almost daily. One lecture bureau offered him fifty thousand dollars, which Washington declined.[14] Former president Cleveland, to whom Washington had sent his address, thanked him "with much enthusiasm for making the address." In his letter to Washington, he added, "Your words cannot fail to delight and encourage all who wish well of your race, and if our colored fellow-citizens do not from your utterances gather new hope and form new determinations to gain every valuable advantage offered them by their relationship, it will be strange indeed."[15]

Even Harvard University was swept up in the fever when, a year later, it bestowed on Washington an honorary degree—the first time a New England university would so recognize the achievements of a black man.[16] Washington dissuaded black voters from political activism while mollifying white supremacists who perpetrated atrocities that embarrassed the nation to the world. His philosophy of accommodation promised acceptance of the status quo. For commercial interests in both the Republican and Democratic parties, the economic benefits were immeasurable: Washington offered cheap and useful labor that would benefit the employer.

The reaction in Minnesota was somewhat different. It was doubtful that the average white Minnesotan cared much about the exposition or Washington's speech because both addressed issues and places far removed from their daily experience. The reaction of the state's chief opinion makers was striking in their low-key assessment of the events, in contrast to the optimism they felt for sectional reconciliation. The editor of the St. Paul *Dispatch* wrote:

> The cordial manner in which the Northern manufacturers of the United States have responded to the invitation to be represented at the exposition have made it one of the finest displays of American genius, enterprise, and mechanical industry ever seen.

He added: "Thousands of Northern people will go down there as visitors during the continuance of the exposition and in that way any lingering prejudices which are the result of the war will be wholly eliminated, and the North and the South will come to a better understanding of each other than ever before. None will more rejoice at the ultimate success of the exposition than the Northern people themselves."[17]

Although the three largest newspapers—the *Dispatch,* St. Paul *Pioneer Press,* and the Minneapolis *Tribune*—all reported on the exposition, such stories were coupled with articles about the rededication of the battleground at Chickamauga.[18] With such actions, "sectional lines," reported the *Dispatch,* "[would be] wiped out."[19] The *Pioneer Press* declared that "The Mason-Dixon line is practically wiped away."[20] All three papers acknowledged Washington as "representative of the colored people," and the *Dispatch* printed his complete speech; but all references to him were written without comment. Praise would come later.[21]

Washington's participation clearly reflected an effort by the enlightened few in the Deep South to forge a long-overdue link between the region's whites and blacks, but his message was essentially one of a Southerner to fellow Southerners. Notwithstanding the desire to see the North and South come together as one nation, Minnesota was still Minnesota, and the South was still the South, one nation but not one people.

The black community of Minnesota, like other Northern blacks, and unlike their white Northern neighbors, did not believe that economic and cultural benefits outweighed the civil rights of Southern blacks. Rather, black Minnesotans—many of whom had recently arrived in the state to escape conditions in Dixie—saw these events in the South as evidence that whites could not be trusted to be true partners with their black neighbors, notwithstanding Washington's hopes and dreams. Throughout the 1890s, Minnesota blacks condemned white-supremacist activities against black Southerners. In virtually every issue of the *Appeal* between January and April 1892, a racial atrocity occurring somewhere in the South was reported.[22] In a desperate need to do something, St. Paul blacks met at St. James AME Church to express "their indignation with the outrages in the South."[23]

That May, taking the lead from the blacks of St. Louis, the St. Paul black community sponsored a day of fasting and prayer in hope "that Almighty God will so work upon the hearts of the American nation that the murderous lynchings to which we are subjected may cease from the land."[24] As long as such crimes were being perpetrated, the civil-rights community was not interested in sectional reconciliation, as reflected in an article titled "A People on Their Knees":

> When the people of the North are thoroughly aroused to the terrible condition of affairs which exists in the South some means will be found to change it. It may require another civil war to right the wrongs of the Afro-Americans; if so, let it come. When all things else fail men fight for their rights, such as are guaranteed by the constitution under which we live—life, liberty, and the pursuit of happiness—and who doubts that we are men, or that we will fight, in the face of our record in the civil war.[25]

Such fury in Minnesota did not diminish at the time of Washington's rosy prescription for racial harmony. Therefore, it was quite understandable that Minnesota's civil-rights community would join its voice to the criticism from other black Northern communities against Washington's speech of accommodation, despite the accolades from Northern whites and Republican leaders. About this reaction, Washington observed:

> [A]fter the first burst of enthusiasm [for his speech] began to die away, the colored people began reading the speech in cold type, some of them seemed to feel that they had been hypnotized. They seemed to feel that I had been too liberal in my remark toward the Southern whites, and that I had not spoken out strongly enough for what they termed the "rights" of the race. For a while there was a reaction, so far as a certain element of my own race was concerned, but later these reactionary ones seemed to have been won over to my way of believing and acting.[26]

Indeed, the civil-rights leadership of black Minnesota raged against white supremacy in the Deep South; yet, their admiration for the man who preached that Southern blacks should accommodate themselves to conditions in the very same South where white supremacy thrived seemed just as firm. The question was, why?

Washington strongly preached some of the most basic Republican values that Minnesota civil-rights leaders had long espoused—dignity in labor and creativity to make it more efficient—but these were not the sole essence of their vision. Washington believed that these values were the means to become business entrepreneurs and to share in the profits of business. "We must not only teach the Negro to improve the methods of what are now classed as the lower forms of labor, but the Negro must be put in a position, by the use of intelligence and skill, to take his part in the higher forms of labor, up in the region where the profits appear."[27] He also taught his students about the importance of property ownership: "A man never begins to have self-respect until he owns a home."[28]

To the small black middle class in St. Paul, despite its misgivings, Washington's message was not entirely without merit. His philosophy of accommodation was a call to blacks to surrender to a social, political, and economic system of white supremacy and black degradation. On the other hand, despite the homes and businesses they owned, the education they possessed, the refined and cultivated manner they acquired, the powerful white people they knew, and the proof they embodied of the promise of their race, they knew that when white patrons looked at them, they only saw in the color of their African skin the irredeemably wretched black masses down South. In his pronouncements of self-respect and responsibility, Washington seemed to offer a prescription to the stereotype of the trifling Southern Negro that haunted the black middle class in the North.

9

The Renaissance
of the Cakewalk

"The Afro-American must learn that when he aspires to a position that will place him over white men as well as those of his own race, his fitness must be judged, not by his own, but by the white man's standard."

—The *Appeal*, April 16, 1892

The readers of the *Appeal* were familiar with Dr. Booker T. Washington before most Americans were. The newspaper had dedicated itself to showcasing the achievements of African Americans during a time when few in the nation saw any reason to take note. Washington's work at Tuskegee—training the untrained black man and woman— was indeed noteworthy. But the fact, as the story line went, that even white Southern men who had terrorized them saw these trained former slaves as useful to the Southern economy elevated the work at Tuskegee to a new level of respect. Washington's was indeed a front-page story. But it was compelling for another reason, for it unintentionally spotlighted the great paradox confronting the black middle class and race men, as well—their ambivalent reaction to the tackiness of racial stereotype. Sympathetic to their Southern brethren and outraged by their treatment at the hands of Klansmen, they nonetheless remained highly sensitive to being perceived by white people in the same light as "certain colored folks." This class of African Americans, by virtue of being citizens, deserved the same opportunities to advance themselves, but their boisterous lack of cultivation and apparent disregard for sober industry fueled the stereotype of racial inferiority with which all black people were stained. For the sake of their own sense of credibility as leaders striving for respect from a white community that was either uncomprehending or suffused with casual disregard, the race men struggled for control over how black people should be viewed. To do so, they used their press, which highlighted both the potential and proven success of black advancement, and, as they celebrated their culture, race, and history, they demanded as loyal Republicans a seat at the table, with the ever-present specter of "certain colored folks" hanging over them. They needed to draw attention to themselves and away from that specter—indeed, from their fear of association with that specter. The paradox is that while embracing the caricature of their race to entertain themselves, they sought to distance themselves from the stereotype. By wearing blackface, they sought to be seen worthy of dignity.

In 1891, the *Appeal* featured Washington in a series on black educators and colleges in the South.[1] Sprawled over the entire front page, which was typically reserved for society news from Chicago, St. Louis, and other cities where the *Appeal* was printed, under the expansive title "Afro-Americans at Work: One of the Practical Ways of Settling the So-called 'Race Problem' Successfully Carried Out by Afro-Americans in the Heart of the Sunny South," appeared an article featuring the work at Tuskegee Institute that taught young black people skills that were useful to the economy of the immediate area.[2]

The correspondent reported that around the campus were shops "where colored boys were making wagons to sell to white merchants of Tuskegee, harnesses, buggies, house, office, and church furniture for white people to buy; boots and shoes, clothing, bed mattresses, and in fact carrying on in a small way almost every industry known in the South." Tuskegee was a school that stood out from the rest that the *Appeal* covered, including liberal arts schools like Clark College in Atlanta and professional schools like Meharry Medical School in Nashville. Neither of the other schools received such benevolence from white neighbors surrounding the campuses as Tuskegee did. "The change is still further emphasized by the relations existing between the school and town. The students and teachers at the institute are of the colored race, but they are respected for what they are doing."[3]

As proof of the county's success in "settling the so-called race problem," the correspondent captured the view of its most influential white man, a scion of "an old family, who also inherited lands and now owns most of the stock in the railroad which connects Tuskegee with the Alabama Western Road":

> I tell you, sir. Professor Washington is a remarkable man. He has done remarkable work here in this county. He has done more to settle the Negro problem than any other one man in the South. He is making the colored boys and girls useful men and women … The school is now the life of the town. We would not have it removed if we could. Indeed we are much more opposed to talk of removal than we ever were of having it come among us.[4]

Here were two reasons why the Minnesota black leadership supported Washington: despite their condemnation of the abuses of Southern white supremacy, the Minnesota civil-rights leaders remained hopeful of an end to violence, and that in the process any program that made blacks indispensable would be heartily endorsed. Ending violence and making blacks useful were reasons Minnesota black leaders supported Washington.

The prominence of the feature in the *Appeal* on March 12, 1892, which filled page 1, clearly indicated the respect that the editor felt for Washington's work. Making "colored boys and girls useful men and women" was clearly paramount, "usefulness" being the central concept. But it was a concept that meant more than simply being vocationally beneficial to a community.

The concept also spoke to how the race at large would be perceived, and, more significant to the black middle class, how it would be perceived by whites in association with *certain* poor blacks. In Minnesota it was not that all low-income blacks were to be kept at arm's length. As Paul Nelson observed, "[T]he social scene was much more egalitarian than elsewhere. Janitors, porters, and artisans held leadership positions, along with the handful of professionals and well-to-do."[5] For example, Samuel Hardy, a leader of the St. Paul League, was a janitor at city hall before being replaced by a political appointee in 1892.[6] Indeed, character distinguished these men; they were noble in their usefulness. If they were useful, then the race had hope and the black middle class would embody that hope. If, on the other hand, poor blacks were without usefulness, the entire race would be denigrated. It was therefore important for blacks to distance themselves from the stereotype of useless blacks. This attitude was often reflected in black middle-class criticisms of the infamous "cakewalk."

The cakewalk began with slaves who competed through dance to amuse their masters on special social occasions. The best dancers received cakes, prompting them to develop extravagant steps and prancing struts that parodied their own masters' dances and costumes. After the Civil War, the cakewalk appeared in theaters and music halls often frequented by poor blacks, beginning in New York City and spreading to other black communities in Northern cities. In time, the practice took a sharp turn toward the grotesque, when white society adopted it as a fad. White performers began to parody the black "cakewalkers," "[imitating] a colored man strutting in a prize contest, the distinguishing features being the head held high, chin up, elbows out, shoulders thrown back, and, especially prominent, an exaggerated frontal protuberance." "What bothers some people about the cakewalk," wrote Paul Nelson in his biography of attorney Fredrick McGhee, "played directly into the stereotype of black men as shiftless caperers."[7] The spectacle came to St. Paul in 1892.

On March 12, the *Appeal* published an article titled "The Renaissance of the Cake Walk," which began with a brief history: "Within the last few weeks enterprising white men have been arranging 'Cake Walks' in various parts of the country. The scheme originated in New York City where the first 'walk' was given and it was a decided financial and social success. It was attended by 13,000 whites including Ward McAllister and other leaders of New York white society. Very few colored people were present and these were as a rule of the lower classes." Adams reported where else they had appeared: "A 'Cake Walk' had just been given in Chicago, and others are being arranged for St. Louis, Minneapolis, Cincinnati, Kansas City, and other large cities, and in every case the persons who will do the walking will be found to be from the lower classes of Colored people."

Then Adams began a critique of the spectacle: "In view of the fact that the 'Cake Walk' is a scheme managed by white men, who hire some fourth rate colored people to walk for the amusement of a motley crowd of white people, it is disgusting to all refined Afro-Americans. And to have the daily papers say that the persons who participated were the elites in colored circles, that the colored 400 were present in all their glory, that Prof. (?) Somebody, (a well-known levee tough) who led the walk, is the leader of colored society, is an outrage. As a matter of fact, the better element of colored people has been conspicuous by its absence from the recent 'Cake Walks.' Intelligent Afro-Americans repudiate all connection with or interest in such back number amusements."[8]

The "refined Afro-Americans" worked hard to disassociate themselves from "useless" poor blacks, those who were unskilled or interested only in "sliding" through life. Many felt that if more blacks were industrious, the stereotype of the shiftless Negro—a burden that the black race in white society was required to shoulder—would fade away. In other words, useless blacks weighed down the standing of the black middle class in the larger community. Useless blacks frustrated the advancement of the race. Indeed, as historian Earl Spangler observed, "Many negro leaders felt that economic discrimination was a major factor in preventing better race relations."[9] In Minneapolis in 1890, the New England Furniture Company was congratulated for employing black laborers. A black Minneapolis newspaper commented: "Let a few more businessmen break down the barrier of race prejudice and we will soon have a solution for the race barrier." Spangler noted: "At the same time, many responsible Negroes realized that, as in any group, some of their more irresponsible members could harm the cause of fair employment practices. One Negro paper stated its hope that the loafers and gamblers, could be rounded up and sent to the workhouse or be given jobs that would keep them out of trouble."[10]

By the mid-1890s, the world of black America had become so stratified by class and region that it was inevitable that the interests among black people had become both multiple and divergent. There was scant support for working-class blacks trying to secure employment or improve working conditions. Readers of the *Appeal* learned only after a settlement had been reached that black waiters had been on strike. The paper was content to report the end of the strike rather than call for support during the strike.[11]

Two years later, the *Appeal* called for a campaign to secure employment "for some of our intelligent, capable, young Afro-Americans, as clerks, salespersons, or salesladies in the business houses of St. Paul." It called for blacks to patronize those businesses that hired blacks, while being careful to avoid using the word *boycott*. This "call," unlike the per-sistent "call" to patronize white businesses that advertised in the *Appeal* that appeared in several issues, was made only once.[12]

Despite their concern over the victimization of Southern blacks at the hands of white supremacists, Northern blacks knew that if large numbers of their Southern kinsmen were to arrive in their midst, trouble would follow. This was the experience in Minnesota. In 1863, the Hickman Pil-grims were met by a mob on the levee in St. Paul.[13] Nine years earlier, fear-ing that the Mississippi River would become a conduit for runaways and fugitives heading North, legislators considered enacting a Black Code. For all his shortcomings, Booker T. Washington clarified in terms never before uttered this very real distinction that existed within black America.

In fact, during the first two decades of the twentieth century, in the spirit of Douglass and Washington who spoke against black relocation, many black leaders of Minneapolis and St. Paul did not welcome the arrival of Southern blacks into the state. Historian David Taylor explained:

> The influx of Southern black migrants [many of whom found work on the railroads and meat-packing plants as redcaps, porters, janitors, waiters, and cooks] generated feelings of hostility among established members of the black community in both cities. Unfamiliar with urban living and with the subtle nuances of northern racial detente, they were castigated for their shortcomings by both blacks and whites. Often the black community placed them at the bottom of its social hierarchy.[14]

During the same period, a number of newly arrived blacks who were regarded as "[criminal] undesirables" arrived from Southern states. "As a result," Spangler wrote, "'native' Minnesota Negroes attempted to pro-tect themselves against this influx. In many cases, local Negro leaders and organizations 'screened' the migrants and selected only those deemed 'worthy' to enter the state."[15]

Indeed, there was a distinct bias against Southern blacks, who tended to be the least skilled laborers in Minnesota. To be unskilled was to be someone who survived by his wits, and that often bred criminal activity. On the other hand, Southern unskilled blacks faced a terrible challenge. Despite the fact that slavery had been abolished, economic slavery—the unbreakable cycle of poverty created in the sharecropper system—held most of them in a hopeless state. Paraphrasing Richard Kluger, wherever they went and whatever they tried to do with their lives, they were badly disabled, irreparably so for the most part, by the malnourishment that the poverty and meanness of their Southern birthright had inflicted upon them during their developing years.[16]

Considering the dilapidated state of the segregated public school system in Southern states where the quality of education for black children was abysmal, their only hope, black Minnesota leaders felt, was to be trained to work with their hands. In some instances, they even believed that a liberal-arts education for Southern blacks was wasteful effort and that they should accept a manual-arts education. In his commencement address at Tuskegee, which appeared on the front page of the June 4, 1895, issue of the *Appeal,* Washington stated, "Of course everyone admits that the supreme need of the Afro-American race in the country is education; yet we also must admit a qualification, if the education be the right kinds. [Liberal-arts] education . . . does not lift men and women to the plane of intelligence and nobility of motives is readily seen in a thousand ways. You and I know a great many so-called educated people who are very ignorant."[17]

For many black leaders, manual education seemed to be a remedy for making young black men and women in the South useful and they felt their skills could best be utilized in the South. They regarded Washington's words as a clarion call to remain in the South: "It is well to bear in mind that whatever other sins the South may have called to bear, when it comes to business, pure and simple, it is in the South where the Negro is given man's chance in the commercial world."[18]

The message was clear: Southern blacks who were industrious and exceptionally skilled were welcome in Northern communities, but those who were merely useful should stay in the South where both communities might benefit. Washington's program would help these blacks, provided they remained in the South.

The common interests in education, being useful, property ownership, ending antiblack violence, and encouraging Southern blacks to remain in the South where they could better take advantage of opportunities to prosper were reasons black Minnesota leaders were attracted to Booker T. Washington, even though they diverged as to the degree they felt Southern whites were capable of becoming racially enlightened.

In fact, the contents of Washington's message—*cast down your buck-ets*—were hard to swallow: he was telling blacks to accept their increasing disenfranchisement; accept the fact that segregated public schooling of black children made a mockery of education; and accept the legal and customary system of racial segregation spreading into every corner of human endeavor. It was hard indeed to criticize degradation while supporting the man who told blacks to accommodate themselves to systemic degradation; yet the black Minnesota leadership did just that. One practical and overriding reason compelled them to make the compromise: political expediency, the price of a seat at the political table.

Across the country, Northern whites accepted Washington's speech as hope for the cessation of racial conflict that had been an obstacle to their investments in the South. "Moreover," explained sociologist E. Franklin Frazier, "northern industrialists regarded Washington's espousal of industrial education for the Negro as a logical program for the training of black industrial workers for a South that was becoming industrialized."[19] Minnesota opinion makers echoed these views, and this meant that the political patrons of the civil-rights community felt the same way. Periodically, honorific articles appeared in the *Appeal* touting Tuskegee's latest success. Sometimes the article had to stretch to find a topic. The following announcement appeared on the front page:

> The Tuskegee Afro-American Conference occurs here in February, as usual . . . The work done in our harness shop compares favorably with that done in factories. This was shown at the Atlanta and Nashville Expositions . . . Our canning department put up 35,000 cans of black-berries this year.[20]

The relationship between blacks and whites in Minnesota had always been relatively benign. The majority of Minnesota whites had passed a referendum that extended suffrage to black men two years before Congress enacted the Fifteenth Amendment. Within six months of passing the referendum, a Republican legislature passed a law punishing any school district that discriminated against black children. When the U.S. Supreme Court declared the Civil Rights Act of 1875 unconstitutional, the Minnesota legislature passed its own public accommodations act. By the 1890s, blacks were attending some of the state's finest centers of higher learning. Although racism prohibited blacks from residing in certain all-white St. Paul neighborhoods, Jim Crow was not the official policy of the city. Many of the state's political, civic, religious, and business leaders had long supported black civil rights and cultural advancement.

Notwithstanding the irritating persistence of discrimination perpetrated by individuals acting in their own behalf, for the most part white Minnesotans—especially the political establishment—demonstrated enlightened attitudes toward their black neighbors. Black leaders took note of this. A white Methodist bishop argued that Northern whites were "practically no different" from Southern people "in regard to the color line." "It is drawn as unmistakably in one section as it is in the other. The people in the North declaim against caste and radical distinctions, but they draw the line just as closely as we do in the South." The *Appeal's* response, while acknowledging the presence of racism in the North, said the differences were considerable:

> [T]here are no Jim Crow cars, no Mississippi constitutions, no cunningly devised laws intended specifically to disenfranchise Afro-American voters . . . An Afro-American can vote in safety anywhere in the North, can attend the best universities and put up in many of the best hotels. All these things constitute practically a great difference. In reference to the lynching business, the Bishop strays still more widely from the truth.[21]

The relative benevolence of white Minnesota had been generally constant and black leaders enjoyed a relatively high degree of access to the power elite. Therefore, it was more than gratitude that compelled blacks to support Washington; it was a manifestation of character. Black leaders experienced the consequence of selecting the wrong national leader when they attended the first national convention of the Afro-American League in 1890. Now, in Minnesota, maintaining and building on their accomplishments required securing relationships with the white establishment. This principle, they came to realize, took precedence over everything else.

Indeed, no black man or woman espousing the radical tactic of direct action against white supremacy or denouncing America for its hypocrisy on the race question was embraced by Minnesota's black leaders. After 1890, Fortune's name did not appear in the pages of the *Appeal* even though he had once been praised by the same newspaper. When the great Frederick Douglass criticized the *Appeal* for the spotty coverage of lynchings and other forms of antiblack abuse and for wasting its journalistic resources on superficial matters, the *Appeal* characterized his statement as "preeminently foolish." The paper let loose its derision, recalling how Douglass had declined to accompany John Brown to Harpers Ferry:

> It calls to mind the fact that Mr. Douglass was quite a leading spirit in organizing the John Brown movement, but upon the first news of the arrest of John Brown, Mr. Douglass at once sped away, via Canada and Europe, and moreover, Mr. Douglass has announced to deliver a commencement oration at an Oklahoma college in a week or two. After making that speech Mr. Douglass had better prepare for his Oklahoma trip by packing a few dozen bombs in his grip-sack. He may need them before he finishes his journey. Even anarchists have sense enough to not run around in advance, threatening to make and throw bombs.[22]

Booker T. Washington would be the appropriate "leader of the race," for he at least was someone who did not criticize the white or black establishment, someone who did not anger white folks, someone who did not endorse bomb throwing, and who did discourage agitation. The political landscape had grown tense with the growing efficacy of Populism. Although third-party politics was a constant in Minnesota since the 1870s, as well as an irritant to the Republican Party, by the 1890s a tentative coalition of urban laborites and black and white farmers in the South posed a real threat. Although Washington argued that Southern blacks should be apolitical, Minnesota's black leaders seized the moment to demonstrate their support for the established order. In both cases, theirs would be positions of support for the status quo; in this they were of one mind.

By the time Washington ascended the platform to speak at the Atlanta Exposition in 1895, the Populist movement in Minnesota was in decline. The year 1892 had been a turning point. Black leaders worked to secure their community's vote for the Republican Party, and as the November elections approached, they stepped up their attack on the Populists: "The People's Party is composed of the illiterate truck farmers, moonshiners, and loafers, who pick up a precarious subsistence by hunting, fishing, and shining around. Their hatred for a rich white man because he had 'learning' and wealth, and, of course, their hatred for the colored man who has neither of these things can scarcely be denied. To this class, a lynching is a grand event, as much a past time of the wolf hunt."[23]

Black leaders were painting the movement with broad strokes, portraying the Populists of the South and Minnesota in the same light. The *Appeal's* readership was primarily urban and black, readers who had become wary of white farmers in both North and South. This was a far cry from the benevolent view they had in 1887 when the *Appeal* reported that black delegates were well received in Minneapolis at the joint convention of the Knights of Labor and the Farmers' Alliance.[24] But in Minnesota, blacks who in 1892 sympathized with the state's Populist movement—which, like other Northern Populist parties, was more benign in racial matters than in the South—nonetheless faced the derision of civil-rights leaders:

> It is exceedingly important that the colored voters of this country should observe and analyze critically the movement now in progress within the Republican Party. The evidence is conclusive that a reactionary element within the party is struggling desperately to force it to adopt a policy as essentially hostile to the colored man as the most bourbonistic Democrat would desire.[25]

To vote Populist was to vote Democratic: "The colored man who voted the Democratic ticket is false to himself, to his country, and to his God."[26] Such loyalty mandated that a black man be seated at the party's table. The election of 1892 was therefore not only a campaign against white supremacy, but a test of Republican inclusiveness.

Since 1888 when James K. Hilyard ran an unsuccessful campaign for alderman-at-large as the Republican-endorsed candidate, blacks were mentioned or nominated for public office with increasing frequency, often accompanied by frustration. In 1892, Fredrick McGhee, representing Ramsey County, went to the state convention and sought support to be a delegate at the national convention. Black leaders called on state party officials to select McGhee in order to give voice to black Minnesota Republicans. They argued that the party owed it to the "constant . . .

fealty" of its black voters. "We do not ask this . . . because of our race, yet we do urge that it will be good, practical politics and just dealing."[27]

However, Scandinavian Republican delegates were intent on leveraging their own influence. "Are our countrymen going to stand for such treatment?" a writer queried in an editorial in the *Svenska Amerikanska Posten* before threatening, "When a political party which depends for its very existence in Minnesota upon the Scandinavians, treats them in such a manner, then it is simply our countrymen's duty to chastise the 'bullies' at the ballot box."[28] At the convention, McGhee won a vote to serve as presidential elector, but party leaders took the office from him and gave it to "a Swedish professor" named J. S. Carlson of Northfield, in an effort to recall "to Republican allegiance great numbers of electors of Scandinavian parentage who had strayed away into the wilderness of Populism and Prohibition."[29] At the Republican National Convention that convened in June, 13 percent of the delegates who attended were African American. None, however, were from Minnesota.[30]

In Minneapolis, a black attorney named William Morris sought the Republican nomination to the legislature. Many blacks said that if he did not get the endorsement, "they would feel that their services to the party had not been appreciated." Black elected officials would work for everyone, not only for black citizens. A black Minneapolis newspaper made it clear that they would not go into the convention seeking "recognition as colored men, but as loyal republicans who have been tried and never found wanting." However, he too was frustrated by party officials, and when denied the endorsement, he described the rejection in racial terms.[31] In biting fashion, the *Appeal* commented, "The Afro-American must learn that when he aspires to a position that will place him over white men as well as those of his own race, his fitness must be judged, not by his own, but by the white man's standard."[32] The efforts of blacks to aid their party against the tide of Populism were for naught. In August, a committee of black leaders—which included McGhee, Morris, Lyles, Hazel, Parker, and Adams—called on a state party official to express their frustration. Although the meeting went well, the official committed a verbal faux pas that was received as a racial slight.[33]

The committee was composed of eight men, none of whom was younger than than thirty. Two were lawyers, one was a real-estate agent, one was an insurance solicitor, one was steward of a prominent club, one was a manager of a business where stained glass was made, one was an ex-newspaper man, and one was an editor. They were cordially received by the aforementioned official and the consultation proceeded in a proper manner until just about the end when the officer addressed the gentlemen as "boys." This one word, of course, knocked the whole thing in the head. The official, manifesting frontier casualness, did not understand that he was dealing with men who comported themselves with Victorian formality. The editor reflected darkly:

> One of the things we have never been able to understand is that white people as a rule get it into their heads they must patronize and get unbecomingly familiar with Afro-Americans to have them believe they are familiar. Whatever courtesy or dignity is necessary in dealing with white people will be fully sufficient in dealing with Afro-Americans, no more, no less.[34]

In September, blacks met at Cunningham Hall in Minneapolis to protest the way Minnesota Republicans had treated them. Many speakers from Minneapolis appeared. Fredrick McGhee also spoke, "relat[ing] how badly he had been treated by the leaders of the party, only because his skin happened to be somewhat darker than that of the Swede." It was decided at the meeting not to organize Negro clubs for the campaign in Minnesota until it had been learned "with certainty" what the Republican Party intended to do with the "elector" McGhee. "Should the party-machine refuse to reinstate him in the office to which he was elected, then the 700 black voters intend to 'bolt' the ticket."[35] The party chose not to respond. By the end of the year, black leaders were despondent. Nationally, Democratic candidate Grover Cleveland once again won the presidency; statewide, however, the Republicans were firmly in control. In neither instance was the Minnesota black vote critical to the outcome. The *Appeal* commiserated: "The Afro-American vote of the North was, at one time, the almost exclusive property of the Republican Party. There are good reasons for thinking that it was largely alienated in the late struggle."[36]

In a broader sense, observed Spangler, the participation of the Minnesota black vote in politics followed much the same trend, and had the same results, as in other Northern states. In too many cases, including Minnesota, the black voter "married himself to the Republican Party."

Between 1885 and 1920, that party was no longer the sole possessor of the traits that had brought about such loyalty. However, it may be that by the 1880s, "separation had become difficult if not impossible," while many black leaders, out of self-interest, kept to the party line.[37]

Spangler continued: "It is perhaps just as true to say that the white man often used the Negro but did not accept him." Although the black vote was exceedingly low, more perceptive blacks used every means possible to increase their influence. As early as the 1880s, the black vote in the North was looked on as a balance of power, particularly in Ohio, Indiana, and Illinois. As the Republican Party began to lose interest in the black vote by the turn of the century, the Democrats paid more attention to it. But with few local exceptions, the Minnesota black vote was too small to affect the balance of power.[38]

During these lean years, political clubs nonetheless proliferated. Among them were the Central Colored Republican Club of St. Paul, Hennepin County Republican Club, the Wedge (nonpartisan), Afro-American Republican Club, the Federation of Colored Men of St. Louis County, Young Men's Colored Club of Minneapolis, Ramsey County Afro-American Republican League, Afro-American Democrats of Ramsey County, Ramsey County Colored Democratic League, and the Negro Independent Progressive Club of Hennepin County (during the 1912 campaign). Many proclaimed themselves permanent organizations, but few lasted more than two years.[39] And because laborers did not participate, and in most instances were not invited, political activism seemed not just middle-class but elitist.

Occasionally, some were revived or merged with other organizations to carry on the same function.[40] Sometimes the members of one club might also be members of another club, as was true of the Afro-American Republican Club and the Colored Citizens Union of 1890.[41] As Spangler noted, a cynical editor would decry all these organizations and declare that black leaders should perfect the ones they had rather than constantly start new ones.[42] Theirs was an endless exercise in ineffectiveness.

On May 19, 1896, the St. Paul *Pioneer Press* reported that the U.S. Supreme Court had just ruled that a Louisiana separate coach law was constitutional as long as segregated coaches provided equal accommodations for black and white passengers.[43] In a small article titled "Jim Crow Car Law

O.K.," the newspaper characterized *Plessy v. Ferguson* as a Southern case springing from a Southern law that reflected the Southern way of life.[44] Opinion makers did not appear to be concerned about the decision for it was irrelevant to Minnesota, where blacks enjoyed a better quality of life and full respect from their white neighbors.

The South, on the other hand, was another world. This was a period of sectional reconciliation when Northerners and Southerners felt they would mutually benefit from the new American economy, when old hostilities from the war would be laid to rest at last, yet just beneath the surface Northerners—Minnesotans—viewed Southern race relations as proof of the backward nature of their white Southern cousins.

The Jim Crow law was further proof that the Democratic-controlled South was only doing what it was always inclined to do: perpetuate the degradation of the black man and woman. The problem with that assessment was that it was the Supreme Court, not the Louisiana legislature, that ruled the coach law constitutional; that the high court was predominantly Northern and Republican; and that the decision itself was the latest in a string of decisions reflecting a Court that believed in the sovereign authority of states' rights. As the author of the opinion, Massachusetts-born Justice Henry Billings Brown, stated:

> Laws permitting, or even requiring, [racial] separation in places where [the races] are liable to be brought into contact do not necessarily imply the inferiority of either race to the other, and have been generally, if not universally, recognized as within the competency of the state legislatures in the exercise of their police power.[45]

In the clearest, most incontrovertible terms, the Court declared that state-sanctioned racial segregation, if the separate facilities were equal, was constitutional.

This was no doubt a hard sort of justice for the blacks who lost the decisions and suffered under their consequences, but it was different for the blacks in Minnesota, where no similar law existed. *Plessy* was a Southern phenomenon. The Northern Republicans who predominated on the Court only granted Southerners the legal and constitutional permission to enact such laws. The *Appeal* criticized neither the Court nor the sincerity of Northern Republicans who influenced Court appointments.

The burden fell heaviest on those in the South, and therefore the legally sanctioned impact of Southern abuses, however egregious, remained for Northern blacks largely something abstract. In the election of 1896, the black civil-rights leaders solidly supported the Republican ticket. An entire issue of the *Appeal* was given over to Republican candidates and issues, and Minnesota Populism, when characterized at all, was portrayed as an economic threat rather than a vehicle for white supremacy, as reflected in a political cartoon depicting a Populist seated in a throne, laughing as Minnesota businessmen fled from the state.[46] What resentment had been felt by black leaders against the state Republican Party by 1896 was set aside. They had solidly returned to the fold.

In April 1897, the editor of the *Appeal* published an advertisement for a Grand Cake Walk and Ball by the Iolathe Club. "The management will endeavor to make this one of the finest Cake Walks ever given in the city."[47] In five years, St. Paul's black elite had come to think more kindly of the spectacle. One year later, the "cakewalk" appeared in a Summit Avenue residence, having become a society fad for the city's white elite.[48]

In November 1898, the Twin Cities black community put on what must have been one of the most remarkable demonstrations of patriotic enthusiasm ever witnessed in Minnesota, a pageant that celebrated America's victory over Spain.[49] But it was more: the spectacle *Cuba* was a notable display of the connections that the black leadership had developed with the white political and commercial elite of both cities who also were the leaders of the state Republican Party. The wives of the white elite raised the money, and the black women, who as Nelson observed represented a major portion of the black middle class, orchestrated the pageant, "a four-act pastiche of tableaux vivants, speeches, songs, and dramatic scenes written and directed by Mrs. Cora Pope and performed by an all-black cast of 300."[50]

Although one performance was given in St. Paul, the enthusiastic reception in Minneapolis resulted in two performances. "The audiences were integrated, and one house was estimated at 2,000 people." Of the many acts that were performed, the one that aroused the audience the most was the stirring and, as the *Pioneer Press* termed it, "decidedly dramatic" oration that McGhee gave in the role of Cuban General Antonio Maceo, a former slave who led the Cubans against Spanish rule. In a speech that Nelson characterized as "optimistic and patriotic," McGhee intoned that just as no color line was observed in the trenches before San Juan Hill, the color line was fading in Minnesota.[51] The production was a success, its very embodiment depicting a state that was becoming a New Jerusalem of enlightenment and racial harmony.

But the celebration was not without controversy. The complex nature of Fredrick McGhee's character reflected the ambiguous racial pride of the black middle class, for it played out not between blacks and whites but within the black leadership. In a sequence of *Cuba,* the cakewalk was performed. McGhee supported the spectacle; a black businessman named J. C. Reid did not. Reid had enjoyed the pageant, in which his wife performed, and said as much in a letter that appeared in the *Appeal* on December 3, but he did not like the cakewalk. Black people lived under constant scrutiny of the white majority that required them, out of pure self-preservation, to maintain a higher standard of conduct and propriety than what was expected of whites. The heroic deeds of black soldiers in Cuba and the otherwise marvelous production of *Cuba* helped the race by winning praise from white America. The cakewalk undid this good: "While [the white man] enjoys it," Reid wrote, "[his] innermost thoughts are: 'all coons are alike.'" Simply put, he did not want the respectable black community of Minneapolis and St. Paul associated with the degradation of the cakewalk in the minds of respectable white people.[52]

One week later, Mattie McGhee, Fredrick's wife, responded with a letter of her own, defending the fad. She said she had first heard of the dance in connection with the Vanderbilts of New York, and it first made its appearance in St. Paul "when Miss Abbie Warner, daughter of the head of a well-known business firm in St. Paul, gave a cakewalk at her residence on Summit Avenue." It was only then that the colored people of St. Paul concluded that they could do the cakewalk too. The cakewalk, she concluded, "is a modest and refined dance . . . indulged in by some of the most refined and cultured people in the Northwest, and who are a credit to the race to which they belong."[53] The McGhees found no peril to their race in the fad. Two weeks later Fredrick McGhee challenged Reid to a public debate to be held in Minneapolis on February 6, 1899. McGhee, the experienced and highly successful trial lawyer, won the debate. In his view, the cakewalk had been vindicated.[54]

In the final analysis, the cakewalk was a reflection of McGhee's provocative temperament, for even then he realized that he had trained his considerable skills on battles far bigger than defending a mere fad. The challenge to civil rights remained deeply embedded in the very fabric of Minnesota society. But was McGhee the man to lead that effort or had he lost standing among his peers because of his independent and prickly style? Could the struggle be truly won within the bounds of state politics or was the core challenge to civil rights a national matter? Indeed, had the time come when the moderate approach needed to give way to a more radical agenda? Would he and his small circle of allies, who included W. E. B. DuBois, have the courage to pay the price of social and political isolation? The cakewalk paled in comparison.

PART III
The
RADICALS

10

WHEATON AND MCGHEE
A Tale of Two Leaders

"Throughout the North there was not only acquiescence among the white population in the 'Southern Way' of solving race problems but a tendency to imitate it in practice."

—C. VANN WOODWARD, *The Strange Career of Jim Crow,* 1955

I t would be wrong to conclude that Fredrick McGhee, in his 1899 defense of the cakewalk, intended to demean his own race. That the celebration included the cakewalk at all revealed a much more complex dynamic that reflected the shifted grounding of racial identity during this period among the black middle class of the Twin Cities. Beyond a doubt, McGhee was a proud black man who demanded respect and the opportunity to fully develop his gifts, of which he had many. He was, in other words, the epitome of a "race man." To be sure, by the 1890s he had become the leader of leaders within the Twin Cities black community because, with his striking good looks, he was sharp, articulate, and impassioned, and he had the time and energy to be a prominent figure, being seemingly ever-present at important events and always prepared with the quotable statement.

His name was familiar because it routinely appeared in the *Western Appeal,* and his words were well documented. Both were gauges for the status of "leader," a role he enjoyed immensely. Being a lawyer granted him special status among blacks, for his bearing had been honed from the verbal jousting matches with white attorneys in the intimidating formal arena of the courtroom, where black men typically came as defendants sitting in obsequious silence, eyes downcast, hands clasped, nervously waiting as other men determined their fate. McGhee was their voice, their brains, their defender. This made him a black leader outside the courtroom as well, for the very nature of his profession made him an equal to white men in a way that black barbers and even newspaper editors could never be. Knowing and understanding the arcane doings of legal practice and speaking with authority, he possessed the gravitas to pronounce unequivocally about what was right and what was wrong, a sign of supreme confidence that few men could ever possess. This too made him a leader of leaders. But in 1897, his path uneasily crossed that of another black man, a younger man, yet just as proud and considerably talented. His name was Frank Wheaton. In both temperament and style he possessed three things McGhee wanted but would never get—the kind of respect that went to a genuine political insider, elective office, and the authorship of two civil-rights laws. The intersection of their paths would be brief and uneasy, yet it would stamp the very nature of civil rights in Minnesota at the end of the nineteenth century.

By 1899, McGhee had been a member of the Democratic Party for six years. Not just affiliated with the party, he had become a passionate critic of the Republican Party to which he once belonged. It was an odd association for the region's preeminent race man to belong to the political party whose Southern legacy embraced the disenfranchisement and persecution of the African American, and which in Minnesota routinely mocked black dignity and the right to equality. But McGhee did not fit neatly into any mold. To be sure, since 1868 black leaders had counseled their people to be willing to support any party fully committed to advancing the interests of African Americans. Nationally, a few, angered by Republican policies, did just that in 1882 when they supported Democratic candidate Grover Cleveland. Even so, black voters nationally and statewide, even those who at times wavered, remained loyal to the party of Lincoln. McGhee did not fall into this camp. The party had let him down and he had decided to leave. He challenged that which was practical, that which was predictable.

Fredrick McGhee, circa 1890. Courtesy of the Minnesota Historical Society.

Born into slavery in Aberdeen, Mississippi, in 1861, McGhee grew up with a passion to want more for his life. He attended Knoxville College in Tennessee through the aid of the Freedmen's Bureau, and moved to Chicago in 1879, where he studied law under the the prominent African American attorney Edward H. Morris, brother of William Morris of Minneapolis. While practicing law, McGhee ran for public office and eventually was recognized as a member of black society. In 1889, he left all of this to move to St. Paul, where he became the first black attorney—indeed, the first black professional—to reside in the city. He was the first black man admitted to the bar and to practice law in Minnesota. "As the first of his race to practice so public a profession," wrote his biographer, Paul Nelson, "he could not avoid being seen as a representative of his people, in their eyes and to the community at large."[1]

He was complicated, temperamental, a paradox, an iconoclast. "All of his life," Nelson observed, "Fredrick McGhee seemed compelled to reject the broad and easy path in favor of the narrow and thorny."[2] As noted, McGhee left the prestige and prosperity of a vibrant black community in sophisticated Chicago to move to St. Paul, where at the time few black professionals resided, and with a black population of 1,500 in a city of 130,000. He was a loyal member of the Republican Party who later joined ranks with the Democrats. Born and raised in the Baptist faith, he converted to Roman Catholicism. McGhee revered Booker T. Washington enough to become chief counsel of the organization he controlled, only to join ranks with Washington's rival, W. E. B. DuBois. He could move audiences with a vigorous defense of the black race, yet use the same talent to defend the cakewalk.[3]

In a sense, this instinct to move between two worlds suited the task he confronted in establishing himself within an all-white legal system and a black community eager for a champion.[4] The St. Paul in which McGhee settled had a bubbling underclass where violence and the sex trade offered an ambitious lawyer plenty of work. But to be successful he had to learn the "procedures, customs, and unwritten rules, while at the same time proving himself to lawyers, reporters, witnesses, judges, jurors and jailers, who by experience associated dark skin with defendant rather than defender" (ibid.). His profession suited the sense that he had of himself. "A defense attorney," Nelson observed, "is by definition 'uppity'; his duty is to challenge the system and the people who have accused his client of crime. McGhee could not have known how Minnesotans would react to a black man, a southern black with a Chicago sheen, engaging in the confrontational business of cross-examining witnesses, disputing the police version of events, and contradicting prosecutors. He had to find the places where his race interfered with advocacy and where it might help" (ibid.).

Much of his early work was defending madams and prostitutes in what seemed to be an endless stream of arrests. He got clients the way a criminal defense attorney typically did—by reputation, referral, court appointment, and hanging around the courthouse. His race also helped because a disproportionate number of those who marched through the system were African Americans and they likely found comfort having one of their own defend them (50). Nelson described most of McGhee's cases as "ordinary, a succession of assaults and larcenies enlivened by colorful characters and the absorbing and engaging fast-paced criminal practice" (ibid.). This work honed his rhetorical skills and flair for the dramatic and gave him a captivating presence whenever he stepped up to the podium, which was particularly useful in the theater of politics.

Politics was as important to McGhee as the protection of civil rights, and within three years of his arrival he had established himself as a powerful campaigner for other candidates. But he could not leverage that talent to advance his own political aspirations. Although he tried to attain elective office, his efforts always fell short because of a lack of support from the party leadership. In 1892, after winning a seat as presidential elector, much to the consternation of the Swedish contingent, he was trying a case in Wisconsin when the central committee suddenly declared his post vacant. "Black Republicans had played the game of ethnic politics and lost" (36). Still, he met the challenge and delivered "a rousing speech" at another rally. Because of his sportsmanlike effort for the good of the party, the state central committee promised that "the McGhee matter" would be settled.[5] But nothing happened. Yet, McGhee continued to campaign for the ticket. "What did McGhee get in the bargain?" Nelson asked. "In the end, only promises, promises never fulfilled."[6]

Within the year, the wound would grow deeper. Notably, this was a time when Republican presidents routinely offered patronage to loyal African American leaders, a practice that often filtered down to state and municipal ranks.[7] Even Frederick Douglass received such appointments as the District of Columbia Register of Deeds and later minister to Haiti.[8] With all that McGhee did for the election of Republicans, he surely assumed that such appointments—or something comparable on the local level—would come his way. By 1892, he had established useful party connections that cast him as someone who could get things done. When the mother of one of his clients wanted her son freed from prison, McGhee persuaded Republican congressman Sam Snider to speak to President Benjamin Harrison, who then granted a pardon. When horse thief Frank Conway hired McGhee to get him out of jail, McGhee approached Republican governor Merriam, and Conway walked away a free man. Indeed, two years after he arrived from Chicago, McGhee was appointed to the party's central committee, "a considerable and significant

Frank Wheaton, circa 1899. Photograph by Charles A. Zimmerman.
Courtesy of the Minnesota Historical Society.

honor."[9] Still, bitterness over the party's betrayal over the elector post loss
never left him. The last straw occurred in the spring of 1893.

McGhee had labored hard to help Republicans win the 1892 St. Paul
municipal elections in which they took the mayor's office, city council,
and assembly. With these victories, the party had the power to appoint
a new city attorney and three assistants in March 1893. Leon T. Chamberlain, who knew McGhee from campaigning together, was appointed
city attorney. Senior party officials, recognizing McGhee's dedication,
promised him the post of assistant city attorney, a job that offered a comfortable salary, steady trial work, and important political contacts. On
March 15, Chamberlain appointed Walter Chapin, a qualified man with

past experience, to the job. As Nelson observed, "McGhee's race probably cost him the position."[10] The Democratic St. Paul *Globe* reported on good authority that it knew McGhee did not get the appointment "because the Irish people would never forgive [Chamberlain] if he appointed a colored attorney to prosecute them in the police court."[11] Once again, the Republicans deferred to ethnic politics. Swedish voters outnumbered African American voters statewide, and Irish voters outnumbered African Americans in St. Paul. In the spring of 1893, as McGhee angrily left the Republican ranks, a black twenty-seven-year-old attorney named J. Frank Wheaton arrived in Minneapolis from Washington.

The breeding that Wheaton showed to those who first met him reflected a past that was very different from McGhee's, starting with the environment in which he was born. Hagerstown, Maryland, a hamlet located in an area where the topography was lined with stony ridges of limestone, was a part of the slaveholding border region that could not accommodate the plantation system, so a highly racial caste structure, as in the Deep South, did not exist. Situated close to the Chesapeake and closer to Pennsylvania than to West Virginia and Virginia, near the sites of two of the most significant battles of the Civil War—Antietam and Gettysburg—generations of African Americans lived there as free men and women, accustomed to lives of high expectations. His father was said to be the first black man to serve on a petit jury in his county, as well as the first black man in Maryland to cast a ballot under the Fifteenth Amendment. Jacob and Emily Wheaton both imbued their son with a sense of pride that could only come from knowledge of one's ancestral roots. From them he claimed to trace his lineage to his paternal grandfather, an Englishman named James Buckingham who settled in Virginia as a planter and who had set his slave son free upon his death.

Born in 1866, Frank Wheaton attended school for two years in Ohio and graduated in 1882 from the West Virginia State Normal School and later Storer College. In 1887, he attended the Maryland Republican Convention and in 1888 the National Republican Convention in Chicago, before stumping Illinois, Indiana, and Ohio for Republican candidates. While in Illinois, he took classes at Dixon Business College, and returned to Maryland in 1889 to attend the state Republican convention, where he served as its temporary chair. In 1890, he clerked in the fifty-first Congress and took classes at Howard Law School, from where he graduated with a law degree in 1892. Later that year, he was admitted to the Maryland bar. A month later, black Maryland Republicans nominated him as a delegate to the Republican National Convention in Minneapolis, the same convention that had denied McGhee a seat; but when Wheaton's credentials were not accepted, he did not go.

Despite that experience, he came to view the city in a much more positive light, possibly at the urging of Edward Morris, the Chicago attorney who had mentored McGhee and whose younger brother William was now an attorney in Minneapolis. As meteoric as his professional life was, he nonetheless had encountered more than his share of racism. The Mill City in the North Star State seemed to be a place where he could flourish. "Tiring of his continued struggle to adjust to the disadvantages imposed on him, Mr. Wheaton moved to Minneapolis, May 3, 1893."[12] Shortly after he arrived, despite already holding a law degree, he entered the law school at the University of Minnesota, the finishing school for young men whom he got to know and who were destined to engineer the white establishment in finance and politics in Minnesota. He graduated one year later. That year, 1894, he began his law practice, and later was selected to his first of three terms as a legislative clerk. In 1896, he was the first black Minnesotan to be a delegate to the Republican National Convention, in St. Louis.[13]

These two men—McGhee born in the year the Civil War began, Wheaton in the year following the war's end—first drew lines during the presidential campaign of 1896. The nature of their respective efforts—McGhee the Democrat for William Jennings Bryan, Wheaton the Republican for William McKinley—reflected both their temperaments and their understanding of the roles they were supposed to play in the contest. Minnesota, and Minneapolis in particular, were already solidly Republican and the black vote was not up for grabs. Wheaton's role, therefore, was minimal. Being the first black man to be selected as a delegate to the national convention, a distinction that was recorded in the national press, cast him as the very embodiment of the image of a progressive party with a progressive agenda.[14] McGhee threw all of his energies into getting St. Paul votes for the Democratic candidate.

On October 19, Bryan made a campaign stop in St. Paul. Waiting for him to arrive at the auditorium was a large and restless crowd that was white and working-class, eager to hear their champion of the free coinage of silver, the removal of all tariffs, and populism. Just after 8 p.m., Fredrick

McGhee approached the podium. By now his reputation as an entertaining speaker given to earthy imagery who sometimes mocked himself as a black man preceded him. "His appearance," reported the *Globe,* "was greeted with cries of 'McGhee, McGhee. Speech, speech.'"[15] He began by comparing the election of 1896 to the Civil War—just as the war was fought over the slavery of black men to white men, this campaign dealt with the slavery of labor to capital.[16] Who better than he could speak to them than one who knew the true burden and false nobility of hard labor? The truth was, no rich white man ever wanted to exchange places with either of them.

Touching on the powerful image that had for so long reflexively dissuaded skeptical Republicans from abandoning their party, McGhee exclaimed: "[T]he bloody shirt is dead and I stand upon it. And now from one end of the country to another the common people are waiting to hear the gospel of the new dispensation preached by that great tribune of the people, William Jennings Bryan!" To prolonged cheering, he resorted to the language of class grievance: "Remember that we the people made this country before capital ever breathed in it. It was the common people who laid the foundation for capital and it is too late now to tell the people that the foundation of a house is no part of the house." Then, a crowd of white Democrats attentively listening to a black man speaking to their issues thrilled to his final point, which poked fun at their racial bias: "Who is it that claims that America can't do what she wants to do? It wouldn't be wise for me to discuss the financial situation, since it is said that the common people don't know anything about it and therefore can't talk about it." They and he were now clearly enjoying themselves. "And if the white people don't know anything about it, how can a poor darkey like me be expected to understand it? (Laughter and applause.)"[17]

McKinley and the Republican Party swept the national elections, and the defeat of Bryan and free silver populism in Minnesota was decisive.[18] Minnesota was solidly under Republican control, which clearly favored Wheaton's next move to political notoriety. It also provided the nexus where the public lives of Wheaton and McGhee would intersect.

With *Plessy v. Ferguson* (1896) states were free to enact laws that mandated segregation, leaving to states the power to decide whether the law was reasonable or not. While the segregation laws were vigorously enforced in the South, antidiscrimination laws in the North, when enforced at all, were continuously shown to be toothless. In Cincinnati, school segregation was an active issue.[19] In a study on the impact of Indiana's civil-rights law during this period, C. Vann Woodward notes: "In practice the law proved to be ineffectual in accomplishing its stated purpose, and racial patterns [of segregation] remained unchanged by its passage . . . Throughout the North there was not only acquiescence among the white population in the 'Southern Way' of solving race problems but a tendency to imitate it in practice."[20]

In Minnesota, although a state civil-rights law was passed in 1885 to discourage discrimination by punishing the culprit through fine and imprisonment, whites continued to deny blacks the full enjoyment of public entertainments. White opinion makers insisted that blacks alleging discrimination did not know how good they had it in Minnesota. By spring 1897, several civil-rights suits were filed by "very respectable people who had no mercenary motive in doing so."[21] Yet, the perceived ambiguity of the law allowed juries to find holes in the law. Two black Minneapolis attorneys, William Morris and J. Frank Wheaton, drafted an amendment to the civil-rights law and began lobbying it through the legislature.[22] Wheaton had his own experience to further motivate him, for he had been a plaintiff in a suit in 1895 after being refused service in a St. Paul restaurant. On April 6 that year, he and two white friends, Representative Wright and D. M. Scribner, went to a St. Paul restaurant at which time owner Louis McDonald said that "he drew the line." The waitress then served the white men soup and plates of food but, reported the *Globe*, "the colored brother, like the little pig in the nursery fable, got none." Wheaton sued and McDonald's defense was that he could not force his waitress to serve "the prize colored speaker of the Republican state central committee," "in spite," as defense counsel John O'Reilly insisted, "all orders." However, Wheaton's counsel, Stan Donnelly, got McDonald to concede that he could have served Wheaton despite the resolve if his employee, "Maggie," agreed that he was the boss, not his waitress. Before a crowded courtroom, Judge Tuohy took the matter under advisement. Nothing more was reported of the case.[23] Because of the possibly sensitive nature of a legislative clerk being indiscreetly in the midst of litigation, or a calculation motivated by political ambition, Wheaton may simply have decided to drop charges. In any event, the issue did not go away. Two months later, after Wheaton spoke at Trinity AME Church on race relations in the South, Representative Dingham commenced his speech on the prejudice that exists in Minnesota and, to illustrate how no African American was protected, no matter how upstanding he was, he referred to the discomfort of the man he was about to name, "to the late insults offered Mr. Wheaton on account of color."[24]

On April 23, 1897, the Wheaton–Morris amendment was adopted. The law imposed substantial criminal penalties on violators and subjected them to fines of one hundred to five hundred dollars plus jail terms of at least thirty days, with a maximum of one year.[25] The amendment specified the places where blacks would have legal protection—"hotel, inn, tavern, restaurant, eating house, soda-water fountain, ice-cream parlor, public conveyance on land or water, theatre, barbershop, or other place of public refreshment, amusement, instruction, accommodation, or entertainment." It dropped the phrase "subject . . . to conditions and limitations established by law" and specified that it also applied to the owners, managers, and lessees of such places that fell under the listed categories. Plaintiffs could receive civil damages of twenty-five to five hundred dollars. Criminal penalties were reduced to between twenty-five and one hundred dollars and thirty to ninety days in jail; a finding of guilt could lead to a fine or jail, but not necessarily both.[26]

The purpose was threefold: (1) to cover all eating establishments, not just restaurants; (2) to encourage juries to award damages; and (3) to encourage criminal prosecution. In other words, it was believed that white judges would be more inclined to rule justly when they knew the penalties would not be heavy: "[The] minimums [of the old law] probably struck prosecutors and judges as far out of line with the offense of refusing someone a meal or a hotel room or a shave on the basis of race."[27] Justice was doable if the price was low enough.

In essence, chapter 349 of the General Laws of 1897, as the second public accommodations enactment was called, meant to fill any loopholes by referencing saloons and any other similar but unforeseeable place where blacks had experienced the greatest discrimination: "other place of public refreshment, amusement, instruction, accommodation or entertainment."[28] The legislators were favorably disposed to the bill. The *Appeal* agreed:

It is a deplorable fact that we need a civil rights law in Minnesota, or anywhere else, for that matter, but we do. And that there must be some sort of flaw in the existing [law] no one more than Mr. McGhee gives evidence, as he has brought all of his civil rights suits under the common law.[29]

The *Appeal* insisted that the *Pioneer Press* had it wrong when it editorialized that such a law was unnecessary. Despite the sense that Minnesota's "people were proud to treat every man according to his merits," and that "if he is a gentleman, he is recognized as such, whatever the color of his skin," no less than the great Booker T. Washington, upon visiting St. Paul, was denied full service at one of the city's prestigious hotels, the Metropolitan. Only after he agreed to take his meals in his room did the hotel permit him to register.[30] Twenty-four years earlier, Frederick Douglass was likewise denied admission by the hotel, and, once admitted, was denied service in the dining room.[31] "And there are scores of others who have pocketed such indignities and borne them in silence," Adams wrote.[32] In 1899, Adams would file the following account about this all-too-common experience:

> Attorney McGhee went into Neumann's restaurant a few days ago, and waiters filled his order with red peppers but he promptly called them down and sat there until he was properly served. He has been in the same place several times and each time some act of discrimination more or less obnoxious has been committed, but McGhee says he will continue to go until he is properly served.[33]

"What we want," Adams wrote two years earlier, "is the absence of any fear of refusal, indignity, or insult solely on account of color, or class."[34] As if anticipating the criticism that the amendment was imperfect, the *Appeal* concluded, "We say by all means pass the amendment and then if that does not meet the requirements, get up another [amendment], until one is found which will, or the people who now refuse our rights become christianized to accord them."[35]

As the amendment wound its way through the legislature, its only critic was Fredrick McGhee, who argued that the mere addition of "saloons" to the list of public accommodations covered by the old law was hardly worthy of "race principle." Actually, saloons as a category were not expressly listed as places covered by the law, though he clearly believed that it was implied: "Ordinarily, we say a law is amended either to cure a defect or make it better, neither of which this amendment does. I admit that saloons are clearly included to the new law, but what race man would prostitute a great race principle to prosecute a saloonkeeper for refusing him drink at his bar."[36] Indeed, how could drinking in dens of iniquity with the likes of the city's baser citizens promote the values of upstanding black citizens? A greater concern, however, was that the new law lowered the maximum amount of damages to the lowest amount required in the old law. According to the old law, a defendant found guilty could be fined between one hundred and five hundred dollars. Under the new law a guilty defendant could be fined only between twenty-five and one hundred dollars. "Fertile indeed must be the brain that by any manner of reasoning can demonstrate that a new law which fixes the highest penalty at what the lowest was under the old law is better than the old law, is of benefit to anyone but the person who is to be punished . . . I have yet to find the person who will explain to me what benefit has or will accrue to my race by thus making lighter the punishment of the man who inflicts the wrong."[37]

In essence, McGhee argued, the new law was weaker because the low fine was hardly significant enough to discourage people intent on denying a black person service. Perhaps from the bitter lesson McGhee learned at the Republican convention of 1892, he considered himself to be the clear-eyed observer who could see through the pretense of advancement in the new bill: "It is no wonder that the bill passed by almost unanimous vote, not even a democrat voting against it, why shouldn't it? [I]t was a measure to reduce the penalty imposed on a white man for refusing to serve the Negro."[38] McGhee was right. Prompted by the whispers of Lincoln and a reputation for racial tolerance to uphold, and realizing that it cost the government nothing, the cause and consequences of discrimination suits were less annoying than a fly buzzing around the ear during a summer night.

McGhee criticized advocates of any bill that diminished the penalty on wrongdoers. Moreover, the biggest concern that *Appeal* editor John Adams had for the old law was in no way addressed in the new law: it did not instruct juries deciding for plaintiffs to require defendants to pay attorney fees. Without this provision, persons of modest means could not afford litigation and thus were discouraged from seeking redress. Without this provision attorneys would be disinclined to represent the aggrieved party. Without this provision, wrongdoers could continue to discriminate with near impunity. Adams's support of the bill could only be explained by his desire to demonstrate loyalty to the Republican Party; and "loyalty" meant simply a willingness to uphold the pretense of governmental magnanimity. For McGhee, the price of loyalty was simply too high. Yet, he did pay a price for "disloyalty," and it was considerable.

McGhee placed a strain on relationships between former friends. According to the *Dispatch,* he reportedly said, in the intemperate terms he often used when he was at his iconoclastic best, that the law was "for the benefit of the crap shooters and blacklegs . . . the most disreputable of niggers." The article continued: "They would work up cases more for the sake of bringing an action. If they could get one half of the $25 . . . they would be enabled to live in luxury for a week or two, or play 'craps' to their heart's content. It would build up a class of blackmailers who have no regards for themselves or for the welfare of the race to which they belong, be a detriment to every colored person who has an ambition to do something and result in more harm to the negro than can be estimated in mere words."[39]

Adams responded by implying that he knew how intemperate McGhee could be, that "friends of Lawyer F. L. McGhee" were not so much surprised at his objection to the amendment "as the manner in which his objections were presented to the public."[40] McGhee's response, which appeared in the following issue of the *Appeal,* was explosive. He accused Adams of bad judgment and bad journalism for believing the *Dispatch* article, and insisted that his record in the defense of his people prohibited him from using such terms as "crap shooters," "blacklegs," and "niggers" "in public speech or in print."[41]

He argued that the amendment's reduced penalties devalued the gravity of the offenses. The limit on damages prevented plaintiffs from seeking higher damages and juries from awarding higher damages. Finally, he made it personal by attacking Adams and his "friends" for believing the *Dispatch* account of McGhee's remarks: "[I]f those friends of mine who are so deeply chagrined at my 'interview' spend as much time and labor as I do in defense of their race, and saving them from shame, without financial recompense they would land themselves securely in the poor house before they went to their reward."[42] As if to put an end to the debate, Adams published the proposed amendment in its entirety in the same issue.[43] Readers would have to draw their own conclusions.

Adams's role in defending the law allowed Wheaton (Morris had already begun receding into Wheaton's shadow) to stay above the fray against the street fighter Frederick McGhee. Indeed, more accustomed to engaging in verbal fisticuffs in the public arena, Adams became the champion for the first black man to pass a law, the first destined for great things. Besides, the law was an important step forward. The minimum fine was a mere pittance. Nonetheless, all-white juries were more likely to find businessmen guilty precisely because they could receive a painless fine. If the minimum remained one hundred dollars, even in the face of incontrovertible evidence, jurors might not want to damage the man's business. It was important for a restaurant to be found publicly guilty by a jury of the owner's peers so that a record could be made in order to improve things in the future. In the end, it would be harder to tolerate discrimination when it was made visible.

Of course, the legislators who supported the amendment were not all sincere in wanting to address discrimination. Many of the Democrats, especially those representing St. Paul, considered the law to be impotent. If the new law truly had teeth, small businessmen—most of whom were the defendants in these suits and many of whom were Democrats' constituents—would be injured. On the other hand, state representatives such as Ignatius Donnelly, who had been a champion for black rights since the war and who had recently introduced a bill to authorize public funding to send black Minnesotans to Tennessee to celebrate the state's centennial, clearly saw the benefit in Wheaton's amendment.[44] Bill No. 853, providing a mere slap on the wrist, did little to provide genuine redress to injured parties or to discourage whites who wanted to discriminate. On the other hand, as weak as the law was, low fines made juries more disposed to find guilt, and this was at least something. A finding of guilt created a record that many otherwise would choose to ignore. Minnesota indeed had a race problem.

McGhee was not so hopeful. He seemed to be saying that as far as the legislature was concerned, racism was something to be endured. Twenty-five dollars was the cost of being black. His complaint was understandable. But his defensiveness, which opponents attacked, undercut the credibility of his argument. The fact that Adams and an establishment newspaper, the *Dispatch*, would attack him illustrates how estranged old friends had become. Although McGhee had replaced old political allies with new ones from the Democratic camp, not even they could be relied on as genuine allies. What influence he had on the main stage of politics had all but died. Adams concluded: "McGhee's opposition to the civil rights amendment counted for nothing and the bill passed quickly into law."[45] Wheaton, on the other hand, understood the ways of the Republican Party in a way that McGhee did not. Ethnic politics had kept McGhee from appointments, whereas Wheaton's standing within the party seemed charmed as he effortlessly moved through the mechanisms of the Republican machinery.

While McGhee came to the state already a lawyer and became the first African American to practice at the bar, Wheaton—likewise a lawyer when he arrived—chose instead to go for a second degree in a school where he could know and be known by the state's political and financial elite. This gave him an advantage, as did his business degree and his instinct to be discreet, generally avoiding controversial issues and minimizing associations with men and demonstrations that only served to draw attention to themselves. While McGhee's world was the courtroom, Wheaton assiduously worked in the far less dramatic confines of the legislative records room. Both men were brilliant and had impressive oratory skills. However, their personalities seemed modified by the jobs they performed: McGhee the coarse, pugnacious litigator, nonconformist, provocateur; Wheaton the smooth operator, audacious but refined. During much of the 1890s, McGhee's life was punctuated with disappointment; Wheaton's was filled with success and opportunity. McGhee believed in the grand demonstration; Wheaton worked the legislative process. McGhee's disposition could not adapt to the simple axiom that politics is all about relationships; Wheaton understood the science of tactical placement—one takes a chess piece only if it advances the player's ultimate goal of capturing the king. Hope was not a factor in this outlook.

In December 1897, William Hazel was again denied service, this time at the Market Restaurant in downtown St. Paul. He planned to sue.[46] In January, a few weeks later, Mr. and Mrs. Thomas Scott of St. Paul were given "cool service" and were served rancid food at the same restaurant.[47] But it would be in Minneapolis that the first suit testing the new law was filed.

McCant Stewart—a graduate of Tuskegee Institute, current law student at the University of Minnesota, and son of a prominent black attorney and school-board member in Brooklyn, New York—was a young man used to comporting himself with dignity and being respected by all men, black and white alike. On March 4, 1898, he went to the Central Avenue restaurant of John Flangstad for a meal. He took a place at a table and waited for the proprietor, who was acting as a waiter, to serve him. Forty-five minutes passed and a number of patrons who had come in after him had been waited upon, yet no effort was made to serve him.[48]

"You can go somewhere else and get your meal," the proprietor allegedly told him.

"I did not know I was in Georgia," answered Stewart. "I thought 1 was in the state of Minnesota, where a colored man was entitled to the same rights as any other citizen."

Flangstad replied: "I employ such as you to clean my backyard. Go out there if you want something to do."

A number of white couples eating there at the time left their tables and went to Stewart to give him their names to be used in prosecuting Flangstad. Stewart tried to get an officer to make an arrest, but the officer refused. Stewart then swore out a complaint. Flangstad was arraigned at the police station and charged with violating the civil-rights statute. At the end of the trial, the jury took only fifteen minutes to decide in Stewart's favor.[49] Even though the state argued a focused case and the jurors who delivered the verdict were all white, *Appeal* editor Adams praised the blacks who attended the trial and encouraged racial solidarity, stating, "there is where we should be all together, fight together, stand together and win together."[50]

The *Stewart* case, a Minneapolis case, was noteworthy on two counts. First, it was the state, rather than Stewart himself, who prosecuted the case under the act. Second, the trial itself involved a number of white witnesses who, as onlookers to the exchange between Stewart and Flangstad, came forward to attest to the defendant's blatant act of discrimination. Even if the outcome of the trial was not unprecedented, the amount of white support for a black man was noteworthy and a hopeful sign as it reflected the extent to which Minneapolis seemed to be a city that was more racially progressive than its twin city east of the Mississippi River.

11

THE ELECTION OF
J. FRANK WHEATON

"A dark horse that won."

—*South Minneapolis Telegram,* November 11, 1898

T his was a time when McGhee, Adams, and other St. Paul community leaders replaced one organization with another in a futile attempt to be politically relevant. Nothing they did attracted votes. Parochial in their approach, they had come to rely on the belief that clubs and rhetoric shaped the political landscape. Without a significant voting bloc, the opportunity to succeed in electoral politics required a different approach that in turn required the black man to understand the ways of the white political establishment. Wheaton's approach—the only approach to date that worked—could only accomplish this by his innocuously working within the white political establishment rather than being a "leader" of the black political community, and do so not as a black Republican but as a Republican who happened to be black.[1] John Francis Wheaton—Frank Wheaton—was such a man. Well situated within the political establishment, he was young and talented, with a reserved but self-assured manner that conveyed his lack of interest in the showy smoke and mirrors of demonstration politics, preferring instead low-key, methodical statecraft. Their goals were inaccessible and grandiose. His was more practical, including sponsoring two amendments to the civil-rights law. By age thirty, and five years McGhee's junior, Wheaton was politically successful in a way that McGhee never would be, and his future clearly extended to the world beyond the Twin Cities. In 1898, one year after he and Morris had successfully lobbied for passage of the civil-rights law, Wheaton would gain the distinction of being the first black ever to be elected to and serve in the state legislature, representing a district that, as Earl Spangler noted, "included less than a hundred Negroes, and [running] ahead of his Republican ticket in a year when the Republicans lost the governorship to Democrat John Lind."[2]

Shortly after one o'clock on the morning of February 22, 1898, Frazier Baker, the black postmaster of the predominantly white hamlet of Lake City, South Carolina, who had been appointed by President McKinley three months earlier, was murdered along with his young daughter by white supremacists while trying to escape his burning house. His wife and infant son were also seriously injured in the attack. The federal government did nothing to prosecute the attackers.[3] As usual, "[t]he Republicans . . . unqualifiedly condemned 'the uncivilized and barbarous practice' of lynching, but made no commitment to put an end to the barbarism."[4] In June, McGhee joined Adams and a handful of others to make plans to form a civil-rights organization in response to the South Carolina tragedy.

In July, the group reconvened and elected black restaurateur Jasper Gibbs, John Adams, William Hazel, William Morris, Fredrick McGhee, and Frank Wheaton, who joined the group late, to be officers and directors of the new organization.[5] Wheaton was an important addition to the group. Although they were all men of standing in the black communities of St. Paul and Minneapolis, it was Wheaton who brought a special prestige even though he was the youngest. He was the rising star, about to be the first black man to be elected to the state legislature, who had found a way to breach the color wall to high elective office, who most prominently with McGhee personified the bipartisan sense of outrage—black Republicans and Democrats standing together to condemn the barbarity of lynching in America. They named the organization the American Law Enforcement League of Minnesota.[6]

In September, the league published its manifesto, which called for the enforcement of the law, the suppression of lawlessness, and the moral, intellectual, industrial, and economic uplifting of the Afro-American. It was a call to action. Central to it was the need to address the issue of lynching so often incited by reports of black men raping white women in a way that "unit[ed] the North and South in sentiment unfavorable to us."[7] Though black Minnesotans, they declared, lived "practically free" of the outrages in the South, they could no longer stand by watching atrocities that routinely were inflicted on their Southern kinsmen.[8] Indicative of their sensitivity to attacking their own city, in contrast, no such formal gesture of outrage had been mounted three years earlier when two black men on two separate occasions were attacked by lynch mobs, nor were the events acknowledged in the *Appeal*.[9]

But, like previous civil-rights organizations born in passion and high principle, they lacked a focused strategy that they had the political courage to fulfill. Nonetheless, typical of such "calls" were pronouncements, as Nelson observed, "[that were] eloquent in the statement of the need for action, vague in describing the action to be taken."[10] On the issue of lynching, "reflecting the political weakness of black America," the league made no specific demand on Congress or the president, but rather placed the responsibility on themselves: "We should endeavor to learn the facts concerning these reports. If they be true, to see that the guilty parties be properly dealt with, but if false, the malicious accuser should suffer the consequences of their own sins . . . Let us prove to the world that we are opposed to crime, no matter who the offender might be."[11] The league also sought to abolish Jim Crow laws, restore black suffrage in Mississippi, and ensure that "the 14th and 15th Amendments be enforced both in letter and spirit." Membership was open to all races, nationalities, or creeds who were in sympathy with the elevation of the African Americans. A legal fund was established and funds solicited for court challenges. John Adams was elected the league's first president.[12]

They knew how difficult the work would be, but they professed to be undaunted: "We have counted the cost, time, labor, and expense, [but] we are willing to make the sacrifice." The reality of what they proposed to do, however, was quite sobering. As Nelson explained: "For the [league] to achieve their goals would have required a mobilization of national will and use of federal power not seen since the Civil War, an undertaking so vast that no sacrifice, no cost of time, labor, or expense, could have brought it about."[13]

Wheaton's participation appeared to diminish from the start. He had many reasons to feel distracted. He may have still been smarting from a humiliating encounter with two officers in January when a white man falsely accused him of stealing his wallet "because [Wheaton's] face happened to show the presence of African blood in his composition."[14] With uncharacteristic pique—at least since he sued Louis McDonald in 1895—he sued his white accuser but apparently dropped his case as soon as it had been filed. It was one thing to draft a law for those choosing to sue, but quite another to be the one who sued: men of stature and ambition like him had to avoid attention-grabbing headlines or appearing to make a quick buck, anything that made him appear "mercenary" or a troublemaker. And it may still have stung that such a white man in a liberal city could besmirch his character and personal history, deny him his dignity, and cavalierly reduce him to the level of the lowest Negro. He had come to Minneapolis because that attitude was not supposed to prevail there. Perhaps he reminded himself that for every one of those kinds of men, there were many more who were vastly better. In this, he agreed with his colleagues, each of whom had moved to Minnesota because, unlike so many states in the Union, it offered a life of civility and potential. The fact that these features were so tragically absent in the South explained why they focused their limited resources there rather than down the street from the office in which they met.

And yet, seated in the July meeting he had to be feeling restless. It had been the consequence of a meeting in June that had followed a March meeting when "they had discussed the many matters of race interest . . . [then appointed] a committee of ten (men) from each of the Twin Cities to meet at the call of the chairman (Gibbs) to discuss the viability of holding a state conference and a convention."[15] He had agreed to join a subcommittee to draft the constitution and bylaws of the organization they were about to form; and now, here he sat knowing that yet another meeting would be called. His short, restless life reflected an energetic temperament that needed to be active in effecting change, not talking to make plans about talking more in the future. This was one more meeting for one more organization. For all of their effort, they could not point to one accomplishment. It was evident that few—not the legislators, certainly not the party itself, not even the black community who seldom showed support for any of their efforts—took them seriously. Rather than instilling in the broader community a sense of urgency to redress wrongs and well-considered tactics to achieve these goals, they had, through all the grand gestures, the platitudes, the bombast, sadly trivialized the work itself and, in some people's eyes, themselves. Wheaton could not afford to be seen this way, especially since in early July he had become a candidate for a seat to represent Minneapolis's 42d district in the legislature.

In the history of black Minnesota, Minneapolis was a logical place for such a campaign to be waged and won. From the early 1850s, settlers of English descent, or "Old Stock," arrived from New England states and upstate New York to settle in communities scattered around the eastern half of the territory but concentrating in the Minneapolis–St. Anthony area surrounding St. Anthony Falls. By the mid-1850s, a growing number of these settlers were motivated to establish abolitionist principles into the body politic to offset the dominance of the Democratic Party that then controlled Minnesota politics. In 1854, Minneapolis was seen to be a place more favorable to black people, for that year, after the St. Paul legislator saw his bill for a black code go down in defeat, he said bitterly that he would propose legislation that would require all Minnesota blacks to live in Hennepin County, which, in the following year, would be the birthplace of the Minnesota Republican Party. Sparked by outrage over the Kansas/Nebraska Act, the Republican Party in large part intended to combat the spread of slavery.[16]

By the end of the decade, the Hennepin County Antislavery Society, the only such organization in Minnesota, was founded, and its members and a sympathetic Minneapolis judge, Charles Vandenburgh, were responsible a year later for freeing a slave woman named Eliza Winston. Disturbances broke out in Minneapolis and the St. Anthony neighborhood and tensions continued until April 1861, when war broke out against the South. Minneapolis men joined other Minnesotans to be the first volunteer regiments in the Union army and the majority of Minneapolis voters supported all three black suffrage referenda.[17]

Yet, enough history had passed to show that attitudes about race could and did change and had refracted into shades of gray. The march of time presented new and unanticipated circumstances that incited new fears, reshuffled priorities, or just wore down old passions. From a time

when black enslavement symbolized all that was evil, the lines of contention were now about labor and class tensions, as well as immigration and
a deepening strain of nativism. The African American population, smaller
than St. Paul's and only now becoming noticeable and active, remained
virtually nonexistent to most Minneapolitans. Yet the people of Minneapolis were a product of their times and felt the race prejudices of whites that
existed throughout the North. In many places, racism was tolerated by
political leaders and sometimes fanned by opinion makers, but was often
left to simmer unattended until it ignited.

In the case of Minneapolis, at least within the 42d legislative district,
the 1898 campaign could be seen as an example of leadership and opinion makers showing how racial opportunity was not an empty phrase and
could in large part be attributed to leading residents within the district.
In addition to including the neighboring villages of Edina, Eden Prairie,
Bloomington, Richfield, and Excelsior, the 42d that Wheaton sought to
represent included the second, seventh, and twelfth wards of Minneapolis.[18] Considered to be the most affluent wards in the city, they would
determine the election. Capping South Minneapolis, they included Lake
of the Isles, the commercial district, the University of Minnesota area, and
south along the west bank of the Mississippi to Fort Snelling.

Here, despite the racial temperament of the man on the street, the
political machinery was very much in control, and at the gears were the
state's political and business elite, Old Stock settlers who had built their
fortunes in lumbering, milling, and banking, whose family names—Pillsbury, Washburn, Crosby—stretched back to the 1850s, men who still
resided in the wards.[19]

In the fashion of nineteenth-century office seekers, a "reluctant" J.
Frank Wheaton "reconsidered his determination made in the spring and
governed by the solicitations of his neighbors in the seventh ward" and
decided to be a candidate for the legislature. "Ever since he had been
old enough to vote Mr. Wheaton had been active in politics and he has
not missed a campaign though he never before sought one as an office
seeker."[20] From the start, it was evident that his labors for the party, going
wherever he was needed to speak on behalf of the Republican agenda,
and the prudent decisions he made—presenting himself as a leader who
embodied the just nature of a political system that had for so long been
vilified as corrupt, and not a victim as one had to be when he publicly

complained (in the manner of a lawsuit) about the injustice done to him because of his race—placed him in the best position to receive the support he needed from the party establishment to wage a successful campaign.

The *South Minneapolis Telegram,* a prominent newspaper whose subscribers resided in the most densely populated area within the 42d district, had thrown its considerable weight behind him. A July edition of the paper dedicated a full page to photographs of Republican candidates. None was more prominent than the handsome likeness of Wheaton that covered two columns. Under the photo the reader learned that he had served as an alternate for Senator Charles Pillsbury to the Republican National Convention in 1896 and "did much effective work for McKinley." So as not to confuse the reader who saw a black face connected with the "white" activity of seeking office, the paper was direct: "Frank was born black and has not faded. He has, however, a spotless character and can long claim much credit for educating himself to [be] an attorney. He seems to be a natural born orator and could certainly make the welkin ring if he goes to St. Paul this winter." Voters had it within their power to make history by electing the first black man to the legislature.[21] On the front page of its August 28 edition, the paper reprinted the photograph of a dignified Wheaton that covered two columns.[22]

He won the nomination from the party in a three-way race, giving him full support for the fall election.[23] Expressing its unequivocal support and by inference the support of the party establishment, as well as perhaps to inoculate white voters from the impulse to vote "white," the paper stated, "We believe the Republicans in the 42nd District are liberal enough not to allow race prejudice to stand in the way of hearty support for Frank Wheaton, nominated for representative . . . He will compare favorably in intelligence, loyalty and devotion to the House from this or any other district."[24] Weeks later the paper formally endorsed him.[25] Nonetheless, as the *Appeal* indicated, reports persisted "of the bias of a number of people in the Seventh Ward who say they will not vote for Frank Wheaton . . . because he is a colored man." Referring to the heroism displayed by black troops in Cuba, the paper argued: "There was no color line there and there should be no color line in our politics. A man is entitled for the office for which he is a candidate."[26]

Despite the support Wheaton had, days before the polls opened the outcome of the race was uncertain. The Minneapolis *Journal,* the city's major newspaper, reported: "[T]he contest is close in the city between J. Frank Wheaton and Albert Dollenmayer. Wheaton is a prominent local colored man, and was reading clerk in the House in 1887. Dollenmayer is a well-known local newspaper man, popular, a competent democrat, and has a strong feeling in the district."[27] The Democrats had chosen well. At a time when Americans were fighting in Cuba, Dollenmayer, a former soldier who had served in Missouri, Dakota Territory, and Wyoming Territory in a military action "to secure the frontier for the expansion of American civilization," as well as in a Texas surveying expedition in 1881, trumped Wheaton's far less heroically adventurous years as a legislative clerk even though it was Wheaton's and not Dollenmayer's party that galvanized popular enthusiasm for American expansionist policy. Voters wanting a nonracial reason to vote against Wheaton could point to his lack of warrior status and find instead their manly candidate of choice in the thirty-seven-year-old Albert Dollenmayer.

Until the campaign, as a reporter Dollenmayer had frequented places where people worked and socialized, forming relationships, massaging contacts, and securing trust with potential informants, all in pursuit of that morsel of information for the story on which he was working. To be successful he had to go to taverns, bars, and pool halls, where men's tongues were loser and stories had more color. They were places Wheaton was not likely ever to go. The way he did his job would surely be a benefit for Dollenmayer, for it cast him as a man's man, a man of the streets, a man of the people. After moving with his family to Minneapolis, he worked for a while at the Minneapolis Glass Company and when it closed he got a job as a reporter at the Minneapolis *Tribune*, where he would cover the gritty police and heady political beats, before getting promoted to city editor. In 1893, he was sent to the nation's capital as the newspaper's correspondent. He returned two years later to became the advertisement writer, hustling shops to place notices in the paper. All the while he remained active in Democratic politics, which may have been the reason he left the Republican *Tribune* in 1898, the year of his legislative campaign.[28]

The immigrant-sounding name of the Democratic candidate would have served him well had the district extended to neighborhoods south of Washington Avenue to include part of South Minneapolis that stretched from Lyndale to the river. Here the city was densely populated with Scandinavians, with Swedes being the largest foreign-born group, followed by

Norwegians and Danes. Although they were largely laborers who worked in the flour mills, lumberyards, and brickworks, while the women were employed in domestic work, many, especially the Norwegians—the third-largest ethnic minority behind the Swedes and the English—owned banks, restaurants, hotels, undertaking business, furniture showplaces, and grocery stores along Washington Avenue South. The Danes, who were also laborers, living in the 1870s on the edge of the Mississippi in an area called Bohemian Flats, located under the Washington Avenue bridge, migrated to the Seven Corners neighborhood and Cedar Avenue, before moving south to live among the Swedes and Norwegians. The people of this neighborhood were disadvantaged immigrants and workingmen "whose interests," Carl Chrislock said, "could not safely be entrusted to the city's 'Puritan-Yankee elite.'"[29] By 1890, Minneapolis had replaced Chicago as the primary destination of Scandinavian immigrants.[30] In fact, the total population of Minneapolis spiked between 1880 and 1890, tripling from 47,000 to 165,000, with Scandinavian immigrants, particularly the Swedes and Norwegians, accounting for a healthy percentage of the growth. Although there were other ethnic groups who peppered the South Minneapolis neighborhoods, the Scandinavian flavor characterized for many Americans what Minneapolis was.[31] One had to search to find a black neighbor. In contrast to Swedish residency in South Minneapolis that numbered nearly 15,000 in 1895 (foreign-born Swedes in Hennepin County numbered more than 22,000), Minneapolis African Americans numbered around 300.[32]

Had the 42d district included those immigrant and labor neighborhoods in South Minneapolis, Dollenmayer, because of his military service, his neighborhood contacts and familiarity, his name, and the fact that many of the southside voters worked for Republican senator and mill owner Charles A. Pillsbury who endorsed Wheaton, might have waged a stronger campaign.[33]

Moreover, Dollenmayer, whose job had been to closely follow the political ebbs and flows of the city and state, albeit for the newspaper of the Republican establishment, had to know that as powerful as the Republican Party was, there were fissures within its ranks. By 1898, the party was at a crossroads when party reformers gathered enough strength to confront the machine politics of former Governor William Merriam. That year, the return to prosperity reduced the intensity of the gold–silver controversy. This controversy was over which currency the nation should adopt—the gold standard that banks and businesses supported or silver, which farmers and populists supported. American victory in the Spanish-American War, which the Republicans had favored, raised the issue of imperialism. In Minnesota, the issue of political "bossism" lost its cutting edge when the 1898 state Republican convention repudiated sitting governor and Merriam surrogate David Clough to nominate William Henry Eustis, former mayor of Minneapolis, a prominent leader of the antimachine faction of the Minnesota party and the *Tribune*'s man. He had, however, alienated such groups as organized labor and Scandinavians, which would contribute to his problems. In the end, he would fail to unify the Republicans. The schism between the party machine faction and the Minneapolis-based "clean government" faction would persist throughout the campaign and contribute substantially to the defeat of Eustis that would lead to the election of Swedish-born John Lind.[34] Wheaton did not face these problems. The party establishment remained focused on his campaign.

The South Minneapolis *Telegram* announced that it would print "some valuable testimonials to Mr. Wheaton's worth [that were] volunteered by leadings citizens."[35] A week before election day, one such letter ostensibly from Senator Charles D. Pillsbury appeared, though he mostly filled his space with a statement in favor of the gold standard, reform, and improved labor relations. Another endorsement was more to the point and the writer's name by itself gave Wheaton credibility with the Scandinavians in the district. It read in part: "It would be a proof that our district is thoroughly 'American' in the noblest sense of the word and that the principle of liberty and equality have overcome the prejudices. And your election by 'white' votes would be a fitting rebuttal to that section of our country where they kick upon it as a duty to shoot down every 'nigger' who dare to aspire to a validation of the great American principle of equality for all citizens." The letter was signed "M. Falk Gjertsen," one of the most prominent clergymen in the Scandinavian community, long-term pastor of Trinity Lutheran Church, and an active participant in civic affairs.[36]

One week later, on November 8, the voters of the 42d district elected Wheaton by one of the largest margins of any elected official. Along with all of the successful candidates, the *Tribune* simply listed as representatives-elect "J. F. Wheaton (R) and John Goodspeed (R)."[37] The Minneapolis *Journal,* a little more discursively, reported: "J. Frank Wheaton, a colored man, has been elected to the house, the first man of his race to be

SOME of the WINNERS.

A DARK HORSE THAT WON.

J. Frank Wheaton ran ahead of his ticket and with John Goodspeed was elected to serve in the legislature this winter. Frank will be
heard from.

Announcement of J. Frank Wheaton's election to the legislature,
South Minneapolis Telegram, November 11, 1898. Courtesy of
the Minnesota Historical Society.

so honored in the history of this state."[38] The front page of the *South Minneapolis Telegram* displayed a two-column photograph of Wheaton with a
caption suggesting a candidate who had won an improbable campaign: "A
Dark Horse That Won."[39]

Historic though his victory was, conventional accounts would consider the election a referendum on black acceptance. That it would happen in Minneapolis, which at the beginning of the decade had become
the state's largest city, with an immigrant population that was still growing
and a black population that was smaller than St. Paul's, made Wheaton's
new and devoted constituents seem as ethnically and socioeconomically

diverse as the city itself. Indeed, if Minnesota was the promised land, Minneapolis in 1898 was its capital. However, a closer look would indicate a more complex picture. Wheaton said, in a letter accepting an invitation to a banquet to honor his election sponsored by the black Republicans of the Twin Cities, "I am proud to inform you that the Republican Campaign Committee put forth a special effort to secure my election. Not a Republican balked. The magnificent display of brotherly feeling in the rank and file of our party, I shall never forget."[40] "Special effort" was an understatement.

As inspiring as Reverend Gjertsen's words endorsing Wheaton were, it is not likely that they alone drew many immigrants in the 42d district into the Wheaton camp. To expand on Chrislock's characterization of the political instincts of immigrants in Bohemian Flats and Cedar-Riverside, they were disinclined to believe that their interests were safely entrusted with the Puritan-Yankee elite. Thus, they probably would not have voted for the man who was endorsed by New Hampshire-born Republican leader and flour mill owner Charles A. Pillsbury. But if Pillsbury's endorsement explains why immigrants and laborers did not vote for Wheaton, it does not explain why large numbers of them did not vote at all. In fact, that year, the electoral gap between the Republican and Democratic candidates was noteworthy: the Democratic organization was all but crippled by the time the polling stations opened on November 8. By late October, voter registration figures indicated a significant drop from two years before, owing apparently to general apathy and the effect of the "citizenship" amendment. "It is," as the *Tribune* reported, perhaps dismissively, "what the politicians expected."[41]

Because fewer Democrats were registered to vote in the election than two years before, even though the city's population had increased, and with it, presumably, the number of residents likeliest to vote Democratic (or, even more likely, for the Fusion candidate Swedish-born John Lind), Democratic candidates, and Dollenmayer in particular, were crippled by the time polling stations opened on November 8. The wards that showed the largest average registration were the second, fourth, and eighth wards, the *Tribune* reported, "and they are reliably Republican." While there could be "some falling off" in some of these wards, it would be "nothing in comparison with the Democratic wards."[42] The St. Paul *Pioneer Press* saw a similar pattern, with Minneapolis Republican strongholds being the second, fourth, fifth, seventh, and eighth wards. In contrast, it listed the first, sixth, and ninth wards as Democratic. "In the aggregate, the Republicans clearly have the best of it."[43] The loss," said officials, "was on account of failure to secure [the right] papers."[44]

The issue of having "papers" in terms of voter registration probably had less to do with immigrant status and more with residency. At the last general election in 1896, an amendment to the state constitution adopted by the state's electors changed the laws governing state citizenship, defining who was entitled to vote, which had a heavy impact on foreign-born residents. The provision as amended increased the length of residency in a precinct from ten days to thirty.[45] One letter writer pointed to the disenfranchising impact of the amendment: "I know from several parties, including myself, who have lately moved into other precincts, they are now advised that this will result in them losing their vote. I was further advised that I cannot return to the old precinct from which I have moved and registered, and I am well aware that I cannot register in the precinct to which I have moved, as I have not lived there the required thirty days." He added: "It appears to me that any law which will require an American citizen who has lived in the state of Minnesota for several years, and in the county of Hennepin and the city of Minneapolis several years, to live in a certain precinct 30 days before an election or to lose the vote, is unconstitutional." The letter was signed "A. H. Young," the retired district court judge.[46]

It is implausible that a man of Young's stature was truly surprised by the amendment, but rather was expressing outrage at its negative impact on vulnerable residents among the immigrant and disadvantaged classes, who had arrived in the city looking for work, moving unwittingly from one precinct to another in pursuit of a place to live, however temporarily, and who were probably semiliterate and sympathetic to the Democratic, Fusion, or Populist rivals of the Republican Party. This had been the political situation in 1896, the year the amendment was approved, and now when it was being implemented. Traditionally, the Scandinavian community had affiliated with the Republican Party and many within it continued to do so, especially those who had moved into the middle class as business and property owners. But in 1896, the swelling underclass and laboring class pinched by a bad economy made a growing number of them volatile. That year, John Lind left the Republican Party because its national convention rejected free silver and embraced the gold standard. Shortly after announcing his decision, he accepted the Silver Republican-Democratic-Populist "draft" to run for governor, nearly defeating the unpopular Republican Governor David M. Clough by only about 2,300 votes.[47] Uncertain whether the economy would soon recover, a citizenship amendment probably seemed the best means to hedge Republican bets. By the end of October, registration in Minneapolis fell to an estimated thirty-five thousand eligible voters. "The falling off," reported the *Pioneer Press*, "is most marked in the Democratic stronghold."[48]

For Wheaton this meant that a large number of potential Dollenmayer votes were disqualified. The Democrats suffered one last blow. With the sense of inevitability of a major loss at the polls, the death knell to any Democratic hope came when party officials convened a meeting of all Hennepin County candidates to inform them that the party had no money in its coffers. One witness described those assembled as "demoralized."[49] Despite these disadvantages, however, the Minneapolis Republicans did not skate through to victory intact. When the votes were tallied, there was, as the *Journal* termed it, "a sad slump to fusion, so far as the head of the ticket is concerned." Fusion-Democrat James Gray convincingly won by a plurality in a field of five candidates with 48.67 percent of the votes.[50] But the "slump" extended beyond the mayoralty. To represent the 42d district in the state senate, Fusion-Democrat S. A. Stockwell, whose support came primarily from Minneapolis, narrowly defeated Republican Gustav Thedan 2,932 to 2,722. And Fusion-Democrat John Lind took the governorship by defeating Republican and former Minneapolis mayor William Eustis by a margin of approximately twenty thousand votes. However, the Republicans kept their majority in all of the statewide offices and the legislature remained "strongly Republican."[51] In addition to electing one senator, voters in the 42d district had to select two representatives. Wheaton outpolled Dollenmayer in every ward (each having been described as strongholds for the Republican party) and every county village within the district by an impressive total of 2,989 to 2,312 votes. Fellow Republican Goodspeed came in second, narrowly defeating Dollenmayer by only 212 votes.[52] Considering all these returns, Wheaton could justifiably claim the sweetest victory.

Black Minnesotans now had reason to feel hopeful about gaining unfettered access to exercising their full citizenship rights as Minnesotans, considering the legal victory of McCant Stewart and the electoral victory of Frank Wheaton. Their optimism was short-lived, however, and few could have known that the real challenge was not with juries, minimal fines, instructions by judges on the law, or even the state's willingness to prosecute the cases. Rather, it was the Supreme Court of Minnesota and its restrictive interpretation of the law that once again infuriated the African American community and the friends of the black man. Two days after Wheaton's election, the Minnesota Supreme Court issued its opinion in the case of *Rhone v. Loomis*.[53] "Now all but forgotten," wrote Kevin Golden, "the decision raised a storm of controversy in 1898 and severely damaged Justice William Mitchell's reputation in the black community."[54]

Events resulting in the case of *Rhone v. Loomis* occurred in September 1897, just a few months after the passage of the amended Minnesota civil-rights law that Wheaton and Morris had authored that spring. Edward T. Rhone, a former slave from Arkansas, had lived in Duluth for ten years. A friend, Thomas Shannon, known by Rhone from the local Republican headquarters, invited him for a drink at a saloon owned by defendant Robert Loomis. According to Rhone, Loomis, who employed a black porter to wait on customers, refused to serve him, stating, "We don't serve colored people in here."[55]

At trial, after receiving corroborating testimony from Shannon, the jury returned a verdict for Rhone and fined Loomis twenty-five dollars, the statutory minimum. The judge denied Loomis's motion for a new trial on grounds that the purpose of the civil-rights act was to "recognize the equality of all men before the law." He reasoned that even though the word *saloon* was not explicitly mentioned in the act, it was encompassed in the statutory language—"other places of public refreshment." Loomis appealed to the Minnesota Supreme Court on the grounds that the judge's interpretation was incorrect. He contended that the legislature did not intend the law to include saloons. More important, he argued that the act did not create a right to demand alcohol.[56]

With his current term coming to an end, Justice Mitchell's decision may have contributed to his failed bid for an endorsement to another term on the high court. He had sought reelection in November after being endorsed by the Democratic-Populist Party, and though he had received substantial support from the Republicans at their convention, he was unsuccessful in getting their nomination. Without official support from the state's most dominant party, he lost his bid. Some thought, "Minnesota lost its greatest judge."[57] Two days after the election, Justice Mitchell, in one of his last opinions, cast the deciding vote in favor of defendant Loomis.

The main issue before the court was whether saloons were implicitly covered by statute along with those establishments that had been explicitly listed. Justice Mitchell wrote: "[W]e are of the opinion that, under the established canons of construction, it must be held that the legislature had excluded . . . saloons, and that the general words do not, and were not intended to include them."[58] While admitting that "other places of public refreshment" could easily be interpreted to include places where intoxicating beverages were sold, Mitchell concluded that because saloons were numerous and more heavily regulated than the combined total of all other places mentioned in the act, the omission must have been intentional.[59]

To criminally penalize a man for refusing to sell liquor, he reasoned, there should be "a reasonable certainty" that the act demanded it.[60] "[The act] nowhere mentions saloons or places where intoxicating liquors are sold."[61] Remarkably, Mitchell reasoned that such an omission had to be intentional for the sake of maintaining public order between the races.

> [T]he legislature might have thought that the right had to be furnished in the statute. Intoxicating drink would be of doubtful benefit to any class of people, and for that reason excluded saloons from the operation of the act. *It is a well-known fact that, owing to an unreasonable race prejudice which still exists to some extent, the promiscuous entertainment of persons of different races in places where intoxicating drinks are sold not infrequently results in personal conflicts, especially when the passions of men are inflamed by liquor.*[62]

In other words, ever-present altercations between white men were one thing, but altercations between blacks and whites were somehow far more insidious. Chief Justice C. M. Start and Justice L. W. Collins, who dissented from the opinion, argued that the phrase "all other places for public refreshment" was meant to be taken literally and that the legislature's omission of the word *saloon* could not reasonably reflect its intent to reserve such an establishment for exclusive use of the white race when all other establishments were to be covered by the law. Justice Collins put it simply: "I am decidedly of the opinion that the saloon is one of the 'other places of public resort, refreshment, accommodation or entertainment' mentioned in the law. If it is not, what place is?"[63]

But the majority of the Minnesota Supreme Court demonstrated its penchant for myopic interpretation. Saloon keepers who discriminated against black customers could do so with impunity. The black community was outraged by the court's decision and Justice Mitchell's reasoning. The *Appeal* criticized Mitchell, who had not received the Republican endorsement, as an "unjust judge," noting that "it was a good thing Justice Mitchell did not get re-elected." The paper called for further action: "It will be a good thing for the friends of equal and civil rights to again amend the [act] so that it will include every place of every kind where any discrimination on account of color is practiced." And it concluded, "Since this damnable decision a number of saloons are refusing to serve Afro-Americans that did so before."[64] If the Minnesota Supreme Court wanted specificity in the language of the law, then it was the duty of the legislature, and Representative-elect J. Frank Wheaton, to provide such language.

In late December 1898, in order to express their pride in Wheaton's electoral success and gratitude to the Republican Party for advancing his campaign, the black leaders of St. Paul and Minneapolis decided to hold a banquet in honor of the representative-elect. On January 5, 1899, and covered by virtually every prominent newspaper in the Twin Cities, the banquet was held at the Beaufort Hotel in Minneapolis, and was attended by 112 African Americans. Festivities were delayed because the guest of honor had not yet arrived—he was still at the legislature in a caucus meeting. When he arrived, the assembly erupted in an ovation. Luminaries of the bench and city hall such as Chief Justice Start, Justice Collins, and Mayor A. R. Keiffor each sent letters of congratulations.[65] During the planning of this event, local leaders must have communicated their hope that Wheaton would lead the effort to amend the law. Wheaton sent a message to his Republican colleagues that such a bill was forthcoming and expressed optimism that the party remained steadfast behind the principle of black equality: "We have reason to be proud that we live in a State where all men enjoy the full and equal blessing of liberty vouchsafed by the Constitution of our great country . . . We live in the most ideal of American States. We have naught to fear if we measure up to the standard of manhood, maintained by our intelligent fellow-citizens."[66]

Within a week of the banquet Wheaton's work to expand civil rights for black Minnesotans would begin. On the surface, he would be working with a receptive legislative body. Indeed, the Republicans in both houses continued to proclaim their support for black equality, although during the ensuing vote, the issue would become thorny. In this session, prohibition was a major issue confronting social and political policy; Wheaton's bill, however high-minded, would fly directly into the eye of the storm. On January 13, Wheaton, "the colored member from Minneapolis," introduced HF No. 66, which would insert "saloons" into the list of places where accommodation of African Americans would be required by law.[67] As Republican leaders in House and Senate committees debated bills that proposed to close all saloons, and even some blacks condemned the Wheaton bill because "they did not want legislation giving them the privilege of buying drinks in all saloons," the issue became a classic debate over the principle of civil rights versus temperance. In their view, civil rights should uplift one's dignity, not make it more possible to degrade it. It was left to Wheaton to make the case.

In committee, he began by saying that he could not avoid the impression that some politics was involved in the recent state Supreme Court decision in *Rhone* that had reversed the lower court on the proposition that saloons were included in the meaning of the language "other places of public accommodation, refreshment, resort, or amusement." Three of the five justices who rendered the decision were Democrats—Buck, Canty, and Mitchell—while Justices Start and Collins, both Republicans, dissented. He spoke at some length on the question of civil rights, disclaiming any personal interest in the bill, as if he wanted to put to rest any lingering suspicion of his long-ago dropped suit against restaurant owner Louis McDonald or any such suit that seemed so characteristic of the educated black man of the day. "Personally," a reporter noted, "I have no complaint to make and nothing but commendation and praise for those of his fellow citizens with whom he, *an unbleached American citizen,* had come in contact."[68] The bill was recommended out of committee to pass. In the end, the issue was decided on the greater principle that it was a black man's right to drink elbow to elbow with any white man in a bar. Accordingly, the Wheaton bill passed both houses along strict party lines. Many of the saloons in question were owned by Democratic constituents. On March 25, 1899, Wheaton's bill to amend the civil-rights act with language that expressly covered "saloons" was adopted.[69] Governor John Lind signed the bill into law.[70]

With this enactment Minnesota demonstrated a will to pass laws to protect the rights of its African American citizens. But the message was qualified, as Wheaton learned. In early March, as his civil-rights bill by now moved smoothly through the lawmaking process, he delivered a speech that "furnished the only sensation of the day."[71] In his clearest voice, sharpened not only by the number of bills he had introduced and speeches he had delivered in the well of the House but by the historical significance of his tenure in the House, Wheaton asked for a resolution directing the House and Senate to direct Congress to preempt Southern state constitutions that denied black citizens the right to vote as the Fifteenth Amendment allowed.[72] Those voters, he contended, were being discriminated against on the presumption that they were not intellectually qualified to exercise their right to vote. Although he agreed with the contention that the intelligent classes of the country should be the rulers and lawmakers, such amendments to state constitutions as Mississippi, Louisiana, and North and South Carolina had adopted did great injustice to his people: they had virtually disenfranchised all black voters.[73] Wheaton wanted his resolution adopted at once. Just as the House was at the point of voting, Democratic Representative W. B. Hennessy of St. Paul reminded the members that only recently it had been agreed upon by common consent that no resolutions should be addressed to the Minnesota representatives in Congress, where the purpose was to direct the senators and congressmen how to vote. He then moved to end debate: "The rules on this point are imperative."[74]

Wheaton never brought the resolution back, perhaps deferring to the relief many of his colleagues felt at not having to take a stance on national racial policy. It is as if he understood that Minnesota's sense of duty to civil rights ended at the state border. Such discretion would later be rewarded with his selection as a member of the Minnesota delegation to the Republican National Convention in 1900. This was the second time he was elected to represent a state at the National Republican Convention. His political and professional fortunes now seemed secured. Since the end of the legislative session, Wheaton's law practice grew to be lucrative, but instead of building his practice he formed a partnership with photographer Harry Shepherd, accompanying him to Omaha to sell prints and making speeches in various cities around the state. In August, he traveled to Kansas City to speak at the Emancipation Proclamation Rally and enjoyed a sumptuous reception in his honor. He had indeed become a prominent figure, not limited to the black community of St. Paul or Minneapolis, but statewide. News accounts of the striking "colored member from Minneapolis" whose speeches, always "masterful" and "spellbinding," and always seeming to draw enthusiastic white crowds wherever he went, swelled the collective chest of black Minnesota with overwhelming racial pride.[75] Wheaton was the best of them all.

Not since the Frazier Baker meeting in July 1898, more than two years earlier, had Wheaton had much, if any, contact with Fredrick McGhee. Adams, in planning the banquet to celebrate Wheaton's election, the singular most significant social event in black Minnesota history since the Convention of Colored Citizens that celebrated passage of the black suffrage referendum in 1868, did not include him. But the banquet was also a celebration of the legacy of the Republican Party that had thrown its considerable weight behind the Wheaton campaign, and Fredrick McGhee was a Democrat. Yet, given the fraternal nature of Minnesota's race men, no eyebrows—not even the Democrats, who most assuredly were not confused over his racial loyalty—would have been raised had McGhee attended the banquet. But he did not attend, nor did he extend any message of congratulations to the newly elected representation of the state's 42d district.

Something had attenuated the bond between McGhee and the other Minnesota race men, stemming, it seemed, from his attack on the Wheaton–Morris amendment in 1897 and exacerbated by his pugnacious defense of, strangely, the cakewalk. At a lavish celebration of black support for the Spanish-American War in 1898, a cakewalk was performed. J. C. Reid, a black clergyman from Minneapolis, who witnessed the display, criticized it as a denigration of African Americans. Mrs. Mattie McGhee had been one of the organizers of the event and took the comments as a personal attack, but it was her husband who took the matter to another level. On the same page in the January 7 edition of the *Appeal* where Adams had dedicated five columns to the Wheaton banquet, he printed in the sixth column McGhee's challenge to Reid to debate the propriety of the cakewalk before a panel of nine judges. Reid, having no forensics experience, would later be judged the loser in the contest. Nonetheless, it was Reid who participated in Wheaton's banquet while McGhee looked on from afar.[76]

Throughout 1899, J. Frank Wheaton was the paragon of leadership in black Minnesota. Through his accomplishments as a legislator and attorney and his acceptance into Minnesota's halls of power, he personified the new optimism that came with the belief that Minnesota—during a time of the most dire straits ever experienced by black America nationally since emancipation and, tragically, before, for slaves had not suffered as freedmen and -women now did—was truly the promised land. He had left an impressive record, having introduced bills to improve roads, increase damages for personal injuries, improve the welfare of railroad workers, empower juries in civil trials to reach verdicts with a 5 to 6 vote, impose penalties for flag desecration, and establish juvenile justice.[77] Yet, while prejudice indeed persisted, it was the enactment of his "saloon" bill that portrayed Minnesota as a place where the spirit of goodwill in support of black rights and dignity and the commitment to political, as well as social, equality flowed as wide and deep as the great Mississippi. With Wheaton, blacks felt, there was no limit to what the state's African Americans could achieve, and no limit to the civility that could exist between the black and white people of the state.

Wheaton had other plans, however. Thirteen months after his election, he moved his residency and law practice to Chicago, where he joined "other African American capitalists" to start the Fraternal Life Insurance Company.[78] But he would maintain a residence in Minneapolis, start a new practice with Frank Curtis, who would later become ambassador to Liberia, and campaign for Republican candidate and steamboat captain Samuel Van Sant for the governorship—all of which substantiated his claim to be a Minnesota delegate at the national convention. Still, Wheaton had become a Chicagoan. Nonetheless, as inspiring as his legacy was, his achievements allowed the race leaders to forget, or ignore, the ugly fact that vestiges of the same bestial form of racism they despised in Southern race relations and wanted to redress in some concerted fashion existed in their own beloved state, in their own saintly city. A "saloon" amendment merely glossed over the ever-present possibility that a poor black man in St. Paul could on any given summer night be the victim of the lynch man's rope.

12

A Call to Action

"He bullied, he obstructed, he belittled, he objected ad nauseum, he appealed to God, and he appealed to prejudice."

—Adina Gibbs, daughter of John Adams,
speaking about Fredrick McGhee's courtroom style, 1970

At the end of the day, it was one thing to pass civil-rights laws but quite another to provide moral force to fully engage the stultifying element in Minnesota society that allowed otherwise decent white men to grab a rope and take the law into their own hands. This was the issue that confronted Minnesota even as it looked on with horror at racial violence being waged against the Southern black man. The black population by the end of the decade, not even 1 percent of the total population of the state, made it understandably easy for white policy makers, faced with economic and monetary issues, class tensions from unionists and activist farmers, immigration, and balancing (usually not successfully) reform and business interests, to overlook the problems that African Americans still faced. Thus, the black newspapers—there were three in the Twin Cities—and a vocal and educated black leadership to articulate issues and an agenda were crucial to the welfare of the community. But they faced a dilemma: in talking about racism in the Twin Cities, and the failure of state leaders to provide moral force, did they threaten what tentative success they had achieved? Making certain demands might make them look uncivil, unappreciative, ungrateful. Their small number and anemic voting bloc made them vulnerable to the door slamming shut, and it could get really cold in Minnesota, where the winters could last for a long time. The race men of Minnesota, now without Wheaton, their strongest conduit to the Republican establishment, had to choose their issue and agenda with considerable care.

In 1899, about the time Frank Wheaton left Minnesota, a black man named Henry Johnson was released on good behavior from the Minnesota state prison at Stillwater after serving five years of an eight-year sentence for manslaughter, a crime that was reduced from the charge of second-degree murder. His victim was a black man named Henry Rollins.[1] At the trial in 1894, prosecutor Pierce Butler laid out a straightforward case, sticking closely to the facts and avoiding all flash-point references that would set off racial animus. The defense counsel, on the other hand, took a direct tack. Johnson's attorney told the jury in his opening statement that Rollins was a bad black man and handy with a razor. Although he regretted saying so, argued counsel, it was his duty "to lay before the jury the dregs and absolute lewdness of mankind as found in the Negro."[2] Appealing to the racial bias of white jurors, his argument exploited their sense that black men were prone to violence and the dead man's life—because he too was black—was worth less than a white man's. It was a message that was "all the more powerful coming from an educated, respectable black citizen." The defense attorney was Fredrick McGhee.[3]

Butler, an Irish Catholic Democrat who later would serve as one of the most conservative jurists to sit on the U.S. Supreme Court, responded by arguing that race had nothing to do with the severity of the offense. The value of the life of a black man was equal to that of whites. Butler had reason to worry about the effect McGhee's argument would have on the jury: "the clear trend in criminal cases of this era showed," noted Paul Nelson, "that juries were quite willing to acquit on the basis of self-defense when the victim was black."[4] Once again McGhee touched the nerve of the jurors by reminding them of the recently decided Kate Davis case, a particularly inflammatory trial in which a white woman was acquitted of killing a black man she claimed had attempted to assault her. Although the judge sustained Butler's objection that McGhee's tactic hurt the prosecution's case, the die was cast. "By mentioning Davis, McGhee sent this message to the jury: White people routinely discount black lives in other cases—why should this one be any different?"[5] The jury convicted Johnson of manslaughter rather than the more severe charge of murder. Upon hearing the verdict and understanding what it meant in terms of the sentence to be rendered, the defendant reportedly smiled broadly and shook his attorney's hand.[6]

The minimal value the jury placed on a black man's life gave Johnson a sentence more like that of a common thief. McGhee indeed knew the hearts of the white jurors of St. Paul and was more than willing to exploit them. He was willing to do anything to get his client off. "He bullied, he obstructed, he belittled, he objected ad nauseum, he appealed to God, and he appealed to prejudice."[7] Adina Gibbs, daughter of John Adams, offered the same characterization of McGhee's courtroom style: "He was a man that would perform when he had cases in court. He just performed. He would weep . . . just cry when he needed to impress the jury. Or he would go through performances and roar and howl and all that sort of thing to impress the jury."[8] In other words, nothing—not civil rights, not politics, not fighting racism, not even his own dignity—mattered more than the interest of his client. He won at any cost within the bounds of the law, even if it meant that his jurors would return to their civilian lives operating their restaurants, hotels, and saloons and be just as inclined to deny service to the African American. Paradoxically, with each victory, he enhanced his reputation as a community leader, a defender of his people, a champion of the unwashed masses. None of this fully explained the complex view he held of poor blacks who were arrested far out of proportion to their share of the population. Much of his practice was in criminal law, and because of his race he was sought out by a mostly African American clientele.[9] At a time when belief that the life of "the dregs and absolute lewdness . . . as found in the Negro" could be devalued in a court of law by a race man, one committed to seeking justice and equality for all African Americans, the line separating the jury box from the street inevitably blurred.

One year later, in April 1895, Henry Brown, accused of raping a white woman, evaded a mob in the Mount Airy neighborhood, just blocks from the state capitol, long enough to be arrested and jailed by the police. Brown escaped what Houston Osborne did not: the feel of the rope around the neck. In June, Osborne broke into the bedroom shared by Frieda Kachel and her sisters. When Frieda awoke and screamed, he fled from the house, with the woman's brother Anton giving chase. When Osborne was captured and returned to the scene of the crime, a mob that had gathered led him by a rope to a cottonwood tree near Iglehart and Lexington. He was hoisted off the ground until some women persuaded the men to let him down. McGhee defended him at trial and managed to have the charges reduced from sexual assault and burglary to just burglary. Osborne pled guilty, and was sentenced to ten years.[10] If he had killed another black man, considering Henry Johnson's fate one year earlier, McGhee might have got Osborne a reduced sentence. Anton Kachel, who had led the mob, did not face charges.[11]

The Republican *Pioneer Press* called the threatened lynching of Houston Osborne "a burst of righteous wrath" and the Democratic *Globe* called it "thrilling and remarkable."[12] The "brute" Osborne nearly got what he deserved.[13] This was the image that many white St. Paul residents held about the value of a black man's life. It was also a reminder to blacks that such events were not aberrations in the North Star State, as illustrated by the Combs incident twenty years earlier. In 1877, when the Democratic St. Paul *Pioneer Press and Tribune* approved the use of mob violence, the *Dispatch* responded: "That disgraceful practice has long ceased in Minnesota, and if the editor of the *PP&T* would gratify his unnatural propensity for blood he should at once pack his grip sack and 'go West.'"[14] In 1895, the "West" had spread northeastward to St. Paul. On June 15, 1920, twenty-five years later, the "West" returned to a new generation of Minnesotans, who lynched three black men in Duluth. At that late date, Minnesota had not yet defined lynching as a crime.[15] By 1900, Adams worried whether the aberration of the past was spreading to the North from the South, where it was continuing.[16]

By the 1890s, the South had declared full-scale war on the civil and political rights of African Americans, and, on any given hot Saturday night, on the life of a black man accused of assaulting or raping a white woman. Northerners looked down on these practices as a peculiar and colorfully unfortunate trait of Old Dixie, while casting a blind eye to the presence of that same impulse in their own midst, whereby any white man could lead or participate in a lynch mob without fear of legal reprisal. But because the black population throughout the North was miniscule in comparison to the total population, such occurrences were rare. Despite pervasive anti-black discrimination, the relative absence of lynching became the measure of moral superiority in the area of race relations. Logically, the smaller the black population was, the greater was the state's sense of moral superiority. Even so, during the late nineteenth century in Minnesota, which had the smallest black population east of the Upper Mississippi River Valley, the sense of moral superiority continued in the face of the potential lynching of Combs in 1877 and of Brown and Osborne in 1895, cheered on by the leading Republican newspaper in St. Paul.

In other words, that regrettable impulse so characteristic of the South was alive in the North Star State. Still, the race man in Minnesota operated within a realm of paradox. His exceedingly small community, not even 1 percent of the total population, was a factor in why more attempted lynchings of black men did not occur. In fact, its small size contributed to the community's relative safety because it generally posed no significant threat to other groups. Blustering words seldom escalated to fisticuffs, knives, or the rope. Conversely, their small numbers created in black Minnesotans a sense of vulnerability to the constant potential of a shift of racial mood: a situation could turn deadly in the blink of an eye. Moreover, pervasive discrimination "in places of public enjoyment" was the ever-present reminder that white society did not want African Americans in its midst. Black business owners—some of whom were race men—understood all too well how effectively their political patrons could influence their actions. Relying on their business and their investments, displeased patrons would withhold their support, bringing black businesses to their knees. And because the black community was too small and too poor to support business, black entrepreneurs needed the support of whites. Logically, if white patrons were to apply similar pressure on white businesses that discriminated, the practice would be severely curbed. But they did not do this and black businessmen took note.

In this context, the race men in Minnesota, regardless of their class and party affiliation, felt their security was always provisional. They chose their battles carefully, and to preserve the placid calm at home, those battles were seldom in their own backyards. Living in a state that most Americans viewed as being on the edge of the country before the wastelands of the Great Plains, race men needed the community of like-minded souls. That is why they organized. Whatever the failed strategic impact on inequality or the inadequate tactical effort to be relevant, working in the company of like-minded men on a struggle against which all the powerful forces of the nation were opposed made the difference between surviving to fight another day and extinction. Organizing became an act of existential purpose. However, the newest organization at the end of the century would tack even more toward caution.

Throughout the 1890s Americans witnessed a national trend to devalue black people in virtually every sphere of society. The Mississippi legislature led the way by holding a state constitutional convention in 1890 for the express purpose of disenfranchising the African American voter. Practically overnight, 123,000 black Mississippians were without the vote. The rest of the South followed. In 1895, South Carolina adopted more extravagant measures, followed by Louisiana, that initiated the infamous "grandfather clause." In four years, the number of eligible black Louisiana voters dropped from 130,344 to just 5,320.[17] The U.S. Supreme Court further fueled the flames when it ruled in 1898 that such codes to disenfranchise the Negro "do not on their face, discriminate between the white and Negro races, and do not amount to a denial of equal protection of law . . . if it has not been shown that their actual administration was evil but only that evil was possible under them."[18] Richard Kluger saw it otherwise: "[T]hose who would do in the Negro were absolved from their heinous acts so long as they did not proclaim their intentions to the world in so many words . . . The black man was left severely vulnerable."[19] Judicial niceties notwithstanding, Jim Crow reigned supreme.

Leading members of the academic community presented so-called research that verified the inferiority of the African American. As early as 1884, the future dean of Harvard's Lawrence Scientific School cited the Negro's "animal nature" and his innate and allegedly uncontrollable immorality as good reasons for disenfranchising the race. In 1896, Prudential Life Insurance Company issued a report that the Negroes' "race traits and tendencies" naturally caused his high incidences of diseases such as tuberculosis and syphilis. No improvement in his environment would affect his health record because the root of his problem was his "immense amount of immorality" (68). Sociology professor Franklin Henry Giddings of Columbia University developed the racist concept of "consciousness of kind," while his colleague, historian William H. Dunning, argued that granting black men the vote was a "reckless . . . species of statecraft."[20] Yale's William Graham Sumner asserted that "stateways cannot change folkways"—in other words, civil-rights laws cannot civilize the black man (85–86). "Northern men," reported the *New York Times* in the spring of 1900, "no longer suppress the suppression of the Negro vote as it used to be denounced in the reconstruction days. The necessity of it under the supreme law of self-preservation is candidly recognized" (84). Within the decade, the venerable *Saturday Evening Post* began publishing articles by Thomas Dixon Jr., noted for his novels on the Reconstruction period. His most famous novel would be *The Clansman: An Historical Romance of the Ku Klux Klan,* which would later inspire *The Birth of a Nation.* In his books, black men, when not clowns, seemed either to be planning to rape a white woman or fleeing from the act. In the pages of America's magazines and journals, "it was a paper lynching," and popular culture blurred the line between chivalry and mob violence (ibid.).

Americans formed their views about local affairs and the people living among them on the basis of news articles, editorials, cartoons, and photographs. With the obvious exception of Frederick Douglass, who had died in February 1895, and Booker T. Washington, few African Americans were commonly viewed as noble figures. Most whites in the North had no contact with African Americans. Immigrants rather than African Americans were the source of social concern for native-born whites in many cities. Only 10 percent of black people lived in the entire region and made up less than 2 percent of the entire Northern population. They constituted one-fourth of the population in one city, Washington, D.C., a city usually referred to as Southern. Indianapolis stood second with a little over 9 percent. In Philadelphia, Pittsburgh, Cincinnati, and St. Louis, the black population was estimated to be around 5 percent. Yet, the degradation experienced by the blacks of Philadelphia, which epitomized a growing number of black communities throughout the North, inspired W. E. B. DuBois to write *The Philadelphia Negro* in 1899. In New York, Chicago, and New Haven, Connecticut, 2 percent of the total population was African American, and less than 1 percent in Boston, Detroit, Denver, and San Francisco. St. Paul and Minneapolis figured in the lower end of this category. Numerically, therefore, African Americans did not impinge on the white population as much as they did in the South and most Northern whites would have had no contact with them. Still, Northerners ignored the legal qualification of "separate but equal" and continued to embrace racial segregation. In February 1900, the *Appeal* reported that Booker T. Washington was denied a room in a hotel in Indiana even though the state's public accommodations law had been in effect for fifteen years.[21]

In cities where the black population was relatively large, more articles of African Americans committing crimes reinforced the stereotype of the criminal Negro while ethnics—Italians, Poles, Germans, Swedes—were usually grouped under the term "white." A similar emphasis on the characterization of the Negro, and to a lesser degree on Chinese, Indians, and Mexicans, appeared in stories about lynchings. Lynchings were by no means limited to the South, or to one race of victims, or for one particular offense that led to the death of so many black men. Rather, stories of white men in the West accused of cattle rustling helped to characterize the region as a place of rugged self-help justice. But east of the Mississippi where most African Americans resided, lynching articles often exaggerated the facts leading up to the mob violence, if not its frequency.

Hanging a black man on the flimsiest of evidence was not unthinkable. Due process was not in the state of mind of the mob. "[I]n the eighties and early nineties," writes C. Vann Woodward, "lynching attained the most staggering proportions ever reached in the history of the crime."[22] Emboldened by popular culture and a government that, in law, was complicit in devaluing the black man and woman, whites acted with impunity to murder them. The number of lynchings had begun to mount since 1883 and reached 231 in 1892 alone.[23] Nelson noted that "the pace of lynching increased, reaching to an average of three people murdered per week."[24] The *Appeal* reported that by 1903, 3,237 lynchings occurred over a twenty-one-year period.[25] This was part of the national culture by the end of the nineteenth century, and in some instances in the North, it was addressed quite casually.

In 1898, during the same week when Minnesota's league issued its call to respond to the murder of the black postmaster in South Carolina, T. Thomas Fortune, who had watched the demise of the National Afro-American League, called for the revival of the organization. Thirty delegates met in Rochester, New York, to form the National Afro-American Council. After much praise from the national black press, the NAAC met again in late December in Washington, D.C. More than ninety delegates attended. Two came from Minnesota—John Quincy Adams and Fredrick McGhee.[26] National mobilization, it seemed, had begun. The NAAC had the same leadership and the same problems as before—little money, few organizers, and no allies with political clout. Undaunted, its leaders believed that the oppression of African Americans was too severe to ignore. Even with the organization's clear determination to attack racism, this time it took a different tack with a call to action that embraced the hat-in-hand accommodationist philosophy of Booker T. Washington, whose 1895 Atlanta speech had secured his position as the preeminent leader of his race. Defying him—and therefore the Republican establishment—would be political suicide. Thus, the call did not condemn Congress or the president for failing to fight lynching: "[We] indulge the hope that he will use his good offices to settle this matter to the satisfaction of all concerned."[27]

The NAAC called for reform of the treatment of black prison inmates. In Southern prisons, men, women, and children were held together in convict camps and forced to work in the peonage system.[28] The NAAC did not call for federal action. Instead, referring to what regional penal systems had done, it asked, "Why can't the South? We appeal to its inclination."[29] With regard to regaining voting rights for disenfranchised Southern blacks, the NAAC accepted that education and property qualifications were legitimate criteria, provided that they applied to white voters as well.[30] On the questions of suffrage and education, NAAC went a little farther than Washington when it called for Congress to reduce the number of representatives from Mississippi, South Carolina, and Louisiana because of their discriminatory voting laws that denied eligible blacks their voting rights. It also asked for more funding for schools in the South and called for the elimination of racially segregated schools and industrial education (which Washington endorsed).[31]

With this vision, McGhee and Adams returned to St. Paul to organize on the local level. For McGhee, this meant directing the work under the aegis of the Law Enforcement League. To stimulate enthusiasm, the league sponsored two rallies in early 1899, the second of which was even more extravagant than the first. In honor of Frederick Douglass, the league rented space in the chambers of the state House of Representatives.[32] In a city where many halls could have been used, the selection of the legislative chambers was evidently intended to demonstrate that the state political leadership endorsed the league's vision. Much care was taken to celebrate the legacy of black freedom. Portraits of Douglass, Lincoln, and abolitionists John Brown, Wendell Philips, and Charles Sumner were all framed with evergreens. The St. James AME choir and two soloists sang and a number of speakers came to the podium, including Governor John Lind, who entered the chamber to "great applause and made a very acceptable speech of considerable length." Another speaker was Mrs. Rosa Hazard Hazel, wife of William Hazel, a cofounder of the league who criticized it in 1891 for putting on showy meetings that yielded nothing. Finally, Fredrick McGhee, in "his usual masterful, eloquence," concluded the evening by speaking on "Douglass as a Statesman."[33] The rally did not spark much lasting attention.

In April, the league tried a different approach to gain support by sponsoring a dinner at the Minneapolis home of league president Jasper Gibbs. Following a favored method of fund-raising, the group's leaders invited William Washburn, E. H. Peavey, Percy Jones, and former postmaster W. D. Hale to eat and drink and smoke fine cigars, offering a menu "in keeping with the distinguished character of the guests. "Blue points on half shell, radishes, olives; chicken buillon en tasses, Prussian pretzels, fillet of sole, Holland sauce aux pomme naturel, salted peanuts, sliced cucumbers; appolinaris, le Fruit frapee; tenderloin de beuf larded aux champignons, white potatoes; pineapple ice; larded quail on fancy toast, dressing of assorted nuts, Jersey sweets, strawberries and cream, vanilla cookies, neapolitan cream a la General Harrison; petite four, assorted fruits, chocolate, coffee, Admiral Farraguts."[34] The menu was indeed "in keeping with the distinguished character of the guests."[35] Nelson observed: "If blacks could not get into the Minneapolis Club to divide up the world with Senator Washburn, they would recreate the club on their turf and invite him."[36] But nothing—no money, no support, no commitments, and no agenda that addressed the immediate needs of most St. Paul blacks who were not members of the black political and social elite—came from the evening. The league was destined to lapse into dormancy for lack of relevancy.

The league's manifesto proposed a passive solution to a national emergency as it plaintively requested the federal government—"if it was so inclined"—to perform its duty to protect and defend its own citizens' right to be citizens. In response, Congress remained mute to the demand from blacks for a federal law against lynching; as to the lynching of black postmaster Frazier Baker in South Carolina in 1898, in particular, President McKinley's administration first declined to prosecute, referring to the crime as a state and local matter. When neither jurisdiction acted, the federal government indicted suspects but convicted none.[37] The league founders tried to spark action, but they found instead that to be effective their initiative had to inspire something that their pallid and cautious manifesto failed to do. The restraint of their rhetoric may also have resulted from party loyalty because most members were active in the Republican Party. And all were followers of Booker T. Washington, and he did not approve of militancy. Had he known that Representative Frank Wheaton was just then preparing the bill to include "saloons" in the long list of places covered by the public accommodations act, the Wizard of Tuskegee might not have approved. Coincidentally, in January 1900, he would share the same stage in Chicago to celebrate the launching of Wheaton's insurance company.[38]

In January 1900, league officers met to decide how to raise funds to mount a court challenge against the Louisiana disenfranchisement law.[39] None of the methods they had tried were successful enough to sustain their initiatives. This time they proposed something altogether different: they would produce a play, *A Social Glass,* starring Fredrick McGhee.[40] His character was named Charles Thornley, a rich heir and ne'er-do-well. The convoluted and melodramatic plot involved illicit romantic affairs, jealousy, and alcohol, all of which led to murder. Eventually, the main character was redeemed and virtue won out, thanks to the grace of a temperance worker. McGhee had performed the role a month earlier when the St. Peter Clavier Choral Association produced the play. About this performance, the *Appeal* commented: "[It was] without question the best production so far presented by the Afro-American talent of the Twin Cities . . . [Fredrick McGhee] was good in his lines, and one would have thought the Counselor had some experience in tippling. It is difficult to understand how a total abstainer could mimic so thoroughly a man crazed by drink as he did."[41] The second production to raise money for a lawsuit by Louisiana plaintiffs raised insufficient funds.[42]

About the same time, Booker T. Washington, scheduled to speak at Carleton College in Northfield, Minnesota, was persuaded to join a luncheon in St. Paul to meet with McGhee, Jasper Gibbs, John Adams, William Morris, and others who included members of St. Paul's white political and legal elite. "Booker T. Washington was the man both white and black America loved, the perfect figure to draw white and black elites together to talk politely about race and related matters."[43]

McGhee had initially reserved a room at the Metropolitan Hotel, the same place that had refused Washington access to the dining room during his 1896 visit and Fredrick Douglass in 1873, but after accepting the reservation, the hotel reversed itself, which forced him to move the meeting to the Commercial Club. Not even a conciliatory, even newsworthy race talk between the mayor of the city and "the embodiment of the highest type of Afro-American manhood" would be permitted at one of the largest single employers of St. Paul's African American workers.[44]

Discrimination was merely a problem of race and not something the mayor felt obligated to address. Moreover, the reduced fine that McGhee had argued against in Wheaton's amended law—from five hundred to twenty-five dollars—indeed made discrimination more affordable, hardly an afterthought to the offender. But it was ultimately Washington's sense of honor that mattered here. As Nelson surmised, "McGhee must have at least entertained the thought of filing a high-profile civil rights lawsuit, but this was not Washington's style."[45] In other words, don't use the rights that are available to you, don't test for equality; tests led to consequences that Washington could not approve of. When it was his turn to speak, Washington stressed the need for vocational education and financial self-help. Genuine political and economic equality between the races would have to wait. He made no mention of social equality—the basis on which his unclaimed right to be served at the Metropolitan rested.[46] In this he satisfied the desires of powerful white men to have black people patiently sit in the shadows of opportunity. As Nelson noted, "White politicians and business leaders could support Washington because he symbolized a solution to the 'Negro Problem' that took place without conflict and somewhere off in the hazy future. With a kindly helping hand or two, it was assumed that the African American would someday grow up and take his separate but roughly equal place in American history."[47] In other words, Washington appealed to the image white men had of blacks as men who were now too illiterate and too socially ill-equipped to sit beside them rather than the stately and accomplished black men seated before them who embodied black potential. Adams thought the meeting was a huge success.[48] Washington was welcomed to return in March to participate in their effort to raise part of a national endowment fund of five hundred thousand dollars that would not go to fighting segregation, but for the Tuskegee Institute.[49]

13

A DEFINING MOMENT FOR MCGHEE

"In the history of nearly all other races and peoples the doctrine preached
has been that manly self-respect is worth more than lands and houses . . .
that a people who voluntarily surrender such respect, or cease striving for
it, are not worth civilizing."

—W. E. B. DuBois, *The Souls of Black Folk,* 1903

In 1900, the agenda of Minnesota's race men had evolved into Booker
T. Washington's as they accommodated themselves to the discriminatory practices of the Metropolitan Hotel and Southerners' morbid
infatuation with the practice of lynching and Northerners' prurient flirtation with the same practice. A full thirty-five years after the end of the Civil
War, black citizens were imperiled in virtually every sphere of American
society. What now mattered most was advancing the great experiment in
racial advancement as the Wizard of Tuskegee envisioned it, by demonstrating to friendly whites how intelligent African Americans were united
in this hollow venture. In 1902, St. Paul provided the stage for some of
America's most renowned civil-rights leaders, and Fredrick McGhee,
who organized the whole event, hoped to be catapulted onto the national
stage. Instead, the convention ignited a revolution that was sparked not by
speeches or demonstrations, but by a far more banal incident.

National Afro-American Council meeting, St. Paul, 1902. Booker T. Washington and Ida B. Wells-Barnett are in the front row; T. Thomas Fortune and W. E. B. DuBois are in the second row; and Fredrick McGhee is two rows behind Washington. From the *Appeal*, July 19, 1902.

It must have been a great privilege for admirers to participate in any gathering attended by the great man from Tuskegee. The magnetism of Washington's personality, the grandeur of his vision, the force of character and gravitas of his authority brought the best out in both white and black men of standing, and it was only his imprint on the race work at hand that bestowed any semblance of moral integrity and prospect of success. Many had come to believe that no black man before or since Frederick Douglass occupied this level of acclaim. Douglass himself, or rather his memory, now paled in comparison, for his name or views were no longer uttered by intelligent Negro leaders; his image required a periodic dusting off whenever it was needed to adorn some convention hall. The fact that Booker T. Washington was both monumental in stature and black made him the embodiment of hope and pride for many African Americans. But even these two attributes fell short of fully understanding his authority, for his imperial bearing conveyed the impression that he was a man imbued with the support of great white men of power who saw in him the incarnation of the solution to the Negro Problem, or at least its containment. Race men everywhere, whether they were adherents of his philosophy or simply loyal to the man, or whether they were opponents, knew that it was through him that all favors flowed, from whom the imprint of acceptability came, against whom junior men like DuBois—who early in his career curried favor from the Wizard for desperately needed funds to do his research—quietly grappled with their capacity to compromise.[1] His blessing of the next convention of the NAAC was critical. It would not only determine the success of the three-day event but boost St. Paul's prestige and rescue the NAAC from disarray. Fredrick McGhee was responsible for the whole affair, and if he was successful, the event could also elevate his standing as a national race leader.

It was the opportunity McGhee had been waiting for. After a frustrating decade, he had not been able to secure even a toehold within the leadership of either the Republican or Democratic parties. His own position seemed relegated to the sidelines until either party, finding in him a symbol of their own racial enlightenment, needed a rousing speech for a white candidate. In the NAAC, McGhee had found that his place, his passion, and his purpose were not to be found in the Minnesota political landscape but in the national arena of civil rights.

For a decade, McGhee had been heading in this direction, whether by litigating the Tennessee separate car law or the Louisiana disenfranchisement law. Most recently, in 1901 he had defended a black man accused of murdering a white man in Tennessee, against an interstate extradition request. He took his case on appeal before the Minnesota Supreme Court, becoming the first African American to argue before that body. He failed, yet his stature grew.[2] A frequent delegate representing Minnesota at national conventions of various civil-rights organizations, by 1899 McGhee was being recognized by national leaders as a man ready for a larger platform. The leaders of the NAAC decided to hold the convention in St. Paul, and in so doing gave him that platform. For McGhee, the stakes were high.

McGhee demonstrated his value to the NAAC through his success as an organizer of events: securing meeting halls, finding housing for guests and delegates, raising money to cover costs, persuading people to attend while addressing innumerable unexpected diversions and challenges. He labored over the programming and staging of the event and made sure that the convention was well publicized. But even if everything went off without a hitch, there was no guarantee that the convention would draw the slightest attention. The surest draw would be the support and participation of Booker T. Washington. The Wizard of Tuskegee, as he had come to be known, had skipped two of the three previous conventions and there was no sense that he would attend this year's event. As early as March 1902, McGhee began writing to Washington's secretary, Emmett Scott, explaining that any level of participation would be most appreciated. Then he urged Scott to persuade Washington to come: "Our people will feel bad if we do not get him."[3]

A week later, McGhee expressed a new level of urgency to getting Washington's participation, one that went beyond mere invitation and expressed alarm over the very survival of the NAAC. Writing directly to Washington, McGhee mentioned his "deep anxiety concerning your coming to the meeting." The NAAC, he confessed, "has no well-defined course" and the organization could not be trusted to "safely adopt [sound policies and strategy] without your judgment and advice."[4] Echoing an April message to Scott decrying the poor leadership of then-NAAC president Bishop Alexander Walters, McGhee feared that without Washington's restraining influence, others would push their own selfish agendas. Even so, knowing Washington's distaste for controversy and that his critics were growing in number, McGhee assured him that they could "arrange our program so that you will not be placed under an embarrassment."[5] When the *Appeal* printed the official call for the convention, Washington's name appeared nowhere in the program.[6]

By that time, McGhee and his committee (composed of attorney William Francis, John Adams, and prominent black St. Paul photographer Harry Shepherd) had designed and printed stationery featuring photographs of Fort Snelling, Minnehaha Falls, Como Park, and St. Paul's new High Bridge. They had reserved the senate chamber of the old state capitol for business sessions, Central Presbyterian and House of Hope Presbyterian churches for evening entertainment and educational sessions, the University of Minnesota Armory for a banquet, and secured rooms in private homes for delegates and guests, and organized parties, receptions, and musical programs. "[N]early every middle-class black family in the Twin Cities had contributed time and effort to the enterprise."[7] But when the convention began, only fifty delegates were present, fewer than had been anticipated.[8] On the evening of July 7, delegates were treated to a long evening of musical selections that included arias from Bizet's *Carmen,* choral renditions from Gounod's *Faust* and Handel's *Hallelujah Chorus,* piano duets from *Il Trovatore,* violin solos, "Hail to the Chief" sung by a chorus of ten accompanied by organ, and an arrangement of "Ave Maria" sung by two vocalists from the St. Peter Claver Choir.[9] But the real show began on the morning of July 9 at the state capitol when Democratic St. Paul Mayor Robert Smith gave the welcome address, followed by Republican Governor Samuel Van Sant. As more speeches followed, there was a stir in the audience as delegates saw the great man himself, Booker T. Washington, escorted to a growing applause to a seat on the stage.[10] There at last he was, the man who without portfolio wielded more influence than any officer of the NAAC. His presence outshone all other luminaries in the chamber. His solemn stature as he sat there quietly on stage spoke louder than any orator who came to the podium.

That afternoon council president Walters gave the keynote address, focusing on two central themes—black suffrage and whether Southern blacks should leave the South. In both instances, he espoused the Washington line: the requirements that Southern states imposed on blacks should also apply to whites.[11] Superficially, the argument seemed reasonable. But on closer examination, such qualifications as education and property ownership were expressly designed to disenfranchise African Americans who lived in a region where most whites were themselves illiterate and impoverished but were nevertheless permitted to vote. It was naive to assume that such codes would be color-blind—a term believed to be first coined by Albion Tourgee when he argued against state-sanctioned segregation in *Plessy v. Ferguson*—or that it was white county administrators, not the law, that filtered blacks off the voting rolls. Given the current racial climate, there was no reason to believe that such practices would change. Further, there was no way to apply the grandfather clause to whites, for the grandfather of no *true* white man had ever been a slave.

As to the question of black migration, Walters argued that Southern African Americans should remain in the South.[12] But this argument was shortsighted. African Americans were vulnerable because they lacked the political power that came from massive voting. As long as the majority remained in the South where they were disenfranchised, black power could not exist and white politicians could continue to ignore their interests. The only way for blacks to acquire political power (short of federal protections that overturned Jim Crow laws) was for them to migrate to the North where they could vote—to cities like Chicago or St. Paul. McGhee should have understood this, for he had lost the Republican presidential electorship in 1892 to ethnic politics ("There were more Swedish votes in Minnesota than black") and also the assistant city attorney post ("The Irish won't be prosecuted by a black man").[13]

But this was not the Bookerite position. The national agenda for black development was explicitly nonpolitical, and moving to the North with the express intent of creating black political power was diversionary at best. The South, not the North, was where most African Americans resided, where they understood Anglo-Saxon, Protestant whites, unlike the many ethnic groups who streamed into Northern cities from all parts of the world, speaking different languages, having different religions, competing for low-paying jobs in modern urban life. In the South it was easier to be useful, easier to start a cottage industry and to survive among the devils they knew. The data to be presented during the morning session of the second day—except, of course, for the growing number of lynchings that Mrs. Barnett would report—attested to this rosy view. Perhaps McGhee understood the dilemma. He knew that the South was determined to force its black population back to second-class citizenship, and if left unchecked, to unending servitude. He also saw how, with more black voters in Minnesota, the state's political elite would have to share power with its African American partners. As one who literally rose *up from slavery*, he knew that with discipline and hard work Southern black men in the North could attain education, honest work, a profession (if that was their aspiration), and respectability, none of which was likely under the present conditions in the South.

But McGhee also knew the other consequence of black migration to St. Paul, a city many out-of-state blacks may have considered "easy."[14] He had seen the black population grow rapidly during the last decade looking for job opportunities, with the greatest increase coming from young black men from the upper South. These arrivals added to the imbalance between the sexes and a highly transient population along lower Cedar, Minnesota, and Roberts streets.[15] The nature of his profession offered him an intimate arrangement with the growing underclass of St. Paul, where,

W. E. B. DuBois in 1904. George Grantham Bain Collection, Library
of Congress Prints and Photographs Division.

as Nelson noted, "lots of people were on the make."[16] As the decade progressed, "native" Minnesota African Americans renewed efforts to protect
themselves against the influx of "undesirables" as "local Negro leaders and
organizations 'screened' the migrants and selected those deemed 'worthy' to enter the state."[17] The criminal element tainted how white people
viewed all blacks, including those who were respectable.

Here was where the convention was fundamentally flawed: it supported the uplift of poor blacks, while viewing that class of blacks as undesirable. The dilemma facing it (other delegates had to be feeling the same
way) was never aired. Although Walters did not offer a clear course of
action, the weakness of NAAC—and, in time, its failure—was the absence
of debate. No one rose to question. No one rose to challenge. Some
of the delegates—notably, DuBois and Ida B. Wells-Barnett—clearly

understood that the dire conditions in which African Americans lived would not improve by moral suasion alone. Both understood the necessity of political, educational, and economic empowerment.

At the time of the convention, DuBois was compiling what he called "a number of his fugitive pieces" into a single volume he would title *The Souls of Black Folk*. In one of the pieces, "Of Our Spiritual Striving," he wrote: "The power of the ballot we need in sheer self-defense."[18] More poignantly, in "Of Mr. Booker T. Washington and Others," he said that Washington's philosophy of submission "practically accepts the alleged inferiority of the Negro races" as part of the bargain of timid, circumscribed advancement. "In the history of nearly all other races and peoples the doctrine preached has been that manly self-respect is worth more than lands and houses . . . that a people who surrender voluntarily such respect, or cease striving for it, are not worth civilizing." To Washington's belief that black people surrender political power, civil rights, and higher education as a means for advancement, he responded: "If history and reason give any distinct answer . . . it is an emphatic *No*."[19]

As Walters spoke, DuBois ruminated on the absence of criticism, which had helped Washington maintain his power over the civil-rights agenda. DuBois had addressed the issue recently in his review of Washington's book *Up from Slavery,* and it would appear again in *Souls:* "[T]he hushing of the criticism of honest opponents is a dangerous thing. It leads some of the best of the critics to unfortunate silence and paralysis of effort, and others to burst into speech so passionately and intemperately as to lose listeners. Honest and earnest criticism from those whose interests are most nearly touched—criticism of writers by readers, of government by those governed, of leaders by those led—this is the soul of democracy and the safe guard of modern society."[20]

Wells-Barnett had already demonstrated her willingness to confront discrimination rather than capitulate to it. In March 1884, after the U.S. Supreme Court had rendered its decision in *Civil Rights Cases,* she boarded a train in Memphis to Woodstock, Tennessee, where she was teaching, and took a seat in the ladies section of the first-class car. But the conductor refused to take her ticket. He ordered her to the smoking car, reserved for blacks. She refused, possibly recalling the following editorial written in response to the decision, six months earlier: "The colored people of the United States feel as if they had been baptized in ice water. The

Ida B. Wells-Barnett, circa 1905. Courtesy of the Special
Collections Research Center, University of Chicago Library.

Supreme Court now declares that railroad corporations are free to force
us into smoking cars or cattle cars, that hotel-keepers are free to make us
walk the streets at night; that theatre managers can refuse us admittance
to their exhibitions."[21] The writer T. Thomas Fortune at an earlier age had
proposed that black people refuse to accept this treatment. If they were to
be beaten or killed for their resistance, it would be for a good cause. "One
or two murders growing from this intolerable nuisance," he wrote, "would
break it up."[22] Wells-Barnett refused to move. The conductor grabbed her
but she resisted, biting his hand, bracing herself against the seat in front
of her. Two men assisted the conductor in shoving her off the train at the
next station. "Bruised, the sleeves of her linen duster torn, she tumbled
down the steps to the platform while her white fellow passengers stood
up and applauded."[23] In *Wells v. Chesapeake, Ohio & Southwestern Railroad,* the first public accommodations suit to be heard in the South since
Civil Rights Cases, she sued the railroad in state court and was awarded
five hundred dollars, before losing on appeal in 1887 on grounds that "her
persistence was not in good faith."[24] What the Supreme Court considered
"bad faith persistence," Fortune knew better: "She had plenty of nerve;
she is smart as a steel trap, and she has no sympathy with humbug."[25]

In 1892, upon realizing that Memphis officials would do nothing to prosecute those responsible in lynching a black shopkeeper, Wells-Barnett called for a mass exodus of black residents from a city "that will neither protect our lives and property, nor give us a fair trial, but takes us out and murders us in cold blood." The black community responded with people selling their homes and crossing the Mississippi to settle in Arkansas.[26] One minister led his entire congregation to California; another led his parishioners to Kansas. In two months, more than six thousand African Americans left Memphis because Wells-Barnett had asked them to. Soon white businesses that depended on their patronage began to fail. White housewives complained of a shortage of domestic workers. Whole blocks of homes stood vacant. With what Wells-Barnett had experienced in Memphis, knowing what she knew about the economic potential of blacks to effect change, at least in Southern cities, Walters's words had to sound hollow.[27]

Later during the convention DuBois reported that the nation was moving rapidly toward industrialization and blacks needed to be educated and "understand the modern civilization" to avoid the economic enslavement that had already ensnared far too many.[28] More tragic still, as Wells-Barnett reported in a later session, 135 black men were lynched in 1901 alone. Two or three black men per week had been lynched for seventeen years.[29] Both reports attested to the determination of powerful white men who would not share their power willingly, and now apparently was not the right time for black folks to initiate a massive protest. That evening was filled with more speeches and musical numbers, including again *The Hallelujah Chorus,* a piano solo, and a hymn sung by a quartet; "The Rosary" sung in English, French, and German by Cyrus Field Adams, brother of *Appeal* publisher John Adams; five more speeches, including one by Josephine Silone Yates, president of the National Association of Women, who talked about nonpolitical matters. She argued that the future of African American prosperity was in the South, the new colonial territories, even Germany and Africa, but not in America's northern cities. Blacks, she said, must work to develop their own skills, self-reliance, and inventive genius, and stay away from politics. "The product of his imagination . . . will accomplish more toward molding the future of the race than any amount of favorable legislation." Washington probably would have approved, though he wasn't present.[30]

On the second day, after a morning of reports on black commercial enterprise, lynching, race mortality, and the economic status of blacks in the South, the delegates adjourned for lunch. Apparently weary of hearing yet more dreary reports scheduled for the afternoon events, fewer than twenty delegates were present. The more than thirty delegates who went elsewhere—perhaps sightseeing at Como Park, Fort Snelling, Minnehaha Falls, or St. Paul's new High Bridge—had evidently not read the morning edition of the *Pioneer Press*, which predicted that a fight was about to happen.[31]

At 2 p.m., instead of calling for the report from the education bureau as scheduled, the chairman of the day called for the nominating committee's report, which had been scheduled for the following afternoon. The report recommended, among other things, that T. Thomas Fortune and Bishop Walters swap positions, with Fortune assuming the council presidency. In a strange twist of procedure, when the delegates accepted the report, the vote was interpreted to mean that the officers had been elected to the new posts. William Pledger, the day's chairman, an attorney-delegate from Atlanta, and a strident Bookerite, handed the gavel to Fortune, the new president-elect.[32] DuBois and his friend Ida Wells-Barnett participated in the protest against the election. To them, Fortune was thoroughly unfit, suffering under severe money problems, argumentative with almost everyone, and, worse still for an organization that was supposed to be nonpartisan, he was seeking a political appointment from President Roosevelt.[33]

The first to protest the election was Minnesota's lone delegate, noted St. Paul photographer Harry Shepherd, who said, "To place T. Thomas Fortune in the presidential chair of this Council by underhanded means, without allowing delegates to have a vote, means the extermination of the Council as a body." Other voices also spoke out against the vote. In the end, the only discussion President-elect Fortune permitted was a motion to adjourn. Notably, throughout the rancor, Fredrick McGhee remained oddly silent.[34] Not until later that evening did he speak to a reporter: "There is a deep feeling . . . that the way the election was carried out was an outrage. The arbitrary ruling of the presiding officer is subject to no other construction than trickery. One thing is certain, and that is that a Council like this cannot long exist unless such actions as this of today are guarded against and made impossible in the future."[35]

His convention had become uncomfortably controversial. Some of the biggest names in the council had openly rejected the newly elected leadership, which included McGhee himself. He had also benefited by this "trickery" as the council's financial secretary-elect, satisfying, it would seem, his own ambition. The power play had been crude and blatant and the man McGhee admired the most had to have been behind it. McGhee's own reputation may have been sullied as he pleaded with Washington to provide the council with "safe and sound guidance" because it "had no well-defined course": *Come and take over, and all will be arranged for your convenience.* What did he expect? Why the urgency? Prior to the St. Paul convention, opposition to Washington offered no real threat to his leadership. At the conventions of 1899 and 1900, critics tried to pass resolutions that condemned Washington, but they failed because of insufficient organization. In 1901, the fiery Harvard-educated William Monroe Trotter founded and edited the Boston *Guardian* that provided anti-Bookerites—the Radicals—with an uncompromising organ for challenging the Washington machine.[36]

Feeling that Washington's influence effectively lulled the council away from being a strong instrument for justice, Trotter and his supporters conspired to capture the 1902 St. Paul convention by thwarting the election to the presidency of a Washington sympathizer. During the months preceding the convention, rumors circulated about an impending coup by the Radicals. This probably was McGhee's motivation for urging Washington to attend. In the months leading up to the convention, Taylor explained, "Washington and his supporters marshaled their strength in an attempt to bring the Council completely under their domination."[37]

It is not certain what emotional landscape Washington loyalist McGhee covered between the outcry after the election and his interview with the reporter, nor why this single event changed him from sycophancy to disenchantment. What is known is that he became an outspoken critic virtually overnight, initially of the election, then of Washington himself.

The Bookerites may have hoped that the evening events would cool tempers, but delegates and guests attending the House of Hope Church seemed more restrained by decorum than by a short memory. After a music program that included "The Heavens Are Telling," "Lead, Kindly Light," and "Achieved Is the Glorious Work," the audience settled in to hear what they had been waiting for: Washington explaining what had happened.

Instead, he gave his standard speech of patience and self-help and the necessity of blacks learning how to live with their white neighbors.[38]

Then, as if knowing he had to say something about the election controversy, he added, "I am glad to see in this Council so many evidences of the fact that we can sink the individual preferences and differences and unite in the one direction of uplifting the race."[39] However, "uniting in one direction" would be as illusory among the delegates as would Washington's philosophy of accommodation create true black development and racial harmony.

As delegates assembled in the senate chambers the next morning for the last day of the convention, they must have seen that morning's issue of the *Pioneer Press*. Its headline read, "Election Causes a Row on the Afro-American Council: Those in Control Fix Up Slate to Retain Their Supremacy and Rush Ticket through When Majority of Delegates Are Absent."[40]

The headline, which exposed the rift he had hoped to cover over with the veneer of unity, must have humiliated McGhee.[41] The *Pioneer Press* was the city's most prominent newspaper and it called the election that had led to McGhee's advancement corrupt. To many observers, it did appear corrupt. The power grab was blatant, without any semblance of due process, debate, or democracy. This was not how the best of the African American race should comport themselves. And it happened at McGhee's convention, on his watch, in his hometown. His honor was at stake. When the morning session began, McGhee and others were ready to renew the fight.

As if expecting a fair hearing from men he deeply respected, "McGhee," Nelson wrote, "led off with a lawyer's challenge to the election, citing four technical irregularities."[42] The chairman of the day promptly dismissed all of McGhee's points. It was as if a door had been slammed in his face. Delegate Nelson Crews then rose to speak, advising the council to elect future officers fairly and without trickery; he referred to Fortune as the "alleged" council president. At this, Fortune jumped up and called Crews to step outside where they could settle the issue. Crews declined, but said, after provoking Fortune's explosive temper as proof of the president-elect's lack of fitness for the post, "[W]hen you throw a stone amid a pack of dogs and one of them squeals, it is pretty good evidence that he is hit." This caused an uproar among the delegates as Crews demanded that all new officers resign so that new elections could be held. The motion was denied. Then he and Ida Wells-Barnett resigned their posts, and the morning session ended.[43]

That afternoon final reports were read. Louisville was designated the site for the 1903 convention, the resignations of Crews and Wells-Barnett were rejected, and the Annual Address to the Nation was adopted. In the end, the prize of victory was control over the wording of the Annual Address to the Nation that would be printed in both black and white newspapers nationwide. With Fortune securely at the helm, and the Wizard's voice in his ears, "the Annual Address," Taylor noted, "was . . . even more conciliatory than it had been in the past."[44]

Included in the address was the endorsement of President Roosevelt, the man from whom council president Fortune was seeking a political appointment, the man who, by inviting Washington for dinner, became the second U.S. president to invite a black man into the White House.[45] Such an endorsement was in direct contravention to the council's nonpartisan policy. Moreover, Roosevelt was a Republican whom Democrat McGhee had once accused of "slaughter[ing] the [Afro-American] race."[46] But McGhee's opinion did not matter. With this, the delegates ended the official business of adopting sound policies and strategies as influenced by the Wizard of Tuskegee. It was time to celebrate.

The banquet that evening, held in the University of Minnesota Armory, was possibly the greatest African American social event in Twin Cities history, decorated in evergreens and miles of red and white bunting into which sixteen electric arc lights were set "in large red balloon-like covering which caused a rosy glow to cover the scene." In the center of the room was a fountain that sent jets of water sixteen feet into the air and was adorned with palms and flowers "making a fairy-like scene that beggars description." Archbishop John Ireland gave the keynote address.[47]

Following this was the grand march led by Fredrick McGhee, wearing a tuxedo and accompanied by his wife Mattie, who wore a pink silk gown and diamonds. "The evolution [of the grand march] was artistic and the long lines and curves of the column filled with handsomely gowned ladies made a scene long to be remembered," the *Appeal* reported. Then nearly two hundred delegates and guests lined up for a sumptuous buffet dinner, after which, having the floor, they were able to commence the evening dance.[48] "It was a nice twist that music was performed by Kuhn's orchestra; at this dance the only white folks in the hall (except for the Archbishop) were the musicians."[49]

The *Appeal* reported in detail the diamonds, pearls, and emeralds, the robin's-egg-blue organdy, court train ecru cord embroidery, Valenciennes lace insertions and black velvet that the ladies wore. However, it did not report anything about the election controversy.[50] That was left to the *Dispatch,* which went into much detail. The *Pioneer Press,* which had scooped the other newspapers on the brewing turmoil among delegates under the headline "Harmony Seemingly Reigns," wrote simply, "The victory of the ruling faction had not been won without leaving many hard feelings."[51]

The divide between the Bookerites and anti-Bookerites had clearly deepened. But even radical editor William Monroe Trotter criticized his ally DuBois for remaining relatively neutral during the convention, claiming that his friend was "like all the others who were trying to get on the bandwagon of the Tuskegean."[52] Trotter, who didn't care much for the council anyway, always relished an opportunity to attack Washington, and was often impatient with friends who didn't share his zeal.

McGhee, on the other hand, who had argued against the Bookerites and thereby potentially severed connections he needed for personal advancement on the national stage, found solace in the fact that so many editors of the black press took little note of the workings of the council, let alone its viability as a force of relevance to black America. They did agree that McGhee had done a fine job of organizing the convention. McGhee took special pleasure in one editor's criticism of Washington's power play:

> After reading the [*Colored American's*] editorial calling the meeting a farce, he purchased a one-year subscription to the paper, asked for several extra copies to give "to white friends of mine," and commented, "Can you tell me if you ever saw more smoke coming down the pike than we are making for the Council?"[53]

Editorials like the *Colored American's* seemed to show McGhee that there was another route to leadership, that as influential as Washington was in black and white America, a significant and perhaps growing number of African American opinion makers and their readers were not under his sway. Indeed, the Bookerites did not win their victory without cost. Washington's ambitious move alienated several important members of the council who had been his supporters. Their desertion had the effect of strengthening the radical cause.[54] But McGhee's resolve may have been especially piqued by an event that had just occurred in the liberal city across the river. It showed with frightening clarity, and apparently like never before, how bankrupt Washington's approach was. In August 1902, William Hicks, a banjo player, found himself harassed by a small group of white men. He kicked two away and ran across the street. They followed after him and crowded around him menacingly until a harvest hand named Peterson fell to the ground "stabbed in two places." Hicks ran away, but he was soon apprehended by the police amid threats to lynch him. "And this is Minneapolis, too," reported the *Appeal*. "Just think."[55]

It is ironic that one more voice alleging the irrelevancy of the council came in a letter before the end of the year from none other than council president T. Thomas Fortune as he was about to take a six-month leave of absence to take a federal appointment he had just been awarded by President Roosevelt. "The main difficulty and drawback to the National Afro-American Council today," Fortune wrote, "is that it has no substantial basic organization. The masses of people do not belong to it or support it with their sympathy and money . . . The official board of the organization really constitutes the only membership . . . No organization constituted as the National Afro-American Council is today, as to its basic membership, can do the important work mapped out by its founders and expected by the people at large."[56]

This was the portrait of an organization the Wizard wanted to control at any price. This was the impact of his patronage over a once promising but now confused young leader. This was the circumstance that now seemed to conjure the soul of the great Frederick Douglass, inspiring McGhee to take his next step in a different direction:

> Those who profess to favor freedom, and yet deprecate agitation, are men who want crops without plowing up the ground. They want rain without thunder and lightning. They want the ocean without the awful roar of its water. This struggle may be a moral one, or it may be a physical one, but it must be a struggle. Power concedes nothing without demand. It never did, and it never will.[57]

Aware that Washington's vision for black advancement was fundamentally flawed, and seeing the future of African Americans rested firmly upon a new agenda, McGhee set his sights on Louisville.

14

After St. Paul, Niagara

"The honor of founding the organization belongs to F. L. McGhee, who first suggested it."

—W. E. B. DuBois, 1905

The convention in St. Paul was ultimately not all that it was intended to be: a spectacular showcase of black life in the Twin Cities and the special relationship that existed between African Americans, especially their social and political elite, and the state's white political and business establishment. The state's governmental leaders had opened the doors to the senate chamber for black men and women to discuss the new civil-rights agenda and it was Minnesota's business leaders who made the opulent festivities possible. But still it all went wrong. Booker T. Washington had exposed his imperial temperament and insistence on absolute control in a way that alienated many, including Fredrick McGhee, arguably Minnesota's most talented race leader. He had organized the event with the intent to secure an affiliation with Washington that would catapult him to national prominence, as a willing acolyte of the great man. But McGhee learned that he was expendable to Bookerite maneuvering at the convention in a blatant move to maintain power over dissenting voices and proceed not in the interest of black America but in the Wizard's behalf. A change of agenda needed to be made, and the next convention in Louisville would provide the stage for confrontation. As he prepared, mindful of all that was at stake—damage to the relations that Washington had established with powerful white men of national prominence, damage to his own reputation nationally and at home to relations with other black leaders who had signed on as Bookerites, damage to the potential of any future civil-rights effort—McGhee, perhaps not even realizing it himself, was inexorably approaching his own defining moment as a genuine national race leader. For the cause and the right side of history, and not personal advancement, he was about to take the side of the small group of black activists called simply "The Radicals" who were led by Ida B. Wells-Barnett, William Monroe Trotter, and a man to whom he would become very close, William E. B. DuBois.

By February 1903, John Adams, William Morris, William Francis, a black St. Paul attorney, and other members of the Twin Cities black elite remained within the ranks of both the Republican Party and the Bookerite faction. Although they knew McGhee to be a Democrat and one who had challenged the council election of Washington's men in 1902, they maintained a collegial relationship with him. In fact, it was likely that few truly understood the intensity to which McGhee felt alienated from the Wizard. Those like Adams and Francis who had seen him argue the irregularities of the election only to be summarily rejected saw him remain disciplined and professional, even remarkably good-natured in defeat. The differences that existed between them—McGhee on one side, the Bookerites on the other—were either purely philosophical or subordinated to a determination to refrain from exacerbating the cleavage between the two warring camps. In fact, McGhee was simply biding his time, waiting for the right moment to strike.[1]

In any event, in early February 1903, these loyal Bookerites elected him to be president of the St. Paul chapter of the NAAC.[2] On February 19 he presided over the Frederick Douglass Day gathering held in the chamber of the House of Representatives at the state capitol and shared the dais with Governor Van Sant, the governor's son, who gave an impromptu speech, and the Reverend Reverdy Ransom, a prominent clergyman from Chicago and future member of the Niagara Movement.[3] It was Ransom's comments that foretold McGhee's vision for a new agenda for equality:

Some questions may be left to time to work out their solutions and others must be settled. To dodge them or leave them for the future is cowardice and criminal. We have never lacked men of courage . . . So with the "Negro Question," we have men who will not dodge but will settle it. It may be said of Frederick Douglass that he achieved greatness in spite of his environments. He stood as the champion of liberty, civilization, and manhood.[4]

But more, he said, needed to be done. Black people voted and paid their fair share of taxes, because they took their role as citizens seriously. It was now time for the nation to face its responsibility. To McGhee, black people had to continue to become aggressive:

Meetings like this and resolutions will not settle the question. We have got to get together. It means you have got to go down in your pockets and fight the battle in the courts and until we do this there will be no settlement of this question.[5]

He was referring to supporting the St. Paul chapter's campaign to litigate the Louisiana separate car law, an un-Bookerite initiative that McGhee was able to have the chapter sponsor, an indication of Washington losing his grip on the organization. McGhee had just been promoted to one of the legal directorship positions for the council after being head of its legal bureau.[6] Later that evening, at the Frederick Douglass Day banquet, before dignitaries who included judges, black and white clergymen, the state's attorney, and city council members, Ransom intensified his message:

Now is the time for every man who has a drop of Negro blood in his veins to speak, and speak so well that the whole civilized world shall hear him . . . There is a time when things have got to be stirred up, and now is the time when the Afro-American has got to stir things up to preserve his rights and franchises.[7]

In April things were indeed stirred up with the release of DuBois's *The Souls of Black Folk*. To many the book was to civil rights what *Uncle Tom's Cabin* was to the abolition of slavery. Surprisingly, it was John Adams, still a Bookerite, who articulated this sentiment: "It is probable that quite a large percentage of the Caucasian people in the United States, if one judges by the spirit of prejudice which exists here, really doubt the existence of souls under black or colored skin. The wave of color prejudice which has recently swept over the country, threatening the absolute undoing of one-seventh of the citizens of this land, by the denial of their simplest rights, and the attempt now being made by the South to relegate all Afro-Americans without regard to character and intelligence, to the condition of practical serfdom, the *Souls of Black Folk* ... is one of the most striking books in contemporary literature."[8] The book review appeared every week in the *Appeal* until July 4, just before the Louisville convention, taking two full-page columns on page 2. Apparently, his Bookerite patrons, who contributed considerable funding to the *Appeal,* as they had to other black newspapers, now felt it necessary to rein him in. Elsewhere Adams wrote an essay that touted Washington's call for patience, self-sacrifice, and humility.[9]

DuBois's book also stirred mass criticism in the white national newspapers and journals and that had the effect of discouraging continued support for his work. At the same time, notes DuBois's biographer David Levering Lewis, "Tuskegee's endowment, thanks to a single night of fundraising at Madison Square Garden, was overflowing."[10]

That night former President Grover Cleveland spoke of "a grievous amount of ignorance . . . laziness and thriftlessness" among nine million African Americans. Edgar Gardner Murphy of the Southern Education Board characterized those types of African Americans as "a rotting body ... polluting the atmosphere we breathe," and Lyman Abbott, a theologian and author, praised the superiority of the white race. Assembled that night were America's leadership of finance, philanthropy, and higher education, including such titan families as the Baldwins, the Ogdens, the Peabodys, the Carnegies, Oswald Villard (later a founder of the NAACP), and many others. Ten days after the fund-raiser, not quite three weeks after the release of DuBois's book, Andrew Carnegie gave Washington six hundred thousand dollars in U.S. Steel bonds for the Tuskegee endowment fund, $150,000 of which was to be "set aside for the personal use of the Wizard and his family."[11] All of this placed Tuskegee in the ranks of the country's richest educational institutions.[12]

In St. Paul, nothing more was mentioned about the separate car lawsuit: insufficient funds were raised for a court challenge. McGhee's attentions now lay elsewhere. Throughout the spring, he appeared to remain a loyal supporter of Washington, but as the Louisville convention grew near, he contacted Trotter to make plans to wrest the council from Bookerite control. In a letter dated June 15, he pushed for Trotter to send as many of his followers from Boston as possible: "We will need your men to help overthrow the present officers of the Council."[13]

Days before he left for Louisville, McGhee at last proclaimed his true feelings in a speech he delivered in St. Paul: "We negroes have become tired of the manner in which we have been made toys for forty years. We have pursued a path of humility only to be trampled all the more." As reported in the Democratic *Daily Globe*—the *Appeal* did not report the plan—McGhee outlined the role that the council henceforth should play. He said black people should abandon the traditional exhortation and protest in favor of the exercise of voting power, along the lines of modern political efforts.[14] The council, McGhee argued, should "go to the politicians and say, 'You must give us our rights; for if you do not we will, in the coming election, take care of the districts that we control, and the results will not be the most beneficial to you.'" The council—indeed, black people as a whole—must truly free themselves from dogged loyalty to a single party, and support whichever will receive them and defend their best interests.[15] To make this happen, its leadership had to change. He wanted the Radicals to take over the leadership and support him to unseat Fortune as president, and he hoped that Trotter, coming to Louisville "with a quiver full of anti-Washington resolutions," would help to make this happen.[16]

In some ways, it was a naive prescription for action. In Southern districts where black residents were the numerical majority, Jim Crow policies denied them access to the polls. This was the problem. Southern politicians had created Jim Crow laws precisely to divest black majorities and keep them in a state of powerlessness. The council would have to transform the demography of African Americans nationwide, to the point of concentrating blacks in districts where the franchise had not been lost, and that meant embracing black migration to Northern cities.

It meant being willing to receive Southern blacks in Minnesota. It meant amassing a political base that challenged powerful white patrons who might view McGhee as an "ingrate," just as abolitionists did when Frederick Douglass broke from his mentor William Lloyd Garrison to start his own newspaper in 1847.[17] It meant threatening Northern and Southern businesses with loss of their cheap black labor. And it meant frightening black Minnesotans who worried that "undesirable" Southern blacks would flood the state. This attitude most clearly presented itself during the World War I and postwar migration when "native" Minnesota African Americans attempted to protect themselves against the influx. "In many cases," Earl Spangler recounted, "local Negro leaders and organizations 'screened' migrants and selected only those deemed 'worthy' to enter the state."[18] For McGhee, quite publicly it meant going toe-to-toe against a very crafty man they all called the Wizard.

Washington's supporters, resorting to tricks similar to those at the St. Paul convention, humiliatingly defeated McGhee, Trotter, and all of the Radicals on the first day of the convention.[19] On the second day, McGhee made a formal report to the council on its business affairs and criticized it for financial mismanagement. This could have been a vicious blow to an organization whose benefactor, Washington, possessed holdings that were flush in money from white patrons whose donations were so massive as to intimidate all rivals and silence critics. McGhee's assault would draw attention to the morally corrupt nature at the core of the Tuskegee machine, perhaps thin the ranks of misguided Bookerites and draw them into the ranks of the Radicals, perhaps even peel away some well-intended philanthropists and redirect their giving to a new movement. But this did not happen. The council, in a maneuver that outflanked McGhee's attack, responded by electing him financial secretary, "the organization's most difficult and thankless (and futile) position." It was a trap. Rejecting the post meant that McGhee was more interested in embarrassing Washington rather than in contributing to solving the problem. Taking it meant that he would be sullied by such an undoable job and any accusation of impropriety hurled at the council. Either way, he knew that he had lost this engagement. This was the last convention he would attend, the last council duty he would perform.[20]

The rancor that characterized the Bookerite and anti-Bookerite factions did not carry over to Minnesota's black political elite. After the Louisville convention, McGhee was alone in renouncing the Wizard, yet he appeared to continue to have cordial relations with William Francis, William Hazel, William Morris, and attorney Charles Scrutchin, all of whom maintained strong ties with the Republican Party and the Bookerite faction. Francis, a rising star in the black community, Republican activist, soon-to-be corporate counsel for the Northern Pacific Railway, and session chair at the St. Paul convention, would eventually be handed McGhee's practice by his widow.[21] Hazel, who in 1891 had been critical of the St. Paul League for being ineffective, and sued restaurants for discriminating against him, took a teaching position at Tuskegee from 1909 to 1919.[22] Scrutchin, whom McGhee had encouraged to start a successful law practice in Bemidji, Minnesota, was vice president of the Minnesota Afro-American Association, became a devotee of Washington's when he saw the Wizard speak at the St. Paul convention, and eventually became the eighth vice president of the council.[23]

One can only speculate about the degree to which these men supported Washington, for Minnesota, where the quality of life for African Americans was better than in most states and far removed for the desperate conditions in the South, seemed to lessen the intensity of the debate. McGhee and his pro-Bookerite friends all supported the principles of self-help, industry, property ownership, racial harmony, and legal recourse, and condemned discrimination and racial violence. Indeed, they seemed to hold more views in common than not. The clearest distinction, rather, appeared primarily to be in the label "Bookerite" and the expectations that came with it.

Being a Bookerite granted men access to station and influence that the Radicals could not provide, as well as the imprimatur of acceptability that attracted a predominately white or middle-class clientele. But it also meant adhering to the Wizard's wishes and the discipline of the Tuskegee machine. But by 1903, for a growing number, being treated as a cog in the Tuskegee machine was hard to bear, especially as Washington's semidictatorial methods grew harder to accept. John Adams viewed the Bookerite tactics at Louisville with disfavor and began to entertain second thoughts about supporting Washington; but he was not yet prepared to take his misgivings farther. He had been elected to be the council's fourth vice president, and as editor of the *Appeal* he continued to be Minnesota's voice for Washington's views, publishing in every summer issue the Annual Address that he helped to draft. But although he outwardly supported Washington, he did not like the way the rules were bent to perpetuate the Wizard's control of the council. It may have bothered him more to see even an erstwhile friend like fellow Minnesotan Frederick McGhee at the 1902 and 1903 conventions be as disrespected as he was, which showed that the council would rather destroy a man of obvious brilliance and talent than find a way to work with him. Adams remained, at least for the time being, a "nominal" supporter of Booker T. Washington. After the "Boston Riot" on July 30, his ambivalence deepened.[24]

The Boston chapter of Washington's National Negro Business League met at the Columbus Avenue AME Zion Church on the stifling hot night of July 30, 1903. Hundreds of people, black and white, filled the church to hear Washington speak. William Lewis, a critic who five years earlier converted to being a fervent Bookerite just before becoming the first African American to be assistant U.S. attorney for the state of Massachusetts, introduced Fortune: as he did, members of the audience hissed and scraped their feet. At least a score of Trotter's followers sprang into action, shouting and filling the aisles as they moved toward the dais. The police arrived and tried to restore calm. About this time, Fortune introduced Washington and pandemonium took over.[25] Fistfights broke out. Trotter's sister allegedly stabbed a policeman with her hatpin. Women swatted adversaries with hats and purses while others fainted in the heat. Trotter jumped up and down on a pew, yelling at Washington until he was overwhelmed by police. Washington, in turn, remained expressionless as many shouted at him, "We don't like you!" and "Your views and aims are not what we sympathize with or think best for our race!" When he finally spoke, he had nothing new to say:

> The morning after the Columbus Avenue church assembly, newspapers across the nation carried reports of riotous clashes, bodily ejections, one knifing, and the arrest of Monroe and Maude Trotter and two others. To horrified northern philanthropists and alarmed southern segregationists, as well as to Washington's vast numbers of African American admirers, the "Boston Riot" was as unexpected as an earthquake. If the Wizard had failed to find the words to restore his authority that hot July night, his Tuskegee Machine clanked immediately into high gear in order to achieve that goal.[26]

In its August 8 issue, the *Appeal* reported simply that "hoodlums" attempted to disrupt "the Booker Washington meeting in Boston." There was reference neither to Monroe Trotter being one of the "hoodlums" nor to the nature of the disruption.[27] The denunciation of the disruption ran only a few lines without a headline and was not prominently situated on the page; it seemed halfhearted, more perfunctory than principled.

Indeed, throughout 1903 the articles Adams published increasingly reflected a halfhearted advocacy for the Bookerite platform, depicting present-day accomplishments of black folks as vindication and unspeakable atrocities as a spark to outrage the reader. For example, in one article he highlighted George Woodson, the first black to become a judge in Iowa and "a personal friend of Booker T. Washington."[28] In another he graphically reported, without attribution, that "while the body [of a falsely accused black woman] was dangling in mid-air it was riddled with bullets by the superior southern savages."[29] The accommodationist philosophy called for black people to avoid challenging Jim Crow laws, yet Adams condemned the highest court in the land for decisions that strengthened them:

> The Supreme Court of the United States has again held to the hidebrand policy of giving the Afro-American a slap in the face every time he pokes his head within the door ... How men who claim to represent can so degrade their high calling is beyond our comprehension unless the honorable court still holds to the Taney decision—"the black man has no right that a white man is bound to respect."[30]

The intent of another story is confusing. A white chambermaid in an Indianapolis hotel refused to change the sheets on the bed in which Washington slept. The article praised the proprietor who discharged her, then in subsequent articles reported funds being raised to support her.[31] In a glass-half-full sense, the black man's dignity was apparently defended by the grace of a white man; in a glass-half-empty sense, the chambermaid was a racial cause célèbre. Taken as a whole, a reader of the *Appeal* during this period would have had difficulty assessing the editor's opinion of Washington's vision.

Throughout this period Adams seemed also to publicly distance himself from McGhee. For instance, he failed to report McGhee's address at the Frederick Douglass Day celebration. In fact, the *Appeal* hardly mentioned McGhee's presence even though he had presided over the event. McGhee's opening salvo against the Bookerites—his outline for the council—went unreported, as did his accusation of financial mismanagement. As far as the *Appeal* was concerned, McGhee seemed to be persona non grata. Washington's exposure in the *Appeal* also diminished considerably and along with it the paper's usefulness to him. Thus, the flow of Bookerite funds that had allowed the *Appeal* to become a national newspaper began to end. During this period, the once-heralded "National Afro-American newspaper" printed in several cities between January and October closed its offices in Washington, St. Louis, and Louisville.[32] The council too lost some of its stature. Still, despite it all and for the time being, Adams stayed with the Bookerites. It was an affiliation that McGhee, whom Adams never criticized in print, did not trust.

In late February 1905, DuBois came to St. Paul to raise money for Atlanta University where he taught. McGhee had arranged his speaking itinerary and played host during the professor's visit. Together they conspired to keep the visit as nonprovocative as possible. Indeed, Nelson surmised, "[t]he innocuous title of his address ('Atlanta University') probably belied, perhaps concealed, a political purpose."[33] That purpose was to establish a new organization that would confront Washington and the Tuskegee machine. At some point, DuBois and McGhee discussed the need for African Americans to become politically active and compel the federal government to enforce the constitutional protections embedded in the Fourteenth and Fifteenth Amendments, and this could not happen unless they were organized. There was no organization to carry out the work. "[T]he Council was on a fast track to oblivion."[34] McGhee argued that they must do something.[35]

DuBois suggested that they convene a meeting of like-minded men in Buffalo, New York. A month later, he was in St. Paul to deliver a lecture at Plymouth Congregational Church, and once again stayed with McGhee as a houseguest. They made further plans for the meeting.[36] Finally, in early June, DuBois drafted and circulated the call from a select group of race leaders who would be the vanguard of what he called "the Talented Tenth"—educators, lawyers, publishers, physicians, ministers, and several businessmen secure enough to risk the Wizard's retribution.[37] The proclamation for the new agenda read:

> The time seems more than ripe for organized, determined, and aggressive action on the part of men who believe in Negro freedom and growth. Movements are on foot threatening individual freedom and our self-respect. I write to you to propose a conference during the summer for the following purposes:

1. to oppose firmly the present methods of strangling honest criticism, manipulating public opinion and centralizing political power by means of improper and corrupt use of money and influence;
2. to organize thoroughly the intelligent and honest Negroes throughout the United States for the purpose of insisting on manhood rights, industrial opportunity and spiritual freedom;
3. to establish proper organs of news and public opinion.[38]

Deferring to the gender bias of some of the invitees, most notable of whom was Monroe Trotter, DuBois reluctantly did not invite any women. This, however, would be remedied for the second annual gathering in 1906 over the initial objection of Trotter, who in time conceded.

Twenty-nine men and the son of one of the delegates arrived in Buffalo, where the hotel they had booked for the meeting declined to serve them. Then, on July 10, they relocated to the comfortable Fort Erie Beach Hotel on the Canadian side of Niagara Falls. In a peculiar twist of fate, more a comedy of errors, a Boston attorney named Clifford Plummer was sent to Buffalo to spy on the group, disrupt the meeting if possible, or at least identify the men in attendance and telegraph it all back to the Wizard in Tuskegee; but they were meeting in Canada. Not knowing this, Plummer reported to Tuskegee from Buffalo that he had stationed himself there "from Wednesday morning until Friday" and that "none of the men named in the report were present except Du Bois."[39]

On July 10, DuBois and his group began to discuss the new agenda for black America. Working harmoniously with the equally prickly Monroe Trotter, DuBois, no doubt nodding to his commitment at least symbolically to be inclusive of women and their right to equal citizenship, drafted the document defining and excoriating the wrongs inflicted against the race, borrowing the same rhetorical device that Elizabeth Cady Stanton, Lucretia Mott, and Frederick Douglass had used fifty-seven years earlier at Seneca Falls in their Declaration of Sentiments. "Men have endeavored in every way they could to destroy [woman's] confidences in her own powers, to lessen her self-respect, and to make her willing to lead a dependent and abject life." The Niagara Declaration of Principles declared: "We refuse to allow the impression to remain that the Negro American assents to inferiority. Through helplessness we may submit, but the voice of pro-test of ten million Americans must never cease to assail the ears of their fellows, so long as America is unjust."

DuBois wanted to make it clear that the plight of the African American was the plight of all working men and women, a position that race men inclined to focus on middle-class goals were not willing to take. "The practice of employers of importing ignorant Negro American laborers in emergencies, and then affording them neither protection nor permanent employment, and the practice of labor unions in proscribing and boycot-ting and oppressing thousands of their fellow toilers simply because they were black. These methods have accentuated and will accentuate the war of labor and capital, and they are disgraceful to both sides." Boldly summing up the heart of the protest that race men had struggled with and failed to carry out for half a century, in terms that surely would have alienated white patrons and cautious blacks, DuBois and Trotter declared: "The Negro race in America stolen, ravished and degraded, struggling up through diffi-culties and oppression, needs sympathy and receives criticism, needs help and is given hindrance, needs protection and is given mob-violence, needs justice and is given charity, needs leadership and is given cowardice and apology, needs bread and is given a stone." With the judgment of John Brown and the thunder of Jeremiah, they insisted, "This nation will never stand justified before God until these things are changed."[40]

They ended with a demand for an end to segregation, equal treatment in places of public entertainment, better schools, health care, and hous-ing. Most important, perhaps, the Niagarites, as they would be called, insisted that white people did not know what was best for black people. McGhee and some of the other men assembled had to recall how incendi-ary this stance had been regarded ten years earlier when the once-militant Fortune-led National Afro-American League had similarly rejected white participation. The white newspapers pilloried the organization and white political and financial supporters in Minnesota withheld their support, essentially bringing the organization to its knees. Today, in Niagara, they knew what this simple provision would cost them, and still they proceeded forward. "We repudiate the monstrous doctrine that the oppressor should be the sole authority to the rights of the oppressed."[41]

Three days later they adjourned, inspired by what they had done and knowing that they had made history in the political, social, and economic

Twelve of the twenty-nine founding members of the Niagara
Movement in 1905. W. E. B. DuBois and Fredrick McGhee are in the
second row. Library of Congress Prints and Photographs Division.

development of their race. Before they departed, they posed for a photograph in front of a mock background of the cascading falls, twelve men
and the son of one of them with proud but sober expressions reflecting
the gravity of their work, the risks they were taking, the sense they felt
that they had no other choice but to make change. Prominently seated
were W. E. B. DuBois and, to his left, Fredrick McGhee. Together they
had created a new agenda for equality that over time would be bloodied,
but not, in principle, bowed. It would be the agenda not just for the new
African American, but for the new America.

15

THE LEGACY

"And while we are demanding, and ought to demand, and will continue to demand the rights enumerated above, God forbid that we should never forget to urge corresponding duties upon our people—the duty to vote, respect the rights of others, to work, to obey the laws, to be lean and orderly, to send their children to school, and to respect ourselves even as we respect others."

—Declaration of Principles for the Niagara Movement, 1905

B ut it would be a long while before America was truly "new," and the twenty-nine men who founded the Niagara Movement had no illusions about the work that lay ahead of them. They faced the full weight of racial oppression and Washington's Tuskegee machine, as well as skepticism from most middle-class African Americans in Minnesota who questioned whether such a radical notion of demanding full and equal rights through complete integration was such a good idea. The paradox was that while they, as many in Minnesota's black middle class, could accept for themselves the Niagarite agenda—indeed, embrace the movement's Declaration of Principles—they nonetheless shied away from any association with critics of Booker T. Washington, who preached the soothing precepts of accommodation. The term "radical," meaning not the agenda itself but the aggressive and intemperate manner in which one demanded that the agenda should be met, scared them. In the end, it was the accumulation of those external pressures, lack of support from their own people, weak finances, and internal dissension that sprang from the bitter feud within the Massachusetts branch, the movement's most important chapter, that led to its demise. Within five years, the momentum slowed and, by 1910, the Niagara Movement was disbanded. However, the spirit was not lost, for that year a new organization, the National Association for the Advancement of Colored People, was formed. An overworked Fredrick McGhee, head of the underfunded and overextended legal department for the Niagara Movement and DuBois's intended successor as general secretary, would become the champion for the new organization in Minnesota, for there was work yet to be done there.

In the weeks following the Niagara conference, readers of Adams's *Appeal* would not have gathered that, as DuBois biographer David Levering Lewis wrote, "the first collective attempt by African Americans to demand full citizenship rights in the twentieth century" had recently occurred.[1] In fact, how significant it would become to history could only be known over the course of time. Otherwise, it was just another group in a long list of groups in which race men gathered together to figuratively howl at the moon. And not just *any* race men, but radicals, troublemakers, men who were willing to forget all that African Americans had achieved under the stewardship of Republican patrons, impatient men who refused to understand that during these unsettling times, the last thing the nation, and in particular black America—indeed, black Minnesota—needed was rancor, provocation, conflict.

In Minnesota, African Americans lived relatively better than their brethren in the South and in parts of the North; they had attained this quality of life because of their industry, hard work, and commitment to middle-class values that included understanding the important link between discretion and protecting one's investments in property and social standing. That they belonged to a race that was too few in number to threaten the masses of the white and immigrant working class crowding into the city provided at once a proprietary sense over their racial identity and racial vulnerability to Saturday night mob violence. Yet, from their rarefied vantage point at the top of the nation, they could see, or at least sense, the direction in which history was ineluctably going. Despite their measured endorsement, they knew that Booker T. Washington's solution

Fredrick McGhee House at 665 University Avenue in St. Paul, circa 1918. Courtesy of the Minnesota Historical Society.

to the so-called Negro Problem was flawed; John Quincy Adams seemed to embody this outlook.

Adams informed his readers of the Niagara Movement in a short article ten days after the session had adjourned. It was buried on page 5 of the *Appeal* and written in a calm and straightforward fashion, free from the rhetoric of protest that DuBois and Trotter used in the Declaration of Principles, free even from some of the heated copy that Adams had employed just weeks earlier on a different theme. In a statement against American imperialism in China, Adams had referenced the arrogance of white chauvinism against peoples of color, likening it to white supremacy in America: "[The] stupid indulgence of race prejudice of the Caucasian of the United States is the most unreasoning and unreasonable biped that struts upon the face of the earth. He regards it as one of his inalienable rights to degrade and Jim Crow and defraud and lynch the man of different color at his pleasure, always, if that the victim aforesaid is defenseless."[2] This was not the sort of statement that a sworn adherent of Booker T. Washington would write, and instead reflected the streak in Adams that often lay dormant until that moment when he could safely give vent to

John Quincy Adams, circa 1915. Courtesy of the Minnesota Historical Society.

it. As he raged against a society that tolerated racism and oppression, he supported a man who tolerated the same society that was at once racist and oppressive. In this, he was, as DuBois termed it, a man of two warring halves. Although Adams and his *Appeal* lived tenuously under the Bookerite tent, he enjoyed just enough independence to exhibit ambivalence to the Bookerite line.

In the next two issues, he published, this time on page 2 and without comment, DuBois's Declaration of Principles in their entirety. The principles began with congratulating African Americans on "certain undoubted evidences of progression in the last decade, particularly the increase of intelligence, the buying of property, the checking of crime, the uplift of home life, the advance in literature and art, and the demonstration of constructive and executive ability in the conduct of great religious, economic and educational institutions," and continued:

> We believe in manhood suffrage.
>
> All citizens have the right to equal treatment in places of public entertainment according to their behavior and desserts.
>
> We complain against the denial of equal opportunities in economic life.
>
> Common school education should be free to all American children and compulsory.
>
> We demand upright judges in courts, juries selected without discrimination on account of color.
>
> We plead ... for an opportunity to live in decent houses and localities, for a chance to rear our children in physical and moral cleanliness.
>
> We refuse to allow the impression to remain that the Negro-American assents to inferiority, is submissive under oppression, and apologetic before insults.
>
> Any discrimination based simply on race is barbarous.
>
> We protest against "Jim Crow" cars.
>
> We regret that the nation had never seen fit adequately to reward the black soldiers who, in five wars, have defended their country with their blood.
>
> We urge upon Congress the enactment of appropriate legislation for securing the proper enforcement of the articles of freedom.
>
> Of the above grievances we do not hesitate to complain, and to complain loudly and insistently.
>
> At the same time we want to acknowledge with deep thankfulness the help of our fellowmen from the Abolitionist down to those who today still stand for equal opportunity and who have given and still of their wealth and of their poverty for our advancement.

The Declaration concluded: "And while we are demanding, and ought to demand, and will continue to demand the rights enumerated above, God forbid that we should never forget to urge corresponding duties upon our people—the duty to vote, respect the rights of others, to work, to obey the laws, to be clean and orderly, to send their children to school, and to respect ourselves even as we respect others."[3]

Black Minnesota had demanded these very principles since Maurice Jernigan and the Golden Key Literary Society first called on voters to extend suffrage rights to black men in 1865, 1866, and 1868, and again when they lobbied the legislature for school integration. They sued for equal access on railway cars, and demanded better public accommodations legislation, respectful treatment from newspapers of note, and a seat at the political table. Indeed, throughout the 1880s and 1890s, black Minnesotans sued restaurants for denying them service on account of their race and they successfully tested the school integration law. Two discrimination cases were litigated in 1906 alone.[4]

In 1909, McGhee litigated a case concerning the education of black school-age children, putting the integration law to the test. The Crispus Attucks Home was a residence for black orphaned and neglected children that had been located in the railroad district. It was subsequently moved to open land that happened to be near an all-white, one-room public school named Mattocks Elementary. Here the Crispus Attucks children were to be educated. But in the summer of 1909, white parents demanded that school officials divide Mattocks into two rooms, or build an additional room. In either case, the black children, they insisted, needed to be taught separately. The *Pioneer Press* agreed with the parents: "It would be illogical to take half the colored orphans and put them under the same teacher. In fact, the natural thing to do, would be to have all the orphans in one room under one teacher."[5]

When the school board considered the issue on September 1, 1909, it was met by a delegation of black children accompanied by Mrs. Lillian Turner, president of the Federation of Colored Women's Club, and attorney Fredrick McGhee, who reminded them of the language and spirit of the statute that banned school segregation. In the face of angry white parents who shouted, "Would you have colored children steal pencils from your children? . . . Would you? . . . Would you?" the school board ruled to comply with the law, with the superintendent saying that McGhee's argument was unnecessary because the law was clear on the matter. McGhee responded that in his twenty years of civil-rights work in Minnesota and around the country he had learned a few things. One of them was that African Americans could never afford to assume that the law would be enforced to protect their rights and privileges. Experience had taught him that black people must assert those rights, not assume them, even in

Minnesota. That is why he had come to St. Paul in 1889, and that is why, twenty years later, he still felt the same way.[6] Demanding rights was not a foreign expression among the black middle class of the North Star State.

Some black Minnesotans built businesses and a few became quite affluent, as the Twin Cities became a destination for black professionals. And while their demands often fell short, the fact that they demanded at all, usually for rights that were coincidentally aligned with the Declaration of Principles, suggested that many black Minnesotans than were seen in the mass meetings were more oriented to the Niagarites than to the Bookerite disciples of accommodation.

Adams's readers could see that accommodation was not working as he kept them apprised of the state of race relations across the country. Indeed, it was not just the country but the Republican Party that stood complaisant as Southern states continued to erode the civil rights of African Americans in every aspect of their lives. Florida in 1903 had already banned intermarriage with a Negro, mulatto, or any person with one-eighth Negro blood: violators were to be imprisoned for up to ten years or fined not more than one thousand dollars. The following year, a race riot erupted in Springfield, Ohio, while Kentucky enacted a segregation law for all public and private schools.

In 1905, the year the Niagara Movement was founded, Georgia allowed private citizens donating public spaces such as parks to designate the exclusion of blacks with the expectation that it would be legally enforced. Florida allowed black maids to sit with white children in the white section, but denied a white maid in charge of a black child to sit in the white section. Thomas Dixon Jr. published *The Clansman: An Historical Romance of the Ku Klux Klan,* the second installment of his Reconstruction trilogy, a national best seller and inspiration for the 1915 movie *The Birth of a Nation.*

Then, starting in January 1906, race riots erupted in Springfield, Missouri, and Chattanooga, Tennessee, and in April, in Greensburg, Indiana, perhaps the first sparked by black migration to a Northern city. Then it was Brownsville, Texas. Since arriving in Fort Brown in July, black soldiers had been subjected to intense racial harassment from Brownsville's white citizens. As a result of this racial tension, a fight broke out between black soldiers and a white merchant. The city council barred the soldiers from setting foot in town. On the night of August 13, 1906, just days before the second annual conference of the Niagara Movement, a race riot erupted when a white bartender was killed and a police officer was wounded by gunshot. Townspeople accused members of the 25th Infantry Regiment, a unit of the famous Buffalo soldiers stationed at nearby Fort Brown. Although their commander testified that all soldiers had been in their barracks that night, evidence was planted against them. In that election year, President Theodore Roosevelt, anxious to string along black voters during his campaign while currying favor with white Southerners, decided to wait until after the election to decide the soldiers' fate.[7] But the racial temperature did not cool.

On September 22, less than a month after Brownsville, an estimated ten thousand white people beat every black person they could find in Atlanta. Even the post office, train station, and a number of white-owned businesses were ransacked by the mob when it sensed that terrified black employees might be hiding inside. At Five Points, Atlanta's busy commercial intersection where the city's network of trolley cars converged, black passengers were pulled off and murdered. The Atlanta *Constitution* reported that "In some portions of the streets, the sidewalks ran red with the blood of dead and dying negroes." DuBois, who had been out of town at the outbreak of violence, rushed home by train to sit on the steps of South Hall to protect his wife and daughter with a shotgun on his lap.[8] The moment was no doubt seared into his thinking and was reflected in a resolution two years later, before the Fourth Annual Niagara Conference, when he endorsed violent self-defense: "Obey the law, defend no crime, conceal no criminal, seek no quarrel; but arm yourselves, and when the mob invades your home, shoot, and shoot to kill." McGhee was one of the signers.[9]

The whole bloody episode took place in the heart of the New South, where Bookerites and their white allies, some of whom considered themselves racial liberals, had ten years earlier, in an elaborate coming-out celebration for the "leader of the race," touted the arrival of a new era of interracial enlightenment. Now, many of these same men had to face the unavoidable fact that the tactically bankrupt accommodation path that Washington had set for so long had failed to blunt the bestial impulse of white supremacy. An exact tally of the dead was never known, though records estimated more than twenty blacks and five or six whites. A few days after he returned to the city, DuBois wrote: "The Atlanta riot was if anything worse than reported."[10] The *Appeal* saw the nightmare through a similar lens.

> The massacre of Afro-Americans at Atlanta Saturday night was the most horrible that has ever occurred in this country . . . and rivals the massacre of the Jews at Kishnieff, Bialystola and Siedlce . . . Many of the newspapers dignified the outbreak as a "race war" when as a matter of fact it was nothing but a bloody massacre of innocent Afro-Americans by white Southern Christians.[11]

In November, after a resounding reelection victory, Roosevelt finally issued his order for the black soldiers at Brownsville. Against the counsel of Washington and Secretary of War William Taft, even in the face of questionable evidence, Roosevelt ordered all of the 167 black soldiers in Brownsville, Texas, to be dishonorably discharged without a hearing or the possibility of appeal. Many were longtime enlistees, a few were close to retirement, and six were Medal of Honor recipients.[12] The news electrified African Americans, for they felt betrayed by a man once viewed as a friend in the White House, but whose policies increasingly ignored any semblance of racial justice, prompting mass protest meetings in several cities. In St. Paul, at Pilgrim Baptist Church, Fredrick McGhee spoke against the hypocrisy of the Republican Party and, with a delegation of race men, sent the president a telegram in protest.[13] Washington had counseled Roosevelt not to issue the order, but when the president did so, Washington remained publicly silent. If anything, he continued to preach patience and accommodation.

The social events that occurred in St. Paul during the first months of 1908 made it abundantly clear just how little ground had been closed between the two groups. The Wizard was scheduled to deliver the Lincoln Day speech, something that McGhee typically would have done. In the same week, Chicago attorney Edward H. Morris, recognized to be "the leading Afro-American lawyer in the United States," a close friend and mentor of McGhee, longtime critic of Washington, and one of the signers of the first Niagara call, was scheduled to speak before a gathering of St. Paul's black Odd Fellows. The *Appeal* reported that "there was a large crowd present," which, given the size of the hall, could have been anywhere from twenty to thirty people. In contrast, Washington's speech was delivered in the chamber of the House of Representatives, the site of his victory at the 1902 NAAC meeting. The day's events began with a grand procession to the office of Democratic Governor John Johnson. "For about an hour," Adams reported, "these two great men talked of matters of interest, both giving and receiving valuable information." Later, when he went to deliver his speech, Washington was greeted at the chamber "by some 500 or 600 people," who, when he appeared, "rose en masse and gave him a Chautauqua salute."[14]

This begs the issue: black Minnesotans enjoyed rights and the expectation to dignity that the Declaration of Principles outlined. Yet, it seemed that most were enthusiastic Bookerites, even though some who identified themselves as Bookerites attended both functions. In fact, the man who introduced both speakers was Bookerite William Trevane Francis.[15] This was the nature of the relationship that existed between both factions: members interacted easily and frequently. Some of the same Minnesota Bookerites had initiated lawsuits against discrimination and railed against the state of race relations across the nation. Indeed, in view of the fact that protest was antithetical to Bookerite orthodoxy, the apparent overwhelming support for the Wizard would seem to be a contradiction. But such was the nature of race work in advancing the agenda for opportunity in Minnesota—being sensitive to national matters of racial justice, tempered by a concern for local racial matters, while maintaining comity with white Republican patrons. This was possible provided one juggled several balls at once—support the "leader of the race" even though he had been anointed by the white political and financial establishment, contain one's own doubts about his vision, or, more fundamentally, his integrity, and openly keep his critics as well as any hint of radicalism at arm's length. In Minnesota, the chief critic and racial radical was now Fredrick McGhee, the state's leading black Democrat. The events of 1908 underscored if not abject support for Washington and the Republican Party, at least reluctance to support the agenda set out by the Niagara Movement.

It would be hard not to imagine McGhee's delight when DuBois, at that year's annual meeting of the Niagara Movement, issued a call to the black voters of America to reject all Republican candidates in the coming elections. Indeed, several state delegations were already pursuing this line. DuBois would even endorse—reluctantly, it turned out—William Jennings Bryan in 1908, and four years later, Southern-born Woodrow

Wilson.[16] And when DuBois issued a resolution justifying violent self-defense, the Bookerites from the Twin Cities could only imagine seeing in McGhee's combustible temper the dangerous spark that might threaten the survival of black Americans in Minnesota. Washington's calming approach to race relations was the only option.

In 1909, a gathering of "intelligent blacks and well-meaning whites" convened at Cooper Union in New York City to discuss setting a new agenda for racial progress. The "intelligent blacks" included many persons such as Ida B. Wells-Barnett of Chicago, William Monroe Trotter of Boston, and W. E. B. DuBois of Atlanta, who had been three of Washington's most severe critics. The whites who joined them were intellectuals and reformers, and some were socialists. Together they would work to set a new and "radical" agenda for racial progress, and it would be called the National Association for the Advancement of Colored People, the NAACP. Yet, despite appearances that it was hostile to Washington's Tuskegee machine, it was not intended to be a radical organization. Oswald Garrison Villard, grandson of abolitionist William Lloyd Garrison and publisher of the New York *Evening Post* and the *Nation,* said that no civil-rights organization could be credible if it was led by radicals. To this end, it became important to drive away Ida Wells-Barnett and William Monroe Trotter, two of the movement's most aggressive leaders, and minimize any "damage" that could be done by the high-profile DuBois, whom the organization now needed to give it credibility. Villard had even proposed maintaining good relations with Tuskegee, assuring Washington that the NAACP was not intent on being anti-Bookerite, When word got to Wells-Barnett, she had a fit, and, referring to Villard's dictates, said she felt that Washington had seemed to sit astride them during the Cooper Union proceedings.[17]

She and Trotter stormed out of Cooper Union and out of the NAACP, leaving their irksome friend and colleague DuBois to make the best of the situation. Later, in a 1914 response to a request to assure a letter writer that the new organization was a legitimate heir to the Niagara Movement, DuBois reassuringly stated: "I beg to say that the platform of the Niagara Movement is probably more radical, at least more out-spoken, from anything that the National Association for the Advancement of Colored People has published. At the same time the general paths of the two organizations are practically identical."[18]

Fredrick McGhee was not able to attend the inaugural meeting, and perhaps it was just as well, for his uncompromising passion for racial justice was as intense as Wells-Barnett's and Trotter's and he had been suspicious of the tempering influence of white people in civil-rights organizations. But clearly, now his mood had changed. He followed what he could of the proceedings, but may have missed the drama as it unfolded between the radicals and Villard. In fact, McGhee's attention was divided. The legal department that he ran for the Niagara Movement remained, as always, desperate for funds, relegating the frustrated litigator to largely administrative matters and fighting civil-rights battles from the sidelines; all his department could afford to do in supporting discrimination lawsuits across the nation was, "due to the lack of funds," "to offer advice and assistance in the preparation of briefs."[19] Now, with the NAACP, its contacts with prominent names, and the independent sources of wealth that the names represented, he saw the potential for the kind of legal defense that civil-rights work desperately needed. Until then, he would have to make do what he could with very little help. This caused a different kind of problem, for as important as the work was, it did not pay his bills. In his St. Paul office he had to balance the needs of his race with satisfying the demands of his creditors by defending some of the county's most unsavory characters, and in doing so, he necessarily lived within the pendular realm of the sacred and the profane. Nonetheless, he probably had mixed feelings that accompanied the benefit of being relieved from all of the mounting administrative responsibilities when word came that DuBois was shifting his focus to the new organization, effectively ending the Niagara Movement, and therefore the legal department.

For McGhee, civil rights would continue to be his work, but because he needed to tend to his law practice, it would take a year before he could bring the NAACP to the state. Finally, in November 1911, he launched his first effort to organize it by managing a recital and fund-raiser. With successes like the *Cuba* production in 1898 and the 1902 NAAC conference, despite Washington's heavy-handed treatment of the proceedings, people recognized him as someone who could put on a good show. Therefore, sponsors saw him as the right man to put on a recital and fund-raiser. McGhee, for his part, had other plans, and he obviously knew that establishing a local chapter in the Twin Cities would be an uphill struggle. To start with, the sponsors, especially the two newspaper publishers, Adams

Fredrick McGhee, circa 1910. Courtesy of the Minnesota
Historical Society.

and Charles Sumner Smith, were Washington supporters. Moreover,
Smith in particular felt he had reason to worry that McGhee would exploit
every opportunity to promote the NAACP while denigrating the great
leader's good works. In fact, he was still angered by an open letter that
DuBois had drafted to European leaders in 1910 that humiliated Washington by refuting the Wizard's impressions of the state of black people
in America. McGhee had been one of the signers.[20] Nonetheless, Smith
decided to go against his better judgment and back McGhee to manage
the affair.

Now McGhee needed to be careful not to show his hand. Advertisements leading up to the event only featured Clarence Cameron White,
the nationally known African American violinist, in hopes that this would

attract a large crowd.[21] In the end, that did not happen. Although it was judged "one of the sweetest and artistic musical events of the season" and an "unqualified" success, as it was characterized by the *Appeal,* it failed to attract a large gathering of St. Paul's prominent black residents.[22] Nonetheless, once McGhee had an audience, he took advantage of the moment to act, talking about the "hopes and aims [of the NAACP] and distributing copies of the *Crisis,* the official journal of the organization edited by DuBois." Ultimately, the event was merely an anemic opportunity to spread the word. Its sponsors were anything but pleased. In a final accounting, the receipts of the affair came to $79.50, with $72.75 in expenses, for a profit of $6.75.[23]

If McGhee was going to establish a beachhead in Minnesota with an NAACP chapter, he would need to employ the skills he had used so often in the 1890s. Rather than issuing a public call and hoping that people would be inspired to attend, he contacted a few specific men from the Twin Cities that he knew would turn out. Then, on March 12, 1912, he called a meeting to formally consider the proposal to launch a new civil-rights organization. With McGhee as chairman of the meeting and Adams as secretary, in bipartisan fashion, those present proceeded to discuss the proposal, which they unanimously approved. Consensus broke down, however, over considerable opposition to being specifically affiliated with the NAACP, which, Smith argued, would tend to promote and encourage strife between the two leaders, DuBois and Washington.

That a tiny affiliate in Minnesota would promote any more strife than already existed between the two leaders seemed incredible. Nonetheless, McGhee, in a move that was at once conciliatory (for he knew he already had a majority to support establishing an affiliate) and tactical (for if it worked, he might draw Bookerites into the NAACP's orbit), appointed a committee on organization. The name of the fledgling organization was changed to the Twin City Protective League—another concession to the reality of the wider community's bias against the NAACP label. On March 29, when the committee recommended proceeding as proposed, nine of the twelve men present voted to approve the new constitution that made it an affiliate of the NAACP and the group's St. Paul chapter. One of the dissenters was Charles Sumner Smith, editor of the *Twin City Star,* and absent from the vote was John Quincy Adams, perhaps because he, a citizen of St. Paul, did not want to go against these men from his own city.[24] Indeed, it was becoming harder for black leaders to accept the gospel of accommodation, even if it was in behalf of their impoverished black brethren in the South. Times were inexorably changing. In October 1913, the Minneapolis chapter was founded; with this the NAACP would have a foothold on both sides of the Mississippi to establish a new agenda for opportunity, inclusion, and dignity.[25]

EPILOGUE

TIME FOR A DIFFERENT TONE
OF ADVOCACY

I n 1912, with an affiliate in place, McGhee and physician Valdo Turner
went as delegates to the national NAACP convention in Chicago that
May, stopping briefly in Milwaukee, where McGhee spoke against
lynching before a Catholic gathering. At the convention McGhee was
elected to the national committee.[1] When they returned, they knew that
they had a lot of work ahead of them, for the struggle for civil rights was
being waged everywhere, including in Minnesota, not just in the South.
Even though African Americans could ride in first class on Minnesota
trains, hotels and restaurants continued to discriminate and black laborers could still be subject to mob violence. One such case, the attack on
Arthur Lewis, occurred just days after McGhee and Turner's return from
Chicago.[2] To race men, it was not sufficient when state leaders viewed
themselves as liberal because they contained mob violence when the
underlying causes of such violence remained. And it was inadequate for
black leaders to decry Southern white supremacy while saying little about
the quality of life for laboring blacks in their own midst. The work left to
be done was, in a sense, the most dangerous because it challenged the
self-interest as well as the sensibilities and insecurities of even their truest
patrons—Republican and Democratic, black and white. The work that lay
ahead in the North Star State alone required the kind of immense energy
that McGhee had had in abundance for his entire professional life, and he
would need every ounce of it for the coming struggle.

It was the season for electioneering in the summer of 1912 and Woodrow Wilson, running for president of the United States, had promised

African Americans a fair shake. Upon returning from Chicago, McGhee leaped with both feet into campaigning for him and Democratic candidates for state and local offices. The Republican establishment that he accused of betraying African Americans who had been so loyal to the party needed to be dethroned, and McGhee was determined to do his part to see that happen, including against powerful opinion makers. On July 10, the *Pioneer Press* printed a short editorial complaining that Republicans in Alabama, almost all of whom were black, were being given delegate representation at the Republican National Convention "far out of proportion of actual votes." They had delivered to the party a little over nineteen thousand votes for the entire state compared to more than twenty-one thousand in Ramsey County alone; yet Alabama received twelve delegates to Ramsey County's two.[3] In response, McGhee wrote, "Why is it that there is no Republican Party in the South? Is it because the people are indifferent and won't vote, or because by reason of grandfather clauses, educational tests, and other make-shifts put in the hands of registrars by which Negroes . . . are denied the right to vote? . . . Is there no power in the country to re-enfranchise these Negroes? Yes, there is, but those who have the power have stubbornly refused to exercise it and now these same men who have stood by, saw the ballot taken from the Negro, refuse to raise a finger to restore it."[4]

For McGhee, a reformed Democratic Party was the only practical alternative to Republican dominance. Even DuBois, despite his socialist leanings, had reluctantly endorsed first William Jennings Bryan, then, by 1912, Woodrow Wilson, whose Southern roots made him suspect—and, as history would record, with good reason. But in 1912, motivated by the conviction that the welfare of African Americans would be forever lost as long as they slavishly supported the Republican Party, McGhee and DuBois both felt, along with their NAACP allies, that the black vote was sizable enough to leverage concessions. They would soon face disappointment when the Democratic Party rejected a civil-rights plank, but they nonetheless organized local chapters of the National Colored Democratic League around the country.[5]

McGhee attended the state Democratic Convention in Duluth and was elected to represent the state at the National Colored Democratic League convention later that summer. Canvassing in St. Paul to mobilize black Democrats in support of candidates in the city elections, at one rally for the Ramsey County Colored Democrats McGhee attracted an esti-mated 150 people. In May, the *Twin City Star* mocked his politics:

> Attorney McGhee had contributed an excellent article, "Sound of the Dollar," to *The New Era,* the official publication of the National Democratic Colored League. He is one of them—McGhee met with "Pitchfork Ben" in Kansas City and Tillman refused to receive the "nigger"—Mac is either forgetful or forgiving, probably both. But the "Sound of the Dollar" will obliterate the past and cause such as he who "to kick the foot that kicked him."

The paper noted the first sign of wear from his speaking engagements when it reported that he "was affected greatly Thursday by hoarseness which he contracted when speaking to the overflow meeting of Demo-crats in St. Paul. We were surprised to hear this, as the morning newspa-pers had made no reference to the problem."[6]

Later that summer, McGhee and his family closed up their home and relocated to their cabin, which he had named "DuGhee," on the Apple River in Wisconsin. He and DuBois had relaxed, fished, and talked about the state of the Niagara Movement there, and now he would do basically the same thing, except that this time he would reflect on plans for the Pro-tective League. Occasionally, he came back to the city to deal with various matters before returning to the cabin. But on one such excursion, friends, including his priest, noticed that he relied on crutches to get around. He insisted that his injury was benign—the result of a bad fall—but in fact he had developed an infection in his leg and his breathing was labored. By late August, his condition seemed to improve, but by September it wors-ened. Because his physician, Dr. Valdo Turner, like most physicians of the day, had no antibiotics that could be of help—such was the state of med-icine at the time—all McGhee could do was remain at home bedridden. Finally, on September 19, he passed away. The cause of death was injury to the right leg, resulting in thrombosis that moved to the lung causing pneumonia. He was fifty years old.[7]

"No death that had occurred in St. Paul in a quarter of a century has been more sadly and generally deplored," The *Appeal* reported. But the significance of his demise—the man to whom the black middle class went to prosecute civil-rights actions and poor black men went for help with criminal defenses—only warranted coverage on the third page of a four-page paper.[8]

Had Fredrick McGhee, as a delegate to the National Colored Democratic League, been able to attend the conference in Baltimore in the late summer of 1912, he would have seen the New York delegate from Harlem and former colleague and rival J. Frank Wheaton. A man who by any calculation was viewed as a rising political star, had left for Chicago before settling finally in New York City, where he led an active life in civic and political affairs. His political allegiances were kaleidoscopic. In 1910, after the founding of the NAACP, he immediately sent ten dollars to Washington's organization, a token donation intended as much to show his unwavering support for the besieged leader of the race as to adjust his own stance on a tectonic political plate that was about to violently shift underfoot. Soon, in his adopted home, a long-term stronghold for Democratic politics, he changed his party affiliation, frequently appearing over the next several years onstage with DuBois to reject Republicanism. He attempted and failed to be elected to the state assembly and focused increasingly on his activities in the Elks fraternal order's real-estate schemes and a flashy legal practice (he represented Amy Garvey in a divorce action from black nationalist leader Marcus Garvey), but he could never quite sustain financial stability. Increasingly, he led a life that became spectacularly banal.

On January 15, 1922, while his wife attended Sunday Mass, J. Frank Wheaton, the first black man to serve in the Minnesota legislature, who had authored two amendments to the state civil-rights law, which had kept his name alive years after he left the state, was found dead by suicide—"illuminating gas poisoning"—in his apartment in New York City.[9] Although a leader among New York blacks, he had been operating close to his financial limits, made more urgent when he posted ten thousand dollars in bail money for one of his clients. When his client jumped bail, followed by a desperate search to find him, Wheaton became despondent. His son Richard found his body.[10] Later that same year in St. Paul, on September 22, longtime editor John Quincy Adams stepped down from a streetcar and was hit by a passing car and died soon afterward.

Not until Washington's passing in 1915 did Adams finally, and completely, sever his ties to the Bookerites, though he clearly had been drifting away from their camp. For some time, his personal relationship with McGhee had been complicated, though they seemed, each for his own reasons, to respect and need the other. When the Niagara Movement was born, though Adams remained within the majority Bookerite camp in Minnesota's black leadership, he seemed to know that he was on the wrong side of history, being relegated, even as early as the founding of the Niagara Movement, to the sidelines of the protest movement.

With the demise of the Washington-controlled council, the *Appeal* found itself outside the mainstream of organized black activism, a position it had not been in since its inception. Adams's passive endorsement of the NAACP in 1910 did not endear him to either the Niagarites or the Bookerites; and though he participated in 1912 in laying plans for the NAACP affiliate, he was absent when the critical vote was taken to launch the new organization, seeming to prefer the role of deriding the excesses of white supremacy while largely ignoring race issues in Minnesota.

Yet, even while playing it safe, ostensibly to hedge his bets against alienating important patrons who still cleaved to the Bookerite line, Adams's journalistic empire was in decline. From a paper that once had editions in Dallas, Washington, St. Louis, Louisville, and until 1913 Chicago, the once-heralded national newspaper was reduced to a local newspaper that published political endorsements of Republican candidates and social events in St. Paul and Minneapolis. Occasionally, the *Appeal* would print stories of racial outrage, injustice, and discrimination; but in time the once mighty voice that provided the critical service of amplifying issues, documenting activities, introducing black leaders, and preserving their legacy for posterity weakened in relevance to shaping a new agenda for opportunity. In the end, his family selected a young African American journalism major from the University of Minnesota to run the *Appeal.* His name was Roy Wilkins, who would later become president of the NAACP.[11]

After Booker T. Washington's death in 1915, DuBois became the preeminent moral leader of African American civil rights and a figurehead for the NAACP as publisher and editor of the organization's journal, *Crisis.* He died in his adopted homeland in Ghana, West Africa, in 1963, on the eve of the historic March on Washington.

A hundred years earlier, in 1863, Maurice Jernigan stepped from the shadows to become one of Minnesota's first and most prominent race men; after only a few years of contributing to momentous events in the cause of racial equality, he returned to the anonymity of shadows. He had long ago learned the twin arts of nuance and discretion that in the coming years would be so characteristic of racial discourse in Minnesota, and he used them to good ends. But he also may have realized that the time when such tactics were governed by genuine sentiment was being replaced by a time when nuance, in the hands of a new generation of white patrons, even "true friends of the black race," was increasingly becoming a polite way to say "no," or at least "not yet." Getting these white men to say "yes"—some of whom were well-intentioned, some not, but all availing themselves to various degrees of genteel indirectedness—required a different sort of black man, one not weighted down by Jernigan's inclination for restraint and decorum. For this new kind of engagement, the barber seemed to realize that a different, perhaps more assertive, tone of advocacy was needed.

NOTES

1. When America Came to St. Paul

1. Depositions of Jacques Lefevre and François Chevalier taken by Henry Hastings Sibley, January 27, 1841, 26; Henry H. Sibley Papers, 1815–1936, Minnesota Historical Society (hereafter, MHS). The warrant is in the Sibley Papers; Henry H. Sibley, "Reminiscences of the Early Days of Minnesota," *Minnesota Historical Society Collections* 3 (1880): 266.

2. The warrant is in the Sibley Papers; Henry H. Sibley, "Reminiscences of the Early Days of Minnesota," 266.

3. Ibid.

4. Governor Robert Lucas, whose Jacksonian penchant for the executive veto had brought him into fierce conflict with the legislature, signed into law a bill that limited public education to "every class of white citizen," a bill on elections that barred anyone "not a free white male citizen" from voting, a militia bill that required enrollment only of "free white male persons," and a bill regulating judicial practice, one specification of which mandated that "a negro, mulatto, or Indian, shall not be a witness in any court or in any case against a white person" (Robert R. Dyskstra, *Bright Radical Star: Black Freedom and White Supremacy on the Hawkeye Frontier* [Cambridge: Harvard University Press, 1993], 26, citing *Laws of the Territory of Iowa [1839]*, 180–81, 188, 330, 404, and *Laws [1840]*, 33). See also Leon F. Litwack, *North of Slavery: The Negro in the Free States, 1790–1860* (Chicago: University of Chicago Press, 1961), 93.

5. Eugene Berwanger, *The Frontier against Slavery: Western Anti-Negro Prejudice and the Slavery Extension Controversy* (Urbana: University of Illinois Press, 1971), 32–33.

6. Ibid.

7. Lawrence M. Friedman, *A History of American Law* (New York: Touchstone/Simon & Schuster, 1985), 160.

8. Mary's sisters were the wives of Indian agent Lawrence Taliaferro and Fort Snelling commandant Seth Eastman (Mary Lethert Wingerd, *North Country: The Making of Minnesota* [Minneapolis: University of Minnesota Press, 2010], 148).

9. Jim Thompson, "Affidavit No. 68," Miscellaneous Reserve Papers; Sioux Affidavits Roll of Mixed-Blood Claimants, 1856. Relinquishments by Lake Pepin Half-Breed Sioux (Record Group 75, Bureau of Indian Affairs, National Archives); Roll #150, Sarah Thompson; Roll #151, George Thompson.

10. St. Paul *Daily Press*, June 3, 1871, 4, column 1; Minneapolis *Daily Tribune*, June 2, 1885, 8, column 3.

11. Northwest Ordinance, sec. 9.

12. Northwest Ordinance, secs. 3–8, as modified by the act of August 7, 1789, Statute at Large, 1:50. For a discussion on the interrelationship between the Northwest Ordinance and the Missouri Compromise, see William Anderson, *The History of the Constitution of Minnesota* (Minneapolis: University of Minnesota Press, 1921), 11.

13. *Congressional Globe,* 29th Congress, 2d sess., 53, 71, 441–45, 540, 572; *Congressional Globe,* 30th Congress, 1st sess., 136, 656, 772, 1052; *Congressional Globe,* 30th Congress, 2d sess., 693, 699; Statute at Large, 9:403–9.

14. St. Paul *Pioneer,* June 28, 1849. See also Litwack, *North of Slavery,* 30–112; Berwanger, *The Frontier against Slavery,* 7–59.

15. J. Fletcher Williams, *A History of the City of Saint Paul, and of the County of Ramsey, Minnesota, to 1875* (St. Paul: Minnesota Historical Society Press, 1983), 149. See also Anderson, *The History of the Constitution of Minnesota,* 9.

16. Ibid., 304. See also "The Story of Afro-Americans in the Story of Minnesota," *Gopher Historian* (winter 1968–69): 5.

17. Thomas S. Williamson letter to former Governor Vermont Slade, written in 1846 (Williamson Papers, MHS). See also Williams, *A History of the City of Saint Paul, and of the County of Ramsey, Minnesota, to 1875,* 162.

18. Williams, *A History of the City of Saint Paul, and of the County of Ramsey, Minnesota, to 1875,* 235, 163; C. C. Andrews, ed., *History of Saint Paul* (Syracuse: D. Mason & Co., 1890), 58; University of Minnesota, Wilson Library (hereafter, UMWL). For a discussion of the "Americanization of the West" movement among missionaries during the preterritorial period of Minnesota, see Albert Barnes, *Home Mission: A Sermon in Behalf of the American Home Missionary Society Preached in the Cities of New York and Philadelphia* (New York, 1849). The sermon was first preached before the Society for Promoting Collegiate and Theological Education in the West, in 1846. See also Barnes's sermon in "The Puritan Tradition in the 'New England of the West,'" *Minnesota History* (spring 1966): 2–4. For an excellent synthesis of the movement in Minnesota, see J. K. Benson, "New England of the West: The Emergence of the American Mind in Early St. Paul, Minnesota, 1849–1855," master's thesis, University of Minnesota, 1970 (UMWL MHS).

19. St. Paul *Pioneer,* April 25, 1850; *Minnesota Census of 1850.*

20. St. Paul *Pioneer,* April 25, 1850. For a count in June 1849, see Williams, *A History of the City of Saint Paul, and of the County of Ramsey, Minnesota, to 1875,* 214.

21. Williams, *A History of the City of St. Paul, and of the County of Ramsey, Minnesota, to 1875,* 165, 170–71. Thompson's was Lot #80; Brunson's, Lot #79; Cavalier's, Lot #85; future senator Morton Wilkinson's, Lot #86; Larpenteur's Lot #73; Forbes's, Lot #72; Ramsey's, Lot #68; Jacob Bass's, Lot #69 (*Minnesota Territorial Census, 1850,* ed. Patricia Harpole and Mary Nagle [St. Paul: Minnesota Historical Society Press, 1972], 43–44).

22. *Acts passed by the First Legislative Assembly of the Territory of Minnesota* (St. Paul, 1850), 53–54. That blacks were prohibited from holding office in villages is also found in *Revised Statutes,* 183, Minnesota Territorial *House Journal* (1854), 255. See also Gary Libman, "Minnesota and the Struggle for Black Suffrage, 1849–1870: A Study in Party Motivation," Ph.D. thesis, University of Minnesota (1972), 11–13.

23. The bill prohibiting blacks from being referees is found in *Revised Statutes of the Territory of Minnesota* (St. Paul: James M. Goodhue, Territorial Printer, 1851), 358. See also Libman, "Minnesota and the Struggle for Black Suffrage," 11–13.

24. The bill prohibiting blacks from holding office in villages is also found in *Revised Statutes of the Territory of Minnesota*, 183, and Minnesota Territorial *House Journal* (1854), 255. See also Libman, "Minnesota and the Struggle for Black Suffrage, 11–13.

25. Minnesota Territory *Journal of House and Council* (St. Paul: Brown & Olmsted: Territorial Printers, 1854), 258–59. For the 1807 Ohio "black law," see Salmon P. Chase, ed., Ohio Statutes I, 555–56, cited in Berwanger, *The Frontier against Slavery,* 23; Paul Finkelman, *An Imperfect Union: Slavery, Federalism, and Comity* (Clark, N.J.: Lawbook Exchange, 2000), 156.

26. William D. Green, "Race and Segregation in St. Paul Schools, 1849–1869," *Minnesota History* (winter 1997): 138–49.

27. Ibid., 144.

28. Ibid., 141–42.

29. Territorial Census of Minnesota, 1857, 183.

2. Maurice Jernigan Takes a Stand

1. "Joseph Farr Remembers the Underground Railroad in St. Paul," ed. Deborah Swanson, *Minnesota History* (fall 2000): 123, 124–25, 127.

2. Ibid., 127. William and Adeline Taylor arrived in St. Paul from Galena, Illinois, in 1850, and immediately set up his barbershop.

3. Ibid., 124.

4. Minnesota Territory, *Journal of the House and Council (1854),* 258–59. For the 1907 Ohio "black code," see Salmon P. Chase, ed., *Ohio Statutes* I, 555–56, cited in Eugene Berwanger, *The Frontier against Slavery: Western Anti-Negro Prejudice and the Slavery Extension Controversy* (Urbana: University of Illinois Press, 1971), 23; Paul Finkelman, *An Imperfect Union: Slavery, Federalism, and Comity* (Clark, N.J.: Lawbook Exchange, 2000), 156.

5. Darlene Clark Hine, William C. Hine, and Stanley C. Harrold, *The African American Odyssey: A Concise History,* 4th ed. (New York: Prentice Hall, 2000), 208; John Hope Franklin and Evelyn Brooks Higginbotham, *From Slavery to Freedom,* 9th ed. (New York: McGraw-Hill, 2001), 204: Leon Litwack, *North of Slavery: The Negro in the Free States, 1790–1860* (Chicago: University of Chicago Press, 1961), 248–49; Melvin Urofsky and Paul Finkelman, *A March to Liberty: A Constitutional History of the United States,* vol. 1 (New York: Oxford University Press, 2002), 384; Swanson, "Joseph Farr Remembers the Underground Railroad in St. Paul," 124–27.

6. *Minnesota Pioneer,* June 5, 1851, August 5, 1852.

7. Douglas Walter Bristol Jr., *Knights of the Razor: Black Barbers in Slavery and Freedom* (Baltimore: Johns Hopkins University Press, 2009), 80, 82, 90.

8. J. Fletcher Williams, *A History of the City of Saint Paul, and of the County of Ramsey, Minnesota, to 1875* (St. Paul: Minnesota Historical Society Press, 1983), 249.

9. Mankato *Semi-Weekly Record,* June 14, 1862; Earl Spangler, *The Negro in Minnesota*

(Minneapolis: T. S. Dennison, 1961), 50; Theodore C. Blegen, *Minnesota: A History of a State* (Minneapolis: University of Minnesota Press, 1975), 136; Williams, *A History of the City of Saint Paul, and of the County of Ramsey, Minnesota, to 1875,* 173–74;

10. Bristol, *Knights of the Razor,* 12.

11. Ibid., 10–11n10.

12. Ibid., 90n7.

13. This view of farming will be discussed in the next chapter.

14. Bristol, *Knights of the Razor,* 91.

15. Ibid., 15.

16. Ibid., 1,19–20.

17. National Archives and Records Administration (NARA), Washington, D.C., Consolidated Lists of Civil War Draft Registration Records, Provost Marshal General's Bureau (Civil War); Collection Name: Consolidated Enrollment Lists, 1863–1865 (Civil War Union Draft Records), 2d Congressional District of Minnesota, 282 (hereafter, "Draft Registration Records"). See also *St. Paul City Directory 1863,* 64, 122.

18. Swanson, "Joseph Farr Remembers the Underground Railroad in St. Paul," 128.

19. *Dred Scott v. Sanford,* 19 Howard (U.S.) 393 (1857).

20. *Minnesota Journal of the Senate 1859–1860,* 599–601; *Falls Evening News,* March 6, 1860. *Dred Scott* did not address the legal status of slave ownership by masters as tourists. Mackubin's bill was intended to fill this legal gap.

21. Minneapolis *Plain Dealer,* August 25, 1860. See also *Falls Evening News,* September 22, 1860; *Pioneer and Democrat,* August 23, 1860.

22. *Minnesotian,* July 23, 1860.

23. *Minnesotian,* July 21, 23, 25, August 1, 1860.

24. For an in-depth account of the Winston incident, see William D. Green, "Eliza Winston and the Politics of Freedom in Minnesota, 1854–1860," *Minnesota History* (fall 2000): 107–22.

25. For a discussion on the tensions that existed between abolitionists and moderate Republicans in Minnesota, and the Henry Sparks incident, see William D. Green, *A Peculiar Imbalance: The Fall and Rise of Racial Equality in Early Minnesota* (St. Paul: Minnesota Historical Society Press, 2007), chapter 6.

26. Bristol, *Knights of the Razor,* 92–94.

27. For a complete account and analysis relating to competition felt by white workingmen in St. Paul, see Green, *A Peculiar Imbalance,* chapter 8.

28. *St. Paul City Directory 1863,* 64, 122 (MHS). Joseph Farr, who had partnered with his uncle since 1857, now carried on alone. William Taylor, the first of Minnesota's race men, died the year before, in 1862. Taylor had accompanied an annuity party that went to the Lower Sioux Agency on the Minnesota River to make payments from the federal government to the Dakota (Sioux). It was not uncommon for civilians to go with such parties, treating the trip as a pleasant outing, and Taylor apparently went to socialize and cut hair at the agency. Tragically, he was caught up in the hostilities and shot to death. See Gary Clayton Anderson and Alan R. Woolworth, eds., *Through Dakota Eyes: Narrative Accounts of the Minnesota Indian War of 1862* (St. Paul: Minnesota Historical Society, 1988), 241; Swanson, "Joseph

Farr Remembers the Underground Railroad in St. Paul," 128–29, 7; *St. Paul City Directory, 1857–1858,* 125; *St. Paul City Directory 1863,* 122 (MHS).

29. Bristol, *Knights of the Razor,* 64–65.

30. Ibid., 4.

31. Draft Registration Records, 282.

32. Enrollment Act (March 3, 1863).

33. Tyler G. Anbinder, *Nativism and Slavery* (New York: Oxford University Press, 1992), 271; Iver Bernstein, *New York City Draft Riots* (New York: Oxford University Press, 2001), 43; Williams, *A History of the City of Saint Paul, and of the County of Ramsey, Minnesota, to 1875,* 412. For an example of Democratic condemnation of the conscription act in St. Paul, see St. Paul *Weekly Pioneer and Democrat,* March 27, 1863.

34. Black troops would distinguish themselves for valor at Fort Wagner, Port Hudson, Millikin's Bend, and Petersburg. See James McPherson, *The Negro's Civil War: How American Blacks Felt and Acted during the War for the Union* (New York: Vintage Books, 1967); Benjamin Quarles, *The Negro in the Civil War* (Boston: Little Brown, 1989).

35. Letter from Thomas Montgomery to parents, September 22, 1865 (MHS).

36. Bristol, *Knights of the Razor,* 4.

37. *St. Paul Press,* January 20, 1865, 4, column 3.

38. Gary Libman, "Minnesota and the Struggle for Black Suffrage, 1849–1870: A Study in Party Motivation," Ph.D. thesis, University of Minnesota (1972), 49, citing James McPherson, *The Struggle for Equality: Abolitionists in the Civil War and Reconstruction* (Princeton, N.J.: Princeton University Press, 1964), 176–77.

39. Emily O. Goodridge Grey, "The Black Community in Territorial St. Anthony: A Memoir," *Minnesota History* (summer 1984): 49. For an account of the controversy faced by clergymen who preached antislavery sentiments from the pulpit, see Charles W. Nichols, "Henry M. Nichols and Frontier Minnesota," *Minnesota History* 19 (September 1938): 254–55.

40. St. Paul *Daily Press,* January 21, 28, 31, 1865; St. Paul *Pioneer,* January 28, 31, February 2, 7, 1865.

41. *St. Paul City Directory, 1864,* 63, 128.

42. For a discussion of the Philadelphia societies, see Jacqueline Bacon and Glen McGlish, "Reinventing the Master's Tools: Nineteenth-Century African American Literary Societies of Philadelphia and Rhetoric Education," *Rhetoric Scholar Quarterly* 30:4 (autumn 2000): 19–47.

43. Bristol, *Knights of the Razor,* 90.

44. "Negro Suffrage," *St. Paul Press,* January 20, 1865, 4, column 3. The other cosigners were A. Jackson, H. Hawkins, Ed. James, and W. Griffin.

45. Ibid.

46. In the House, the vote was 31 to 8. In the Senate, the vote was 16 to 4 (*Minnesota Journal 1865,* 142, 154, 165).

47. St. Paul *Pioneer,* February 7, 1865.

48. *Minnesota House Journal, 1865,* 65, 66, 101, 109, 122, 139; St. Paul *Daily Press,* January 21, 28, 31, 1865; St. Paul *Pioneer,* January 28, 21, February 2, 7, 1865.

49. Mankato *Free Press,* February 4, 1865.

50. Chatfield *Democrat,* August 19, 1865.

51. Bristol, *Knights of the Razor,* quoting Henry A. Murray, *Lands of the Slave and the Free: Cuba, the United States, and Canada* (John Parker & Son, 1855), 19.

52. Minnesota Secretary of State, "Census of the State of Minnesota," *Annual Report* (1865), 119.

53. The tally from Winona County was 735 to 892. In contrast, Marshall received 1,169 votes to 735 for Henry Rice ("Census in the State of Minnesota, 1865," extracted from Minnesota Secretary of State, *Annual Report for 1865* [St. Paul: MHS, 1865], 119).

54. *Minnesota House Journal, 1865,* 318.

55. "An Interesting Scene—Cane Presentation to Mr. Chas. Griswold," *St. Paul Press,* March 1, 1865, 4, column1. A similar gesture was made to Senator Levi Nutting.

56. Ibid.

57. Ibid.

58. Bristol, *Knights of the Razor,* 120–21.

59. See chapter 5 for a profile of C. D. Gilfillan.

3. On Becoming a Good Republican

1. William D. Green, *A Peculiar Imbalance: The Fall and Rise of Racial Equality in Early Minnesota* (St. Paul: Minnesota Historical Society Press, 2007), 151–63.

2. See *Proceedings of the Convention of Colored Citizens of Minnesota* (St. Paul: St. Paul Press Company, 1869); *Legislative Manual, 1869,* 89; *1871,* 133.

3. *Proceedings of the Convention of Colored Citizens of Minnesota,* 10–11.

4. David V. Taylor, "Pilgrim's Progress: Black St. Paul and the Making of an Urban Ghetto, 1870–1930," Ph.D. thesis, University of Minnesota (March 1977), 75–77, 77n66.

5. H. P. Hall, *Observations from 1849–1904* (St. Paul, 1904), 61–62, 170.

6. *Proceedings of the Convention of Colored Citizens of Minnesota,* 19–20.

7. Even though the act was signed into law on May 20, 1862, section 1 stated the act would be enacted on January 1, 1863.

8. *The Homestead Bill: Speech by Hon. M. S. Wilkinson, of Minnesota (Senate, April 3, 1860, Congressional Globe,* 36th Congress, 1st session, 1508–1512), 3–4, 8. See also John Ashworth, *Slavery, Capitalism, and Politics in the Antebellum Republic,* vol. 2 (Cambridge: Harvard University Press, 1995), 270–71.

9. *The Homestead Bill: Speech by Hon. M. S. Wilkinson,* 3.

10. Ibid., 4, 8.

11. 37th Congress, Sess. II, Ch. 75, secs. 1 and 2.

12. William Deverell, "The American West," in *The American Congress: The Building of Democracy,* ed. Julian Z. Zelizer (New York: Houghton-Mifflin, 2004), 271.

13. *Congressional Globe,* 36th Congress, 1st sess., 1509–10.

14. Deverell, "The American West," 270–71.

15. Ibid., 271.

16. Ibid.

17. Mary Lethert Wingerd, *North Country: The Making of Minnesota* (Minneapolis: University of Minnesota Press, 2010), 336.

18. David A. Nichols, *Lincoln and the Indians: Civil War Policy and Politics* (Columbia: University of Missouri Press, 1978), 122.

19. Retrieved from http://www.abrahamlincolnsclassroom.org/Library/newsletter.asp?ID= 50&CRLI=130. Wilkinson acknowledged the potential for enrichment that one holding this position could gain when he recounted an exchange at the White House between an official and President Lincoln. The Indian agent (whom he did not name) asked the president to appoint the agent to the rank of brigadier general to fight the Dakota in Minnesota. With this command, the official claimed that he would put down outbreaks and save thousands of lives as well as millions of dollars for the government, and that "he thoroughly understood the Indians and how to handle them." The agent rambled on until the president, whose patience gave out, interrupted him: "Sir, since the war began, I have received a great deal of advice from all classes of men, and a great many promises that have been made, and my experience and observation had been that those who promise the most do the least." This ended the interview. Wilkinson noted, "Mr. Lincoln was a keen judge of character and saw through the fellow at once, and that his object was to make money out of the scheme" (Carl Sandberg, *Abraham Lincoln: The War Years*, vol. 3 [New York: Harcourt, Brace & Company. 1939], 452).

20. William J. Stewart, "Settler, Politician, and Speculator in the Sale of the Sioux Reserve," *Minnesota History* (fall 1964): 85.

21. "Statement by William Dodsworth Willard," in *Semi-Centennial of Mankato, 1852–1903* (Mankato: Free Press, 1903), 115 (Southern Minnesota Historical Center, University of Minnesota, Mankato).

22. Stewart, "Settler, Politician, and Speculator in the Sale of the Sioux Reserve," 85.

23. Montgomery to his mother, June 14 or 27, 1864, Thomas Montgomery Papers, MHS; Minnesota Census 1865, Cleveland Township, Le Sueur County. Roll 2 (MHS).

24. Montgomery letter to his father, March 22, 1865, Thomas Montgomery Papers, MHS; emphasis added. See also Earl Spangler, *The Negro in Minnesota* (Minneapolis: T. S. Denison, 1961), 48, 54; Muster rolls, 67th Regiment, Company B United States Colored Infantry; Montgomery to his brother, October 22, 1864 (MHS).

25. *Congressional Globe,* 38th Congress, 1st sess., Senate, June 28, 1864, 3329.

26. Ibid.

27. Ibid., 3329–30.

28. Ibid., 3330.

29. Ibid.

30. Ibid. On April 8, 1864, Wilkinson (and Alexander Ramsey) "voted for passage of the joint resolution submitting to the Legislatures of the several States the proposition to amend the Constitution of the United States," joining a majority of thirty-eight yeas to six nays.

31. Ibid.

32. Herman Betz, *A New Birth for Freedom: The Republican Party and Freedmen's Rights, 1861–1865* (New York: Fordham University Press, 2000), 90–91.

33. Ibid., 91.

34. Ibid.

35. *Congressional Globe,* 38th Congress, 1st sess., Senate, June 28, 1864, 3330.

36. Montgomery to his brother James, October 18, 1865. Montgomery had a special interest in

William R. Marshall for he had been a lieutenant colonel and beloved commanding officer of the 7th Minnesota, rising eventually to the rank of brevet brigadier general. In 1865 he was elected governor of Minnesota and served for two terms. He campaigned for black suffrage, played an active role in the 1868 referendum, and, as governor, in 1869 signed legislation that denied state funds to school districts that separated children on the basis of race. However, in 1865, despite his support for black suffrage, the question failed statewide by a vote of 14,651 to 12,138; Marshall defeated Democrat Henry Rice, 17,318 to 13,842. Montgomery's skepticism about the success of black suffrage was well-founded, especially in light of his understanding of his own community. In 1865, black suffrage and Marshall both fell short: Marshall lost 422 to 729; the black suffrage amendment lost 224 to 839. See *Minnesota in Civil and Indian Wars, 1861–1865* (St. Paul: Pioneer Press Co., 1890), 367; Census of the State of Minnesota, 1865, *Annual Report for 1865* (St. Paul: Minnesota Historical Society), 119.

37. Mankato *Weekly Record,* February 13, 1865, 2, column 2.
38. Montgomery to father, March 22, 1865.
39. In Nicollet County, Marshall defeated Rice 475 to 380; the amendment narrowly failed 331 to 374 (Census of the State of Minnesota, 1865, extracted from the Minnesota Secretary of State's *Annual Report for 1865* [St. Paul: Minnesota Historical Society], 119). For a discussion of the Minnesota campaign for black suffrage, see Gary Libman, "Minnesota and the Struggle for Black Suffrage, 1849–1870: A Study in Party Motivation," Ph.D. thesis, University of Minnesota, June 1972; see also "The Long Road to Black Suffrage, 1849–1868," *Minnesota History* (summer 1998): 68–84.
40. Thomas Hughes, *History of Blue Earth County* (Chicago: Middle West Publishing, 1978), 159; (Southern Minnesota History Center, University of Minnesota, Mankato).
41. Mankato *Union,* August 17, 1866, 3, column 2.
42. Hughes, *History of Blue Earth County,* 163.
43. Stewart, "Settler, Politician, and Speculator in the Sale of the Sioux Reserve," 89. See also Edward Duffield Neill and Charles S. Bryant, *History of Minnesota River Valley, Including the Employers and Pioneers of Blue Earth County* (Minneapolis: North Star Press, 1882), 549.
44. Stewart, "Settler, Politician, and Speculator in the Sale of the Sioux Reserve," 89–90.
45. Ibid., 90.
46. Ibid.
47. Ibid., 92. See also *Monthly Abstract of Land Sales, St. Peter: Sioux Lands,* December 1867–69.
48. Stewart, "Settler, Politician, and Speculator in the Sale of the Sioux Reserve," 90. See also *Monthly Abstract of Land Sales, St. Peter: Winnebago Lands,* December 1865–67 (National Archives and Records Administration [NARA], 49).
49. Stewart, "Settler, Politician, and Speculator in the Sale of the Sioux Reserve," 92n29.
50. Ibid., 91.
51. Ibid., 92.
52. Theodore C. Blegen, *Minnesota: The History of a State* (Minneapolis: University of Minnesota Press, 1975), 340, 304.
53. Ibid., 304–5.
54. Ibid., 306–7.
55. David V. Taylor, "Blacks," in *They Chose Minnesota: A Survey of the State's Ethnic Groups,* ed.

June Drenning Holmquist (St. Paul: Minnesota Historical Society Press, 1981), 87, citing U.S. Census 1860–80.

56. Ibid.
57. Richard Kluger, *Simple Justice* (New York: Knopf, 1976), 43.
58. Eric Foner, *Reconstruction: America's Unfinished Revolution, 1863–1877* (New York: Harper & Row, 1988), 245–46.
59. Kluger, *Simple Justice*, 43.
60. Ibid., 44.
61. Spangler, *The Negro in Minnesota*, 46.
62. Ibid., 55.
63. St. Paul *Daily Press*, May 16, 1863, 1, columns 2 and 3.
64. Frederick L. Johnson, *Uncertain Lives: African Americans and Their First 150 Years in the Red Wing, Minnesota Area* (Red Wing: Goodhue Historical Society, 2006), 17.
65. Ibid., 19.
66. Ibid., citing Ben Densmore to Orrin Densmore, September 22, 1863 (Benjamin Densmore papers, MHS).
67. Ibid.
68. Ibid., 20, citing Orrin Densmore to Daniel Densmore, April 28, August 29, 1864.
69. Spangler, *The Negro in Minnesota*, 46.
70. "Statement by William Dodsworth Willard," 115.
71. In Blue Earth County in 1867, the black suffrage amendment won 1,246 to 1,168, and in Nicollet County, 551 to 503; but in Le Sueur County, the amendment failed 516 to 1,010. In 1868, the amendment passed in Blue Earth County, 1,588 to 1,108, and in Nicollet County, 647 to 486, while it failed in Le Sueur County, 791 to 1,159 (*Tribune Almanac for 1868* [New York: New York Herald Tribune], 56–57; *Legislative Manual, 1869,* 89; *Legislative Manual, 1871,* 133).
72. Spangler, *The Negro in Minnesota*, 46.
73. St. Peter *Free Press*, June 15, 1907; St. Peter *Herald*, June 14, 1907; St. Peter *Tribune*, January 20, 1869; Neill and Bryant, *History of the Minnesota Valley, Including the Explorers and Pioneers of Minnesota,* 665.
74. Edward J. Pluth, "'A Negro Colony' for Todd County," *Minnesota History* (fall 2009): 312–24.
75. *Legislative Manual of the State of Minnesota, 1869,* 89.
76. V. Jacque Voegeli, *Free but Not Equal: The Midwest and the Negro during the Civil War* (Chicago: University of Chicago Press, 1967), 7.
77. Taylor, "Blacks," 87.
78. *Proceedings of the Convention of Colored Citizens of Minnesota,* 19–20.
79. Sterling D. Spero and Abram L. Harris, *The Black Worker* (New York: Atheneum, 1959), 11–12. See also Noel Ignatiev, *How the Irish Became White* (New York: Routledge, 1995).
80. Spero and Harris, *The Black Worker,* 13.
81. St. Paul *Daily Press*, May 16, 1863, 1.
82. St. Paul *Daily Press*, May 6, 1863.
83. Minnesota Territorial *House Journal, 1854,* 258–59; *Minnesota House Journal, 1860,* 242.
84. St. Paul *Daily Press*, May 16, 1863, 1.

85. Ibid.
86. Spero & Harris, *The Black Worker,* 17–19.
87. Spangler, *The Negro In Minnesota,* 56–57.
88. *Proceedings of the Convention of Colored Citizens of Minnesota,* 18.
89. Wilkinson went to the House of Representatives and served a term. As his career progressed, he became increasingly critical of federal policy that advanced the interests of business and railroads at the expense of farmers.

4. The Sons of Freedom

1. Richard Kluger, *Simple Justice* (New York: Knopf, 1976), 43.
2. St. Paul Board of Directions, "Minutes," 1865; St. Paul *Daily Pioneer,* October 9, 1865, 1, column 2; St. Paul *Daily Press,* October 10, 1865, 4, column 1.
3. For a detailed history of segregation in St. Paul schools, see William D. Green, *A Peculiar Imbalance: The Fall and Rise of Racial Equality in Early Minnesota* (St. Paul: Minnesota Historical Society Press, 2007), chapter 10.
4. St. Paul *Daily Pioneer,* November 30, 1867.
5. *Proceedings of the Convention of Colored Citizens of Minnesota* (St. Paul: St. Paul Press Company, 1869), 29.
6. For a review of the debate on the Fourteenth Amendment and school desegregation during the deliberations of the Civil Rights Act of 1875, see Kluger, *Simple Justice,* 732.
7. Carter G. Woodson, *Education of the Negro* (Brooklyn: A & B Publishing, 1999), 189.
8. Ibid., 190–206.
9. Accolades appeared in the St. Paul *Daily Press,* January 8, 1869, and Minneapolis *Tribune,* January 8, 1869. Even the *Pioneer* was positive. See *Daily Pioneer,* January 3, 1869; *Weekly Pioneer,* January 8, 1869.
10. William D. Green, "Race and Segregation in St. Paul Schools, 1846–1969," *Minnesota History* (winter 1996–97): 139.
11. St. Paul *Pioneer,* November 14, 1868, 1, column 1.
12. Republican Mayor Stewart, for example, said, "Very likely they will shut him out from the schools, but they will insist with pathetic emotion that he is intelligent, and if, perchance, a colored man is found who couldn't read his vote, what a hue and cry would be raised" (*Proceedings of the Convention of Colored Citizens of Minnesota,* 10–11). See also Green, *A Peculiar Imbalance,* 155.
13. St. Paul *Pioneer,* January 3, 1869, 3. See also St. Paul *Weekly Pioneer,* January 8, 1869, 5.
14. St. Paul *Pioneer,* January 8, 1869, 4, column 1.
15. Mankato *Union,* March 17, 1865.
16. *St. Paul Press,* January 20, 1869.
17. William H. C. Folsom, *Fifteen Years in the Northwest* (St. Paul: Pioneer Press Company, 1888), 732. See also J. Fletcher Williams, *A History of the City of Saint Paul, and the County of Ramsey, Minnesota, to 1875* (St. Paul: Minnesota Historical Society Press, 1983), 434.
18. *Minnesota Laws, 1869,* 7; St. Paul *Daily Press,* March 14, 1869, 4, column 1. For a full account, see Green, *A Peculiar Imbalance,* 169–71.

19. St. Paul *Daily Press,* March 14, 1869.

20. St. Paul *Daily Pioneer,* March 14, 1869.

21. For an account of this trial, see Green, *A Peculiar Imbalance,* chapter 11.

22. St. Paul *Weekly Pioneer,* March 26, 1869.

23. Moffit and Hickman were whitewashers. (A whitewasher is one who applies plaster to walls.) Hickman was also the spiritual leader of the Pilgrim Baptist Church though he was not yet ordained. Moffit was a member of his church (Church Record Book, November 14, 1866; First Baptist Church papers, MHS).

24. St. Paul *City Directories, 1863–1869; U.S. Census 1870.*

25. St. Paul *Weekly Pioneer,* March 26, 1869.

26. For example, Robertson owned as part of his library the newspaper published in 1791 by James Franklin, older brother of Benjamin (*St. Paul Press,* May 16, 1869).

27. Robertson expressed these views in a letter to his son then traveling in Paris (D. A. Robertson to Victor Robertson, January 31, 1885; Daniel A. Robertson and Family Papers, 1814–1933, MHS).

28. For a biographical sketch of Robertson, see Williams, *A History of the City of Saint Paul, and the County of Ramsey, Minnesota, to 1875,* 283; Charles Flandrau, *Encyclopedia of Biographies of Minnesota: History of Minnesota* (Chicago: Century Publishing and Engraving, 1900): 1:43432; T. M. Newson, *Pen Picture of St. Paul and Biographical Sketches of Old Settlers from the Earliest Settlement of the City up to and Including the Year 1857,* vol. 1 (T. M. Newson: St. Paul, 1886), 217–18. See also Green, *A Peculiar Imbalance,* 178–79.

29. St. Paul *Daily Press,* May 15, 26, 1869.

30. St. Paul *Daily Pioneer,* April 13, 1869; Earl Spangler, *The Negro in Minnesota* (Minneapolis: T. S. Dennison, 1961), 35.

31. St. Paul *Daily Pioneer,* April 13, 1869.

32. St. Paul Board of Education, "Minutes," April 19, 1869 (MHS).

33. As late as 1909, a delegation of white parents appeared before the board of education to protest the admission of blacks students at Mattocks School (St. Paul Board of Education, "Minutes," September 1, 1909).

34. *Proceedings of the Convention of Colored Citizens of Minnesota,* 18.

35. Thomas A. Wood, *Knights of the Plow: Oliver H. Kelley and the Origins of the Grange in Republican Ideology* (Ames: Iowa State University Press, 1991), 91, 118–30.

36. Ever since 1862 when senators debated the Homestead Act, Wilkinson strongly advocated for the interests of farmers. However, during his congressional term, he became a greater critic of monopolies on behalf of farmers and the common man (*Congressional Globe,* 37th Congress, 2d sess., 2857, columns 2–3, June 21, 1862; *Congressional Globe,* 41st Congress, 1st sess., 871–72, January 29, 1870).

37. Spangler, *The Negro in Minnesota,* 58–59.

38. St. Anthony *Falls Democrat,* December 24, 1869, 1, column 1.

39. See Donald J. Woods, "Playhouse for Pioneers: The Story of the Pence Opera House," *Minnesota History* (winter 1972): 169.

40. Minneapolis *Daily Tribune,* January 4, 1870, 4, column 2.

41. This is conjecture, but considering the times, it is likelier than not that because the Pence Opera House catered to the "upper crust," it would have denied admission to black patrons.

This practice, which occurred across the North, was the reason the Civil Rights Act was passed in 1875.

42. Minneapolis *Daily Tribune,* January 4, 1870, 4, column 2; St. Anthony Falls *Democrat,* January 4, 1870, 1, column 4; St. Paul *Daily Pioneer,* January 5, 1870, 1, column 1.

43. *St. Paul Press,* January 8, 1870, 1, column 2.

44. Ibid.

45. *St. Paul Press,* January 16, 1870, 4, column 3. See also Eric Foner, *Reconstruction: America's Unfinished Revolution, 1863–1877* (New York: Harper & Row, 1988), 74; and David H. Donald, ed., *Inside Lincoln's Cabinet: The Civil War Diaries of Salmon P. Chase* (New York: Longmans, Green and Company, 1954), 264–66.

46. Foner *Reconstruction,* 461; Allan Nevins, *The Emergence of Modern America, 1865–1878* (New York: McMillan Company, 1927), 31–37; Clarence H. Danhof, *Change in Agriculture: The Northern United States, 1820–1870* (Cambridge:Harvard University Press, 1969), 10.

47. Foner, *Reconstruction,* 461.

48. William Watts Folwell, *A History of Minnesota,* vol. 3 (St. Paul: Minnesota Historical Society Press, 1969), 61.

49. Mary Lethert Wingerd, *Claiming the City: Politics, Faith, and the Power of Place in St. Paul* (Ithaca, N.Y.: Cornell University Press, 2001), 34.

50. Ellen Carol DuBois, *Feminism and Suffrage: The Emergence of an Independent Women's Movement in America, 1848–1869* (Ithaca, N.Y.: Cornell University Press, 1980), 130.

51. Wingerd, *Claiming the City,* 34.

52. St. Paul *Daily Press,* June 3, 1871, 4, column 1.

53. Richard Edwards, *St. Paul Census Report and Statistical Review Embracing a Complete Directory of the City of St. Paul, Minnesota* (1873), 422.

54. For reference to Jackson, see the Duluth *Tribune,* December 23, 1871, 2, column 3. For Grey, see Minnesota State Census, 1875. For Hickman, see my forthcoming book *The Children of Lincoln: Four White Patrons of Black Freedom, 1860–1876.*

55. *St. Paul Press,* May 14, 1871, 4, column 2; May 21, 1871, 4, column 3.

56. Douglas Walter Bristol Jr., *Knights of the Razor: Black Barbers in Slavery and Freedom* (Baltimore: Johns Hopkins University Press, 2009), 121–22.

57. W. E. B. DuBois, *The Souls of Black Folk* (New York: Fawcett Premier Books, 1969), 18.

58. David V. Taylor, "Blacks," in *They Chose Minnesota: A Survey of the State's Ethnic Groups,* ed. June Drenning Holmquist (St. Paul: Minnesota Historical Society Press, 1981), 76.

59. Ibid., 74.

60. Until the mid-1860s, the black population was distributed throughout St. Paul's five wards. But by the late 1860s, blacks began to concentrate in the commercial district in Lowertown, which one newspaper editor called "a negro rookery" (ibid., 76).

61. DuBois, *The Souls of Black Folk,* 16–17.

62. Minneapolis *Tribune,* January 19, 1973, 4, column 3.

63. Frederick Douglass, "Self-Made Man," in *The Frederick Douglass Papers,* ed. John Blassingame and John McKivigan, series 1, vol. 4 (New Haven: Yale University Press, 1992), 545–75.

5. Mr. Douglass and the Civilizable Characteristics of the Colored Race

1. *Proceedings of the Convention of Colored Citizens of Minnesota* (St. Paul: St. Paul Press Company, 1869), 25.
2. *St. Paul Press,* February 8, 1873, 4.
3. Ibid.
4. William S. McFeely, *Frederick Douglass* (New York: W. W. Norton, 1991), 277. By the beginning of the 1870s, some of the Republican Party's most liberal members began to challenge the Grant presidency because of rampant corruption, a deteriorating national economy, and a protracted military presence enforcing Reconstruction policies in the South. Two notable members of the movement were Minnesota's own Morton Wilkinson and Ignatius Donnelly. See Martin Ridge, *Portrait of a Politician* (Chicago: University of Chicago Press, 1962), 137–38, 143–47. See also the Wilkinson section in my forthcoming book *The Children of Lincoln: Four White Patrons of Black Freedom, 1860–1876.*
5. *St. Paul Press,* February 8, 1873.
6. St. Paul *Daily Dispatch,* February 8, 1873, 1, column 1; St. Paul *Daily Dispatch,* February 14, 1873, 2, column 2.
7. St. Paul *Daily Pioneer,* February 8, 1873, 4, column 4.
8. "Resolved, That the Judiciary Committee be instructed to explore the expediency of enacting a law punishing by severe penalties any landlord or inn-keeper within the state, who shall refuse entertainment to any person based on account of race or color, said committee to report by bill or otherwise" (*Journal of House and Senate,* 1873, 170).
9. St. Paul *Daily Press,* February 8, 1873, 1, column 2; St. Paul *Daily Dispatch,* February 14, 1983, 1, column 2.
10. Richard Kluger, *Simple Justice* (New York: Vintage, 1975), 50, 626–34.
11. *St. Paul Press,* March 4, 1873, 2, column 1.
12. Ibid.
13. St. Paul *Daily Pioneer,* May 15, 1873, 4, column 2; May 16, 4, column 4; St. Paul *Dispatch,* May 16, 1873, 4, column 1.
14. For a thorough account of the infestation, see Annette Atkins, *Harvest of Grief: Grasshopper Plagues and Public Assistance in Minnesota, 1873–78* (St. Paul: Minnesota Historical Society Press, 2004).
15. St. Paul *Daily Pioneer,* May 15, 1873, 4, column 2; May 16, 4, column 4; St. Paul *Dispatch,* May 16, 1873, 4, column 1.
16. *Civil Rights in America: Racial Desegregation in Public Accommodations* (Washington, D.C.: U.S. Department of the Interior, 2004), 13.
17. *Washington, Alexandria and Georgetown Railway Co. v. Brown,* 84 US 445 (1873).
18. Leslie H. Fishel, "Repercussions of Reconstruction: The Northern Negro, 1870–1883," *Civil War History* 14 (December 1968): 328.
19. *Civil Rights in America,* 13.
20. 18 Statute, Part 3, chapter 114, 335 (Act of March 1, 1875).
21. L. E. Murphy, "The Civil Rights Act of 1875," *Journal of Negro History* 12:2 (April 1927): 110–27; 18 Statute, Part 3, chapter 114, 335 (Act of March 1, 1875), section 3.

22. C. Vann Woodward, *The Strange Career of Jim Crow* (New York: Oxford University Press, 1966), 28.

23. Howard Rabinowitz, "From Evidence to Segregation: Southern Race Relations, 1865–1880," *Journal of American History* 63:2 (September 1976): 346.

24. Ibid., 347.

25. Eric Foner, *Reconstruction: America's Unfinished Revolution, 1863–1877* (New York: Harper & Row, 1988), 556.

26. John Hope Franklin, "The Enforcement of the Civil Rights Act of 1875," *Prologue* 6 (winter 1974): 225–35.

27. Foner, *Reconstruction,* 556.

28. Avery Craven, *Reconstruction: Ending the Civil War* (New York: Holt, Rinehart, and Winston, 1969), 307n, citing the *Nation,* August 24, 1876. See also Foner, *Reconstruction,* 24.

29. Henry Ward Beecher reportedly said to Wendell Phillips in Chicago in 1873: "Ah, Phillips, we are getting old . . . for I feel that there is nothing left now to fight against—nothing that excites my antagonism as did those questions of our younger days. They are settled, and you and I are no account any longer" (St. Paul *Dispatch,* February 17, 1877, 4, column 5). For commentaries on the shift of focus from black civil rights by the Republicans, see Foner, *Reconstruction,* 343–44; Kluger, *Simple Justice,* 55.

30. McFeely, *Frederick Douglass,* 289.

31. Frederick Douglass, *Life and Times of Frederick Douglass* (Hartford, Conn.: Park Publishing, 1882), 453.

32. McFeely, *Frederick Douglass,* 300.

33. Ibid.

34. Foner, *Reconstruction,* 472.

35. David V. Taylor, "Pilgrim's Progress: Black St. Paul and the Making of an Urban Ghetto, 1870–1930," Ph.D. thesis, University of Minnesota (March 1977), 43–44.

36. Rochester *Post,* June 18, 1869, 2, column 2; St. Paul *Pioneer,* June 11, 1869, 4, column 3.

37. St. Paul and Minneapolis *Pioneer Press,* June 12, 1877, 6, column 2.

38. St. Paul *Dispatch,* June 11, 1877, 2, column 3.

39. Ibid.

40. Ibid.

41. David V. Taylor, "Blacks," in *They Chose Minnesota: A Survey of the State's Ethnic Groups,* ed. June Drenning Holmquist (St. Paul: Minnesota Historical Society Press, 1981), 78–80.

42. Ibid., 79.

43. Ibid.; Taylor, "Pilgrim's Progress," 38.

44. Taylor, "Pilgrim's Progress," 39.

45. Douglass came to St. Paul in 1868, 1869, and 1873. Regarding train service, see St. Paul *Daily Pioneer,* May 15, 1873, 4, column 2.

46. "Afro-Americans in Minnesota," *Gopher Historian* (winter 1968–69): 18; St. Paul and Minneapolis *Pioneer Press,* December 11, 1887; St. Paul *Daily Dispatch,* July 7, 1876, 1, column 7.

47. Taylor, "Pilgrim's Progress," 38.

48. St. Paul *Dispatch,* February 25, 1875, 4, column 1.

49. St. Paul and Minneapolis *Pioneer Press,* December 11, 1887; *St. Paul City Directories 1876.*

50. Taylor, "Pilgrim's Progress," 158.

51. Ibid.

52. Ibid.

53. Ibid.

54. St. Paul *Daily Pioneer Press,* August 3, 1875, 4, column 1. See also Minneapolis *Tribune,* July 27, 1875, 4, column 1.

55. Minneapolis *Tribune,* August 7, 1875, 4, column 2.

56. St. Paul *Daily Dispatch,* September 23, 1876, 1, column 1.

57. St. Paul *Sunday Pioneer Press,* September 26, 1875, 4, column 5.

58. *Pioneer Press and Tribune,* May 24, 1876, 6, column 3.

59. Minneapolis *Tribune,* June 26, 1876, 4, column 1. See also June 3, 1876, 4, column 3; March 9, 1876, 4, column 2; August 1, 1876, 4, column 2; July 31, 1879, 4, column 4; August 1, 1879, 4, column 5; June 18, 1880, 7, column 2; St. Paul *Daily Dispatch,* July 7, 1876, 1, column 7; St. Paul *Pioneer Press,* March 29, 1877, 7, column 2; February 11, 1880, 7, column 2.

60. St. Paul *Pioneer Press,* April 10, 1879, 3, column 1.

61. St. Paul *Daily Globe,* April 11, 1879, 3, column 5.

62. St. Paul *Pioneer Press,* April 28, 1879, 6, column 3; Stillwater *Gazette,* May 7, 1879, 1, column 3.

63. St. Paul *Daily Globe,* June 24, 1881, 1, column 6.

64. Earl Spangler, *The Negro in Minnesota* (Minneapolis: T. S. Dennison, 1961), 42. See also William Watts Folwell, *A History of Minnesota,* vol. 3 (St. Paul: Minnesota Historical Society Press, 1969), 58, 139.

65. 18 Stat. 335, Sections 1, 2 (1875).

66. The cases selected were from Kansas, southern New York, California, western Missouri, and western Tennessee. African American citizens protested their exclusion from a hotel dining room in Topeka, Kansas, from an opera hall in New York City, from the better seating of a San Francisco theater, and from a car seat set aside for ladies on the train.

67. *Civil Rights Cases,* 109 U.S. 3 (1883).

68. *St. Paul City Directory 1883,* 391; *Cincinnati Ohio City Directory 1885,* 682.

69. Thomas M. Newson, *Pen Pictures and Biographical Sketches of Old Settlers,* vol. 1 (St. Paul, 1886), 12.

70. Minneapolis *Daily Tribune,* June 2, 1883, 5, column 3.

6. Senate Bill No. 181

1. V. Jacque Voegeli, *Free but Not Equal: The Midwest and the Negro during the Civil War* (Chicago: University of Chicago Press, 1967), 179.

2. Minneapolis *Tribune,* March 6, 1885, 5, column 2.

3. Minneapolis *Tribune,* January 27, 1885, 5, column 3; St. Paul *Pioneer Press,* January 28, 1885, 4, column 1.

4. Minneapolis *Tribune,* January 6, 1885, 4, column 4; *Legislative Manual 1885,* 536; J. Fletcher Williams, *A History of the City of Saint Paul, and of the County of Ramsey, Minnesota, to 1875* (St. Paul: Minnesota Historical Society Press, 1983), 435n, 461, 436; *Journal of the Senate 1885,* 84; Minneapolis *Tribune,* March 7, 1885, 4, column 5; T. M. Newson, *Pen Pictures of*

St. Paul, Minnesota, and Biographical Sketches of Old Settlers, from the Earliest Settlement of the City, up to and Including the Year 1857 (St. Paul, 1886), 442–44.

5. Journal of the House 1885, 606, 656; Journal of the Senate 1885, 331.

6. Chapter 225 of the General Laws of Minnesota for 1885, 295–96.

7. Civil Rights Cases, 109 U.S. 3 (1883), 37–42; Richard Kluger, Simple Justice (New York: Knopf, 1976), 81.

8. "The powers not delegated to the United States by the Constitution, nor prohibited by it to the states, are reserved to the states respectively, or to the people" (U.S. Constitution, amendment 10).

9. Milton R. Konvitz, A Century of Civil Rights (Westport, Conn.: Greenwood Press, 1983), 157–58.

10. Ibid., 158.

11. Ibid.

12. Theodore Blegen, Minnesota: A History of the State (Minneapolis: University of Minnesota Press, 1975), 287.

13. Journal of the Senate 1885, 331.

14. General Laws of Minnesota for 1885, chapter 224, section 1.

15. In 1880, a second black newspaper was established in St. Paul called the St. Paul Review. Like the Western Appeal, it was short-lived (Earl Spangler, The Negro in Minnesota [Minneapolis: T. S. Dennison, 1961], 61).

16. In 1885, the percentage of the African American population was 0.16 percent. The white population was 1,115,984 and the black population was 1,814, of whom 1,100 were African American men (Minnesota Census, 1885; David V. Taylor, "Pilgrim's Progress: Black St. Paul and the Making of an Urban Ghetto, 1870–1930," Ph.D. thesis, University of Minnesota [March 1977], 59).

17. Minneapolis Tribune, March 6, 1885, 5, column 2.

18. St. Paul Dispatch, March 5, 1885, 1, column 2.

19. St. Paul and Minneapolis Pioneer Press, March 6, 1885, 5, column 4, and 3, column 3.

20. Ibid., 3, column 3.

21. Oliver Wendell Holmes, "The Path of the Law," 10; Harvard Law Review 457 (1897).

22. For the remedy, see General Laws of the State of Minnesota for 1885, chapter 224, section 2.

23. Western Appeal, June 27, 1885, 1, column 5.

24. St. Paul Daily Pioneer Press, June 30, 1885, 8, column 5.

25. Western Appeal, July 4, 1885, 1, column 2.

26. Ibid.

27. Ibid.

28. Western Appeal, July 11, 1885, 1, column 3.

29. Rayford W. Logan, Betrayal of the Negro: From Rutherford B. Hayes to Woodrow Wilson (London: Collier Books, 1969), 56.

30. Heather Richardson Cox, West of Appomattox: The Reconstruction of America after the Civil War (New Haven, Conn.: Yale University Press 2007), 212–13. See also Logan, Betrayal of the Negro, 56.

31. Logan, Betrayal of the Negro, 57. See also Cox, West of Appomattox, 213–14.

32. Census data from 1890. See William Watts Folwell, A History of Minnesota, vol. 3 (St. Paul:

Minnesota Historical Society Press, 1969), 192; Earl Spangler, *The Negro in Minnesota* (Minneapolis: T. S. Dennison, 1961), 63.

33. *Western Appeal,* May 7, 1887, 1, column 1.

34. Ibid., 2.

35. *Western Appeal,* March 3, 1887, 1, column 1; March 12, 1887, 1, column 1; March 26, 1887, 1, column 1. For examples of the newspaper telling readers to patronize advertisers, see December 3, 1887, 1, column 4; April 23, 1887, 1, column 2.

36. *Western Appeal,* May 5, 1887, 1, column 2.

37. *Western Appeal,* December 24, 1887, 1, column 1; September 7, 1889, 2.

38. *Western Appeal,* March 12, 1887, 1, column 1.

39. Ibid., column 2; emphasis added.

40. Ibid.; emphasis added.

41. *Western Appeal,* October 1, 1887, 1, column 1.

42. *Western Appeal,* December 24, 1887, 1, column 1.

43. *Western Appeal,* June 6, 1887, 1, column 1.

44. *Western Appeal,* February 2, 1887, 1, column 2.

45. *Western Appeal,* April 2, 1887, 1, column 1.

46. *Western Appeal,* June 13, 1887, 1, column 2.

47. *Western Appeal,* December 24, 1887, 1, column 4.

48. *Western Appeal,* September 7, 1887, 2.

49. Ibid.

50. *Western Appeal,* March 5, 1887, 2.

51. Taylor, "Pilgrim's Progress," 284, 288. See also Kevin Golden, "The Independent Development of Civil Rights in Minnesota, 1849–1910," *William Mitchell Law Review* 17 (1991): 449, 459.

52. *Western Appeal,* July 4, 1885, 1, column 3 (pro-laborer rights and antimonopolyism); June 27, 1885, 1, column 4 (support of a woman's right to practice law).

53. Minneapolis *Tribune,* June 1, 1885, 4, column 6.

54. *Western Appeal,* September 4, 1885, 1, column 2.

55. *Western Appeal,* October 15, 1887, 4, column 2.

56. Ibid.

57. *Western Appeal,* July 16, 1887, 1, column 1.

58. Taylor, "Pilgrim's Progress," 288.

59. *Western Appeal,* December 3, 1887, 1, column 1; December 17, 1887, 1, column 1; March 19, 1887, 1, column 2.

60. See, for example, *Western Appeal,* March 26, 1887, 2.

61. *Western Appeal,* September 24, 1887, 4, column 2; October 1, 1887, 1, column 2; October 8, 1887, 1, column 4; October 15, 1887, 1, column 2, and 4, column 1.

62. *Western Appeal,* December 24, 1887, 1, columns 1–2, and December 31, 1887, 1, column 3.

63. David V. Taylor, "John Quincy Adams: St. Paul Editor and Black Leader," *Minnesota History* (winter 1973): 284.

64. Ibid., 285.

65. Ibid., 290n41.

66. Ibid., 290.

67. *Western Appeal,* October 15, 1887, 1, column 1.

68. *Western Appeal,* November 26, 1887, 1, column 2.

7. A Certain Class of Citizens

1. David V. Taylor, "Pilgrim's Progress: Black St. Paul and the Making of an Urban Ghetto, 1870–1930," Ph.D. thesis, University of Minnesota (March 1977), 62.

2. Ibid., 62n51, citing *Western Appeal,* June 27, 1885.

3. Ibid., 63.

4. *Western Appeal,* July 4, 1885, 1, column 3.

5. *Western Appeal,* March 19, 1887, 1, columns 1–2.

6. St. Paul *Daily Pioneer Press,* March 26, 1874, 4, column 2; June 25, 1874, 6, column 1; Minneapolis *Tribune,* March 20, 1875, 3, column 2; March 24, 1875, 3, column 4; May 4, 1875, 4, column 3; St. Paul *Daily Pioneer,* June 5, 1877, 4, column 4. For DuBois's summer job on Lake Minnetonka, see David Levering Lewis, *W.E. B. DuBois: 1868–1919: Biography of a Race* (New York: Henry Holt, 1993), 82–83.

7. W. E. B. DuBois, *Darkwater: Voices from within the Veil* (New York: Schocken Books, 1969), 111. See also Lewis, *W.E. B. DuBois,* 82–83.

8. *Western Appeal,* July 18, 1885, 2, column 2.

9. DuBois, *Darkwater,* 113.

10. David V. Taylor, "John Quincy Adams: St. Paul Editor and Black Leader," *Minnesota History* (winter 1973): 291.

11. Ibid. See also *Western Appeal,* May 21, 1887, 1, column 2.

12. *Western Appeal,* October 15, 1887, 4, column 2.

13. Ibid.

14. *William A. Hazel v. Michael E. Foley & Thomas J. Foley (Foley Brothers),* 25515 Civil Court of the Second Judicial District, State of Minnesota, Judgment, October 17, 1887, Ramsey County Courthouse, St. Paul.

15. *Western Appeal,* October 22, 1887, 1, columns 1–2. See also Taylor, "John Quincy Adams," 292 n36.

16. *Western Appeal,* October 22, 1887, 1, column 1.

17. Ibid.

18. *Western Appeal,* December 3, 1887, 1, column 2.

19. Ibid.

20. *Western Appeal,* November 19, 1887, 1, column 2.

21. A year earlier, the Republicans, similarly disposed to co-opting voices of dissent, allowed delegates from the joint convention of Minnesota Alliance and the Knights of Labor, whose platform embodied the demands of both farmers and laboring men, to sit at the Republican convention. See Theodore C. Blegen, *Minnesota: A History of a State* (Minneapolis: University of Minnesota Press, 1975), 388.

22. *Western Appeal,* November 19, 1887, 1, column 1; December 3, 1887, 1, column 5; December 19, 1887, 1, column 1.

23. *Minneapolis Spokesman,* May 16, 1958, 4. See also Taylor, "John Quincy Adams," 292.

24. Taylor, "John Quincy Adams," 292.

25. Ibid.

26. *Western Appeal,* December 31, 1887, 1, column 3.

27. Ibid., column 2.

28. Blegen, *Minnesota,* 386–88.

29. *Western Appeal,* December 3, 1887, 1, column 3.

30. Taylor, "John Quincy Adams," 292.

31. Ibid., 288.

32. *Western Appeal,* June 11, 1887, 1, column 1.

33. Emma Lou Thornbrough, "The National Afro-American League, 1887–1908," *Journal of Southern History* 27:4 (November 1961): 496.

34. Local chapters of varying size and strength formed in New England, Pennsylvania, New York, Illinois, and even distant San Francisco. In the South, organizations were attempted in Virginia, Texas, North Carolina, Tennessee, and Georgia (ibid., 498). Georgia's black population made plans to organize in January 1888 (*Western Appeal,* January 7, 1888, 1, column 2).

35. *Appeal,* October 19, 1889, 2; October 26, 1889, 2; Taylor, "John Quincy Adams," 293.

36. Thornbrough, "The National Afro-American League, 1887–1908," 499. On the constitution, see *Appeal,* November 9, 1889, 1, column 2. The revised constitution can be found in *Appeal,* December 14, 1889, 2, column 2.

37. *Appeal,* November 9, 1889, 1, column 2; December 14, 1889, 2, column 2.

38. Taylor, "John Quincy Adams," 293.

39. *Appeal,* December 30, 1889, 1, column 1.

40. Thornbrough, "The National Afro-American League, 1887–1908," 498.

41. St. Paul *Daily Pioneer Press,* January 17, 1890, 1, column 3. See also Minneapolis *Tribune,* January 17, 1890, 4, column 5.

42. Earl Spangler, *The Negro in Minnesota* (Minneapolis: T. S. Dennison, 1961), 78.

43. Thomas Fortune, "Why We Organize a National Afro-American League," *Afro-American Budget* I (February 1890): 231, 240; Thornbrough, "The National Afro-American League, 1887–1908," 498–99.

44. Thornbrough, "The National Afro-American League, 1887–1908," 499.

45. Ibid., 500.

46. St. Paul *Dispatch,* January 16, 1890, 2, column 2.

47. Thornbrough, "The National Afro-American League, 1887–1908," 499–500.

48. *Appeal,* May 16, 1891, 1; May 23, 1891, 3; Taylor, "John Quincy Adams," 293; Spangler, *The Negro in Minnesota,* 79.

49. Thornbrough, "The National Afro-American League, 1887–1908," 500; Paul Nelson, *Fredrick L. McGhee: A Life on the Color Line, 1861–1912* (St. Paul: Minnesota Historical Society Press, 2002), 32.

50. Thornbrough, "The National Afro-American League, 1887–1908," 499n11, citing *New York Age,* July 25, 1891.

51. Ibid.

52. *Appeal,* June 27, 1891, 2, column 1. See also Nelson, *Fredrick L. McGhee,* 32–34; Taylor, "John Quincy Adams," 293; Spangler, *The Negro in Minnesota,* 79.

53. Thornbrough, "The National Afro-American League, 1887–1908," 500–501.

54. Ibid., 501n15.

55. Nelson, *Fredrick L. McGhee,* 34–35.

56. Ibid., 37.

57. Ibid.

58. Thornbrough, "The National Afro-American League, 1887–1908," 501.

59. *Appeal,* August 30, 1890, 3, column 3.

60. Ibid.

61. *Appeal,* January 11, 1890, 2, column 2; emphasis added.

62. St. Paul *Daily Pioneer Press,* January 17, 1890, 1, column 3. For a report on Senator Butler's bill, see St. Paul *Dispatch,* January 16, 1890, 1, column 2; Rayford Logan, *The Betrayal of the Negro: From Rutherford B. Hayes to Woodrow Wilson* (New York: Collier Books, 1965), 142.

63. St. Paul *Daily Pioneer Press,* January 17, 1890, 1, column 3.

64. St. Paul *Daily Pioneer Press,* January 18, 1890, 9, column 3.

65. Minneapolis *Tribune,* January 17, 1890, 4, column 5.

66. *Appeal,* February 15, 1890, 2, column 3; February 22, 1890, 2, column 5; March 1, 1890, 3, column 3.

67. *Appeal,* February 22, 1890, 2, column 2.

68. *Appeal,* December 13, 1890, 3, column 2.

69. *Appeal,* December 20, 1890, 6, columns 1–3.

70. *Appeal,* May 24, 1890, 2, column 2.

71. *Appeal,* September 14, 1890, 2, column 2.

72. *Appeal,* May 10, 1890, 2, column 4.

73. *Appeal,* November 15, 1890, 2, column 2.

74. The letter is found in the *Appeal,* November 22, 1890, 3, column 1.

75. Richard Kluger, *Simple Justice* (New York: Knopf, 1976), 67–68.

76. *Appeal,* January 31, 1891, 3, column 3.

77. *Appeal,* December 20, 1890, 3, column 2.

78. Ibid.

79. Ibid.

80. Nelson, *Fredrick L. McGhee,* 29–30.

81. Regarding Adams, for example, see *Appeal,* June 14, 1890, 3, column 2; for McGhee, see August 30, 1890, 3, column 3.

82. *Appeal,* October 11, 1890, 3, columns 2–3.

83. *Appeal,* May 23, 1891, 3, column 3.

84. *Appeal,* June 20, 1891, 3, column 4; June 27, 1891, 2, column 1.

85. *Appeal,* July 18, 1891, 2, column 2.

86. *Appeal,* January 31, 1891, 3, column 3.

87. Ibid.

88. Ibid.

89. Ibid.

8. Professor Washington, Leader of the Race

1. St. Paul *Dispatch,* January 16, 1890, 2, column 2.
2. Ibid.
3. Ibid.
4. St. Paul *Dispatch,* September 19, 1895, 1, column 7.
5. Booker T. Washington, *Up from Slavery* (Oxford: Oxford University Press, 1995), 124–25. Subsequent references are given in the text.
6. Richard Kluger, *Simple Justice* (New York: Knopf, 1976), 69; St. Paul *Pioneer Press,* September 20, 1895, 4, column 3.
7. Kluger, *Simple Justice,* 69; St. Paul *Pioneer Press,* September 20, 1895, 4, column 3.
8. Washington, *Up from Slavery,* 121.
9. Kluger, *Simple Justice,* 69; St. Paul *Pioneer Press,* September 20, 1895, 4, column 3.
10. Rayford Logan, *The Betrayal of the Negro: From Rutherford B. Hayes to Woodrow Wilson* (New York: Collier Books, 1965), 277.
11. Ibid.
12. Ibid.
13. Washington, *Up from Slavery,* 127–28. Subsequent references are given in the text.
14. Logan, *The Betrayal of the Negro,* 278.
15. Washington, *Up from Slavery,* 133.
16. Logan, *The Betrayal of the Negro,* 278.
17. St. Paul *Dispatch,* September 19, 1895, 4, column 2.
18. St. Paul *Dispatch,* September 18, 1895, 1, columns 2–5; St. Paul *Pioneer Press,* September 18, 1895, 2, column 7; Minneapolis *Tribune,* September 18, 1895.
19. St. Paul *Dispatch,* September 19, 1895, 1, column 7.
20. St. Paul *Pioneer Press,* September 19, 1895, 2, column 4.
21. St. Paul *Dispatch,* September 18, 1895, 1, columns 3–4.
22. *Appeal,* January 30, 1892, 2, column 1 (Florida); February 6, 1892, 2, column 2 (Louisiana); February 13, 1892, 2, column 1 (Texas), February 13, 1892, 2, column 1 (Kentucky); February 27, 1892, 2, column 2 (Alabama); March 2, 1892, 2, column 2 (Georgia); April 9, 1892, 2, column 2 (Tennessee).
23. *Appeal,* April 16, 1892, 3, column 3.
24. *Appeal,* May 28, 1892, 3, column 3. See also June 4, 1892, 5, columns 1–2.
25. *Appeal,* May 28, 1892, 2, column 2.
26. Washington, *Up from Slavery,* 134.
27. *Black-Belt Diamonds: Gems from the Speeches, Addresses, and Talks to Students of Booker T. Washington* (New York: Fortune and Scott, 1898), 14.
28. Ibid., 40–41.

9. The Renaissance of the Cakewalk

1. For examples of the features on colleges, see *Appeal,* January 2, 1892, 1, columns. 3–4; January 23, 1892, 1, columns 3–4; February 6, 1892, 1; April 16, 1892, 1.

2. *Appeal,* March 12, 1892, 1, columns 1–2.

3. Ibid.

4. Ibid.

5. Paul Nelson, *Fredrick L. McGhee: A Life on the Color Line, 1861–1912* (St. Paul: Minnesota Historical Society Press 2002), 148.

6. Ibid., 215n1, citing the *Appeal,* August 20, 1892, 4.

7. Ibid., 62–63.

8. *Appeal,* March 12, 1892, 2, column 1.

9. Earl Spangler, *The Negro in Minnesota* (Minneapolis: T. S. Dennison, 1961), 90.

10. Ibid., 91.

11. *Appeal,* May 10, 1890, 2, column 4.

12. *Appeal,* May 21, 1892, 3, column 3.

13. On the Hickman Pilgrims, see William D. Green, *A Peculiar Imbalance: The Fall and Rise of Racial Equality in Early Minnesota,* 127–39 (St. Paul: Minnesota Historical Society Press, 2007).

14. David V. Taylor, "Blacks," in *They Chose Minnesota: A Survey of the State's Ethnic Groups,* ed. June Drenning Holmquist (St. Paul: Minnesota Historical Society Press, 1981), 81.

15. Spangler, *The Negro in Minnesota,* 67.

16. Richard Kluger, *Simple Justice* (New York: Knopf, 1976), 7.

17. *Appeal,* June 4, 1895, 1, columns 1–2.

18. Booker T. Washington, *Up from Slavery* (Oxford: Oxford University Press, 1995), 128.

19. E. Franklin Frazier, *Black Bourgeoisie: The Book That Brought the Shock of Self-Revelation to Middle-Class Blacks in America* (New York: Collier Books, 1969), 61.

20. *Appeal,* October 16, 1891, 1, column 2.

21. *Appeal,* June 4, 1892, 2, column 1.

22. *Appeal,* June 11, 1892, 2, column 2. Implicated as a coconspirator in John Brown's raid on Harpers Ferry, Douglass left the country to avoid being arrested, and only returned to the United States from Great Britain when he learned of the North's acceptance of Brown's martyrdom. He gave penitence for not having had the courage to join Brown in the raid. See William S. McFeely, *Frederick Douglass* (New York: W. W. Norton, 1991), 198–200, 212.

23. *Appeal,* October 8, 1892, 4, column 2.

24. "The colored delegates were accorded a patient hearing on all subjects in which they took an interest. The colored people have much to hope from their connection with the Order [the union]. They already derived many benefits and many more are in store for them, from this organization, the only one that knows no creed, nationality or color" (*Appeal,* October 22, 1887, 2, column 2).

25. *Appeal,* January 1, 1892, 2, column 1.

26. *Appeal,* August 8, 1892, 8, column 2.

27. Nelson, *Fredrick L. McGhee,* 35, citing St. Paul *Pioneer Press,* April 24, 1892, 5.

28. Ibid., 36, citing *Svenska Amerikanska Posten,* May 10, 1892, 4; translated in Peg Meier, *Bring Warm Clothes: Letters and Photos from Minnesota's Past* (Minneapolis: Neighbors Publishing, 1981), 189.

29. *Appeal,* April 2, 1892, 3, column 3. See also Nelson, *Fredrick L. McGhee,* 36; Spangler, *The Negro in Minnesota,* 83–84; *Svenska Amerikanska Posten,* September 20, 1892, 5, column 2; William Watts Folwell, *A History of Minnesota,* vol. 3 (St. Paul: Minnesota Historical Society Press, 1969), 195.

30. For an account of black participation during the National Republican Convention of 1892, see Iric Nathanson, "African Americans and the 1892 Republican National Convention, Minneapolis," *Minnesota History* 61:2 (summer 2008): 76–82.

31. Nelson, *Fredrick L. McGhee,* 35–36; Spangler, *The Negro in Minnesota,* 81.

32. *Appeal,* April 16, 1892, 2, column 2.

33. *Appeal,* August 6, 1892, 8, column 2.

34. Ibid.

35. *Svenska Amerikanska Posten,* September 20, 1892, 5, column 2.

36. *Appeal,* December 3, 1892, 2, column 2.

37. Spangler, *The Negro in Minnesota,* 81–82.

38. Ibid.

39. Ibid., 80.

40. Ibid.

41. *Appeal,* October 11, 1890, 3, columns 2–3.

42. Spangler, *The Negro in Minnesota,* 80.

43. *Plessy v. Ferguson,* 163 U.S. 537 (1896).

44. St. Paul *Pioneer Press,* May 19, 1896.

45. Ibid., 544.

46. *Appeal,* October 31, 1896, 1–4.

47. *Appeal,* April 17, 1897, 3, column 2.

48. Nelson, *Fredrick L. McGhee,* 63.

49. Ibid., 61.

50. Ibid.

51. Ibid., 62.

52. Ibid., 64, citing *Appeal,* December 3, 1898, 4.

53. Ibid., 65, citing *Appeal,* December 10, 1898, 4.

54. Ibid., citing *Appeal,* February 11, 1899, 4.

10. Wheaton and McGhee

1. Paul Nelson, *Fredrick L. McGhee: A Life on the Color Line, 1861–1912* (St. Paul: Minnesota Historical Society Press, 2002), 4. See also Earl Spangler, *The Negro in Minnesota* (Minneapolis: T. S. Dennison, 1961), 68; *Appeal,* June 22, 1889, 1.

2. Nelson, *Fredrick L. McGhee,* 4.

3. Ibid., 13. See also "Afro-Americans in Minnesota: Biographies of Black Pioneers," *Gopher Historian* (winter 1968): 19; Spangler, *The Negro in Minnesota,* 68.

4. Nelson, *Fredrick L. McGhee,* 13. Subsequent references are given in the text.

5. *Appeal,* September 24, 1892, 2.

6. Nelson, *Fredrick L. McGhee,* 37.

7. President James Garfield had set the precedent of creating "Negro jobs" with the executive branch, which were typically filled by aging lions of the abolitionist movement. John M. Langston was minister of Haiti and consul general to the Dominican Republic; Henry Highland Garnet, minister to Liberia; ex-Senator Blanche K. Bruce, register of the treasury. See Rayford W. Logan, *The Betrayal of the Negro: From Rutherford B. Hayes to Woodrow Wilson* (London: Collier Books, 1965), 54.

8. Ibid. Douglass was appointed by President Hayes to be Marshal for the District of Columbia, recorder of deeds, and minister to Haiti. See William S. McFeely, *Frederick Douglass* (New York: W. W. Norton, 1991), 289, 306, 335.

9. Nelson, *Fredrick L. McGhee,* 80–81.

10. Ibid., 82.

11. St. Paul *Globe,* March 19, 1893, 3. See also St. Paul *Pioneer Press,* March 11, 1893, 4; St. Paul *Daily News,* March 15, 1893, 5.

12. *Progressive Men in Minnesota* (1897 Book), 350–51 (MHS).

13. Ibid., 350, 341; *Appeal,* January 7, 1899; September 1, 1864; June 12, 1897; St. Paul *Globe,* April 17, 1895;*Who's Who of the Colored Race* (1915), 281. See also Tim Brady, "Barely There," *Minnesota Monthly* (August 2004): 23, 24; Spangler, *The Negro in Minnesota,* 69.

14. Los Angeles *Times,* March 23, 1896, 2.

15. St. Paul *Globe,* October 11, 1896, 2.

16. Ibid.

17. Ibid.

18. Carl H. Chrislock, *The Progressive Era in Minnesota, 1899–1918* (St. Paul: Minnesota Historical Society Press, 1971). 11.

19. *Appeal,* March 22, 1890, 2, column 3.

20. C. Vann Woodward, *The Strange Career of Jim Crow* (Oxford: Oxford University Press, 2002), 72, citing Emma Lou Thornbrough, *The Negro in Indiana: A Study of a Minority before 1900* (Indianapolis: Indiana Historical Collection, 1957), 258.

21. *Appeal,* April 17, 1897, 2, columns 1–2.

22. Nelson, *Fredrick L. McGhee,* 55–56. For Wheaton's lawsuit, see St. Paul *Globe,* April 17, 1895, 2; April 24, 1895, 2.

23. St. Paul *Globe,* April 17, 1895, 2, columns 3–4; April 22, 1895, 2, column 3.

24. *Appeal,* June 1, 1895, 4, column 4.

25. Statutes of Minnesota 1879–1888, vol. 2, chapter 124, sections 203 and 204.

26. *Appeal,* April 24, 1897, 3.

27. Nelson, *Fredrick L. McGhee,* 56.

28. Act of April 23, 1897, chapter 349, section 3, 1897, Minnesota General Laws 616; Statutes of Minnesota 1879–1888, vol. 2, chapter 124, sections 203 and 204.

29. *Appeal,* April 17, 1897, 2, column 1.

30. Ibid., at column 2.

31. St. Paul *Daily Pioneer,* February 8, 1873, 4, column 4.

32. *Appeal,* April 17, 1897, 2, column 2.

33. *Appeal,* June 17, 1899, 3.
34. *Appeal,* April 17, 1897.
35. *Appeal,* June 17, 1899, 3, column 2.
36. *Appeal,* April 17, 1897, 2, column 2; April 24, 1897, 2, column 2.
37. *Appeal,* April 24, 1897, 2, column 3.
38. Ibid., at column 3. See also Nelson, *Fredrick L. McGhee,* 56–57.
39. St. Paul *Dispatch,* April 9, 1897, 9.
40. *Appeal,* April 14, 1897, 2.
41. *Appeal,* April 24, 1897, 2.
42. Ibid.
43. Ibid.
44. On March 23, Representative Donnelly introduced Bill No. 853, "a bill to appropriate money to the Negroes of Minnesota and participate in the Tennessee centennial of 1897." The bill was referred and lost to the Committee of Appropriations (*House and Senate Journal 1897,* 640).
45. *Appeal,* April 24, 1897.
46. *Appeal,* December 25, 1897, 3, column 2.
47. *Appeal,* January 6, 1898, 1, column 3.
48. *Appeal,* March 5, 1898, 4, column 7.
49. *Appeal,* March 5, 1898, 4, column 7; Minneapolis *Journal,* March 3, 1898, 6, column 5; J. Clay Smith, "In the Shadow of *Plessy*: A Portrait of McCant Stewart, Afro-American Legal Pioneer," *Minnesota Law Review* 73 (1988): 495, 502, 504–12.
50. *Appeal,* March 19, 1898, 4, column 1. See also March 26, 1898, 4, column 1; Spangler, *The Negro in Minnesota,* 77.

11. The Election of J. Frank Wheaton

1. Earl Spangler, *The Negro in Minnesota* (Minneapolis: T. S. Dennison, 1961), 69.
2. Ibid.
3. *Appeal,* June 18, 1898, 3; July 2, 1898, 3; July 9, 1898, 3; Paul Nelson, *Fredrick L. McGhee: A Life on the Color Line, 1861–1912* (St. Paul: Minnesota Historical Society Press, 2002), 73.
4. Rayford W. Logan, *The Betrayal of the Negro: From Rutherford B. Hayes to Woodrow Wilson* (London: Collier Books, 1965), 97.
5. David V. Taylor, "Pilgrim's Progress: Black St. Paul and the Making of an Urban Ghetto, 1870–1930," Ph.D. thesis, University of Minnesota (March 1977), 108; Nelson, *Fredrick L. McGhee,* 66.
6. *Appeal,* July 23, 1898, 4.
7. *Appeal,* September 17, 1898, 3–4.
8. Ibid., 4.
9. See St. Paul *Pioneer Press,* June 25, 1895, 2.
10. Nelson, *Fredrick L. McGhee,* 66.
11. Ibid., 68.
12. Taylor, "Pilgrim's Progress," 108–9; Nelson, *Fredrick L. McGhee,* 68.

13. Nelson, *Fredrick L. McGhee*, 68. See also *Appeal*, September 17, 1898.

14. *Appeal*, January 8, 1898, 3, column 2.

15. *Appeal*, March 19, 1898, 4, column 1.

16. In fact, the party was founded in St. Anthony, a community situated on the northern shore by St. Anthony Falls. In 1876, St. Anthony was incorporated into the Minneapolis municipal border. See Lucile M. Kane, *The Falls of St. Anthony: The Waterfall That Built Minneapolis* (St. Paul: Minnesota Historical Society Press, 1987); Jocelyn Wills, *Boosters, Hustlers, and Speculators: Entrepreneurial Culture and the Rise of Minneapolis and St. Paul, 1849–1883* (St. Paul: Minnesota Historical Society Press, 2005).

17. See reminiscence of C. G. Ames in Eugene V. Smalley, *History of the Republican Party from Its Organization in the Present Time, to Which Is Added a Political History of Minnesota from the Republican Point of View* (St. Paul, 1895), 324; William D. Green, *A Peculiar Imbalance: The Fall and Rise of Racial Equality in Early Minnesota* (St. Paul: Minnesota Historical Society Press, 2007), 71–82; Theodore C. Blegen, *Minnesota: A History of a State* (Minneapolis: University of Minnesota Press, 1975), 215–17; Census of the State of Minnesota, 1865, extracted from the Minnesota Secretary of State's *Annual Report* for 1865 (St. Paul: Minnesota Historical Society), 119; *Tribune Almanac for 1868* (New York: New York Herald Tribune), 56–57; *Legislative Manual 1869, 89, 1871*, 1343.

18. *Legislative Manual 1899*, 514.

19. John G. Rice, "The Old Stock Americans," in *They Chose Minnesota: A Survey of the State's Ethnic Groups*, ed. June Drenning Holmquist (St. Paul: Minnesota Historical Society Press, 1981), 62.

20. *South Minneapolis Telegram*, July 1, 1898, 2, columns 1, 3–4.

21. Ibid., 1.

22. *South Minneapolis Telegram*, August 28, 1898, 1, columns 3–4.

23. Ibid., July 8, 1898, 1, column 2; *Appeal*, July 9, 1898, 3, column 2.

24. *South Minneapolis Telegram*, July 15, 1898, 3, column 1.

25. Ibid., September 30, 1898, 2, column 1.

26. *Appeal*, October 1, 1898, 3, column 5.

27. Minneapolis *Journal*, November 3, 1898, 6, column 5.

28. Dollenmayer would eventually become the treasurer of the Democratic State Central Committee (Albert Dollenmayer Family Papers, Box 3, MHS).

29. Carl H. Chrislock, "Profile of a Ward Boss: The Political Career of Lars M. Rand," Norwegian American Historical Association (NAHA) online (vol. 31, 35), a much expanded version of a paper presented at a conference at St. Olaf College, October 25–26, 1984.

30. Holmquist, *They Chose Minnesota*, 233, 251, 260, 264, 284.

31. Ibid.

32. Holmquist, *They Chose Minnesota*, 78, 251.

33. For example, see "Laid the Corner Stone," Minneapolis *Tribune*, September 20, 1886, 5, column 3.

34. Carl H. Chrislock, *The Progressive Era in Minnesota, 1899–1918* (St. Paul: Minnesota Historical Society Press, 1971), 13.

35. *South Minneapolis Telegram*, August 28, 1898, 1, columns 3–4.

36. Ibid., November 4, 1898, 3, column 4. On Gjertsen, see Chrislock, "Profile of a Ward Boss."

37. Minneapolis *Tribune,* November 10, 1898, 1, column 6.

38. Minneapolis *Journal,* November 10, 1989, 7, column 3.

39. *South Minneapolis Telegram,* November 11, 1898, 1, columns 3–4.

40. *Appeal,* December 24, 1898, 3, column 3.

41. Minneapolis *Tribune,* October 26, 1898, 2, column 2.

42. Minneapolis *Tribune,* October 26, 1898,2, column 2.

43. St. Paul *Pioneer Press,* October 26, 1898, 6, column 2.

44. Minneapolis *Tribune,* October 26, 1898, 2, column 2.

45. "Every male person of the age of 21 years and upwards, belonging to either of the following classes, who have resided in the same state six months next preceding any election, shall be entitled to vote at such election, in the election district in which *he shall at the time have been for 30 days a resident,* for all offices that now are, or hereafter may be, elective by the people" (section 1, article 7 of the Constitution of the State of Minnesota; emphasis added).

46. Isaac Atwater, ed., *The History of the City of Minneapolis, Minnesota,* vol. 1 (New York: Munsell & Company, 1893), 111.

47. Chrislock, *The Progressive Era in Minnesota, 1899–1918,* 12–13.

48. St. Paul *Pioneer Press,* October 30, 1898, 6, column 1.

49. Ibid., November 4, 1898, 6, column 1.

50. Our Campaign–Mayors, 1899. http://www.ourcampaigns.com/RaceDetail.html?RaceID=719529.

51. Minneapolis *Tribune,* November 9, 1898, 6, column 2.

52. *Legislative Manual 1899,* 514.

53. 74 Minn. 200, 77 N.W. 31 (1898).

54. Kevin Golden, "The Independent Development of Civil Rights in Minnesota, 1849–1910," *William Mitchell Law Review* 17 (1991): 462. See also *Appeal,* November 19, 1898, 3, column 4.

55. Paper (Case) Book (No. 11048), 7–9, 11–19, 35–36 (MHS).

56. Ibid.

57. Hiram Stevens, *History of the Bench and Bar of Minnesota,* vol. 1 (St. Paul, 1904), 71.

58. 74 Minn. 205.

59. Ibid., 204.

60. Ibid., 203.

61. Ibid., 204.

62. Ibid., 205; 77 N.W., at 32–33.

63. 74 Minn. 206, 207.

64. *Appeal,* November 19, 1898, 3, column 4.

65. *Appeal,* January 7, 1898, 3.

66. *Appeal,* December 24, 1898, 3, column 3. See also *Appeal,* January 7, 1899, 3; *South Minneapolis Telegram,* January 6, 1899, 4, column 2; St. Paul *Pioneer Press,* January 5, 1899, 6, column 1; Minneapolis *Tribune,* January 5, 1899, 7, column 4.

67. St. Paul *Pioneer Press,* January 14, 1899, 5, column 2.

68. St. Paul *Pioneer Press,* January 25, 1899, 9, column 2; emphasis added.

69. *Appeal,* March 4, 1899, 2, column 1; Minneapolis *Tribune,* March 7, 1899, 3, column 4; March 2, 1899, 2, column 2.

70. An Act to Protect All Persons in Their Civil and Legal Rights, chapter 41, section 1, 1899, in *General Laws of Minnesota*, 38–39. Regarding Lind's gubernatorial election, see William Watts Folwell, *A History of Minnesota*, vol. 3 (St. Paul: Minnesota Historical Society Press, 1969), 245–47. Throughout these events, little attention was paid to the wholly separate world of the illegal sales of liquor, federal Indian law, an old Ojibwe warrior named Bugonaygeshig, and the wooded region in northern Minnesota where the Battle of Sugar Point was fought in October 1898, "the first and only serious outbreak of the [Ojibwe] against white man's authority," "the last Indian uprising in the United States." What began as a routine arrest culminated in a bloody incident between warriors of the Bear Island tribe and a regiment of soldiers dispatched from Fort Snelling. The incident got out of hand, leaving embarrassed authorities seeking a speedy conclusion. "Old Bug," as he was called, was eventually released and President McKinley pardoned the warriors who fought beside him (Louis H. Roddis, "The Last Indian Uprising in the United States," *Minnesota History Bulletin* 3 [February 1920]: 270–90; William Watts Folwell, *A History of Minnesota*, vol. 4 [St. Paul: Minnesota Historical Society Press, 1976], 312–23).

71. Minneapolis *Tribune*, March 3, 1899, 3, column 2.

72. Minneapolis *Journal*, March 2, 1899, 2, column 2; Minneapolis *Tribune*, March 3, 1899, 3, column 2. Earlier, Wheaton had introduced a bill to appropriate fifteen thousand dollars to erect a building at the soldiers' home for the accommodations of the wives of ex-soldiers (St. Paul *Pioneer Press*, February 25, 1899, 3, column 4). He had also authored bills on such varied topics as banning flag desecration, bicycle licensing, juvenile justice, a bill to provide for the incorporation of companies formed to provide loans to indigents, and a state training school. Two of his bills were enacted that term—HF 61 (the civil-rights bill) and HF 504 (the flag desecration bill) (*Pioneer Press*, April 18, 1899, 3, column 4).

73. St. Paul *Pioneer Press*, April 18, 1899.

74. Ibid.

75. *Afro-American Advance*, June 17, 1899, 3, column 1; *Appeal*, July 6, 1899, 4, column 2; *South Minneapolis Telegram*, July 7, 1899, 1, column 4.

76. *Appeal*, January 7, 1899, 3, columns 1–5. For an account of *Cuba*, the production that starred Fredrick McGhee in the leading role of General Antonio Maceo, a former slave who led the fight for independence from Spain, see Nelson, *Fredrick L. McGhee*, 61–62; for the circumstances leading up to the debate between McGhee and Reid, see 62–63.

77. *Appeal*, January 21, 1899, 3; St. Paul *Pioneer Press*, January 22, 1899, 9; *South Minneapolis Telegram*, February 3, 1899, 2; St. Paul *Pioneer Press*, February 10, 1899, 3; March 12, 1899, 12; March 15, 1899, 3.

78. *Appeal*, December 9, 1899, 3, column 5; *Afro-American Advance*, December 9, 1899, 12, 1, column 12; *Negro World Newspaper*, May 19, 1900, 1, column 3.

12. A Call to Action

1. St. Paul *Pioneer Press*, March 13, 1894, 8.

2. Ibid.

3. Paul Nelson, *Fredrick L. McGhee: A Life on the Color Line, 1861–1912* (St. Paul: Minnesota Historical Society Press, 2002), 52.

4. Ibid.

5. The trial was reported in St. Paul *Pioneer Press,* March 29, 1892; March 20, 1892, 3; March 31, 1892, 8. For the full account, see Nelson, *Fredrick L. McGhee,* 53.

6. St. Paul *Pioneer Press,* March 16, 1894, 1.

7. Nelson, *Fredrick L. McGhee,* 53.

8. Ibid., 53–54, citing David V. Taylor, "Interview of Adina Gibbs, Dec. 18, 1970," audiovisual library of the Minnesota Historical Society (Adina Gibbs).

9. Ibid., 50.

10. St. Paul *Pioneer Press,* June 25, 1895, 2.

11. St. Paul *Pioneer Press,* June 12, 1895, 2.

12. St. Paul *Pioneer Press,* June 3, 1895, 1; St. Paul *Globe,* June 3, 1895, 1.

13. St. Paul *Pioneer Press,* June 3, 1895, 1.

14. St. Paul *Dispatch,* October 10, 1877, 2, column 4.

15. For a complete account of the 1920 Duluth lynching, see Michael Fedo, *The Lynchings in Duluth* (St. Paul: Minnesota Historical Society Press, 2000); William D. Green, "'To Remove the Stain'": The Trial of the Duluth Lynchers," *Minnesota History* (spring 2004): 22–35.

16. *Appeal,* March 31, 1900, 2, column 1.

17. Richard Kluger, *Simple Justice* (New York: Knopf, 1976), 67–68.

18. *Williams v. Mississippi,* 170 U.S. 213 (1898).

19. Kluger, *Simple Justice,* 68. Subsequent references are given in the text.

20. "Consciousness of kind" is a theory that asserts that a person's state of mind recognizes another person as being of like mind. It served as an explanation for grouping all black people into one category.

21. *Appeal,* February 12, 1900, 2, column 3; Milton R. Konvitz, *A Century of Civil Rights* (Westport, Conn.: Greenwood Press, 1983), 155.

22. C. Vann Woodward, *The Strange Career of Jim Crow* (New York: Oxford University Press, 1966), 43.

23. Ibid.

24. Nelson, *Frederick L. McGhee,* 46.

25. *Appeal,* May 2, 1903, 2, column 2.

26. August Meier, *Negro Thought in America, 1880–1915* (Ann Arbor: University of Michigan Press, 1968), 130; Emma Lou Thornbrough, "The National Afro-American League, 1887–1908," *Journal of Southern History* 27 (November 1961): 501; David V. Taylor, "Pilgrim's Progress: Black St. Paul and the Making of an Urban Ghetto, 1870–1930," Ph.D. thesis, University of Minnesota (March 1977), 107–9; *Appeal,* January 7, 1899, 2.

27. *Appeal,* January 7, 1899, 1–2.

28. The peonage system evolved from forced labor statutes that had been passed in all Southern states, permitting arrests for vagrancy, breach of contract, and other crimes. Once convicted, the defendant could be bound to a term of labor on a chain gang to work off the fines and court costs. See Melvin Urofsky and Paul Finkelman, *A March to Liberty: A Constitutional History of the United States,* vol. 2 (New York: Oxford University Press, 2002), 495–96.

29. *Appeal,* January 7, 1899, 1–2.

30. Ibid.

31. Ibid.

32. *Appeal,* January 21, 1899, 3; February 25, 1899, 3.

33. *Appeal,* February 25, 1899, 3.

34. *Appeal,* April 22, 1899, 3. The errors in French spelling are in the source.

35. Ibid.

36. Nelson, *Fredrick L. McGhee,* 71.

37. Ibid., 73. See also George B. Tindell, *South Carolina Negroes, 1877–1890* (Baton Rouge: Louisiana State University Press, 1966), 255–56.

38. *Appeal,* January 20, 1900, 4, column 1.

39. *Appeal,* January 13, 1900, 3.

40. *Appeal,* February 3, 1900, 3–4; Taylor, "Pilgrim's Progress," 109.

41. *Appeal,* December 16, 1899, 3; December 23, 1899, 5.

42. Nelson, *Fredrick L. McGhee,* 75.

43. Ibid. The white attendees included Mayor Kiefer, Judge Grier Orr, and attorney Thomas P. Kane (*Appeal,* January 20, 1900, 3). See also St. Paul *Pioneer Press,* January 18, 1900, 5.

44. *Appeal,* April 27, 1897, 2.

45. Nelson, *Fredrick L. McGhee,* 75.

46. *Appeal,* January 20, 1900, 3; St. Paul *Pioneer Press,* January 18, 1900, 5.

47. Nelson, *Fredrick L. McGhee,* 75–76.

48. *Appeal,* January 20, 1900, 3.

49. Ibid., January 20, 1900, 2; Taylor, "Pilgrim's Progress," 114.

13. A Defining Moment for McGhee

1. David Levering Lewis, *W .E. B. DuBois: Biography of a Race, 1868–1919* (New York: Henry Holt, 1993), 228–37.

2. In October 1901, McGhee attempted to persuade Governor Samuel Van Sant to deny extradition to Henry Summers, arguing that the man would surely be lynched if he was returned to Tennessee. The governor declined and ordered extradition. Immediately, McGhee sought to persuade the Ramsey County Court to issue a writ of habeas corpus, which it declined to do. Afterwards he appealed to the state supreme court, making him the first African American to do so. His appeal was rejected (*Appeal,* October 5, 1901, 3; October 12, 1901, 3; November 30, 1901, 30.

3. Paul Nelson, *Fredrick L. McGhee: A Life on the Color Line, 1861–1912* (St. Paul: Minnesota Historical Society Press, 2002), 97, citing McGhee letter to Emmett Scott, March 25, 1902 (Booker T. Washington Papers, Library of Congress [hereafter, BTW Papers]).

4. Ibid., citing McGhee to Scott, March 29, 1902 (BTW Papers).

5. Ibid., citing McGhee to Scott, April 5, March 29, 1902 (BTW Papers).

6. *Appeal,* July 5, 1902, 3.

7. Nelson, *Fredrick L. McGhee,* 97–98.

8. *Appeal,* July 19, 1902, 2; David V. Taylor, "Pilgrim's Progress: Black St. Paul and the Making of an Urban Ghetto, 1870–1930," Ph.D. thesis, University of Minnesota (March 1977), 111.

9. *Appeal,* July 19, 1902, 2.

10. Ibid.; St. Paul *Pioneer Press,* July 10, 1902, 2.

11. St. Paul *Pioneer Press,* July 10, 1902, 2.

12. Ibid.

13. *Svenska Amerikanska Posten,* May 19, 1892, translated in Peg Meier, *Bring Warm Clothes: Letters and Photos from Minnesota's Past* (Minneapolis: Neighbors Publishing, 1981), 189; St. Paul *Globe,* March 19, 1892; Nelson, *Fredrik L. McGhee,* 36, 82.

14. Earl Spangler, *The Negro in Minnesota* (Minneapolis: T. S. Dennison, 1961), 67.

15. David V. Taylor, "Blacks," in *They Chose Minnesota: A Survey of the State's Ethnic Groups,* ed. June Drenning Holmquist (St. Paul: Minnesota Historical Society Press, 1981), 77.

16. Nelson, *Fredrik L. McGhee,* 12.

17. Spangler, *The Negro in Minnesota,* 67.

18. W. E. B. DuBois, *The Souls of Black Folk* (New York: Fawcett Premier Books, 1969), 22.

19. Ibid., 48, 49; emphasis in the original.

20. Ibid., 45.

21. Dorothy Sterling, *Black Foremothers: Three Lives* (New York: Feminist Press, 1988), 71–72. See also the documentary film *Ida B. Wells: A Passion for Justice* (William Greaves Productions, 1989).

22. "Railroad Villainies," New York *Globe,* March 31, 1883, 1.

23. Sterling, *Black Foremothers,* 72.

24. Ibid., 73, 76. See also Lewis, *W .E. B. DuBois,* 244.

25. Sterling, *Black Foremothers,* 74.

26. Ibid., 79.

27. Ibid., 80.

28. St. Paul *Globe,* July 10, 1902, 10.

29. St. Paul *Pioneer Press,* July 11, 1902, 3.

30. St. Paul *Globe,* July 10, 1902, 10.

31. St. Paul *Pioneer Press,* July 11, 1902, 3.

32. Ibid. See also Lewis, *W. E. B. DuBois,* 235.

33. Lewis, *W. E. B. DuBois,* 238.

34. St. Paul *Pioneer Press,* July 11, 1902, 3; St. Paul *Globe,* July 11, 1902, 10.

35. St. Paul *Globe,* July 10, 1902, 10.

36. Emma Lou Thornbrough, "The National Afro-American League, 1887–1909," *Journal of Southern History* 27 (November 1961): 502–4.

37. Taylor, "Pilgrim's Progress," 112–13. See also Stephen R. Fox, *The Guardian of Boston: William Monroe Trotter* (New York: Atheneum Press, 1970), 46; August Meier, *Negro Thought in America, 1880–1915* (Ann Arbor: University of Michigan Press, 1968), 173.

38. *Appeal,* July 5, 1902, 3; St. Paul *Dispatch,* July 11, 1902, 3.

39. St. Paul *Dispatch,* July 11, 1902, 3.

40. St. Paul *Pioneer Press,* July 11, 1902, 3.

41. The *Globe* editor, for instance, commented that "by minimizing to [black people] of the pursuit of political ends, . . . [Washington] has shown himself to be at once a profound thinker, a good American and a safe guide for his people" (St. Paul *Globe,* July 12, 1902, 4).

42. Nelson, *Fredrick L. McGhee,* 103.

43. St. Paul *Dispatch,* July 11, 1902, 3.

44. Taylor, "Pilgrim's Progress," 114.

45. Ibid.

46. Roosevelt reportedly talked about having to force black troops at gunpoint to move to the front lines in Cuba, where they often suffered the greatest number of casualties (Nelson, *Fredrick L. McGhee,* 86, citing Chicago *Broad Ax,* July 21, 1900, 1).

47. *Appeal,* July 19, 1902, 2.

48. Ibid.

49. Nelson, *Fredrick L McGhee,* 105.

50. *Appeal,* July 19, 1902, 2.

51. St. Paul *Dispatch,* July 11, 1902, 3; St. Paul *Pioneer Press,* July 12, 1902, 3.

52. Trotter had a point, for as late as 1903 DuBois was seeking financial support from the Wizard (Lewis, *W. E. B. DuBois,* 297–98, 299).

53. Nelson, *Fredrick L. McGhee,* 106, citing *Colored American,* July 19, 1902, 2. See also *Washington Bee,* July 26, 1902, 2; *Indianapolis Freeman,* August 6, 1902, 1; *Cleveland Gazette,* August 16, 1902, 1. For the *Colored American* editorial, see the issue dated July 26, 1902, 2.

54. David V. Taylor, "John Quincy Adams: St. Paul Editor and Black Leader," *Minnesota History* (winter 1973): 295.

55. *Appeal,* August 8, 1902, 4, column 1.

56. Emma Lou Thornbrough, *T. Thomas Fortune:Militant Journalist* (Chicago: University of Chicago Press, 1972), 234–35. See also *Appeal,* December 13, 1902, 4; January 17, 1902, 3.

57. Frederick Douglass in a speech in Canandaigua, New York, August 3, 1857, collected in a pamphlet by the author, *Frederick Douglass Papers, Series One: Speeches, Debates, and Interviews,* vol. 3: *1855–63,* ed. John W. Blassingame (New Haven: Yale University Press, 1985), 204.

14. After St. Paul, Niagara

1. Biographer Paul Nelson makes the case that despite McGhee's disputes with the Bookerites, he did not attack or break with them in public because "in race issues the dirty laundry should not be exposed to the general public" (*Fredrick L. McGhee: A Life on the Color Line, 1861–1912* [St. Paul: Minnesota Historical Society Press, 2002], 182). That is plausible. However, in too many other venues (e.g., before an all-white jury), before the pen and eyes of a reporter, he freely played to commonly held bias. His defensive response to a quote on the Morris–Wheaton amendment in 1897 that he allegedly gave to the *Dispatch* seemed authentic. As Nelson observed, "It is not at all uncommon for people who had risen from misery to achievement to look down upon those had not" (184).

2. *Appeal,* February 7, 1903, 3.

3. *Appeal,* February 21, 1903, 3.

4. Ibid.

5. *Appeal,* February 21, 1903, 3. In May, Ransom's Chicago church was dynamited, allegedly by "policy gamblers" (*Appeal,* May 9, 1903, 2 and 4).

6. *Appeal,* July 18, 1902, 3.

7. *Appeal,* February 21, 1903, 3.

8. *Appeal,* June 20, 1903, 2.

9. Ibid.

10. David Levering Lewis, *W.E. B. DuBois: Biography of a Race, 1868–1919* (New York: Henry Holt, 1993), 298.

11. *Appeal,* May 9, 1903, 2.

12. Lewis, *W.E. B. DuBois,* 298.

13. Charles Puttkamer and Ruth Worthy, "William Monroe Trotter, 1872–1934," *Journal of Negro History* 43 (October 1958): 301. See also Nelson, *Frederick L. McGhee,* 109.

14. St. Paul *Daily Globe,* June 28, 1903, 2.

15. Ibid.

16. Lewis, *W.E. B. DuBois,* 299.

17. William S. McFeely, *Frederick Douglass* (New York: W. W. Norton, 1991), 151.

18. Earl Spangler, *The Negro in Minnesota* (Minneapolis: T. S. Dennison, 1961), 67, citing Minneapolis *Spokesman,* February 28, 1958.

19. Nelson, *Fredrick L. McGhee,* 110–11.

20. Ibid., 111.

21. Douglas R. Heidenreich, "A Citizen of Fine Spirit," *William Mitchell, a Magazine for Freedom Alumni of William Mitchell College of Law* (fall 2000): 2, 3; Nelson, *Fredrick L. McGhee,* 190; St. Paul *Dispatch,* March 30, 1911, 13.

22. Nelson, *Fredrick L. McGhee,* 207.

23. Steven R. Hoffbeck, "Victories Yet to Win: Charles E. Scrutchin, Bemidji's Black Activist Attorney," *Minnesota History* (summer 1996): 65.

24. David V. Taylor, "Pilgrim's Progress: Black St. Paul and the Making of an Urban Ghetto, 1870–1930," Ph.D. thesis, University of Minnesota (March 1977), 116; David V. Taylor, "John Quincy Adams; St. Paul Editor and Black Leader," *Minnesota History* (winter 1976): 296.

25. Lewis, *W.E. B. DuBois,* 299–300.

26. Ibid., 300–301.

27. *Appeal,* August 8, 1903, 2.

28. *Appeal,* August 30, 1903, 4.

29. *Appeal,* August 1, 1903, 2.

30. *Appeal,* May 2, 1903, 3.

31. *Appeal,* May 16, 1903, 2.

32. Taylor, "Pilgrim's Progess," 116; Taylor, "John Quincy Adams," 296.

33. Nelson, *Fredrick L. McGhee,* 128.

34. Ibid., 128–29.

35. Lewis, *W.E. B. DuBois,* 316. DuBois stated: "The honor of founding the organization belongs to F. L. McGhee, who first suggested it" (Herbert Aptheker, *A Documentary History of the Negro People in the United States,* vol. 2 [New York: Citadel Press, 1968], 904).

36. *Appeal,* March 4, 1905, 2.

37. Lewis, *W.E. B. DuBois*, 316.

38. Elliot Rudwick, "The Niagara Movement," *Journal of Negro History* 42 (April 1957): 177–82.

39. Lewis, *W.E. B. DuBois*, 317.

40. Ibid., 321–22.

41. Darlene Clark Hine, William C. Hine, and Stanley C. Harrold, *The African-American Odyssey*, 4th ed. (Upper Saddle Creek, N.J.: Prentice Hall, 2000), 367. See also Richard Kluger, *Simple Justice* (New York: Knopf, 1976), 95; Nelson, *Fredrick L. McGhee*, 130–31; Aptheker, *A Documentary History of the Negro People in the United States*, 900–901; Lewis, *W.E. B. DuBois*, 316–17, 321–22.

15. The Legacy

1. David Levering Lewis, *W.E. B. DuBois: Biography of a Race, 1868–1919* (New York: Henry Holt, 1993), 317.

2. *Appeal*, July 22, 1905, 5, column 2.

3. Niagara Movement "Declaration of Principles" (1905).

4. *Appeal*, February 24, 1906, 3; January 29, 1907, 3. See Ramsey County District Court civil case file 93002, *Samuel Thompson v. G. R. Kibbe*, filed March 16, 1906 (MHS); *Pioneer Press*, July 14, 1911, 14; Ramsey County Court civil case no. 94559, *Richard C. Clark v. May Hee*, *d.b.a. Kong Tong Lo Co*, filed November 21, 1906, Ramsey County Courthouse, St. Paul, Minnesota. See also Paul Nelson, *Fredrick L. McGhee: A Life on the Color Line, 1861–1912* (St. Paul: Minnesota Historical Society Press, 2002), 171–72.

5. St. Paul *Pioneer Press*, September 1, 1909, 14.

6. St. Paul *Pioneer Press*, September 2, 1909, 14; Paul Nelson, "Orphans and Old Folks: St. Paul's Crispus Attucks Home," *Minnesota History* 56:3 (1998): 103, 110–12; Nelson, *Fredrick L. McGhee*, 174–75.

7. See Walter Rucker and James Nathaniel Upton, eds., *Encyclopedia of American Race Riots*, vol. 1 (Westport, Conn.: Greenwood Press, 2007), lvii, 77.

8. Lewis, *W.E. B. DuBois*, 335.

9. A transcript of the resolution appeared in "Denounced Republicans," Oberlin *Tribune*, September 4, 1908.

10. Lewis, *W.E. B. DuBois*, 335.

11. "The Atlanta Massacre," *Appeal*, September 29, 1912, 2, column 2.

12. Louis R. Harlan, *Booker T. Washington: The Wizard of Tuskegee, 1901–1915* (New York: Oxford University Press, 1983), 3–31; James A. Tinsley, "Roosevelt, Foraker, and the Brownsville Foray," *Journal of Negro History* 43 (January 1965): 43–65; Emma Lou Thornbrough, "The Brownsville Episode and the Negro Vote," *Mississippi Valley Historical Review* 44 (December 1957): 469–83.

13. *Appeal*, December 1, 1906, 3.

14. *Appeal*, January 18, 1908, 3. See also January 25, 1908, 3.

15. Nelson, *Fredrick L. McGhee*, 162–63.

16. Lewis, *W.E. B. DuBois*, 340–41, 423–24. For an example of sentiment from a state

delegation, see Niagara Movement, "Report of the Secretary for the State of Pennsylvania," Oberlin, Ohio, meeting, August 31–September 2, 1908, 3.

17. For Wells-Barnett's account of Cooper Union, see Ida B. Wells-Barnett, *Crusade for Justice: The Autobiography of Ida B. Wells* (Chicago: University of Chicago Press, 1970), 321–23. See also Lewis, *W .E. B. DuBois*, 397–98.

18. DuBois letter to A. N. Wolfe, December 15, 1914 (University of Massachusetts, Amherst, Niagara Movement Archives); retrieved November 22, 2012, from http://www.library .umass.edu/spcoll/digital/niagara.htm.

19. McGhee letter to DuBois, August 14, 1909 (ibid.).

20. "The National Negro Conference to Mr. Washington, 1910," in Herbert Aptheker, ed., *Documentary History of the Negro People of the United States,* vol. 2 (New York: Citadel Press, 1966), 884–86.

21. *Appeal,* November 4, 1911, 3, columns 1–2.

22. *Appeal,* November 11, 1911, 3, columns 3–4.

23. Minneapolis *Twin City Star,* December 2, 1911, 1, column 2.

24. Minneapolis *Twin City Star,* March 16, 1912, 2, column 2; March 30, 1912, 1, column 3.

25. Minneapolis *Twin City Star,* October 3, 1913, 3, column 2.

Epilogue

1. Minneapolis *Twin City Star,* May 4, 1912, 2, column 4.

2. Minneapolis *Twin City Star,* "Mob Handles Negro Roughly," May 24, 1912, 2, column 3.

3. St. Paul *Pioneer Press,* July 10, 1912, 6.

4. St. Paul *Pioneer Press,* July 12, 1912, 6.

5. For a list of delegates, see Chicago *Broad Ax,* October 12, 1912, 1, column 5. See also Jack L. Forrest, "New Freedom or New Slavery: Woodrow Wilson and the Emergence of a New Negro Leadership," Proceedings of the Oklahoma Academy of Science for 1963, 134.

6. Minneapolis *Twin City Star,* May 4, 1912, 2, column 2.

7. Death certificate of Fredrick L. McGhee, St. Paul Department of Health; *Appeal,* September 21, 1912, 3. See also Paul Nelson, *Fredrick L. McGhee: A Life on the Color Line, 1861–1912* (St. Paul: Minnesota Historical Society Press, 2002), 200.

8. *Appeal,* September 21, 1912, 3; see also *Appeal,* August 31, 1912, 3; September 7, 1912, 3.

9. Wheaton's name was mentioned in a few civil-rights cases. See Minneapolis *Twin City Star,* December 23, 1915, 4, column 2 (regarding the theater); December 28, 1916, 1, column 5 (regarding a Minneapolis teacher); *Minnesota Messenger,* July 29, 1922, 1, column 1; March 17, 1923, 1, column 1.

10. *Minnesota Messenger,* January 22, 1922, 1, column 6; *New York Times,* January 16, 1922, 28, column 2; New York *World,* January 16, 1922, 11, column 4.

11. David V. Taylor, "John Quincy Adams: St. Paul Editor and Black Leaser," *Minnesota History* (winter 1973): 283, 296.

INDEX

Abbott, Lyman, 283

abolition, 26, 32, 40, 234; Douglass's experiences with, 103, 105, 106, 114, 284; freeing slaves brought north by vacationing slaveholders, 23–25; hypocrisy of, 54, 55. *See also* Emancipation Proclamation of 1863; Thirteenth Amendment

accommodation, philosophy of, 259, 261, 276, 303; black leaders moving away from, 271, 307; weaknesses of, 37, 279, 299; white supremacy not deterred by, 288, 300. *See also* Washington, Booker T.

accommodations, public. *See* public accommodations

acculturation, 20–21

Adams, Cyrus Field (brother of John Quincy), 149, 273

Adams, John Quincy (newspaper editor), 136–38, 296; and American Law Enforcement League of Minnesota, 231, 232; as Bookerite, 262, 263, 281, 286–87, 288–89, 295–96, 304–5, 312–13; on cakewalks, 195–96; death of, 312; fighting discrimination, 151–52, 154, 156, 160–61, 164; McGhee's relationship with, 227, 288, 312–13; and NAAC, 259, 267; and NAACP, 306, 313; and National Afro-American League, 161–62, 165, 167; on the Niagara Movement, 295, 296–97; planning banquet for Wheaton's election, 249; Republican Party relationship, 137–38, 148–49, 150, 162, 171, 203–4, 226, 281; on saloons' refusal of service, 134–35; on *The Souls of Black Folk*, 282–83; and St. Paul League, 163, 164, 171; and Wheaton-Morris amendment, 225–26, 227. *See also Appeal*; *Western Appeal*

African Americans. *See* blacks; blacks, Minnesota

Afro-American League. *See* National Afro-American League; St. Paul League

Afro-American Republican Club (AARC), 175, 205

American House hotel (St. Paul): Lyles's barbershop in, 118

American Law Enforcement League of Minnesota, 231–34, 259–60

Anderson, Robert F.: and St. Paul League, 165

Andrew, John A., 55

antiblack sentiment: among immigrants, 7, 8–11, 66, 67, 71, 122, 219, 269; in the North, 26, 52, 54, 55, 65–68, 200, 254; in public accommodations, 103; in the trades, 65–68; in the West, 56. *See also* discrimination; prejudice; racism

anti-Bookerites, 275, 278, 284–85, 293. *See also* Bookerites; Radicals

Appeal (newspaper), 201, 202, 207, 313; condemnations of white supremacists' activities, 189–90, 207; name change, 160; Niagara Movement covered in, 295, 296–97; society news in, 171–72, 173; on Booker T. Washington, 192, 193–94, 288–89. *See also* Adams, John Quincy; *Western Appeal*

Arthur, Chester A., 139, 140, 148

Atlanta Cotton States and International Exposition: Booker T. Washington's speech at, 179–80, 181–91, 199, 259

Ault, Thaddeus, 58

Austin, Horace, 115

Auter, James, 27

Baker, Frazier: lynching of, 231, 258, 260–61

Baldwin, William H., 183

Baltimore, Maryland: black barbers in, 27

Banks, Robert, 119, 122

Baptist, C. W., 145

barbers, black: attracting influential white customers, 12–13, 17, 25, 27, 31, 63, 151; common features of, 13, 33, 117; history of, 18–21; as leaders of black community, 13, 20, 40–41, 43–44, 214; middle-class status of, 28, 43–44; mob violence against, 26; not serving black customers, 20, 40, 41, 93; Southern, 17, 19, 20–21, 27; suffrage work, 32–41, 43–44. *See also* Grey, Ralph; Jackson, Thomas; Jernigan, Maurice; Lyles, Thomas

Barnard, Henry, 73

Basset, Albert: family farm, 62

Battle of Sugar Point, 342n70

Beecher, Henry Ward, 328n29

Berry, Eugene, 14

Berwanger, Eugene, 4

Bill No. 34 (Minnesota Territorial Legislature), 9. *See also* blacks, Minnesota: territorial laws restricting civil rights of

Bill No. 181 (Minnesota State Legislature). *See* legislation, Minnesota, public accommodations law

Bill No. 198 (Minnesota State Legislature). *See* legislation, Minnesota: antischool segregation

Birth of a Nation, The (movie): based on *The Clansman,* 257, 299

Bishop, Harriet, 76

black laws: in Iowa, 4, 5, 315n4; in Ohio, 9, 15, 26. *See also* blacks, Minnesota: territorial laws restricting civil rights of

blacks: economic potential of, 273; research purporting inferiority of, 256–57; value of life, compared to whites', 252–53, 254; white stereotypes of, 13, 35, 120, 191, 192, 258, 262–63

blacks, Minnesota, 102, 302; as Bookerites, 194, 200, 299, 302, 303; lack of homesteading opportunities for, 45–46, 49–50, 57, 61–64, 68, 71; political involvement of, 203–4, 269, 273; poor, 94–95, 110, 120, 194–95, 196, 270; population figures, 61, 64, 118, 124, 141, 238, 251, 255, 330n16; serving as jurors, 81–84, 107; territorial laws restricting civil rights of, 4–7, 9, 15, 18, 67, 197, 316n22, 317n23, 317n24;

thriving image of, 122–23. *See also* civil rights: in Minnesota; Minneapolis: black population in; Republican Party, Minnesota: blacks' relationships with; St. Paul: black population in

Blaine, James, 140, 141

Blair bill (U.S. Congress), 172

Blegen, Theodore, 60, 159

Blue Earth County: black suffrage vote in, 63–64, 323n71; immigration to, 57–58, 63

Bookerites: black Minnesotans as, 194, 200, 299, 302, 303; divide with anti-Bookerites, 278, 285; facing racial violence, 300–301; at Louisville NAAC convention, 285, 286; McGhee's break with, 278, 284, 285, 288, 346n1; at St. Paul NAAC convention, 275, 280. *See also* Adams, John Quincy: as Bookerite; anti-Bookerites

Boone, John Alfred, 61–62

Boston Riot (1903), 287–88

Bradley, Joseph P., 124–25, 127

breach of contract as legal defense, 169, 343n28

Brissette, John, 116–17

Bristol, Douglas, 18, 26; on black barbers, 19, 27, 28, 30, 40

Brower, Abraham, 64

Brown, B. Gratz, 52

Brown, D. P.: at Emancipation Proclamation commemorations, 173, 175–76

Brown, Henry: threatened lynching of, 253, 255

Brown, Henry Billings, 206

Brown, John: Douglass's connection to, 201, 336n22

Brown, Joseph, 59

Brownsville, Texas: racial harassment in, 299–300, 301, 346n46

Bruce, Blanche K., 338n7

Brunson, Alfred, 8

Brunson, Benjamin, 8–9

Bryan, William Jennings: DuBois's endorsement of, 302, 310; McGhee campaigning for, 220, 221

Buck, Daniel (Minnesota Supreme Court justice), 247

Buckalew, Charles, 52

Buckingham, James, 219

Bugonaygeshig (Ojibwe warrior), 342n70

Bullock, Rufus, 183, 187

Bureau of Refugees, Freedmen, and Abandoned Lands, U.S., 61

Burgett, John T., 144

Burghardt, William Edward, 152

businesses, black-owned, 40, 255, 299. See also barbers, black; professional class, black

businesses, white-owned, 142, 196–97, 273. See also corporations; monopolies

Butler, M. C.: bill to send blacks to Africa, 171

Butler, Pierce, 252

cakewalks, 195–96, 207–9; McGhee's defense of, 208–9, 213, 216, 249

Canada: blacks escaping to, 14, 16, 26, 201

Cane, Mark, 63

Canty, Thomas, 247

Castle, Henry A.: proposal for public accommodations bill, 109, 125, 127, 327n8

Chamberlain, Leon T., 218, 219

Chambers, Samuel, 62

Chapin, Walter, 218–19

chapter 224 (Minnesota state statutes). See legislation, Minnesota, public accommodations law

chapter 349 (Minnesota state statutes). See legislation, Minnesota, public accommodations law: Wheaton-Morris amendment

Chesapeake, Ohio & Southwestern Railroad, Wells v., 272

Chevalier, François, 4

Chrislock, Carl, 238, 241

Christmas, Richard, 24–25

churches: black, 26, 28, 29, 82, 92, 119–20, 139; Kaposia mission, 4, 8; St. Paul's first, 8, 10. See also ministers, black; Pilgrim Baptist Church

citizenship, black, 54, 70, 79, 269, 290, 294; amendment regarding, 241, 242, 243–44. See also Fourteenth Amendment; suffrage, black

civil rights, 31, 141, 146; lawsuits challenging, 111–12, 164, 169, 175, 222, 224, 298; in Minnesota, 90, 164, 168,

189–90, 209, 214, 241, 248, 250, 309; Protective League's advancement of, 158, 160; Republicans' support for, 83, 135–36; in the South, 189–90, 299; Wheaton's work on, 246–47. See also blacks, Minnesota: territorial laws restricting civil rights of; equality, black; Fifteenth Amendment; Fourteenth Amendment

Civil Rights Act of 1875, 110, 112, 113, 124, 160, 326n41; declared unconstitutional, 125, 127, 130, 199–200

Civil Rights Cases (U.S. Supreme Court), 124–25, 130, 132, 139–40, 271, 329n66

Civil Rights Committee, 168, 169

civil rights leagues, 155, 157–58. See also National Afro-American League; St. Paul League

Civil War, 26, 34, 39, 51, 52–53, 61, 64–65; black soldiers in, 29, 30, 31, 35–36, 39, 144, 319n34; draft for, 28–31, 53; slavery as issue in, 25, 82, 107, 221. See also Emancipation Proclamation of 1863; reconciliation, racial/sectional; Reconstruction

Clarendon Hotel (St. Paul): Hazel's suit against, 154–56

class, socioeconomic, 105–6, 196–97, 221. See also blacks, Minnesota: poor; middle class, black; professional class, black; underclass, black; working class, black

Cleveland, Grover, 188, 283; black support for, 140–41; election of, 148, 150, 204, 214; visit to St. Paul, 145, 149

Clough, David, 239, 243

Collins, L. W., 245–46, 247

color-blind: origin of term, 2(

Colored Citizens' Union, 174, 05

Combs, Taylor: attempted lynching of, 115–17, 164, 255

community building, 53, 65, 88

Compton, James, 63

Congdon, Chester A., 134

consciousness of kind: Giddings's concept of, 256, 343n20. See also double consciousness: DuBois's concept of

Conscription Act of 1863, 28–29, 30

Constitution, U.S.: Fifteenth Amendment, 88, 164, 248, 289; Fourteenth Amendment, 30, 110, 172, 289; powers

left to the states, 330n8; Thirteenth
Amendment, 54, 56, 321n30

160; work for black suffrage, 87, 162. *See also* equality, black: Republican Party's support of; Radical Republicans

Republican Party, Minnesota, 23, 33, 53, 174, 231; absence of black officeholders in, 78, 141; black barbers' support of, 40, 93; blacks' relationships with, 130, 138–40, 155, 163, 201–5, 207–8, 214, 246–47; at Convention of Colored Citizens of Minnesota, 77–78; courting immigrants' votes, 150, 203, 219, 220, 239, 242–43, 269; dissatisfaction with Civil Rights Act of 1875, 113, 127; dominance of, 15, 141, 221; and equality for blacks, 36, 80, 83, 95, 96, 109–10, 135–36; fissures in, 150, 238–39, 332n21; founding of, 234, 340n16; McGhee's disillusionment with, 103, 202–4, 213–14, 217–19, 225, 226, 228, 301; and Minnesota constitution of 1857, 32; Populist Party's rivalry with, 201–2, 203, 207, 242; racism in, 42, 64; shifting attention away from black issues, 85–86, 106, 121, 129, 143, 149; values espoused by, 97, 190–91; *Western Appeal's* relationship with, 135–37, 138, 141–49; Wheaton's loyalty to, 235, 236. *See also* Adams, John Quincy: Republican Party relationship

Rhone, Edward T., 244, 265

Rhone v. Loomis, 244–46, 247

Rice, Edmund, 124

Rice, Henry: in 1865 gubernatorial race, 320n53, 322n36, 322n39

Richardson, Heather Cox, 140

riots. *See* violence, racial: riots

Robert Banks Literary Society, 119, 122

Robertson, Daniel A., 82–83, 84, 86, 325n26

Robinson, Henry: suit against Milwaukee and St. Paul Railroad, 111–12

Rollins, Henry, 252–53

Roosevelt, Theodore: and Brownsville, Texas, race riot, 300, 301, 346n46; NAAC endorsement of, 277

Ryan Hotel (St. Paul), 136, 145, 149, 151

saloons: not mentioned in Minnesota public accommodations law, 134–35, 154, 224–25, 244–48, 250, 261

San Francisco, California: black population in, 257; discrimination in public accommodations, 112

Saulsbury, Willard, Sr., 52, 54

Scandinavians: in Minneapolis, 237–38; Republican Party's courting of, 150, 203, 219, 239, 242–43, 269

schools, St. Paul: black students omitted from attendance records, 86, 94; integration of, 80, 83, 84–85, 110; segregated, 9–10, 71–76, 80, 85, 164; trade, 90. *See also* education, public; segregation, school

Scott, Dred. *See Dred Scott* decision

Scott, Thomas (Mr. and Mrs.), 228

Scribner, D. M., 222

Scrutchin, Charles, 285, 286

Secombe, Charles and David, 32

segregation: Democratic Party favoring, 84, 85, 310; in the North, 258; state-sanctioned, 206–7, 221–22, 268. *See also* racism

segregation, school, 9–10, 78–79, 198; Iowa, 75, 315n4; Kentucky, 299; Minnesota bill outlawing, 75–76, 79–86, 107, 199, 298, 299, 322n36. *See also* Ohio: education of black children in; schools, St. Paul: segregated

self-help, principles of, 162, 273; Douglass's speech on, 96–97; Sons of Freedom founded on, 73, 87; Booker T. Washington's promotion of, 137, 262. *See also* social Darwinism

separate but equal, principle of, 113, 169, 205–7, 257–58

separate coach laws: Louisiana, 205–7, 282, 283; Oklahoma, 169; Tennessee, 167, 168–69, 174–75, 266

Shannon, Thomas, 244

Shelton, F. H., 175

Shepherd, Harry: and NAAC convention in St. Paul, 267, 274; Wheaton's partnership with, 248–49

Sherman, William: and burning of Atlanta, 183

Shilloch, John, 58

Sibley, Henry Hastings, 4, 7, 17

silver standard. *See* gold vs. silver standard

Simons, H., 123

slaveholders, Southern: rights of ownership in North, 14, 22–25, 318n20; seeking return of runaways, 14–17, 22, 24–25

slavery, 6, 10, 33, 39; economic, 197–98; politics of, 23–25. *See also* abolition; Emancipation Proclamation of 1863; Thirteenth Amendment; West Indies slaves' emancipation

slaves, runaway: Jernigan as, 21–22, 23, 25, 27; retrieving, 14–17, 22, 24–25; in St. Paul, 13–18; William Taylor's assistance to, 15, 16–17, 18, 22, 23, 25, 107; violence against, 53, 197. *See also* Hickman Pilgrims

Smith, Charles Sumner, 305, 306

Smith, Robert: and NAAC St. Paul convention, 268

Smith, Seagraves, 79

Snider, Sam, 217

social Darwinism, 71, 106, 129

Social Glass, A (play), 261

soldiers, black: in Civil War, 29, 30, 31, 35–36, 39, 144, 319n34; Iowa Territory law against, 315n4; land for, 49–51, 57, 61–62, 64, 65

Sons of Freedom: agenda of, 70–71, 73, 86, 90, 110, 120, 162; decline of, 91–92, 95, 96; education promoted by, 75–76, 85, 86; fighting school segregation, 78–79; fostering racial pride, 70, 87–88; founding of, 73, 82, 87. *See also* Golden Key Literary Society; leadership, black; race men, Minnesota

South, the: black barbers in, 17, 19, 20–21, 27; disenfranchisement of blacks in, 164, 172, 248, 254–56, 268, 269; freedmen/ women living in, 49, 52, 53, 54, 61; lynchings in, 172, 231, 258, 264, 273; race relations in, 145, 182, 183, 189, 206, 250; racial violence in, 142, 143, 233, 251; Reconstruction in, 113, 114–15, 183, 327n4; Republican Party in, 141, 160; runaway slaves from, 15–16, 18, 21; state-sanctioned segregation in, 206–7, 221–22, 268; tourists visiting the North from, 14, 22–25, 318n20. *See also* Civil War; migration, black; white supremacists; *and individual southern states*

South Carolina: Baker's lynching in, 231, 258, 260–61; black barbers in, 27;

disenfranchisement of black voters in, 172, 248, 256

Southern Railway system, 183

Spangler, Earl, 68, 124, 165, 196, 197, 204–5, 231, 285

Spanish-American War, 239; black support for, 207–8, 213, 249

Sparks, Henry, 24

speculators: buying up homestead land, 46–47, 48, 57–59, 64

Sprague, J. W., 58

St. Anthony, 32, 234, 340n16

Stanton, Elizabeth Cady: Declaration of Sentiments, 290

Start, Charles M., 245, 246, 247

State v. Harris, 81–84

Stearns County: black suffrage vote in, 64

stereotypes, racial, 13, 35, 120, 258, 262–63; black middle-class concerns over, 142, 191, 192–93, 194–95, 196. *See also* racism

Stewart, McCant: lawsuit brought by, 228–29, 244

St. Marks, Francis, 27

Stockton, R. J., 73, 82; barbershops of, 41, 92; leadership role of, 43, 117

Stockwell, S. A., 243

Stowell, F. M., 32

St. Paul, 17, 89, 119; black population in, 33, 68, 118–19, 124, 207, 240, 257, 260; boosterism in, 90–91; Democratic Party's dominance in, 15, 17, 34, 76, 82–83, 138, 149, 234; discrimination in, 112, 138, 157, 173, 175, 177, 228, 262; district court in, 7–8; ghettos developing in, 95, 115, 200, 326n60; Grand Army of the Republic encampment of 1896 in, 64–65; McGhee first black lawyer in, 103, 215; migration of blacks to, 123, 269–70; NAAC convention of 1902, 264–79, 280, 281, 304; racism in, 110, 138, 200, 250; Republican victories in, 218–19; runaway slaves coming to, 13–18; settlement of, 3–11, 14, 76, 126; underclass in, 94, 216, 269–70; violence against blacks in, 26–27, 38, 53, 66–67, 69, 197. *See also* Douglass, Frederick: refused rooms in St. Paul hotels; schools, St. Paul

St. Paul and Galena Packet Company: black strikebreakers brought in by, 66

South, the; Supreme Court, U.S.; West, the; *and individual states*

Usher, John, 47–48

Vandenburgh, Charles, 24–25, 48, 234

Van Sant, Samuel, 250, 268, 281, 344n2

Vashon, John, 26

vigilance, black, 157, 160, 162, 167

Villard, Oswald Garrison: and NAACP, 303, 304

violence, racial, 102; mob, 38, 144, 163, 254, 257–58, 291, 294, 309; riots, 25, 53, 299–301; self-defense against, 300, 303; Southern, 142, 143, 233, 251; in St. Paul, 26–27, 38, 53, 66–67, 69, 197. *See also* laborers, black: white laborers perceiving as threat; lynchings

Voegeli, V. Jacque, 64, 128

voters and voting, black: disenfranchisement of, 248, 256, 259, 268, 284, 315n4; loyalty of, 142–43; in Minnesota, 6–7, 269; power of, 68–69, 130, 131, 271

voting: registration for, 172, 241, 242–43, 341n45

Walters, Alexander, 267; speech at NAAC St. Paul convention, 268, 270, 271, 273

Ward, H. W., 62

Ward, T. Harris, 64

Warner, Abbie, 208

Washburn, William, 260

Washington, Booker T., 180, 197, 258, 265, 282, 286, 346n41; Atlanta Cotton States and International Exposition speech, 179–80, 181–91, 199, 259; at Boston meeting of National Negro Business League, 287; death of, 312; dinner with Theodore Roosevelt, 277; honorary Harvard degree, 188; importance of, 257, 265–66; Lincoln Day speech, 301–2; Madison, Wisconsin, speech, 179–80; McGhee's relationship with, 216, 281, 285; at NAAC St. Paul convention, 264–79, 280; refused service at Metropolitan Hotel, 224, 262; self-help promoted by, 137, 262; in St. Paul, 261–63; wealth at disposal of, 285. *See also* accommodation,

philosophy of; anti-Bookerites; Bookerites; Tuskegee Institute

Washington, D.C.: black population in, 257

Washington, George: "Rules of Civility," 18

Wealthwood: blacks settling near, 65

Wells-Barnett, Ida B., 265, 272; discrimination suffered on railroad, 271–72; leaves NAACP, 303–4; lynching protests, 269, 273; as member of the Radicals, 281; at NAAC convention in St. Paul, 270–71, 274, 276–77

Wells v. Chesapeake, Ohio & Southwestern Railroad, 272

West, the, 22, 56, 127, 130; farming in, 47, 89; public education in, 74, 75; violence in, 23, 58

Western Appeal (newspaper), 118, 122, 330n15; blacks criticized by, 143–45; as organ of St. Paul League, 165, 167; Republican Party relationship, 135–37, 138, 141–49; whites criticized by, 145–46. *See also* Adams, John Quincy

West Indies slaves' emancipation: commemorations of, 118, 121–22

Wheaton, Frank (John Francis), 214, 218, 219–21, 240; and amendments to public accommodations law, 222–28, 262; and American Law Enforcement League of Minnesota, 231, 233–34; bills introduced in Minnesota Legislature, 342n72; confrontations with McGhee, 220–21, 224–28; as delegate to Republican National Convention, 248, 250; first black man elected to Minnesota legislature, 231, 234–40, 244, 246, 249; first black man to pass a bill in Minnesota, 227, 230; insurance company founded by, 250, 261; move to Chicago, 250, 252; move to New York City, 312; partnership with Shepherd, 248–49; Republican Party membership, 220, 228, 235, 241

Wheaton, Jacob and Emily (parents of Frank), 219

Wheaton-Morris amendment, 222–28, 230–31, 249, 262, 346n1

White, Clarence Cameron, 305

whites, 26, 229, 258, 266, 291; in NAACP, 303, 304; philanthropy of, 89–90, 118;

prejudice of, 95–96; stereotypes of blacks, 194–95, 196, 262–63; value of life, compared to blacks', 252–53, 254; working-class, 94, 106. *See also* elite, white; immigrants and immigration, white; laborers, white

whites, Minnesota, 64, 103, 330n16; benevolence of, 118, 199–200; bigoted actions of, 145–46; poor, 94–95, 110; preferred as settlers in Minnesota, 59–60; school integration rejected by, 80, 83, 84–85, 325n33; as supporters of black suffrage, 39–40

white supremacists, 123, 179, 202, 295; *Appeal*'s condemnations of, 189–90, 207; black Minnesotans' concerns over, 194, 197; Southern, 131, 160, 288, 300. *See also* discrimination; prejudice; racism

Wiley, Mrs. J. J.: lawsuit brought by, 145–46, 149, 161

Wilkins, Roy, 313

Wilkinson, Morton S., 13, 78, 162, 321n19, 327n4; on black homesteading, 57, 111; at Convention of Colored Citizens of Minnesota, 61, 65, 68–69, 71, 85, 86; elected to House of Representatives, 56, 321n30, 324n89; on Homestead Act, 44–47, 325n36; overseeing sale of Winnebago lands, 47–51

Willard, John, 48, 58, 63

Willey, Waitman T.: relocation amendment, 51–57

Williams, Fletcher, 7

Williamson, Thomas S., 7

Wilson, Henry, 56

Wilson, Woodrow, 302–3, 309–10

Wingerd, Mary, 89

Winnebago people: sale of reservation land, 47–51, 59, 63

Winona County: black suffrage vote, 320n53

Winston, Eliza: emancipation trial of, 24–25, 48, 107, 234

Winston, P. B., 175

Wisconsin: school segregation banned in, 75. *See also* Madison, Wisconsin

Wizard of Tuskegee. *See* Washington, Booker T.

Wolf, Albert, 60

women: leadership positions in black community, 119; suffrage for, 121, 146–47, 290. *See also* Wells-Barnett, Ida B.

Woodson, Carter G., 74

Woodson, George, 288

Woodward, C. Vann, 222, 258

working class, black, 74, 94, 196, 291

Wright, George B., 58, 222

Yates, Josephine Silone, 273

Young, A. H., 242

William D. Green is professor of history at Augsburg College in Minneapolis and the author of *A Peculiar Imbalance: The Fall and Rise of Racial Equality in Minnesota, 1837–1869* (Minnesota, 2015).